Lincoln Christian College
11.75

HEBREW AND SEMITIC STUDIES

Godfrey Rolles Driver

HEBREW AND SEMITIC STUDIES

PRESENTED TO

GODFREY ROLLES DRIVER

M.C., C.B.E., M.A., Hon. D.D. (Aberdeen and Manchester)
Hon. D.Litt. (Durham), F.B.A.

Professor of Semitic Philology in the
University of Oxford 1938–1962
Fellow of Magdalen College

IN CELEBRATION OF
HIS SEVENTIETH BIRTHDAY
20 AUGUST 1962

EDITED BY
D. WINTON THOMAS
AND
W. D. McHARDY

OXFORD
AT THE CLARENDON PRESS
1963

Oxford University Press, Amen House, London E.C.4
GLASGOW NEW YORK TORONTO MELBOURNE WELLINGTON
BOMBAY CALCUTTA MADRAS KARACHI LAHORE DACCA
CAPE TOWN SALISBURY NAIROBI IBADAN ACCRA
KUALA LUMPUR HONG KONG

© *Oxford University Press 1963*

PRINTED IN GREAT BRITAIN

492.082
T45

GODFREY ROLLES DRIVER

WE, who edit this volume, and those who have contributed to it, offer to Professor Driver our most sincere congratulations on his seventieth birthday, which fell on 20 August 1962. For us it is indeed a happy occasion, for it gives us an opportunity to express to Professor Driver our deep gratitude for the outstanding services which for over forty years he has rendered to Hebrew and Semitic studies, and at the same time the high personal esteem and affection in which we hold him.

Professor Driver's eminence in Hebrew and Semitic studies has long been recognized by scholars throughout the world, and many honours have been conferred upon him. He has been President of the Society for Old Testament Study and of the International Organization for Old Testament Study. He was elected a Fellow of the British Academy in 1939, and he has received honorary doctorates from the universities of Aberdeen, Manchester, and Durham.

The knowledge of ancient Semitic languages which Professor Driver commands is truly remarkable in its range and depth, and with it he combines a fine knowledge of the classical languages. His success in recovering a large part of the lost vocabulary of ancient Hebrew has been a major achievement in Semitic lexicographical research in the last generation, and in so far as his discoveries have thrown fresh light upon countless dark places in the Hebrew text of the Old Testament, he has made a contribution for which not scholars alone are grateful, but all those too whose concern is the true meaning of the Old Testament text. His close familiarity with Eastern ways of life and thought, gained more particularly in the course of military and national service in two world wars, has led him frequently to a fresh and more convincing elucidation of the Old Testament. Whenever new discoveries in the Semitic field have been made, whether of seals, potsherds, tablets, papyri, or scrolls, Professor Driver has greeted them with lively zest and accepted the challenge which they present to the interpreter. The select bibliography of his writings, which is included in this volume, impressively reveals his prodigious labours, and at the same time gives some

19892

indication of the extent to which future generations of scholars will be indebted to him for them.

Professor Driver's inspiring teaching has been enjoyed by a long succession of pupils, among whom we, the editors, feel proud and privileged to be counted. His intellectual honesty and his enthusiasm for his subject have been for them an abiding example, while his youthful exuberance has always been a source of sheer delight. Many could testify to his ready generosity in the giving of his time and help, as well as encouragement, in their work. The cause of good learning has at all times found in him a staunch ally, always willing to lend practical assistance where the project seemed to him worth while. The recently created Institute of Oriental Studies in Oxford stands as a monument to his energy and vision.

In presenting this volume to Professor Driver, we add to our expression of gratitude for his great services to scholarship our hope that he may enjoy many more years in which to continue his work and to bring to fulfilment those tasks already begun but not yet ended. In this hope, as well as in our gratitude, we believe that the entire international circle of Hebrew and Semitic scholars will wish to join us.

D. WINTON THOMAS
Regius Professor of Hebrew, Cambridge

W. D. McHARDY
Regius Professor of Hebrew, Oxford

CONTENTS

PLATES

ARCHAIC SURVIVALS IN THE TEXT OF CANTICLES

By WILLIAM F. ALBRIGHT, *Baltimore*

THE problem of the Song of Songs is far from being solved, but material continues to accumulate. Indications that it goes back to some sort of dramatic composition like the Chester Beatty Papyrus published by Sir Alan Gardiner[1] are balanced by its refractory content, which refuses to conform to any proposed reconstruction. The striking archaisms which will be assembled in this paper are offset by a number of certain Iranian loanwords. Contrary to assertions in the past, there is not a single Greek loanword,[2] and therefore there is no evidence for the frequently assumed Hellenistic date.[3] A date in the fifth–fourth century B.C. for the collection and editing of Canticles thus appears to be certain.

That the contents were gathered from oral sources of North Palestinian origin becomes highly probable when we note such linguistic peculiarities as the frequent use of the northern relative *še* and the dominance of northern geographical terms. Oral transmission is also suggested by the role played by Solomon, as well as by the curious deformation of some notable archaisms. For instance, we find in vi. 8 a lyric tricolon (preserved as 2:2:3):

There are sixty queens, And eighty concubines,
And unnumbered maidens!

In Ugaritic poetry the numerical gradation 'seventy–eighty' is common, and there are well-attested cases in Hurro-Hittite literature, so it is reasonably certain that 'sixty' is a later substitute for 'seventy' at a time when the numerical gradations of the second millennium had ceased to be normative.

In this brief paper we shall limit ourselves to a few passages where both content and style suggest archaism, as well as to a very few other

[1] *The Library of A. Chester Beatty* (London, 1931), Papyrus I.

[2] *Appiryôn* is also Iranian; see G. Widengren, *Sakrales Königtum im Alten Testament und im Judentum* (Stuttgart, 1955), p. 112. The derivation from Greek φορεῖον was always linguistically unlikely.

[3] See most recently Moses Hadas, *Hellenistic Culture: Fusion and Diffusion* (New York, 1959), pp. 147–64. His parallels are all of the most indefinite type.

places where new light can be shed on obscurities. We do not aim at an exhaustive treatment, since our data are far from being adequate for any such attempt. The principal indication of archaistic style is the repetition of words and phrases according to known patterns in Ugaritic and other early North-west Semitic literature from the Bronze Age. Since repetitive patterns have proved to be excellent clues in analysing archaic Hebrew verse,[1] and since it can be shown that the nature of archaic repetition was no longer understood in later times,[2] their recurrence in late texts is a clear proof of archaism, or at least of archaic survivals in material of otherwise later date.

In i. 2b–3a we find an unusually clear example of archaic style; the consonantal text requires no revision and even the vocalization may be correct:

כי־טובים דדיך מיין   לריח שמניך טובים

Truly[3] thy love is sweeter than wine,
It is sweeter than[4] the scent of thy perfume!

Since the M.T. is consistently archaic, while the Greek offers in the second colon a similar text which renders the Hebrew of the final colon in iv. 10 literally, we must follow it here. The Greek substitute presupposes a bicolon, 2:2, which does not fit into the otherwise exclusively 3:3 context of verses 2–4.

In ii. 15 we have a couplet, 2:2–2:2, which is again perfect as it stands:

Catch for us the foxes, The little foxes,
Which despoil the vineyards— Our vineyards being in blossom![5]

[1] See especially my treatment in the *Robinson Volume, Studies in Old Testament Prophecy* (Edinburgh, 1950), pp. 3–8 and *passim*, where earlier treatments are referred to. Among more recent discussions note especially 'A Catalogue of Early Hebrew Lyric Poems' (*H.U.C.A.* xxiii, 1950–1, pp. 1–39), *passim*, and my remarks in *Studi Orientalistici in Onore di Giorgio Levi Della Vida*, i (Rome, 1956), pp. 8 ff. Recently the writer has analysed all Hebrew poems which he would date before the tenth century B.C., as well as other scattered material in the O.T., obtaining striking evidence for stylistic sequence dating, in full agreement with the general incidence of linguistic archaisms and of historical allusions; cf. provisionally *Vet. Test.* ix, 1959, p. 346.

[2] See *Interpretationes* (*Mowinckel Volume*, Oslo, 1955), pp. 8 f. A Johns Hopkins thesis on this subject has not yet been published.

[3] The asseverative *kî* is far commoner in Hebrew than generally supposed, as will be shown in an unpublished Johns Hopkins dissertation.

[4] On *lĕ* used instead of classical Hebrew *min*, see below, p. 4, n. 1.

[5] The word *sĕmādár*, already well attested in much later Aramaic dialects, has now been found in an inscribed sherd from eighth-century Hazor, which reads *lpqḥ smdr* 'belonging to Pekah, *semadar*'. Possibly the second word referred to wine flavoured with vine blossoms. At all events the word was already known in Hebrew by the eighth century B.C. It is not impossible that Aramaic *smâdrâ* (from which the vocalization of the

In the three bicola we have examined there are three cases of repetitive parallelism of the single-word type. In Ugaritic as well as in the Song of Miriam (Exod. xv) we have two-word repetitions but not single-word examples. The two-word repetition occurs also in an Egyptian translation of a Canaanite magical text from the thirteenth century B.C. (though the original Canaanite spell may be considerably older).[1] Single-word repetitive parallelism is particularly common in the Song of Deborah, and appears frequently in the Balaam Oracles and other poetic compositions which the writer dates in the twelfth–eleventh centuries.[2] Interestingly enough, assonance became paronomasia before the end of the eleventh century,[3] and continued chiefly in this form in subsequent centuries—*except* where clear archaism is involved. In narratives dealing with events of the thirteenth–twelfth centuries we often find archaic quotations or reminiscences with double or single-word repetition, suggesting the poetic originals from which many of these narratives were derived.

In iv. 8 we have an obvious reference to Canaanite mythological literature, as first recognized by Alfred Bertholet in the *Baudissin Festschrift* (1918), pp. 47–53, and then discussed by the writer in the *Robinson Volume*, p. 7. The three bicola in the metrical scheme 3:3–3:3–2:2 have one perfect example of two-word repetitive parallelism (*'ittî mil-Lĕbānôn*) and one of one-word repetition (*mē-rôš*). In this connexion it may be observed that we may have here a case of misunderstanding caused by the ambiguity of the preposition *la/i* in North-west Semitic usage. In Ugaritic it is sometimes uncertain whether it is

Hebrew is presumably derived) may stand for older **sumaddar* (cf. *'elpâ* from *elippu*, and many other similar Aramaic loans from Accadian) and be derived from the peculiar *sumaktar*, attested in the meaning 'slave born in the house', Latin *verna*. An original sense like 'blossom' would be quite possible. Meanwhile cf. the discussion of the word by Kemal Balkan, *Kassitenstudien, I. Die Sprache der Kassiten* (New Haven, 1954), pp. 138 ff., which follows B. Landsberger. There is no proof, however, that the word is of Cossaean origin; it may be Indo-Aryan or from some native Anatolian tongue. (For the inscribed sherd from Hazor see, for example, Y. Yadin, *Illustrated London News*, 1 Dec. 1956, p. 952.)

[1] See R. T. O'Callaghan, *Orientalia*, xxi, 1952, pp. 37 ff.

[2] Cf. p. 2, n. 1, above.

[3] Contrast the Song of Deborah (*c.* 1150–1125) and the Blessing of Moses (Deut. xxxiii) with the Blessing of Jacob (Gen. xlix); the two latter may be dated before *c.* 1050 and after that date, respectively. Since there are many cases of assonance in the Song of Moses and the Blessing of Moses, but no examples of plays on words, such as become so common in the Blessing of Jacob and later, the inference is clear. Plays on words in the later Hebrew sense do not appear in the Ugaritic poems—nor are they found in older Babylonian literature. In Egyptian they are common in all periods, but this Egyptian practice apparently did not establish itself among the North-western Semites until very late in the second millennium B.C.

to be rendered 'to' or 'from'. In the Old Testament there are many examples where the preposition in question should be translated 'from'; the latter alternative seems to have been forgotten before the time of the LXX.[1] If we suppose that the original Canaanite song referred to Adonis' invitation to go hunting on Lebanon and Antilibanus, addressed to his beloved, a Phoenician goddess identified with Aphrodite by the Greeks, it makes much better sense; Adonis disregarded the warnings of his mistress and was killed by a wild animal while hunting in the mountains.

The following verses, iv. 9–12 (but not verses 13 f., which are late, as shown by Iranian words), also contain several examples of repetitive parallelism: three with one repeated word (*bĕ-'ăḥăd—bĕ-'ăḥăd*, *măh—măh*, *rêaḥ—rêaḥ*) and one with two words, one of which had been reduced to a single beat after the loss of the Bronze Age case-endings (*gan nā'ûl—gan nā'ûl* for older Canaanite *ginnu na'ûlu—ginnu na'ûlu*). Note that the close parallel in wording between Cant. i. 2 f. and iv. 10 occurs in the middle of this archaic passage.

In v. 9 there is a very interesting example of a form of repetitive parallelism which turns up in several Hebrew poems which I should date in the thirteenth–eleventh centuries B.C., where two words appear at the beginning of two bicola instead of in adjacent cola.[2] The M.T. reads as follows:

מה־דודך מדוד　　היפה בנשים
מה־דודך מדוד　　שככה השבעתנו

Since neither the LXX nor any modern translation that I have seen makes grammatical sense of the M.T. we should read the repeated colon: מה־דודך 'כ'מ(ו)־דוד 'What is wrong[3] with thy lover as[4] a lover?' The verse would then mean:

What is wrong with thy lover as a lover,
O fairest of women?

[1] There is now a considerable literature on the use of the preposition *lĕ* in the sense 'from' in the Old Testament as well as in other dialects of North-west Semitic. Note particularly the publications of Mitchell Dahood and his students.

[2] The classical instance is in the text of Deut. xxxii. 43 as restored from M.T., LXX, and a Qumran fragment from Cave IV; see *Vet. Test.* ix, 1959, pp. 340 f.

[3] For this translation, see Brown–Driver–Briggs, *Hebrew and English Lexicon*, p. 552b, and my comments on *mah bĕrî* in Prov. xxxi. 2 (*Levi Della Vida Volume*, i, p. 10). The usage appears in Ugaritic; e.g. Keret i, lines 38 f., in Ginsberg's translation (*A.N.E.T.*, p. 143a), on which see H. L. Ginsberg, 'The Legend of King Keret', *B.A.S.O.R.*, Suppl. Stud. 2–3, 1946, pp. 35 and 50.

[4] See Brown–Driver–Briggs, p. 454a, on the asseverative *kaph*.

What is wrong with thy lover as a lover
  That thou[1] shouldst adjure us so strongly?

In vii. 1 f. we have another transparent borrowing from a North-west Semitic mythological theme. The writer has discussed this passage briefly in the *Robinson Volume*,[2] but would now nuance his treatment slightly. The original should be read:

שובי שובי השולמית
שובי שובי ונחזה בך
מה תחזו בשולמית
כ־׳תחל׳ מחלת המחנים

Come back, come back, O Shulammith,
  Come back, come back,[3] let us watch thee!
How do ye see Shulammith
  When ⟨she dances⟩[4] the dance of the two armies?[5]

The following verses give a vivid description of the charms of the dancer, whose breasts leap like young gazelles as she goes through the rapid gyrations of her dance.

As pointed out in 1950, there can be no doubt that the prototype referred to the war-goddess Shulmânîtu,[6] female counterpart of the war-god Shulman; the Hebrew form is presumably due to a conflation of *Šulmânît* with *Šûnammît* 'the Shunamite woman', appellation of the last consort of King David. Parallels are numerous in Mesopotamian literature. Ishtar is called 'She Whose Dance[7] Is Battle' (*ša mēlultaša tuquntu*), just as in her name Nanaia she is called *ša mēlul⟨ta⟩ša qablum*.[8]

[1] Vocalize as feminine with the commentators.

[2] pp. 7 f.

[3] For a similar fourfold repetition of an imperative, see the Song of Deborah, Judges v. 12.

[4] Vocalize *kî-tāḥōl* (from the stem *ḥll*, as shown by Accadian *elēlu* and the derived *mēlultu* (from **maḥlúlatu*), with a further denominative *melēlu*. The meanings of all these words oscillate between dancing and 'orchestral' singing; cf. the writer's *Archaeology and the Religion of Israel* (1956 edn.), p. 210, n. 96, and the further note on the latter note, p. 230. The verb has obviously dropped out by haplography; it is practically required by the following adverbial accusative, which should be preceded by the cognate verb. Were there further doubt, it should be removed by the fact that LXX inserted a verb of movement, ἐρχομένη, suggesting that there was a verb but that the translator was not sure of its meaning.

[5] Hebrew *maḥăneh*, like Phoenician *mḥnt*, means both 'camp' and 'army'.

[6] On this goddess, see the writer's study, *A.f.O.* vii, 1931, pp. 164 ff. During the past thirty years much new material on Shulman and Shulmânîtu has been gathered, and a paper has been under preparation for some time.

[7] On this word, see n. 4, above.

[8] See K. Tallqvist, *Akkadische Götterepitheta* (Acta Orientalia . . . Fennica, vii, 1938), p. 209.

In the triumphal poem of Tukulti-Ninurta I, from the late thirteenth century B.C., she appears as patroness of the warriors 'who dance into the onslaught (?) of weapons' (*immellū-ma ina šeẖṭūti*[?] *kakkê*).[1] Again at a much earlier date we read in the Agushaya Poem (iii. 7–10):

isinša tamẖara *šūt (i)raqqudū a(na ana)nti*
išātu ul tamẖat a(na ē)teli *itarrū (ana) dašni*[2]

Her feast is the onslaught Of those who dance into battle,
Ere the kindled fire flames up, They are reduced to ashes!

We may safely suppose that the Canaanite prototype of Shulmânîtu–Shulammith is the goddess Anath, whose sanguinary play is so vividly portrayed in the Anath episode of the Baal Epic (V AB, B).[3]

In viii. 5–7 we again have mythological allusions combined with archaic style. There has been some dislocation of the text, as well as two probable losses by homoioteleuton. Rearranging where possible we read:

מי־זאת עלה מן־המדבר
מתרפקת על׳י׳ דודה
שמה חבלתך אמך
שמה חבלה ילדתך
. . . . .
שימני כחותם על־לבך
׳שימני׳ כחותם על־זרועך
. . . . .

This may be rendered:

Who is she who comes from the desert,
Leaning upon her lover?
There thy[4] mother was in travail with thee,
She who bore thee was in travail!
. . . . . .
Place me as a signet on thy heart,
⟨Place me⟩[5] as a signet on thine arm!
. . . . . .

[1] For the text, see E. Ebeling, *Mitt. d. Altorient. Gesellschaft*, xii (2), 1938, p. 8, line 41.
[2] For the text, see H. Zimmern in *Vorderasiatische Schriftdenkmäler*, x, no. 214, col. III, lines 7 ff.
[3] See H. L. Ginsberg's translation, *A.N.E.T.*, p. 136.
[4] The pronominal suffixes should be feminine, with the commentators.
[5] The writer owes this obvious emendation to Dr. Victor Gold; the verb has been lost by haplography.

There can be little doubt that the mother of the beloved was a mythical figure, possibly a girl who had escaped to the desert after having become pregnant by a god. A somewhat similar situation is described in the Poem of the Beautiful and Gracious Gods, where the two infants born to El and two unnamed women are reared in the 'Desert of Kadesh'. The wording is almost the same: *mdbr Qdš ṯm* 'desert of Kadesh. There . . .'.[1] In Rev. xii. 6, in a passage generally recognized as being based ultimately on imagery of mythical origin,[2] we are also told that the mysterious woman clad in celestial imagery, being pregnant with a male child, was miraculously carried off into the desert. In any event, the antiquity of the passage is assured by the certain appearance once, and probably twice, of the Bronze Age repetitive pattern of parallelism: *abc—abd*.

In the following verses we have additional reminiscences of Canaanite mythology: the parallelism of Môt 'Death' and Sheol 'Underworld', as well as the collocation of *'z* and *M(w)t*, as in the Baal Epic; a possible reference to Resheph in verse 6, and a certain allusion to the mythological dragons of the primordial waters, Mayim Rabbîm[3] and Neharôt.[4]

The tenacity with which archaic material dating at the latest from the last centuries of the second millennium, and perhaps even older, persisted into the fifth–fourth centuries B.C., when it was presumably collected by an unknown amateur, is quite extraordinary. Without the taste and collector's enthusiasm of our unknown scribe (or scribes), both secular and religious literature would be immeasurably poorer. Our collector's care should also be commended, since he apparently never conflated his fragments of transmitted lyrics in such a way as to combine Iranian and other obviously late expressions with archaic style and mythical imagery!

[1] Virolleaud, *Syria*, xiv, 1933, plate XIX, lines 65 f.

[2] Naturally not a conscious borrowing from pagan mythology, but presumably an unconscious adaptation through the medium of dreams or visions. Jewish and Christian symbolism and iconography have been immensely enriched in this way.

[3] See H. G. May, 'Some Cosmic Connotations of Mayim Rabbim, "Many Waters"', *J.B.L.* lxxiv, 1955, pp. 9–21.

[4] See especially May, ibid., pp. 19 f.

A SYRO-HEXAPLAR TEXT OF THE SONG OF HANNAH: 1 SAMUEL II. 1–10

By P. A. H. DE BOER, *Leiden*

I

SINCE Ceriani's photolithographic edition of MS. C. 313 Inf., Bibl. Ambros., Milan, 1874, and de Lagarde's edition of six manuscript fragments from the British Museum and one from Paris, *Bibliothecae syriacae . . . quae ad philologiam sacram pertinent*, Göttingen, 1892, some more Syro-hexaplar texts have been published. C. C. Torrey published as variants to de Lagarde's edition of the Syriac apocrypha quotations from Esdras i (iii), to be found in a catena commentary from the ninth century, B.M. Add. 12.168, and fragments of the book of Nehemiah, *A.J.S.L.* xxiii, 1906–7, pp. 65–74. J. Gwynn brought out the same text of Nehemiah together with the fragments of 1 and 2 Chronicles, to be found in the same manuscript, B.M. Add. 12.168, and fragments of the books Genesis, Joshua, Proverbs, and Ecclesiastes, MS. B.M. Add. 7145, London, 1909. M. H. Gottstein published a fragment from the University Library at Cambridge, Or. 929, Deut. xxxii. 8–15, *Muséon*, lxvii, 1954, pp. 291–6. Fragments of the book of Psalms were published by Mme V. V. Pigoulewskaja in *Palestinskij Sbornik*, 1 (63), 1954, pp. 59–60. This Psalm manuscript is from the collection of A. Noroff (cf. *Bibliothèque de M. Abraham de Noroff* 1, Saint-Pétersbourg, 1868, at present in Publičnaja Biblioteka S.S.S.R. im. V. I. Lenina, Moscow; cf. A. Každan, 'Grečeskie rukopisi biblioteki im. V. I. Lenina', in *Voprosy istorii*, x, 1946, pp. 107 f.). A. Rahlfs mentions this manuscript as Norov 74 in his *Verzeichnis der griechischen Handschriften des Alten Testaments* (Göttingen, 1914), p. 141. These fragments of the book of Psalms have the same text as codex Ambr. C. 313 Inf. Finally, Gottstein published Syro-hexaplar texts from the British Museum, B.M. Add. 14.485, Add. 14.486, and Add. 17.195, *Biblica*, xxxvii, 1956, pp. 162–83.[1]

[1] Cf. the discussion and further study in *Biblica*, xxxvi, 1955, pp. 227 f., by G. Mercati, who asks the important question, what relation do the Bible text and the text of the Odes bear to one another, and in *Biblica*, xl, 1959, pp. 199–209, by H. Schneider, who treats the texts of the Odes Exod. xv, Deut. xxxii, Ps. cli, and Dan. iii. 52–88, the song of the three holy children.

II

The Syro-hexaplar text of the song of Hannah published here became known to me during the collection of Bible manuscripts on microfilm for the preparation of a critical edition of the Old Testament Peshiṭta.[1] The text is part of a manuscript from the patriarchal library at Mosul, Bibl. Patr. 1112. This manuscript is not mentioned in A. Scher, 'Notice sur les manuscrits syriaques conservés dans la Bibliothèque du patriarchat Chaldéen de Mossoul', *Rev. d. Biblioth.* xvii, 1907, pp. 237–60, but it belongs to the manuscripts saved from Diarbekir; cf. J. Vosté, 'Notes sur les manuscrits syriaques de Diarbekir . . .', *Muséon*, l, 1937, p. 345: Cod. 2.

Mosul Patr. Chald. 1112 consists of two parts. Fols. 1a–127b are parchment, twelfth century. They consist of 13 quires of 10 fols. each, but the first and the last folio of quire ܐ and fol. 8 of quire ܝ are missing. The second part, fols. 128a–140b, is paper, probably fourteenth to sixteenth century.

The manuscript contains the Psalms, fols. 1a–130a, and seven Odes. The lacunae are: Ps. i. 1–5, xii. 3–xiv. 1, and xxxix. 13–xl. 12. Fols. 128a–130a, from a later hand, contain Ps. cxlvi. 8–cli. The text of the seven Odes is found on fols. 130a–140a. The Odes are:

The song of Moses, Exod. xv, fols. 130a–131a;
The second song of Moses, Deut. xxxii, fols. 131a–134b;
A song of Isaiah, Isa. xxvi. 9–19, fols. 134b–135b;
The song of Hannah, 1 Sam. ii. 1–10, fols. 135b–136a;
The psalm of Habakkuk, Hab. iii, fols. 136a–137b;
The psalm of Jonah, Jonah ii. 2–9, fol. 137b;
The song of the three holy children, Dan. iii. 52–88, fols. 138a–140a.

Fol. 140b has a colophon which is unreadable except the initial words.

III

Mosul Patr. Chald. 1112, fol. 135b.

ܨܠܘܬܐ ܕܚܢܐ ܐܫܬܪܪ ܠܒܝ 1 (1)
ܒܡܪܝܐ. ܐܬܪܘܡ ܩܪܢܝ ܒܐܠܗܝ܀ 2

[1] I owe Mgr Dr. R. Bidawid, Bishop of Amadiyah, Iraq, a debt of gratitude for his good offices in the acquisition of microfilms from the patriarchal library at Mosul. Our Syro-hexaplar text is unique. Even if Masius' manuscript were preserved, we should not have the S.H. text of 1 Sam. ii. 1–10; cf. Rahlfs on the missing parts in Masius, in de Lagarde, *Bibliothecae syriacae* . . ., p. 32h.

3 ܕܝܠܝ. ܐܬܦܬܚ ܦܘܡܝ ܕܝܠܝ ܥܠ

4 ܒܥܠܕܒ̈ܒܝ. ܡܛܠ ܕܐܬܒܣܡܬ ܒ

5 ܒܦܘܪܩܢܐ ܕܝܠܟ. ܠܝܬ ܩܕܝܫܐ ܐܝܟ (2)

6 ܡܪܝܐ. ܘܠܝܬ ܠܒܪ ܡܢܟ. ܘܠܝܬ

7 ܙܕܝܩܐ ܐܝܟ ܐܠܗܐ ܕܝܠܢ. ܠܐ ܬܬܪܘܪܒܘܢ. (3)

8 ܘܠܐ ܬܡܠܠܘܢ ܪ̈ܡܬܐ ※ ܒܪܒܘܬܐ. ܐܦܠܐ

9 ܬܦܘܩ ܡܪܘܪܒܘܬܐ ܡ̈ܠܐ ܡܢ ܦܘܡܟܘܢ

10 ܕܝܠܟܘܢ. ܡܛܠ ܕܐܠܗܐ ܕܝܕ̈ܥܬܐ ܡܪܝܐ.

11 ܘܐܠܗܐ ܕܡܛܝܒ ܐܘܪ̈ܚܬܐ ܕܝܠܗ. ܩܫܬܐ (4)

12 ܕܓܢܒܪ̈ܐ ܐܬܡܚܝܠܬ: ܘܡ̈ܚܝܠܐ ܐܬܚܝܠܘ

13 ܣ̈ܒܥܐ. ܒ̈ܠܚܡܐ ܐܬܒܨܪܘ. ܘܟܦܢ̈ܐ (5)

14 ܕܟܦܢܘ. ܫܒܩܘ ÷ ܐܪܥܐ ↙. ܡܛܠ

15 ܕܥܩܪܬܐ ܝܠܕܬ ܫܒܥܐ. ܘܗܝ ܕܣܓܝܐܬ

16 ܒܒ̈ܢܝܐ ܐܬܡܚܝܠܬ: ܡܪܝܐ ܡܡܝܬ (6)

17 ܘܡܚܐ. ܡܚܬ ܠܫܝܘܠ ܘܡܣܩ.

Fol. 136a.

1 ܡܪܝܐ ܡܡܟܟ ܘܡܥܬܪ. . ܡܡܟܟ (7)

2 ܘܡܪܝܡ. ܡܩܝܡ ܡܢ ܐܪܥܐ ܠܡܣܟܢܐ. (8)

3 ܡܢ ܩܩܠܬܐ ܡܩܝܡ ܠܒܝܫܐ. ܕܢܘܬܒ

4 ܥܡ ܫܠܝ̈ܛܐ ÷ ܕܥܡ̈ܡܐ ܘܟܘܪܣܝܐ

5 ܕܫܘܒܚܐ ܢܘܪܬ ܐܢܘܢ. ܗܘ ܝܗܒ ܨܠܘܬܐ

6 ܠܗܘ ܕܡܨܠܐ. ܘܒܪܟ ܫܢ̈ܝܐ ܕܙܕܝܩܐ.

7 ܡܛܠ ܕܠܘ ܒܚܝܠܬܢܘܬܐ ܗܘ ܓܒܪܐ (9)

8 ܚܝܠܬܢܐ. ܡܪܝܐ ܡܚܝܠ ܢܥܒܕ ܠܒܥܠܕܝܢܐ ܕܝܠܗ (10)

9 ܕܝܠܗ. ܡܪܝܐ ܩܕܝܫܐ. ܠܐ ܢܫܬܒܗܪ ܚܟܝܡܐ (10a)

10 ܒܚܟܝܡܘܬܐ ܕܝܠܗ. ܘܠܐ ܢܫܬܒܗܪ ܥܫܝܢܐ

11 ܒܥܘܫܢܐ ܕܝܠܗ. ܐܠܐ ܒܗܕܐ ܢܫܬܒܗܪ (10b)

12 ܗܘ ܕܡܫܬܒܗܪ. ܒܗܢܐ ܕܡܣܬܟܠ

13 ܘܝܕܥ ܠܡܪܝܐ. ܘܠܡܥܒܕ ܕܝܢܐ

14 ܘܙܕܝܩܘܬܐ ܒܡܨܥܬܗ ܕܐܪܥܐ. ܡܪܝܐ ÷ (10c)

15 ܣܠܩ ܠܫܡܝܐ ܘܪܥܡ ܗܘ ܕܐܢ ܩ̈ܨܘܬܐ

16 ܕܐܪܥܐ. ܘܝܗܒ ܚܝܠܐ ܠܡܠ̈ܟܐ ܕܝܠܢ. ܘܡܪܝܡ

17 ܩܪܢܐ ܕܡܫܝܚܐ ܕܝܠܗ

IV

Ishodad of Merw's commentary has one S.H. quotation from the song of Hannah: ܡܘܣܐ. ܚܣܝܪ̈ܐ ܡܠܝ̈ܐ ܠܚܡܐ B.M. Or. 4524, fol. 120a, line 23, 1 Sam. ii. 5.[1]

Ishodad continues with the still enigmatic ܟܦ̈ܢܐ· ܡܠܝ̈ܐ ܘܣܒ̈ܥܐ. His 'Hebrew' reading is the Peshiṭta version, ܣܒܥܐ being a different spelling for ܫܒܥܐ also found elsewhere.[2]

This reading ܠܐ ܬܡܠܠܘܢ ܪܘ̈ܪܒܬܐ in verse 3, which is neither Peshiṭta nor S.H., is remarkable.

In Bar Hebraeus' *Auṣar Rāzē*[3] occur three quotations from S.H.: *ad* verse 3: ܗ̄ܘ ܡܛܠ ܕܐܠܗܐ ܕܝ̈ܕܥܬܐ ܡܪܝܐ ܘܐܠܗܐ ܕܡܛܝܒ ܐܬܥ̈ܝܐ ܕܝܠܗ, without variants; *ad* verse 5: ܗ̄ܘ ܐܬܒܨܪ, with the following variants: 1 manuscript *praem.* ܘ; 17 manuscripts read the plural ܐܬܒܨܪܘ. And it seems possible to suppose this plural reading too in the basic text of Sprengling–Graham's edition. And *ad* verse 5: ܡܠܝ̈ܐ· ܡܚ̈ܣܪܐ., without variants.

Bar Hebraeus' quotations do not coincide entirely with Ishodad's quotations.

In September 1961 I had an opportunity of seeing in the Vatican Library at Rome two more Syro-hexaplaric readings of the song of Hannah. Bar Hebraeus' three quotations mentioned above occur too in Vat. sir. 489, in the margin of fol. 304a. A remarkable text of the song of Hannah is to be found in Barberiniani orientali 2, fols. 119b–201a, being one column of the manuscript which consists, for the greater part, of five columns—Armenian, Arabic, Coptic, Syriac, and Ethiopic versions. I hope to deal with this text elsewhere. A description of Vat. sir. 489 and Barb. or. 2 is to be found in *List of Old Testament Peshiṭta Manuscripts* (edited by the Peshiṭta Institute of Leiden University, Leiden, 1961), p. 67, and in *Vet. Test.* xii, 1962, p. 128.

Finally, in the Syriac translation of 1 and 2 Clement[4] occurs a quotation (which in the Greek original text is indicated as Jer. ix. 23 f.) of

[1] B.M. Or. 4524 is a manuscript from the seventeenth or eighteenth century; cf. G. Margoliouth, *Descriptive List of Syriac and Karshuni MSS. in the British Museum acquired since 1873* (London, 1899), pp. 45 f. It is the only known manuscript besides Syr. 10 of the Greek patriarchate in Jerusalem, dated A.D. 1380. My thanks are due to Dr. J. B. Segal, who kindly copied the passage on fol. 120a for me.

[2] Cf. Payne Smith, *Thes. Syr.* 4036.

[3] Edited by M. Sprengling–W. C. Graham, *Bar Hebraeus' Scholia on the Old Testament*, Part I (Chicago, 1931), p. 302.

[4] 1 Clement xiii. 1, cf. R. L. Bensly, *The Epistles of S. Clement to the Corinthians* (Cambridge, 1899), p. ܟܗ. I owe this quotation to Mr. W. Baars, who has helped me in many ways.

1 Sam. ii. 10; in choice of words it recalls the S.H. text of 1 Sam. ii. 10:
ܠܐ ܢܫܬܒܗܪ ܚܟܝܡܐ ܒܚܟܡܬܗ: ܐܦ ܠܐ ܚܝܠܬܢܐ ܒܚܝܠܗ. ܐܦ ܠܐ ܥܬܝܪܐ ܒܥܘܬܪܗ.
ܐܠܐ ܗܘ ܕܡܫܬܒܗܪ ܒܗܕܐ ܢܫܬܒܗܪ. ܠܡܣܬܟܠܘ ܘܠܡܕܥ ܕܒܠܐ ܘܪܘܡܘܬܐ.

V

The S.H. text suggests some observations.

Fol. 135b. *Line 1*

ܐܫܬܪܪ] In Ps. xxxiii. 6 S.H. is ܫܡܝ̈ܐ ܐܫܬܪܪܘ, a rendering of *οἱ οὐρανοὶ ἐστερεώθησαν*. A figurative use of the verb is made in Rom. i. 12 P. (= Peshiṭta): ܠܡܫܬܪܪܘܢ ܕܒܗ ܪܘܚ . . .

Line 3

ܐܬܦܬܚ] This form is in Jer. li. 58 S.H., a rendering of *ἐπλατύνθη*. The same verb renders *πλατύνω*, figur., in Ps. cxviii (cxix) 32 S.H.

Line 4

ܐܬܒܣܡ] The Ethpa. of ܒܣܡ is the usual rendering of *εὐφραίνομαι*.

Line 7

ܠܡܫܬܒܗܪܘܢ] ܢܫܬܒܗܪ is 4 times the rendering of *καυχάσθω* in Jer. ix. 23 f. (22 f.) S.H.

Line 8

ܒܪ̈ܒܘܬܐ] *εἰς ὑπεροχήν*. This expression occurs in the Bible only here. But once, in Jer. lii. 22 S.H., *ὑπεροχή*, with its literal meaning, is rendered by ܪܒܘܬܐ. Cf. too Rom. xiii. 1 P. ܫܘܠܛܢ̈ܐ ܕܪܒܘܬܐ < *ἐξουσίαι ὑπερέχουσαι*.

Line 9

ܡܪܘܪܒܘܬܐ (ܡ̈ܠܐ)] A hitherto unknown formation in Syriac, a rendering of the *hapax legomenon* *μεγαλορρημοσύνη*. The verb *μεγαλορρημονεῖν* is rendered by ܪܘܪܒ ܡ̈ܠܐ in the S.H. texts Pss. xxxiv (xxxv) 26, xxxvii (xxxviii) 16, liv (lv) 12, and Ezek. xxxv. 13. Cf. too the rendering of *μεγαλορρήμων* by ܡܬܪܘܪܒܢܐ, e.g. in Ps. xi (xii) 4 S.H.

Line 11

ܐܘܡ̈ܢܐ] A rendering of *ἐπιτηδεύματα*, Judges ii. 19; Ps. ix. 11 S.H.

Line 12

ܐܬܡܚܠ] Ethpa. Cf. Ps. xvii (xviii) 36 S.H., a rendering of *ἀσθενεῖν*, metaphorically.

ܐܬܚܣܢܘ] A rendering of *περιζωννύναι*, cf., for example, Ps. xvii (xviii) 32 S.H.

Line 13

ܐܬܒܨܪܘ] A rendering of ἐλαττοῦν, cf. Ps. xxxiii (xxxiv) 10 S.H.

Line 17

ܡܚܝܐ] Aph. of ܚܝܐ, a rendering of ζωογονεῖν in Exod. i. 17, 18, 22; Judges viii. 19; 3 Kings xxi (xx) 31; 4 Kings vii. 4, all S.H.

Fol. 136a. *Line 1*

ܡܡܣܟܢ] A rendering of *πτωχίζειν*, *hap. leg.* in LXX.

ܡܡܟܟ] In S.H. the usual rendering of *ταπεινοῦν*, cf., for example, Judges xvi. 5.

Line 2

ܡܪܝܡ] A rendering of *ἀνυψοῦν*, cf., for example, Ps. cxii (cxiii) 7 S.H.

ܡܣܟܢܐ] A rendering of *πένης*, e.g. in Exod. xxiii. 3 S.H.

Line 3

ܒܨܝܪܐ] The usual but not exclusive rendering of *πτωχός* in S.H., cf., for example, Job xxii. 8; Jer. v. 4.

Line 4

ܥܫ̈ܝܢܐ] Not the usual rendering of *δυνάστης*, which is rendered by ܫ̈ܠܝܛܢܐ, e.g. Judges v. 9 S.H.: ܫܠܝܛܢܐ ܕܥܡܐ. Our ܥܫܝܢܐ is used in Ps. lxxi (lxxii) 12 S.H.: ܦܪܩ ܠܒܨܝܪܐ ܡܢ ܥܫܝܢܐ < *ἐρύσατο πτωχὸν ἐκ . . . δυνάστου*.

Line 7

ܕܠܗ] Possibly an error; read ܕܠܐ.

ܚܝܠܬܢܘܬܐ] The usual rendering of *ἰσχύς* in S.H.

Line 8

ܒܥܠ ܕܝܢܐ] The rendering of *ἀντίδικος* in S.H., Hos. v. 11; Prov. xviii. 17; Jer. l. 34.

Line 9

ܒܪ ܡܕܥܐ] The rendering of *φρόνιμος* in, for example, 3 Kings v. 7 (21) S.H.

Line 12

ܕܠܡܣܬܟܠܘ] The rendering of *συνίειν*, e.g. in Ps. lii (liii) 2 S.H.: the same construction with ܠ: ܠܡܚܙܐ ܐܢ ܐܝܬ ܕܡܣܬܟܠ ܐܘ ܕܒܥܐ ܠܐܠܗܐ.

Line 15

ܠܥܫܝܢܐ] Without *s*[e]*yāmē*.

ܪ̈ܫܝܗ] A rendering of *ἄκρα*, e.g. in Isa. xli. 5 S.H.: the same construction with ܐܪܥܐ *γῆς*: ܪ̈ܫܝܗ ܕܐܪܥܐ.

VI

A comparison of the Greek text, edited by Brooke–McLean, Cambridge, 1927, with our S.H. text from Mosul gives the following results:

Verse 1

μου 2°] ܕܝܠܝ ÷ *cum* M.T.

ἐπὶ ἐχθροὺς τό στόμα μου] ܦܘܡܐ ܕܝܠܝ ܥܠ ܒܥܠܕܒܒܝ = στομα μου επ εχθρους μου *cum* Aabnopxc_2e_2𝔄𝔅ℭ𝔏[s] Or-lat Chr.[1]

εὐφράνθην] *praem.* ܡܛܠ = οτι *cum* Ap[b].

Verse 2

ὅτι] *om. cum* A.

δίκαιος — σοῦ] ܣܛܪ ܡܢܟ. ܘܠܝܬ ܙܕܝܩܐ ܐܝܟ ܐܠܗܐ ܕܝܠܢ = πλην σου και ουκ εστιν δικαιος ως ο θεος ημων *cum* A.

Verse 3

ὑψηλά] *add.* ܠܪܘܡܐ ⁜ = εις υπεροχην *cum* AMa-hmoswxzc_2e_2𝔖[j].[2]

μὴ 3°] ܐܦܠܐ may be a rendering of και μη *cum* bqtzc_2e_2 or of μηδε *cum* MNac-hm-psv-ya_2b_2𝔏[s]Or-lat⅓. Cf. Ps. i. 5 μηδε (S.H.: ουδε).

γνώσεως] ܕܝܕܥܬܐ = γνωσεων *cum* AMNa-no*p-b_2𝔄𝔖-ap-Barh𝔖[j] Or-lat½ Cyp.

Verse 5

καὶ ἀσθενοῦντες παρῆκαν γῆν] ܘܟܦܢܝܢ ܕܦܫܩܘ. ܫܒܩܘ ÷ ܐܪܥܐ ↙ = οι πεινωντες (*cum* AMNa-hm-e_2𝔄𝔅ℭ𝔏𝔖[j] Or-lat) derelinquerunt ÷ terram (*cum* Or-lat).

Verse 8

καὶ 1°] *om. cum* —; cf. M.T.

λαῶν] ܕܥܡܡܐ ÷ *cum* M.T. Cf. om. in 𝔏[B] (inter potentibus).

δικαίου] ܕܙܕܝܩܐ = δικαιων *cum* Aqtyz*a_2𝔄𝔅ℭℭ𝔏[bs]𝔖[j].

Verse 10a

καὶ 1° — αὐτοῦ 2°] *om. cum* p𝔏[e].

Verse 10b

συνίειν] *praem.* ܒܗܘ ܕ = εν τω *cum* a-fi[a]m-pswxzc_2e_2𝔖[j] (vid) Thdt.

Verse 10c

÷ after ܡܠܟܐ?

VII

S. R. Driver observed in his *Notes on the Hebrew Text . . . of the Books of Samuel* that the Alexandrian manuscript exhibits a text which has

[1] Cf. Berlin MS. Or. Oct. 1019, edited by M. Black, *A Christian Palestinian Syriac Horologion* (Cambridge, 1954), pp. 164 ff. and 24 f. [2] Ibid., pp. 165 and 25.

been systematically corrected so as to agree more closely with the Hebrew.[1] How did they correct the Greek manuscript? F. C. Burkitt stated: 'In all four books of Kings and in some other parts A has been conformed to the Hexaplar text. . . . In fact A is often little more than a transcript of the fourth column of the Hexapla, but without the critical signs by which Origen's additions were marked off from the rest.'[2] H. B. Swete, quoting Burkitt's words in his *Introduction to the Old Testament in Greek*, continues: 'In other words, adaptation to the Hebrew has been effected not by direct use of the official Hebrew text, but through the medium of Origen's work.'[3]

The S.H. text published here seems to prove the correctness of the thesis that the Alexandrian manuscript is based on the Hexapla. Similarity with A is striking. Only in two cases S.H. does not follow A: verse 3 *αυτων* A and verse 8 *καθισαι αυτον* A. Origen's influence is obvious too in the second part of the variant reading in verse 5. And the use of Origen's *sigla* points in the same direction.

Striking similarity in a rather short passage, however, is not sufficient to form a general rule. In the S.H. texts of 1 and 2 Samuel published by Gottstein in *Biblica*, xxxvii, only one case occurs where S.H. + A vary from the other manuscripts: 2 Sam. xxiii. 13 ܩܣܘܪ // A *κασωαρ*. The same fragments, on the other hand, have many cases of unique A readings without support in S.H., e.g. 1 Sam. vii. 6, 11, xx. 12, 16, 19, 20, 22, 41; 2 Sam. vii. 1, xxi. 5, xxiii. 16. It remains remarkable that in all these cases A differs from M.T.

It seems very probable that G. Mercati's important questions, *Biblica*, xxxvi, do find an answer in our S.H. text. The text appears to be quoted from a Bible manuscript and not from a manuscript of the Odes. It is striking that the S.H. text in a number of cases follows the Bible text of the Alexandrian manuscript and not the text of Odes to be found in the same codex: verse 2 *οτι*; verse 2 *πλην σου κτλ.*; verse 8 *δικαιων*. A conclusive answer, however, is made difficult by the fact that fols. 135b and 136a do not belong to the original Psalter manuscript and may have been copied from a Bible manuscript.

[1] 2nd edn., Oxford, 1913, p. xlvii.

[2] *Fragments of the Books of Kings according to the Translation of Aquila* (Cambridge, 1897), p. 19.

[3] 2nd edn., Cambridge, 1914, p. 489.

A NEW LIST OF SO-CALLED 'BEN NAFTALI' MANUSCRIPTS, PRECEDED BY AN INQUIRY[1] INTO THE TRUE CHARACTER OF THESE MANUSCRIPTS

By A. DÍEZ-MACHO, *Barcelona*

I

IN *M.d.W.* ii, pp. 52*–56*, a double list of 'Ben Naftali'[2] manuscripts prepared by P. Kahle and R. Edelmann may be seen. The first describes typical 'Ben Naftali' manuscripts (MSS. A, B, C, . . . O). The second lists 18 'Ben Naftali' manuscripts—many of them previously known as such, more or less influenced by and adjusted to Ben Asher tradition.

In 1956 an article was published (*Estudios bíblicos*, xv, pp. 187–222) which I had written in New York a year before, 'Un manuscrito hebreo protomasorético y nueva teoría acerca de los llamados MSS. Ben Naftalí'. In this article I intended to publish a new 'Ben Naftali' manuscript—MS. 558 (E.N.A. 2640), fols. 21–22, and to examine the whole problem of the so-called 'Ben Naftali' manuscripts. My conclusion was that this type of manuscripts is prior to Ben Naftali, that their characteristics are proto-Tiberian, that many of these characteristics derive from the 'Palestinian' punctuation, and, if there be a resemblance between the real Ben Naftali manuscripts and the so-called 'Ben Naftali' manuscripts, this resemblance could be explained by the same origin—the Palestinian punctuation—of the features common to the two types of manuscripts.

In connexion with the true character of the Ben Naftali school, three other studies appeared at that time: H. Yalon's article on the *parasha* Num. xiii–xv of the MS. Heb. 8° 2238 of the Hebrew University,

[1] The present writer wishes to thank Dr. Manfried Dietrich, who put at my disposal a copy of his Dissertation, *Neue palästinisch punktierte Bibelfragmente, veröffentlicht und auf Text und Punktation hinuntersucht*, presented in the Faculty of Theology of Tübingen University, 1960, and kindly gave me permission to quote from this excellent study. During Dr. Dietrich's recent visit to Madrid I had the opportunity of discussing with him many of the points involved in this introductory inquiry.

[2] When Ben Naftali is written in this article with ' ', the pseudo-Ben Naftali manuscripts are meant; the so-called 'Ben Naftali' manuscripts.

Jerusalem (*Kiryath Sepher*, xxx, 1955, pp. 257–63), showing that this manuscript, considered by U. Cassuto a pure Ben Asher manuscript, is, in fact, a typical Ben Naftali manuscript, and two articles by F. Pérez Castro of Madrid: '¿Ben Ašer — Ben Naftalí?: Números 13–15 en cinco MSS. a la luz de Mišael Ben Uzziel' (*Homenaje a Millás-Vallicrosa*, ii (Barcelona, 1956), pp. 140–8) and the important study 'Corregido y Correcto' (*Sefarad*, xv, 1955, pp. 3–30). In this last article Pérez Castro lists the Ben Asher and Ben Naftali readings of MS. B 19a and Or. 4445 for the Pentateuch, Jer., and Job, following as criterion the *ḥillufim* of Mišael Ben Uzziel. After these studies it appears evident that Ben Naftali differs from Ben Asher in some 900 small details, mostly in the use of the *metheg*.

In 1957 Jos. Prijs published an article on MS. B I 13 of Basel, a new 'Ben Naftali' manuscript ('Über Ben Naftali-Bibelhandschriften und ihre paläographischen Besonderheiten', *Z.A.W.*, N.F., lxix, 1957, pp. 171–84).

In the same year, 1957, Abba Ben David published (*Tarbiz*, xxvi, pp. 385–409) his first contribution in this field, ''Al mah neḥlĕqū Ben Asher ū-Ben Naftali?', which was followed in 1958 by another study, 'Ḥillūfē Ben Asher ū-Ben Naftali 'al pī bĕdīqāh bi-mqōrōt qĕdūmīm' (*Bēt Miqrā'*, iii, 1958, pp. 1–20). In this article the author studies the *Diqdūqē ha-Ṭĕ'āmīm* and the Grammar *Hōrāyat ha-Qōrē'* in connexion with the differences of the two great Masoretes. The continuation of this article will study such differences in the following sources: the Qaraite manuscripts written in Arabic letters and pointed according to the Tiberian system, Codex Prophetarum Petropolitanus of 916, Codex Reuchlinianus, published by A. Sperber in 1956, and other manuscripts attributed, as the said codex, by P. Kahle to the 'Ben Naftali' school.

I have just mentioned the (facsimile) edition of the 'Ben Naftali' manuscript known as Codex Reuchlinianus. In the same Collection, *Corpus Codicum Hebraicorum Medii Aevi, Pars II: The Pre-Masoretic Bible*, Sperber published in 1959 two other 'Ben Naftali' manuscripts, the Parma Pentateuch (MS. Parma 1848, formerly De Rossi 668) and the Parma Bible (MS. Parma 2808, formerly De Rossi 2).

Shelomo Morag has devoted a detailed criticism to Sperber's presentation of the Codex Reuchlinianus as 'the *Pre-Masoretic* Bible': 'The Vocalization of Codex Reuchlinianus: Is the "Pre-Masoretic" Bible Pre-Masoretic?'[1] (*J.S.S.* iv, 1959, pp. 216–37). The conclusion of Morag's study is that 'some of the peculiarities of Codex Reuchl. are distinctly

[1] Hereafter Morag.

Palestinian. . . . We can regard it [CR] as representing a certain Palestinian school. . . . In its principles this school is rather *post*- than *pre*-Masoretic, it represents a later stage in the development of the Masorah' (p. 237).

Last year, 1960, Israel Yeivin published a Hebrew fragment, Prov. xxv. 26–xxvii. 8, of the Antonin Collection in Leningrad, no. 243 (no. 170 of Abraham I. Katsch, *Ginze Russiyah, Catalogue of Hebrew MSS. Preserved in the U.S.S.R.*, ii (New York, 1958), facs. 25 and 26), in his article 'Qeṭaʿ Miqrāʾ bĕ-niqqūd ṭĕbarnī lō-māsortī' (*Tarbiz*, xxix, 1960, pp. 345–56). This manuscript is another 'Ben Naftali' manuscript, not so old as MS. 558, fols. 21–22, of the Jewish Theological Seminary of New York (see above), but older than the 'Ben Naftali' manuscripts described in *M.d.W.* ii. In this manuscript, as in MS. Add. 21161 of the British Museum, and Add. 4709 and Vat. 6 and in most 'Ben Naftali' manuscripts of the poetical books of the Bible, *tĕbir* substitutes *dĕḥi*, a phenomenon which I noted in my article on MS. 558, fols. 21–22, and Prijs in his study of MS. B I 13a of Basel, and which one can see in the Babylonian punctuation of the poetical books.

From this short outline of the recent work on assumed or real Ben Naftali manuscripts it results that we have now more material for knowing the exact nature of such peculiar manuscripts. But we still need further material, especially old 'Ben Naftali' manuscripts of the type of MS. 558, fols. 21–22, of the J. Th. S., and of the type of the fragment published by I. Yeivin. The material studied by Kahle and Prijs or published by Sperber gives an idea of what the 'Ben Naftali' manuscripts are in an evolved stage of punctuation. Of the primitive stage there is so far little evidence. For this reason our concern in this article is not only to add a great number of new 'Ben Naftali' manuscripts, but to add especially a good number of old, primitive 'Ben Naftali' manuscripts.

We can group the manuscripts[1] of this list in three categories: (i) 'Ben Naftali' manuscripts in a very early stage of development: MSS. 1, 3, 4, 7, 13; (ii) 'Ben Naftali' manuscripts showing a very developed punctuation: MSS. 2, 8, 9, 14, 15, 19, 24, 25; and (iii) 'Ben Naftali' manuscripts of later date, greatly influenced by the Ben Asher tradition and more or less adjusted to this prevailing tradition: MSS. 11, 21, 22.

[1] Owing to the scanty material preserved or available for this study, not all the manuscripts listed in this paper are classified. The Ben Naftali manuscripts of the poetical books are not included in these groups.

In this division one can, of course, distinguish transitional stages, for instance the proper place of MSS. 10 and 12 is between i and ii. The tendency to a complete and accurate punctuation is observed in group ii, the group to which Codex Reuchlinianus and the Parma manuscripts edited by Sperber belong. The manuscripts of this group show a great many of the features listed by Kahle in *M.d.W.* ii, pp. 57*–60*, and give the impression of being rather post-Masoretic than pre-Masoretic manuscripts. However, this impression vanishes when from a comparison of group i with ii it becomes apparent that the latter is only an evolution in the direction of completeness and accuracy of the punctuation of group i, which is very primitive, very imperfect and inconsistent, and similar to the Palestinian punctuation. Only the manuscripts of group iii can be termed post-Masoretic, due to consistent adjustment of their punctuation to that of the *textus receptus* and to the small number of 'Ben Naftali' characteristics which survived this accommodation. The materials I present in this article help to establish the theory advanced in my aforementioned study ('Un manuscrito hebreo protomasorético y nueva teoría acerca de los llamados MSS. Ben Naftalí' (hereafter 'U.M.P.')):

(A) *The 'Ben Naftali' manuscripts are not of the real Ben Naftali school*: see in nos. 1, 2, 8, 9, 10 typical Ben Asher readings according to Mišael Ben ʿUzziel; in nos. 10, 11, 14 typical Ben Naftali readings.

(B) *The real Ben Naftali school has some features of punctuation in common with the so-called 'Ben Naftali' manuscripts*

(1) Initial *shewa*, when preceding a *yod* with a *ḥireq*, is vocalized with *ḥireq* consistently in the real Ben Naftali school, inconsistently in the false 'Ben Naftali' manuscripts. See examples of such use in MSS. 1, 6, 9, 12, 15 of this study and in Codex Reuchlinianus (Morag, p. 236). This representation of *shewa* by a *ḥireq* occurs, too, several times in the so-called 'Ben Naftali' manuscripts when the following *yod* is vocalized with a vowel other than *ḥireq*: see MSS. 1, 4, 9, 13?, 18.

Both types of vocalization are typically Palestinian.

(2) A more limited use of the *maqqeph* than in the Ben Asher school (Morag, p. 236, n. 12; Abba Ben David, ''Al mah neḥlĕqū . . .', p. 391). See examples in MSS. 1, 7, K, 11, 12, 13 (no *maqqeph*).

The conjunctive dot of the Palestinian punctuation in which the *maqqeph* originates is sparingly used in the old Palestinian manuscripts;

its use increases in more recent Palestinian manuscripts (Dietrich). 'Ben Naftali' MS. 18 already uses the *maqqeph* with great frequency.

(3) A more frequent use of the *metheg* than in the Ben Asher school, but this applies only to the real Ben Naftali and to the 'Ben Naftali' manuscripts of group ii. The manuscripts of group i, as a matter of fact, exhibit very few *mĕthāgīm*. In MS. 2 there is no trace of any *metheg*; in MS. 13 only a few. This absence or infrequent use of *metheg* is found in old Tiberian manuscripts (Bauer–Leander, *Histor. Gramm. der hebr. Sprache*, p. 155 i′). In Palestinian and Babylonian punctuations there is no *metheg*.

(C) *Many characteristics of the so-called 'Ben Naftali' manuscripts are found in the Palestinian punctuation*

(1) The confusion of the vowels *segol/ṣere* and *pataḥ/qameṣ*. In the 'Ben Naftali' manuscripts sometimes one vowel sign is used consistently for two vowels (*pataḥ* for *qameṣ* in the Targum of MS. 1, *ṣere* for *segol* in MS. 4), sometimes both vowel signs are interchangeably used, sometimes there is no confusion of vowels, or the confusion occurs very seldom. From the study of the Palestinian manuscripts worked out by Dietrich for his Dissertation he draws the conclusion that in the beginning there was in Palestinian only one *e* and one *a* sound; in the second stage the vowel signs for *segol/ṣere* and *pataḥ/qameṣ* were interchangeably used and finally they were distinguished.

Confusion of *o/u*, of which there are examples in MS. 13 of this list, although not general in Palestinian manuscripts, appears, however, in some Palestinian manuscripts (cf. A. Díez-Macho–S. Spiegel, 'Fragmentos de Piyyuṭim de Yannay en vocalización babilónica', *Sefarad*, xv, 1955, pp. 298–9), for instance, in MSS. T.–S. Coll. K 25/108, T.–S. Coll. N.S. 249/9, and T.–S. Coll. N.S. 249/5 and in MS. T.–S. Coll. K 26/8, Heb. d 44, fols. 1–4, d 37, fols. 38–39, of the Bodleian Library (Dietrich's Cb 1 and Ob 2/Cb 3). Dietrich does not follow Kahle's assumption of a general confusion in Palestinian of *o/u* (see *The Cairo Geniza*, 2nd edn., pp. 66 f., and Murtonen,[1] p. 32. 8, 9).

(2) In Palestinian vocalization *shewa* is either not indicated or is rendered by *pataḥ*, *ṣere*, or *segol*, and by *ḥireq* before *yod*. (On this last treatment of the *shewa* in our 'Ben Naftali' manuscripts, see above, (B) (1).) The Palestinian representation of *shewa* by *pataḥ* probably explains the vocalization פְּרַעֹה found in MSS. 3, 4 of this list.

[1] A. Murtonen, *Materials for a Non-Masoretic Hebrew Grammar*, i (Helsinki, 1958).

Unusual punctuations of MS. 4, as Exod. xix. 25 ונְחת, xvii. 12 ושֲויר, &c., are found in the Tiberian punctuation of MS. 594, box B, envelope 12, of the J. Th. S. of New York, a very primitive punctuation added to the first-hand Palestinian pointing.

(3) In different manuscripts of our list one can find, instead of the Tiberian *ḥaṭeph*, the corresponding full vowel or a simple *shewa* (cf. examples in MSS. 3, 4, 6, 7, K, 9, 13). When this old 'Ben Naftali' punctuation is evolved as in manuscripts of group ii, the *ḥăṭephim* appear either in the ordinary Tiberian form or in the form described in *M.d.W.* ii, p. 58*, nn. 9, 10.

In the Palestinian manuscripts vowelless gutturals are given a full vowel or remain unvocalized. A primitive representation of these unvocalized Palestinian gutturals is their pointing with simple Tiberian *shewa* as found in the oldest 'Ben Naftali' manuscripts.

In several Palestinian manuscripts discovered and analysed by Dietrich (MS. Heb. d 29, fols. 17–20, of the Bodleian Library, MS. Ob 2/Cb 3, MS. T.–S., 2nd Coll. 2/71 = Cb 7, and MS. T.–S. Coll. N.S. 249/8 = Cb 10) we find, in their second hand, archaic Tiberian vocalization: the same proto-Tiberian pointing which is exhibited by our 'Ben Naftali' manuscripts of group i, namely a full vowel or *shewa* instead of *ḥaṭeph*: אְדום , אְלהים; Joshua xiv. 6 הָאֶלהים, xviii. 27 ותְרַאלה (for ותראֲ'), xxi. 27 מֶחַצי (for מֶחֱ'); Ezek. xvi. 20 לֶאֶכל, xvii. 23 אשתָלנו (B.H.[3] אשתֳלנו), &c.

The contrary use—*ḥaṭeph* instead of a full vowel—of which there are examples in MSS. K, 9, 14, 16 of this list, is paralleled in Dietrich's MS. Ob 1 by an example of a second proto-Tiberian hand: Joshua xiv. 5 וַיְחַלְּקוּ (B.H.[3] וַיַּחְלְקוּ).

(4) The use of *qameṣ* for *ḥolem* (MS. 4), or *pataḥ* for *ḥolem* (MSS. K, 11), and the use of *ḥolem* for *qameṣ ḥaṭuph* (MS. 16) are well attested in Palestinian pointing. This last use is, according to Dietrich, a good indication of the Palestinian manuscript being uninfluenced by Tiberian pointing.

(5) Incomplete vocalization. Common and proper nouns, and particles, in the 'Ben Naftali' manuscripts are very often partially or completely without vocalization. This happens especially in the case of the word *'asher*. Such a lack of vocalization, chiefly in the case of proper nouns and *'asher*, is well attested in Palestinian manuscripts.[1]

[1] Cf., for instance, the Palestinian manuscript published in *The Cairo Geniza* (2nd edn.), Appendix III.

(6) Although a given word in 'Ben Naftali' manuscripts and in the Palestinian pointing remains unvocalized, it is, as a rule, accented. There is also a lack of accentuation in both 'Ben Naftali' manuscripts and in Palestinian punctuation, but it is restricted to single accents, not to a type of word.

(7) A peculiar case of defective vocalization in both types of manuscript—'Ben Naftali' and Palestinian—is that of the 'segolata': often only the first vowel is marked.

(8) Another characteristic shared by both classes of manuscripts is defectiveness in regard to the *pataḥ gĕnubah* (cf. 'U.M.P.', p. 207).

(9) Defectiveness in the accents is shown in Palestinian manuscripts by the omission of *soph pasuq*, or *silluq*, or *atnaḥ*: MSS. Cb 1 and Ob 2/Cb 3 of Dietrich's study omit *soph pasuq*—the first completely, the other regularly. MS. Cb 10 (= T.-S. Coll. N.S. 249/8 = Judges vi. 2–viii. 24) writes the *silluq* only once (Dietrich), MS. Ob 1 (= MS. Heb. d 29, fols. 17–20 = Joshua xiv. 3–xxi. 31) exhibits the same accent irregularly (Dietrich), and MS. Cb 6 (= T.-S., 2nd Coll. 1/130) omits the *atnaḥ* entirely (Dietrich).

In MSS. 1, 3, 4, 7 *silluq* is missing or very sparingly used. MS. T.-S. Coll. A 4/1 (= Num. xxiv. 12–xxv. 22), according to Dietrich a manuscript with early defective punctuation, uses the *silluq* irregularly.

MS. T.-S. Coll. N.S. 249/12, Dietrich points out in his study, has two forms for *soph pasuq*: two dots and one dot. Both forms are attested in MS. 7 of this list.

(10) In MSS. 1, K, 8, 9, 10, 12, 15 of the following list one can see examples of postpositive *pashṭa* not repeated on the stressed syllable. The Palestinian manuscripts have one sign (–̈) for *pashṭa* and it is not located on the stressed syllable.

(11) In many 'Ben Naftali' manuscripts *geresh* occurs in the form of simple *geresh* and not as *gerĕshayim* (cf. *M.d.W.* ii, p. 58*, n. 14, and MSS. 1, 4, K, 8, 10, 12, 14, 15).

In Palestinian manuscripts *geresh* occurs, not *gerĕshayim*, and, as a rule, as prepositive accent (in MS. Cb 10 *geresh* is normally *post*positive, Dietrich).

(12) In old 'Ben Naftali' manuscripts accents are not always located on stressed syllables: cf. MSS. 1, 3, 4, K, and what is written above, (10) and (11). The same phenomenon is observed regularly in the Palestinian manuscripts, but in some Palestinian manuscripts there is a tendency to put the accent on the stressed syllable. Cf. MS. Cb 2 = T.-S. Coll.

K 26/1 = Ezra iii. 1–iv. 2 of Dietrich's Dissertation; and cf. ibid., the second-hand proto-Tiberian punctuation of MS. Cb 7 = T.–S., 2nd Coll. 2/71 = Ezek. xvi. 18–xviii. 6, xxvii. 36–xxx. 21: *pashṭa* is postpositive and written only with the mark ‒̀: xvii. 16 הַמֶּלֶךְ, &c.

(13) As regards conjunctive accents, one will notice in the description of the following 'Ben Naftali' manuscripts many deviations from Ben Asher tradition: often the conjunctive accents are missing, often *maqqeph*, *merka*, and *shophar* are interchangeably used (cf. the following description of manuscripts and 'U.M.P.', pp. 202–4).

Such accents are not original in the Palestinian and Babylonian pointings. They were introduced after the disjunctive accents in the form of a dot in between the words, a dot sparingly used in the earliest manuscripts and increasingly used afterwards. This dot was differentiated in several conjunctive accents and *maqqeph*, but confusion of *maqqeph*, *merka*, and *shophar* is noticeable, too, in Palestinian manuscripts, for instance in MS. Cb of Dietrich's study.

(14) As far as the poetic accents are concerned, the deviations of the 'Ben Naftali' manuscripts from the Ben Asher accentuation is here more discernible. Instead of *rebiaʿ mugrash* (‒), MSS. 16 and 18 of this list furnish simple *rebiaʿ* as ‒ (the same form in Palestinian MS. L of *M.d.W.* ii, p. 30*, and in MS. Cb 8 = T.–S. Coll. N.S. 249/3 = Sl. 74. 11–77. 21) in MS. 16, and in the form of a dot (‒) in MS. 18. In Palestinian manuscripts there is no composite accent corresponding to the *rebiaʿ mugrash* of the Ben Asher tradition. There is no *rebiaʿ mugrash* in the 'Ben Naftali' manuscript described in 'U.M.P.', p. 200.

(15) Instead of *ṭiphḥa* (prepositive) or *dĕḥi* of the Ben Asher tradition, 'Ben Naftali' manuscripts (almost all which I have examined, cf. MSS. 16, 17, 18, and what I write in the description of MS. 16; cf. too the manuscript described in 'U.M.P.', pp. 201–2) are provided with *tĕbir*.

This use is paralleled in Palestinian MSS. T.–S. 20/58, Sl. 44. 20, 21; 45. 18 (mistakenly omitted in Murtonen's edition), and in MS. T.–S. 20/52, Sl. 57. 9 (omitted in Murtonen's edn.) and in MSS. T.–S. 20/53 and T.–S. 20/54. Cf. N. Allony–Díez-Macho, 'Dos MSS. palestinenses más de la Geniza del Cairo', *Estudios bíblicos*, xvii, 1958, pp. 87 f.; idem, 'Lista de variantes en la edición de los MSS. palestinenses T–S 20/58 y 20/52', ibid. xviii, 1959, pp. 293–8; idem, 'Otros dos MSS. palestinenses de Salmos', *Sefarad*, xviii, 1958, pp. 255 f., 265.

Therefore, four out of the five Palestinian manuscripts of poetical books so far known—MS. L of *M.d.W.* ii and Cb 8 = T.–S. Coll. N.S.

249/3 of Dietrich's Dissertation are the same manuscript—attest the substitution of *dĕḥi* by *tĕbir* so consistently introduced in 'Ben Naftali' manuscripts.

(16) As regards diacritical marks, 'Ben Naftali' manuscripts are usually thought to be very complete—although not very accurate—in the provision of them. As a matter of fact, it is only to manuscripts of group ii that these marks are attached regularly and in great quantity. The use of such diacritical signs is inconsistent and moderate in early 'Ben Naftali' manuscripts. This inconsistent and restricted use of diacritical marks is peculiar to Palestinian manuscripts.

(17) In the 'Ben Naftali' manuscripts of this study, as in general in 'Ben Naftali' manuscripts, *shin* and *śin* are distinguished by a dot inside the letter: *shin* ש, *śin* ש (*M.d.W.* ii, p. 60*). In MSS. Cb 1 and Cb 9—two Palestinian manuscripts influenced by the Tiberian pointing (Dietrich)—the mark of *shin* is ש and that of *śin* ש. In Palestinian MS. T.-S. Coll. N.S. 249/13 = Gen. xxxiii. 2–xxxv. 20 *śin* is marked שׂ as in many of the 'Ben Naftali' manuscripts of our list and as in Tiberian punctuation. In MS. 13 ·שׁ for שׁ. In MS. 8 אש·יג for B.H.[3] אֲשִׂיג. In Murtonen, p. 33. 1, ·ש *shin* and p. 34. 2 ש or שׂ *śin*.

In 'Ben Naftali' manuscripts the old form (dot inside) often alternates with the later one (dot on the letter).

(18) *'Aleph* with *mappiq*. This is considered one of the more typical features of 'Ben Naftali' manuscripts. In fact, a great many of such manuscripts bear this dot. But note that manuscripts of group i—except MS. K—do not have this dot. Palestinian manuscripts with such a dot are few. To the Palestinian evidence which I collected in 'U.M.P.', pp. 207 f., can be added further evidence from Palestinian MS. Cb 1 of Dietrich's study: אּ (B.H.[3] מַמְאֶרֶת Lev. xiii. 52); אּ (B.H.[3] הָבִיאִי Isa. xliii. 6); אּ (B.H.[3] הַבְּרִיאָה Ezek. xxxiv. 3); נֹאּל (B.H.[3] נֶאֱלָמָה Isa. liii. 7). Cf. also ibid. תֹּהּ (B.H.[3] תֶּהְדֹּפוּ Ezek. xxxiv. 21). Dietrich quotes an example from Levias גֹּאּוותך.[1]

In MS. 4 of this list בעֹּם is paralleled in Dietrich Cb 8, Sl. 77. 5 עינֹּי; cf. ibid. ואֹּהֹּמיה Sl. 77. 4; תהֹּמות Sl. 77. 17. Cf. also MS. 250a (= E.N.A. 1328, p. 6), fols. 8–15, and MS. 55: *he*, when pronounced, is always pointed הּ. *Raphe* on *'aleph* is very common in the manuscripts of our list. Palestinian evidence: Dietrich MS. Cb 9 אֿל·ה (B.H.[3] בֵּאלֹהֶי

[1] Another example in Murtonen, p. 33. 1.

1 Chron. v. 25), and Ob 2/Cb 3, 2 Kings ii. 21 רפֿאתי. Two other examples: Murtonen, p. 33. 2.

(19) Final *he* with *mappiq* (הּ). This *mappiq* is usually under the *he* in the 'Ben Naftali' manuscripts. Cf. 'U.M.P.', p. 208, for Palestinian evidence and MS. 594, box B, envelope 12, of the J. Th. S. of New York, Lam. i. 2 להּ (*The Cairo Geniza*, 2nd edn., p. 342) and Dietrich Cb 10, Judges vi. 37, 39 לבדהּ.

(20) *Raphe* and *dagesh* on *waw* or *yod*. A dot under *yod* and one or two dots in the form of Tiberian *shewa* under *waw* when they are final letters (־יּ; ־וּ or ־וְ).

For these 'Ben Naftali' features, cf. Palestinian evidence from MSS. L, H, J of *M.d.W.* ii, in 'U.M.P.', pp. 210–11. Dietrich provides further Palestinian evidence: MS. Cb 8 = T.–S. Coll. N.S. 249/3 = Sl. 74. 11–77. 21 (a new fragment of MS. L of *M.d.W.* ii): Sl. 74. 14 לויתן; 74. 19 עיניך, and Murtonen, MS. a, p. 33.

(21) *Raphe* and *dagesh* on consonants other than *bgdkft*. This characteristic of the 'Ben Naftali' manuscripts, sparingly and inconsistently used in early 'Ben Naftali' manuscripts, is found in almost every consonant—except gutturals and some final letters—in 'Ben Naftali' manuscripts of more developed punctuation.

Parallel use to the first type of practice is found in Palestinian MSS. L, A of *M.d.W.* ii, and Dietrich Cb 8, Sl. 74. 21 יהללו; 77. 8 הלעו למים and Dietrich Cb 9 ובונה (B.H.[3] וּבוּנָה 1 Chron. ii. 25). Cf. 'U.M.P.', pp. 209 f., and Murtonen, p. 33. 1, 2.

The use of *raphe* and *dagesh lene* in 'Ben Naftali' manuscripts, contrary to the rules of these diacritical marks, is attested in MSS. K, L of *M.d.W.* ii (cf. 'U.M.P.', p. 209). In MS. Cb 1 Dietrich remarks the presence of Palestinian *raphe* (ׄ) where a *dagesh lene* would be expected.

Such inconsistencies are well explained on the assumption that these manuscripts are punctuated in a primitive way.

(22) As regards the consonantal variant readings, the manuscripts of our list as a rule exhibit deviations in the *matres lectionis* from B.H.[3], and very few 'real' consonantal or textual variations. The deviations are minor as compared with those usually found in Palestinian manuscripts. As far as the text is concerned, Dietrich divides his eleven Palestinian manuscripts into four groups: three of them are 'Vulgar Texts' and the fourth a 'Hafṭarah Text'. Second-hand Tiberian corrections in several

of these Palestinian manuscripts attempt to accommodate, not always successfully, the Palestinian text to Ben Asher tradition. There are, therefore, different textual traditions deviating—more or less—from Ben Asher tradition, but little by little all traditions were accommodated to the latter. The more recent a Palestinian or a 'Ben Naftali' manuscript is, the more the deviations from Ben Asher tradition vanish. Inasmuch as Palestinian and 'Ben Naftali' manuscripts reflect a textual tradition confirmed by other manuscripts and old versions, they are 'Masoretic' manuscripts. As a matter of fact, there was a Palestinian Masora as shown by MS. Ob 2/Cb 3, which is a manuscript of Palestinian–Tiberian Masora, and by the use of *qĕrē–kĕtib* in Palestinian manuscripts. The 'Ben Naftali' manuscripts are also Masoretic because in many of them Masoretic notes can be seen, not many, however, and not always in accord with B.H.³ Masora parva. And, as Palestinian manuscripts can be considered early Masoretic, the 'Ben Naftali' manuscripts too can be called early Masoretic Tiberian. It is quite reasonable to assume that the Palestinian manuscripts were the work of different punctuators and the result of a multiplicity of types of punctuation. When it was deemed necessary to substitute the Palestinian punctuation for a more practical system, namely for the Tiberian punctuation, the multiplicity of punctuators and the variety in punctuation continued in existence within the early Tiberian pointing. These primitive Tiberian *naqdanim* reflect by the new signs the various Palestinian ways of pointing, complement the defective punctuation, and introduce new practices of pointing, some of them finally rejected by the mature Tiberian system represented by Ben Asher. Only after a long period of tentative and imperfect punctuation could the perfection of Ben Asher pointing be reached. To this period of variety, inconsistency, defectiveness, and primitivism of the Tiberian punctuation belong the 'Ben Naftali' manuscripts of groups i (early period) and ii (later period).

Mĕnaḥem ben Saruq, writing his *Maḥberet c.* 960, witnesses in this Dictionary to the existence of manuscripts in which all the consonants—except *'ayin* and *ḥeth*—have *dagesh* or *raphe*. In this book the wide use of the 'Ben Naftali' manuscripts of group ii is clearly attested. Around this time the Ben Asher tradition was finally fixed (cf. Bauer–Leander, *Histor. Gramm.*, pp. 128 f.).

From all this it seems that so-called 'Ben Naftali' manuscripts should be regarded as proto-Tiberian manuscripts deriving from the Palestinian tradition.

II

1. MS. Bodl. Heb. c 51, fols. 1–2

2 fols. From the Geniza. Hebrew text with Onqelos alternating. Gen. xxxv. 1–15 (fol. 1), xxxviii. 18–xxxix. 4 (fol. 2). Described in the Add. Catalogue as 'Syr. squ. char., vellum, 11¾ × 9½ in.'. Two columns per page; 25 lines in each column. Damaged and obliterated, especially fol. 1a. There is only one hand. Tiberian vowels and accents, these only in the Hebrew text. There is no Masora or *lĕgarmeh* in the margins.

This manuscript is very old, a conclusion drawn from the primitive way of punctuating. For instance, Gen. xxxix. 3 f. בְּיָדוֹ,[1] a typical Palestinian punctuation to be found in Biblical fragments with Palestinian *niqqud* and 'almost always in the piyyuṭim' [with Palest. *niqqud*]: cf. Abba Ben David's review of A. Murtonen, *Materials for a Non-Masoretic Hebrew Grammar*, i, *Qiryat Sefer*, xxxiii, 1958, pp. 487 f. Cf. also xxxviii. 24 לֽיהודה, Hebrew and Targum (B.H.³ לִֽיהוּדָה); xxxv. 11 and *passim* אֱלהים; but it appears in Hebrew and Aramaic xxxv. 12 וּלְיִצְחַק, xxxv. 15 יַֽעְקב. Often one vowel for two: xxxv. 7 וּבְנָא; xxxv. 12 הָאָרֶץ; xxxviii. 30 זָרח (B.H.³ זָֽרַח); xxxix. 4 נָתן (B.H.³ נָתַֽן). In Aramaic there are many *matres lectionis*. xxxv. 12 אשֶׁר; xxxviii. 18 אֲשֶׁר־, but often אֲשֶׁר.

There is regular confusion of *pataḥ/qameṣ*, *segol/ṣere*, a confusion common in Palestinian vocalization. In the Targum of our manuscript only *pataḥ* is used. xxxv. 12 נַתַּתִּי (B.H.³ 'נָתַ); xxxv. 14 וַיֶּסֶךְ (B.H.³ וַיֵּ֥סֶךְ); xxxv. 11 שַׁדָּי (B.H.³ שַׁדַּי); xxxviii. 20 לָקַחַת (B.H.³ לָקַ֫חַת); xxxviii. 18 חֹתַמְךָ (B.H.³ חֹֽתָמְךָ); וַתֹּאמֶר (B.H.³ וַתֹּ֫אמֶר); xxxviii. 20 וַיִּשְׁלַח (B.H.³ 'לַח).

Often the accents are not on the tonic syllable as in Palestinian and Babylonian punctuation: xxxv. 8 וַתָּמָת; מִתַּחַת; תַּחַת (B.H.³ תַּ֫חַת); xxxv. 14 נֶסֶךְ (B.H.³ נֶ֑סֶךְ); xxxviii. 18 אֶתֶּן (B.H.³ אֶתֶּן־); וּפתילֶךָ; xxxviii. 24 תָמָר (B.H.³ תָּמָ֑ר); xxxviii. 26 לְשֵׁלָה (B.H.³ לשֵׁלָ֣ה); xxxviii. 29 פרצְתָּ (B.H.³ 'פָּרַ֥צ).

[1] In I. Yeivin, 'Qeṭa' Miqrā' . . .', p. 352: Prov. xxvi. 6, 9 בְּיַד־; xxvii. 1 בְּיום. Yeivin remarks: 'Such a punctuation is found in the Palestinian pointing, but not in the Babylonian one. Undoubtedly there is a link between this pointing and the typical Ben Naftali punctuation בִּישראל (Kahle, characteristic no. 6).'

The *silluq* is almost always absent. The *pashṭa* many times, if not always, is not repeated on the stressed syllable: xxxviii. 23 שַׁלָּחְתִּי (B.H.³ שִׁלחתי); xxxviii. 25 חמיה (B.H.³ חמיה); xxxix. 4 וַיָּפְקִדֵהוּ (B.H.³ 'דהו).

There are many variations in the use of the Tiberian accents: xxxv. 8 דבורה (B.H.³ 'רה); שְׁמוֹ (B.H.³ שְׁמוֹ); xxxv. 11 ויאמר לוֹ (B.H.³ ויאמר לו); xxxviii. 20 בְּיד (B.H.³ ביד); xxxviii. 21 אַיֵּה (B.H.³ אַיֵּה); xxxviii. 23 תִּקַּח לָהּ (B.H.³ תִּקַּח־לָהּ).

And yet this manuscript, so old, has many of the characteristics of the so-called Ben Naftali school: xxxv. 7 אַחִיו; xxxv. 13 מֵעָלָיו; xxxviii. 18 לָהּ; xxxviii. 19 צְעִיפָהּ; xxxviii. 21 וישאל (B.H.³ 'אל); xxxv. 8 האלון; xxxix. 3 וַיַּרְא; xxxix. 2, 3 מַצְלִיחַ; xxxviii. 27 תְּאוֹמִים; confusion of vowels; אשר, &c.

But the *ga'yah* is very scarce, and not so frequent as in B.H.³ is the use of the *maqqeph*: xxxviii. 18 הערבון (B.H.³ 'הָע); xxxviii. 25 שִׁלְחָה (B.H.³ 'שָׁל); xxxviii. 26 ולא (B.H.³ וְלֹא־), &c.

In xxxv. 12 very probably there is a *ga'yah* in וְּלְזַרְעֲךָ, a Ben Asher reading; Ben Naftali reads 'וּלְ.

This manuscript, in conclusion, is a very good example of a proto-Tiberian manuscript. There are the 'Ben Naftali' characteristics in it, but in a very early stage of development. For instance, there is little use of *raphe* and, especially, of *dagesh*. Even *dagesh forte* is missing many times; this too is characteristic of 'Ben Naftali' manuscripts.

2. MS. Bodl. Heb. b 4 (Cat. 2611), fols. 13–16

4 fols. Hebrew with Onqelos following the Hebrew text: Gen. xxxvii. 15–xxxviii. 29 and xli. 2–46. Two columns in small folio; 27 lines each column. Handwriting not 'Spanish' as stated in Catalogue but oriental. No Masora in the margins, nor *lĕgarmeh*.

Only the Hebrew text has punctuation according to the 'Ben Naftali' school: Gen. xxxvii. 22 אָבִיו׃; xxxvii. 30 אחָיו׃; xxxvii. 34 שמלתָיו׃; במתנָיו׃, &c.

Dagesh and *raphe*, especially *raphe*, not confined to *bgdkft*. *Dagesh lene* especially in a consonant—chiefly *lamed*—beginning a word after a disjunctive accent or after a closed syllable. The use of these signs is moderate. Examples: xxxvii. 28 וַיִּמְשְׁכוּ; xxxvii. 34 בְּמָתְנָיו; xxxviii. 18 וּמָטְךָ (B.H.³ וּמַטְּךָ); xxxviii. 19 וַתָּסָר; אַלְמְנוּתָהּ; xli. 8 הַמַּשְׁקִים [*sic*].

Raphe on consonantal *yod*: xxxvii. 28 מִדְיָנִים; xli. 8 מצרַיִם.

Ḥaṭeph qameṣ instead of *qameṣ ḥaṭuph*: xxxvii. 34 בּמֳתְניו; xxxviii. 9 נְתָן־.

Ḥaṭeph pataḥ: xli. 3 אַחֲרֵיהֶן; xli. 11 חֲלוֹם.

Final *he* with *mappiq*: xxxviii. 18, 22 לָהּ.

Occasional confusion of *qameṣ/pataḥ*: xxxviii. 18 וּמָטְךָ (B.H.³ 'וּמַטְ); xxxviii. 19 (xli. 42) וַתָּסָר (B.H.³ 'סַר).

The relative *'asher*: written אשר or אֲשר; seldom (xli. 43) אֲשֶׁר. But the accentuation is not missing on this word.

Pataḥ gĕnubah is used in the ordinary way, but in xli. 37 probably רוּח.

Shin and *śin*: שׁ, שׂ.

Occasional deviations in the accents: xli. 19 והנֵּה שֶׁבַע פרות (B.H.³ והנֵּה שֶׁבַע־פָּרוֹת); xli. 27 וְשֶׁבַע (B.H.³ ושֶׁבַע); xxxviii. 14 וַתָּסַר (B.H.³ ותסר).

Variant readings regarding the *matres lectionis*: xli. 20 הראשונות; xli. 22, 24 וטבת (B.H.³ וטבות); xli. 23 צמחת (B.H.³ צמחות); xli. 27 והרעות; xli. 42 רְבִיד; xli. 27 שְׁדוּפוֹת.

Characteristic of this manuscript is the absence of *ga'yah* and *metheg*, which, as a rule, occur with great frequency in the 'Ben Naftali' manuscripts. In xli. 45 פַּרְעֹה, a Ben Asher reading (Ben Naftali פַּרְעֹה). Textual variation: xli. 19 עֹלוֹת אַחֲרֵיהֶן מן היאר דַּלּוֹת (the addition מן היאר is unvocalized).

3. MS. T.–S. B 6_5 of the University Library, Cambridge

1 fol.[1] Vellum, lacking part of the margins. Two columns per page; 22 lines per column. Hebrew text and Onqelos alternating for Gen. xli. 24 (Aramaic)–43. Very few notes of Masora parva and in agreement with that of B.H.³ as far as I can determine from fol. 3a, of which a photostat is in my possession. The handwriting is similar to that

[1] On my last visit to Cambridge I discovered that nine fols. are preserved: (1) Gen. vi. 6–vii. 15; (2) xviii. 23–xix. 6; (3) xli. 24–43 (the one here described); (4) Exod. xxxi. 3–xxxii. 1; (5) xxxix. 10–28; (6) Lev. iv. 32–v. 11; (7) v. 11–25 (parts); (8) vii. 32–viii. 12; (9) xiii. 42–56.

of MS. T.–S. B 6_1 (Deut. xvi. 16–xvii. 7), a 'Ben Naftali' manuscript to be described later (no. 7 of this list), and to that of MS. T.–S. B 6_2 (2 fols. containing Num. xxiii. 4–27, Deut. ix. 5–21), another 'Ben Naftali' manuscript listed by Kahle as MS. K (*M.d.W.* ii, p. 53*). Handwriting similar, too, to MS. 503, fols. 15–16 (E.N.A. 2116), of the J. Th. S. in New York to be described later (no. 4 of this list). Similar, for instance, is the shape of the *'ayin* and the oblique *pataḥ*s. In fact, all these manuscripts have similar characteristics.

MS. T.–S. B_6 mixes *qameṣ/pataḥ*, *ṣere/segol*: xli. 25 וְאַמָר; xli. 33 וְעָתַּה; יֵרֶא (B.H.³ יֵרֶא). Sometimes well-known words appear without vowels: xli. 32 החלוֹם; xli. 31 הַרָעָב; xli. 33 פרעֹה. But always אֲשֶׁר. One vowel for two: xli. 24 טָבָתָא as in MS. 1 of this list and in the manuscript published by Israel Yeivin, 'Qeṭa' Miqrā' bĕ-niqqūd ṭebarnī lō-māsortī', *Tarbiz*, xxix, 1960, p. 352. We find xli. 25, 28 הָאֱלֹהִים; xli. 32 הָאלֹהִים and הָאְלֹהִים.

At least twice (xli. 28, 32) פְּרְעֹה, a very strange second-hand vocalization to be found again in MS. 503, fols. 15–16 (MS. 4 of this list), of the J. Th. S. of New York. In my opinion, this representation of *pataḥ* by *shewa* witnesses to the old pronunciation of the *shewa* as a *pataḥ* as in many 'Palestinian' manuscripts, chiefly in those published by Falk Bar (cf. on this the above-mentioned review of Murtonen's book by Abba Ben David, pp. 486 f. and n. 8). But it still remains strange that in two different manuscripts only the name פרעה appears vocalized several times in such a strange way. However, in xli. 33 there is another case of second-hand *shewa* instead of a full vowel: וְיְשִׁיתֵהוּ (B.H.³ וְיָשׁ׳), and perhaps we may relate to this old use of the *shewa* such curious punctuations as xli. 31, 32 אְרֵי and second-hand punctuation of xli. 32 האְלהים. Notice also xli. 30 וְיִתְּנְשֵׁי. Also reflected is the Palestinian usage of putting *qameṣ* instead of *ḥaṭeph qameṣ*, as in xli. 26 הַשִּׁבָּלִים (B.H.³ הַשִּׁבֳ׳).

Another hint of the great age of this manuscript is the recurrent omission of the *silluq*, a feature consistently found in MS. 1 of this list.

This old manuscript has several characteristics attributed to the Ben Naftali school, for instance *raphe* over נ, מ, final ה, ף: xli. 30 סִיבְּעַה; xli. 31 תַּקִּיף; xli. 32 [הַשָּׁנ[ות; כִּי נָכֹון (B.H.³ כִּי־נָכוֹן); וּמְמַהֵר; דְאִיתְנֵי.

Raphe also over י: xli. 33 וְיָשִׁיתהו; וְימַנְיֵּה. Regularly *dagesh forte* is missing: xli. 28 דִבַּרְתִּי.

Shin is written שׁ and שׁ.

As usual in these manuscripts, there are small deviations in the accents, which are not always on the stressed syllable: xli. 25 אֶֽת־אֲשֶׁ֣ר (B.H.^{3} אֶ֣ת אֲשֶׁ֣ר); xli. 26 שֶׁ֣בַע־ (B.H.^{3} שֶׁ֣בַע); xli. 28 דִּבַּ֖רְתִּי (B.H.^{3} דִּבַּ֖רְתִּי); דְּמַלֵּילְ[ית]; xli. 31 וְלֹא יוּדַ֖ע (B.H.^{3} וְלֹֽא־יוּדַ֖ע); xli. 32 כִּֽי־נָכ֤וֹן (B.H.^{3} כִּֽי־נָכ֣וֹן); xli. 33 אֶ֣רֶץ (B.H.^{3} אֶ֣רֶץ); xli. 31 הַשָּׂבָ֖ע (B.H.^{3} הַשָּׂבָ֖ע).

The evidence cited surely gives proof that the manuscript here studied belongs to the company of proto-Tiberian manuscripts.

4. MS. 503 (E.N.A. 2116), fols. 15–16, J. Th. S. of New York

2 fols. Vellum. Two columns on both sides; 24 lines in each column. Upper part of fol. 16 torn or obliterated. Hebrew text and Onqelos alternating for Exod. xvii. 10–xviii. 12; xix. 20–xx. 18. A few Masoretic notes on the margins. Handwriting similar to that of MSS. T.–S. B $6_{1,\ 2,\ 5}$ (see no. 3 of this list). The present manuscript shows a striking resemblance to these manuscripts regarding the punctuation. In the present manuscript, however, the connexions with Palestinian punctuation and 'Ben Naftali' characteristics are more numerous.

The manuscript shows first- and second-hand punctuation. During my stay in New York I copied this manuscript, distinguishing first- and second-hand punctuation. In his additions or corrections, the second hand uses a different black ink. The first *naqdan* omits the vocalization of some words, particularly proper, and very common, nouns. The second *naqdan* adds the missing vowels. The first hand is more accurate and complete regarding the accents. The second hand tries to correct the confusion in the vowels of the first hand and to bring the text of the first punctuator more into agreement with the punctuation prevailing in later times. But this goal is not achieved and, as a matter of fact, the second-hand punctuation still retains several deviations from the *textus receptus*, for instance xviii. 12 לֵֽאלֹהִ֑ים; xx. 12 לְמַ֙עַן֙. The first hand represents an old proto-Tiberian punctuation, the second hand a further development in the direction of the canonical Masoretic punctuation. The corrections are introduced largely into the Hebrew text, the Targum being neglected, as a rule, by the correctors.

Let us examine the main characteristics of the manuscript.

Exod. xviii. 4, 10 פַּרְעֹה as in MS. 3 of this list.

Exod. xvii. 12 בְּיָדָיו (B.H.^{3} בְּיָדָ֑יו) as in MS. 1 of this list, and in

'Qeṭa' Miqrā' bĕ-niqqūd lō-māsortī', *Tarbiz*, xxix, 1960, and in Palestinian punctuation.

Exod. xx. 7 בֵּשְׁמֵיה. *Ṣere* is used consistently by the first hand for *segol*, and both, *ṣere* and *segol*, are used in Palestinian punctuation for our *shewa*; cf. A. Díez-Macho–S. Spiegel, 'Fragmentos de Piyyuṭim de Yannay en vocalización babilónica', *Sefarad*, xv, 1955, p. 302, n. 8. But in this case בֵּ׳ takes the place of בִּ׳, a common Palestinian usage: cf. ibid., p. 300.

As in Palestinian punctuation, the representation of *shewa* in our manuscript lacks uniformity: Exod. xviii. 1 וּלְישראל (2 h. וּלְיִשְׂרָאֵל); xix. 25 וּנְחתָּ (1 h.), וּנְחַתָּ (2 h.); xx. 11 וּנַּח (1 h.), וּנָּח (2 h.); xvii. 12 ושׁנָיו (2 h. וּשֵׁנָיו). A parallel punctuation of *shewa* is repeated in MS. 594, box B, envelope 12, of the J. Th. S. of New York published by me in 'La cantilación protomasorética del Pentateuco', *Estudios bíblicos*, xviii, 1959 (see p. 244, nn. 46, 49, 50, 52). See also this manuscript published by Kahle in *The Cairo Geniza*, 2nd edn., 1959, pp. 336–44.

Another use of *shewa*: xvii. 15 וְשַׁן; xvii. 12 וְמִזֶה (2 h. vocalization). For this last example, see MS. 594, box B, envelope 12, 'La cantilación . . .', p. 246, line 2 (וְמֵרַב). Many times *waw* (*conjunctivum*) remains without a vowel.

Another Palestinian vestige: xix. 22 הַכָּהֲנִים (2 h. and B.H.[3] הכֹּהנים). In Palestinian not only is there confusion of *qameṣ/ḥolem*, but even confusion of *pataḥ/ḥolem* (see my article, 'La cantilación . . .', p. 243, n. 42. Cf. ibid., p. 244, n. 59 (וְיָתֵר), a proto-Tiberian *qameṣ* for *ḥolem*). For examples of Palestinian confusion of *qameṣ/pataḥ* and *qameṣ ḥaṭuph/ḥolem*, see my article, 'Tres nuevos MSS. bíblicos palestinenses', *Estudios bíblicos*, xiii, 1954, p. 252.

First hand prefers *ṣere* instead of *segol*. First-hand *segolim* are few: xvii. 12 אֶבֶן (not corrected by 2 h.); וַיֵּשֶׁב (2 h. וַיֵּשֶׁב); xvii. 13 חָרֵב׃ (2 h. חָרֶב׃); xvii. 14 אֵל־ (2 h. אֶל־).

Gutturals are given either *shewa*, full vowel, or no sign. In Palestinian *niqqud* they are given either full vowel or no sign. Examples in our manuscript: xvii. 12 עְלָה; וַהְוַאָה; xvii. 13 ויחְלֹשׁ (2 h. וַיַּחְלֹשׁ; B.H.[3] וַיַּחֲלֹשׁ); xvii. 14 אְרֵי; xviii. 11 ארֵי; xvii. 15 עְלוֹהִי; דְעַבַד; xvii. 16 וְאַמַר; xvii. 13 עְמַלֵק; xvii. 11 (Onqelos), but עֲמלק (Hebrew).

'Asher is written defectively: xviii. 5 אשר (2 h. אֲשֶׁר); xviii. 1 אְשׁר (2 h. אֲשֶׁר); xvii. 11 כַאְשר (2 h. כַּאְשֶׁר; B.H.[3] כַּאֲשֶׁר).

Pataḥ gĕnubah is a second-hand addition: xvii. 10 יהושע (2 h. יְהוֹשֻׁעַ); xvii. 15 מִזְבֵּחַ (2 h. מִזְבֵּחַ); xvii. 11 יַנִּיחַ.

The use of *raphe* and *dagesh lene* is similar to that of MSS. 1 and 3 of this list, and *dagesh forte* is not indicated: xvii. 12 וידי (B.H.³ וִידֵי); xviii. 1 דְּמִדְיָן; xvii. 12 וַיִּתְמְכוּ; וַיָּשִׂימוּ; וַיְהִי; תָּמְכוּ (B.H.³ תָּמְכוּ); אֱמוּנָה; הַשָּׁמֶשׁ; xvii. 14 וַיֹּאמֶר; זֹאת; מָחֹה; אֶמְחֶה; xvii. 15 שְׁמוֹ; xvii. 16 מִדֹּר (B.H.³ 'מִ); xviii. 3 שְׁנֵי; בָּנֶיהָ; xviii. 5 וּבָנָיו; חֹנֶה; xix. 21 בעם (2 h. בָּעָם; B.H.³ בָּעָם).

Silluq is missing as in MSS. 1 and 3 of this list.

There are differences in the first- and second-hand accents. Several accents are not located on the stressed syllable: xviii. 1 כֹּהֵן (2 h. כֹּהֵן); וַיִּשְׁמַע (Hebr.) but וּשְׁמַע (Onq.); xviii. 5 וַיָּבֹא (B.H.³ ⸗); xviii. 7 וַיִּשַּׁק (2 h. וישק; B.H.³ וַיִּשַּׁק); xviii. 12 וַיִּקַּח (B.H.³ ⸗).

On the margins *paseq* (פס) is indicated. According to Bauer–Leander, *Histor. Gramm.* (p. 149. 9, n. 3), *paseq* and *lĕgarmeh* are indicated in old Tiberian manuscripts.

In three words there are Babylonian superlinear vowels but, at least in one case, the vocalization is not real Babylonian—it is Palestinian: xix. 21 יֶהֶרְסוּ (2 h., B.H.³ יֶהֶרְסוּ); רָב; xix. 22 יתקדשו (2 h. יִתְקַדָּשׁוּ).

5. MS. T.–S. B 6_3 and MS. T.–S. B 6_4, University Library, Cambridge

MS. T.–S. B 6_3 has 6 fols., all badly mutilated: Lev. xxiii. 41–xxvi. 25. From this manuscript I have studied fols. 1a, 2a, and 3a.

MS. T.–S. B 6_4 is a fragment containing Lev. xiv. 4–17.

These two manuscripts belong to the same manuscript: a manuscript in vellum, with two columns per page, badly damaged and obliterated. In all these fragments, nevertheless, there are several legible lines which afford enough material to recognize the true character of this manuscript, which comes from the Cairo Geniza. The Hebrew text alternates with Onqelos.

The handwriting is oriental and peculiar to 'Ben Naftali' manuscripts. The handwriting is old and, furthermore, the features of the punctuation point to an early date. The punctuation, although almost complete in the

Hebrew text, is defective in the Targum—especially in the accentuation. Particles are sometimes left without vowels. There is confusion of *pataḥ/qameṣ* to a limited extent. *Pataḥ gĕnubah* is missing. *'Aleph*, when it is a consonant, has an inscribed dot. *Raphe* and *dagesh lene* are not only on *bgdkft*, but also on other consonants. In Onqelos the vocalization retains many features of the superlinear *Vorlage*. Final *ḥeth* is written as חּ, *shin* and *śin* as שׁ or שׁ and שׂ.

We list here several examples:

Lev. xxv. 10 Onq. וְתְתוּבוּן (Bab. pointing); וּגְבַר (Bab.); xxv. 11 Hebr. שָׁנָה; לָכֶם; אֶת־; תִבְצְרוּ; Onq. שְׁנַת; xxv. 12 תֵּאכְלוּ; יוֹבֵל; xxv. 13 אִישׁ; אֶל־; xxv. 16 כִּי מִסְפַּר; xiv. 4 Onq. וּצְבַע; וְאַעַא (for וְאָעָא); חַיַּן (for יְיָן'); xiv. 5 הָאֶחָת; אֶל־; Onq. מַבּוּע; חְדָא; דַחְסַף; xiv. 6 יִקַּח; אֹתָהּ; שְׁנֵי; הָאֶרֶז; xiv. 8 וְגִלַּח (B.H.[3] וְגִלַּח); בַמַּיִם; הַמַּחֲנֶה; שִׁבְעַת; Onq. שַׁבְעָה (Bab.); לְמַשְׁרִיתָא; לְמַשְׁכְּנֵיה; וְיִצַּבַע and וְיַגַּלַּח instead of 'וְי of Ben Naftali; וּבתר; xxiv. 15 גְּבָר, גְּבַר; קֳדָם; וְיִקַבֵּל; xxv. 16 תַּזְעָר (for 'עַר); xxiv. 17 אֲרֵי.

One can see in the above examples a good number of the characteristics of the so-called 'Ben Naftali' manuscripts. In xxiv. 16 בנקבְו שֵׁם (Ben Naftali בנקבְו שֵׁם); שֵׁם· יהוָה (conjunctive Palestinian dot).

The manuscript, however, does not belong to the group of MSS. 1, 3, 4 of this list. It is similar to MS. 6.

6. MS. T.–S. B 5$_{13}$, University Library, Cambridge

1 fol. Much like the foregoing manuscript (no. 5): same handwriting, excellent script. It also comes from the Geniza, and the text is without Masora. In the present manuscript only in Deut. xxi. 16, 22 is there Masora (לֿ) in the margins. As in MS. 5, the text is arranged in two columns, but in MS. 6 they are complete, although somewhat dirty. Also MS. 6 has Hebrew text (Deut. xxi. 15–xxii. 8) alternating with Onqelos. Both manuscripts have Ben Naftali characteristics, but more frequently in the Hebrew than in the Aramaic. In MS. 6 accents are usually confined to the Hebrew text. In this manuscript *segol/ṣere, pataḥ/qameṣ* are mixed, *raphe* and *dagesh lene* are indicated in great numbers and in consonants other than *bgdkft*. One finds some variations, as usual, in the conjunctive accents and in the *matres lectionis*. There

is no *pataḥ gĕnubah.* Some particles remain unvocalized. *Metheg* does not occur with great frequency.

Below I give some examples:

Deut. xxi. 15 סְנוֹאַתָא; וַחְדָא; רְחוּמְתַא; וּסְנוּאַתַא; xxi. 16 וְהָיָה; הַנְחִילוֹ; בָּנָיו; יִהְיֶה; אֶת בֵּן הָאֲהוּבָה (B.H.³ אֶת־בֶּן־הָאֲהוּבָה); xxi. 17 יִמָּצֵא לוֹ; אוֹנוֹ (B.H.³ אֹנוֹ); אֲרֵי; xxi. 18 שֹׁמֵעַ; xxi. 19 מְקֹמוֹ (without *silluq*); xxi. 20 שֹׁמֵעַ בְּקֹלֵנוּ; xxi. 21 וָמֵת (B.H.³ וָמֵת); וְיִרָאוּ a Ben Naftali vocalization (B.H.³ וְיִרָאוּ); וִימוּת; מִבֵּינָךְ; וְיִרְגְּמוּנֵּיה; אֱינָשֵׁי.

As in MS. 4, so also in the present manuscript there are a few Babylonian vowels: xxi. 16 לְבַכָּרָא, but one of them (the last ‾) does not agree with the real Babylonian pointing. Another example above (xxi. 15).

The preceding examples are taken from one page of the manuscript which was available, in photostat, for study.

7. MS. T.–S. B 6_1, University Library, Cambridge

Fragment of a vellum manuscript. Two columns. In page *a* only 12 lines in one column and 13 in the other are preserved. The fragments come from the Geniza of Cairo. In its handwriting and pointing, the manuscript belongs to the group of MSS. 1, 3, 4 and MS. K of *M.d.W.* ii, p. 53*.

As in all these manuscripts, Hebrew (Deut. xvi. 16–xvii. 7) and Onqelos alternate. Due to lack of material—only one page was available for study—a good many of the 'Ben Naftali' characteristics are not present in the part of the manuscript which has been studied. Even so, we can list enough readings to convince us that the manuscript is 'Ben Naftali', and that it is proto-Tiberian in the same group as the aforementioned manuscripts. Common nouns and particles are left unvocalized, and the vocalization of gutturals is very primitive. *Pataḥ/qameṣ* and *ṣere/segol* are confused. *Pataḥ* prevails over *qameṣ* in the Targum, as is the case in the manuscripts of this group. The use of *metheg* is not frequent in the aforementioned manuscripts, and in the present manuscript I have detected very few cases of *metheg* in the verses studied. There are few *silluq*s in our manuscript. There is no *silluq*, or very few, in the said group. There are small differences regarding the conjunctive accents. As far as one can see in the verses examined, *raphe* and *dagesh* *lene* are normally confined to *bgdkft*, but still one finds xvi. 20 קוּשְׁטָא קוּשְׁטָא and final הּ. In xvii. 2 קִירְוָךְ; xvii. 7 לְהֲמִיתוֹ, &c.

In Onqelos there are many traces of the original Babylonian *Vorlage*: xvi. 16 אֱלָהָךְ; דִּיתִירְעֵי; קֳדָם; xvii. 2 לְמֶיעְבַּד.

I present here examples of the readings of MS. T.–S. B 6_1:

xvi. 17 אלהיךָ; אשר־ (B.H.³ אֲשֶׁר); נְתַן לָךְ (B.H.³ נָתַן־לָךְ:); יְדֵיהּ; אֱלָהָךְ; דְּיָהֵב לָךְ; xvi. 18 וְשֹׁטְרִים; תִּתֵּן לָךְ (B.H.³ תִּתֶּן־לְךָ); אשׁר יהוָה אלהֶיךָ (with no other vowels): B.H.³ אשׁר יהוָה אלהֶיךָ; נֹ[תֵן] (B.H.³ נֹתֵן); xvi. 20 צדק צֶדֶק; תחְיֶה (B.H.³ תִּחְיֶה); וְיָרַשְׁתָּ (B.H.³ וְיָרַשְׁתָּ); את־הארץ אשר־יהוָה (without further vocalization); אֱלֹהֶיךָ; נֹתֵן־לָךְ (B.H.³ נֹתֵן לָךְ:); xvi. 21 לֹא תִּטַּע (B.H.³ לֹא־תִטַּע); אֲשֵׁרָה; כל־ (B.H.³ כָּל־); מִזְבַּח; תַּעֲשֶׂה לָּךְ (B.H.³ תַעֲשֶׂה־לָּךְ:); אֶ[שר]תּ כל־; xvi. 22 אֲשֶׁר; את, כל, ית unvocalized.[1]

We have examined a group of manuscripts similar in writing and pointing: MSS. 1, 3, 4, 7. These manuscripts, as already stated, are to be related in handwriting and punctuation to MS. K of the list of 'Ben Naftali' manuscripts made by P. Kahle (*M.d.W.* ii, p. 53*). MS. K is MS. T.–S. B 6_2 of the University Library, Cambridge, containing, in two folios of two columns, Hebrew and Onqelos texts for Num. xxiii. 5–27 and Deut. ix. 5–22. Kahle, who examined fol. 1a (Num. xxiii. 5–14) and fol. 2a (Deut. ix. 5–12), rightly considers the manuscript to belong to the manuscripts that he calls Ben Naftali. I have studied fol. 1b and fol. 2b and I have reached the conclusion, not only that the manuscript is 'Ben Naftali', but that it also has the same characteristics of the writing and pointing of the aforementioned group of manuscripts.

We find in this MS. K pointings such as Num. xxiii. 23 בְּיַעֲקֹב; לְיַעְקֹב; לְיַעֲקֹב; Deut. ix. 10 בְּיוֹמָא, a kind of vocalization already seen in MSS. 1 and 4 of the group. Side by side we find pointings such as Num. xxiii. 20 לְיִשְׂרָאֵל (Onq.); xxiii. 23 בְּיִשְׂרָאֵל; וּלְיִשְׂרָאֵל; Deut. ix. 5 לְיִצְחָק, which appear also in the said group of manuscripts. It is more in keeping with the Ben Asher school than with that of the real

[1] Further examples: xvii. 2 קִירְוָךְ; xvii. 3 וַיֵּלֶךְ; וַיַּעֲבֹד; אוֹ לַיָּרֵחַ | וְלַשֶּׁמֶשׁ; הַשָּׁמַיִם; לְטַעֲוָת; xvii. 5 וָמֵתוּ; xvii. 7 יַד הָעֵדִים (B.H.³ יַד הָעֵדִים).

Ben Naftali. MS. K confuses, too, the vowels *segol/ṣere, pataḥ/qameṣ*. It ignores *qameṣ*, writing invariably *pataḥ* not only in the Targum but in the Hebrew text as well. In MS. K one can see the Palestinian vocalization *pataḥ* כַּל instead of *ḥolem* כֹּל, as we saw *qameṣ* for *ḥolem* (כָהנים for כֹ׳) in MS. 4.

MS. K also ignores *ḥaṭeph segol*, Deut. ix. 6 אֶלֹהֶיךָ, just as in the said manuscripts. Cf. MS. 3 Gen. xli. 25, 28 הָאֶלֹהִים.

Cf. also Deut. ix. 9 of MS. K וְמַיִם with Exod. xvii. 12 וְמִזֶה of MS. 4.

Dagesh lene and *raphe* are not only marked on *bgdkft*, but they are also marked sometimes—though inconsistently—on the other consonants just as in the said group of manuscripts: Num. xxiii. 19, 23 אֱלָהָא; מִתְקַיְּים; xxiii. 21 אַוֶן (B.H.³ אָוֶן); xxiii. 24 יִתְנַשָּׂא; xxiii. 25 וַיאמַר.

In Onqelos, in K, and in the above-mentioned manuscripts *ḥaṭeph pataḥ* is often substituted by *pataḥ*: Num. xxiii. 26 וְאַמַר. In xxiii. 25 K תְקַבְּנוּ (B.H.³ תִקֳּבֶנּוּ). In MS. K there are some features not found in the said group of manuscripts: xxiii. 18 עֲדַי (B.H.³ עֲדָי); xxiii. 24 וְדַם חֲלָלִים (B.H.³ וְדַם־חֲלָלִים); xxiii. 27 אֲקַבֶּךְ; xxiii. 26 הֲלָא; xxiii. 24 וּכְאַרְיָא.[1]

Accents of MS. K are not always on the stressed syllable as in MSS. 1, 3, 4: Num. xxiii. 23 נַחַשׁ (B.H.³ נַחַשׁ); קֶסֶם (B.H.³ ֶ ֶ); xxiii. 21 אַוֶן (B.H.³ אָוֶן).

MS. K does not omit *silluq*. As in the aforementioned manuscripts, so in K there are variations in the accents, especially the conjunctive ones: xxiii. 23 מַה פַעַל (B.H.³ מַה־פָּעַל); xxiii. 24 טֶרֶף (B.H.³ טֶרֶף); Deut. ix. 10 כְּכָל הַדְּבָרִים (B.H.³ כְּכָל־הַדְּ׳).

Metheg is used very sparingly in MS. K and the same group of manuscripts.

In Deut. ix. 10, 11 (Hebrew) יהוֹה (for B.H.³ יהוה) and ix. 11 (Aramaic) יְהַב לִי (for יהב לי).

[1] Further examples of MS. K: Num. xxiii. 6 וַיָּשָׁב אליו (B.H.³ וַיָּשָׁב אֵלָיו).

8. MS. d 79, fols. 5–6, Bodleian Library, Oxford

2 fols. Vellum. Written in two columns of 24 lines, except fol. 5b (Exod. xv) arranged in poetical form.

Fol. 5: Exod. xiv. 19–xv. 15; fol. 6: xxv. 9–xxvi. 5. Only Hebrew text. The material is dirty, especially fol. 5a, which is almost unreadable. The handwriting is oriental.

The text has vocalization and accents. The latter appear even in unvocalized words; for instance *'asher* usually appears with incomplete or with no vocalization at all, and yet it bears accentuation: Exod. xxv. 21 אשֶׁ֣ר; xxv. 29 אֲשֶׁ֥ר.

The punctuation of this manuscript shows a great number of 'Ben Naftali' characteristics. But Exod. xv. 13 גאלת, a Ben Asher reading (Ben Naftali 'גֿא).

The punctuation is already developed: the signs have become more and more diversified and they are used with greater consistency than in the group of manuscripts just described. The present manuscript is clearly recent among the 'Ben Naftali' manuscripts; it has seven vowels and normally it does not confuse *pataḥ/qameṣ* and *ṣere/segol*. It has no *pataḥ gĕnubah*. It has many *ḥăṭephim*. Examples: Exod. xv. 2 עָזִ֤י; xv. 6 נֶֽאְדָּרִ֖י בַּכֹּ֑חַ (B.H.³ נֶאְדָּרִ֖י בַּכֹּ֑חַ); xv. 7 תְּשַׁלַּ֣חְ (B.H.³ 'לַּ֣ח); xv. 8 וּבְר֣וּחַ; נֶֽעֶרְמוּ֙ (B.H.³ נֶ֣עֶרְמוּ); xv. 9 אֲחַלֵּ֣ק; xv. 10 בְּרוּחֲךָ֖; xxv. 23 אָֽרְכּ֔וֹ; xxv. 26 לְאַרְבַּ֥עְ.

For the frequent and strange use of *dagesh* and *raphe*, note the following examples: xv. 4 שָׁלִ֣ישָׁ֔יו (B.H.³ שָׁלִשָׁ֖יו); xv. 8 בְּלֶב־ (B.H.³ בְּלֶב־); xv. 9 אשִׂ·יג֙ (notice ·ש instead of שׂ); נַפְשִׁ֔י (the dot in ש is doubtful); אָרִ֣יק; xv. 10 נָשַׁ֥פְתָּ; יָ֑ם; צָֽלְל֗וּ (B.H.³ צָֽלֲל֗וּ); כָּעוֹפֶ֔רֶת (B.H.³ כַּעוֹפֶ֔רֶת); xxv. 19 קְצוֹתָ֥יו; xxv. 30 לְפָנַ֖י; xxv. 31 וְקָנָ֔הּ.

א, when a consonant, has the typical inscribed dot (א).

With regard to the accents, normally they agree with those of B.H.³, but there are yet some differences: prepositive *tĕlisha* is repeated, *pashṭa* too, as a rule; *geresh* stands for *gerĕshayim*, *lĕgarmeh* is indicated on the margin, *metheg* occurs with abnormal frequency as in later 'Ben Naftali' manuscripts. Notice the following accentuation: xv. 7 חֲרֹ֣נְךָ֔ (B.H.³ חֲרֹ֣נְךָ֔); xv. 10 כָּעוֹפֶ֔רֶת (B.H.³ כַּעוֹפֶ֔רֶת); xv. 12 נָטִ֙יתָ֙ (B.H.³ נָטִ֙יתָ֙); xxv. 31 מִקְשָׁ֔ה (B.H.³ מִקְשָׁ֗ה); xxv. 33 גְּבִעִ֔ים (B.H.³ גְּבִעִ֔ים);

xv. 7 תְּהֳרָס (B.H.^{3} תַּהֲרֹס); xv. 11 מִי כָּמֹכָה (B.H.^{3} מִי־כָ'); xxv. 22 אִתְּךָ (B.H.^{3} אוֹתְךָ).

The Masoretic notes are very few: xxv. 31 הַמְּנוֹרָה = ג מל בת.

There are quite a number of variant readings regarding *scriptio plena* and *defectiva*.

9. MS. Heb. d 80, fol. 6, Bodleian Library, Oxford

1 fol. Vellum. Two columns of 22 lines each. Num. xx. 27, missing in the text, is added in the lower margin. Fol. 6a: Num. xx. 14–28; fol. 6b: xx. 28–xxi. 9. First column of fol. 6b has been redone by a second hand, which has completed the missing vocalization in some words.

This second hand uses indifferently *pataḥ* and *segol* and vocalizes xxi. 2 בְּיָדִי (as the first *naqdan*?). See xxi. 1 מֶלֶךְ (1 h., B.H.^{3} [illegible]); xxi. 2 אַת־ and אֶת־.

The handwriting is similar to that of Codex Reuchlinianus. According to the Catalogue it is 'French square'. The fragment comes from the Cairo Geniza and its script is oriental. This kind of handwriting is peculiar to the 'Ben Naftali' manuscripts.

Owing to the scanty material, not all the characteristics of the 'Ben Naftali' manuscripts can be found in this manuscript; for instance there is no case of *pataḥ gĕnubah*. Yet such characteristics are present in great number: *'aleph* is written א or אֿ, and *dagesh* and *raphe* occur on all the consonants except the gutturals.

We find final ן–, י– and ײ or יֿ in the middle of a word, יֿ at the beginning of a word. See the treatment of the gutturals in the examples below:

Num. xx. 16 וַיִּשְׁמַע; וַיִּשְׁלַח; אֲנַחְנוּ; xx. 20 חֲזָקָה; xx. 25 קַח; xx. 26 אַהֲרֹן; xxi. 1 עֲרָד (2 h., B.H.^{3} עֲרָד).

אשר without vowels but with accentuation.

Proper nouns are always accentuated, sometimes with full vocalization, sometimes with incomplete, or zero, vocalization. There is no confusion of *pataḥ/qameṣ* or *ṣere/segol*. The second hand, as said above, confuses *segol/pataḥ*. But yet there are vocalizations such as xx. 18 אֱלָיו (B.H.^{3} אֵלָיו) and xx. 19 אֵלָיו (= B.H.^{3} אֵלָיו); xxi. 4 אֱדוֹם (B.H.^{3} 'אֱ).

A hint as to the Palestinian origin of the manuscript is found in the following vocalization xxi. 1 בִּישְׂרָאֵל (בִּ 1 h. and 2 h.); cf. above, בִּיָדֵי.

Regarding the accents, *silluq* is expressed, *soph pasuq* is indicated by two little dots—very close to each other—at the left side of the last word of the verse, in the upper part. This indication of *soph pasuq* is the ordinary one in these old manuscripts. The accents are on the stressed syllable. But *pashṭa* is not always repeated: xxi. 1 וַיִּלָּחֶם (B.H.³ וילחם); xxi. 5 הֶעֱלִיתֻנוּ (B.H.³ הֶעֱלִיתֻנוּ); לֶחֶם (B.H.³ לֶחֶם); but xx. 15 אבתינו; xxi. 5 בֵּאלֹהִים; וּבְמֹשֶׁה; xxi. 4 וַיִּסְעוּ.

In the conjunctive accents there are several differences compared with B.H.³: xx. 24 כִּי לֹא (B.H.³ כִּי לֹא); xxi. 5 כִּי־ (B.H.³ כִּי); xx. 19 אֵלָיו (B.H.³ אֵלָיו).

Metheg appears with great frequency, but in xxi. 1—at least in the second-hand punctuation—the reading is הכנעני—a Ben Asher reading—instead of הֽכנעני of the real Ben Naftali school.

Lĕgarmeh is indicated in the margin, but no other Masoretic note is to be found. There are, too, some variant readings in the *matres lectionis* and one word deleted between מִצְרַיִם and וְלַאֲבֹתֵינוּ (xx. 15).

10. MS. Heb. e 43 (Cat. 2610), fols. 17–18, Bodleian Library, Oxford

2 fols. Vellum. According to the Catalogue: 'Syr. sq. Rabb. character, 8°'. Hebrew text without Targum for Deut. xxx. 19–xxxi. 16 (fol. 17) and xxxiii. 27 to the end of Deut. (fol. 18). At the end of Deut. the *sofer* adds a note indicating the number of verses in the Torah.

The text is not arranged in columns, but written in continuous lines. The characteristics of the so-called 'Ben Naftali' manuscripts are reduced in this manuscript to a small group, mostly concerned with the abnormal use of *dagesh lene* and *raphe* on consonants other than *bgdkft*. *Lamed* at the beginning of a word is very often given a *dagesh*: Deut. xxx. 19 לְּמַעַן; xxx. 20 לָּשֶׁבֶת; הָֽאֲדָמָה (B.H.³ הָאֲ׳); xxxi. 2 אֱלֹהֶם [*sic*]; מֵאָה; שָׁנָה; xxxi. 7 נִשְׁבַּע; וְאַתָּה; xxxiii. 29 נוֹשַׁע; xxxiv. 6

קִבַּרְתּוֹ; xxxi. 9 זִקְנֵי; וַיִּתְּנָהּ (B.H.³ 'נָהּ); xxxi. 12 יִלְמְדוּ; xxx. 20 בְּקֹלוֹ.

'Aleph is given *raphe*, but no *dagesh*: xxi. 2 וַיֹּאמֶר; xxxi. 8 הוּא; notice the frequent use of *dagesh* in the *yod* of יִשראל.

The consonantal character of final *yod* or *waw* is not indicated.

The punctuation—vowels and accents—is, on the whole, complete, but not infrequently a vowel, mainly *ḥolem* or *shewa*, or a *dagesh* is missing. Notice the defective vocalization of these 'segolata': xxxiii. 27 קֶדם; ומִתַּחת; and of xxxi. 12 יִשְׁמעוּ.

There is no *pataḥ gĕnubah*: xxx. 20 לִשְׁמֹע; xxxi. 3 יְהוֹשֻׁע; xxxiv. 9 רוּח.

Vowels are not confused.

This manuscript follows Ben Asher readings rather than Ben Naftali. For instance: xxx. 20 לְיִצְחָק; xxxiii. 29 וְיִכָּחֲשׁוּ; xxxiv. 4 לְיִצְחָק; xxxiv. 10 בְּיִשְׂרָאֵל; Ben Naftali reading in xxxiv. 9 בִּן־נּוּן (Ben Asher reads בִּן־נוּן).

In the accents the usual deviations from the accentuation of B.H.³ can be traced, too, in this manuscript: they relate to the conjunctive accents and to the disjunctive as well: xxx. 20 כִּי הוּא (B.H.³ כִּי הוּא); xxxiv. 1 רֹאשׁ הַפִּסְגָּה (B.H.³ רֹאשׁ הַפִּסְגָּה); xxxiv. 3 הַנֶּגֶב (B.H.³ הנגב); xxxiv. 4 זֹאת (B.H.³ זאת); וּלְיַעֲקֹב (B.H.³ וּלְיַעֲקֹב).

Silluq is indicated.

Metheg occurs very often. *Lĕgarmeh* is not indicated in the margins.

There are repeated accents ֞; ֣֣.

The accents are now on the stressed syllable.

There is no Masora, except to state the number of verses, as already said.

There are several variant readings in the consonantal text: xxxi. 1 for אֶת־, our manuscript has אֶת כל with LXX, Pesh., Vulg., and many manuscripts; but this כל has been deleted; xxxi. 7 תַּנְחִלֶנָּה (B.H.³ תנחילנה); xxxi. 12 אלהיהם with other texts, against אלהיכם of B.H.³.

The present manuscript is older than MSS. 8 and 9, but more recent than MSS. 1, 3, 4, 7.

11. MS. 282 of Sassoon Library, Letchworth, England

This vellum manuscript contains the Torah alternating with Onqelos, fol. 1 beginning with Gen. xlv. 14. The folios are numbered with Hebrew letters and the pages (482 is the last page of the codex) are indicated in Arabic numeration. On p. 482b the colophon states that the manuscript was written in A.M. 4949 = A.D. 1189. The handwriting is probably oriental, but the codex, if not written in Germany, at least found its way there, as witnessed by the cursive German writing of p. 482. The text is arranged in three columns, and Masora—parva and magna—is on the margins. Thirty lines in each column.

The manuscript belongs to the third category of 'Ben Naftali' manuscripts, namely to those that, although accommodated on the whole to the prevailing Tiberian text, still exhibit a limited number of 'Ben Naftali' characteristics. These features are retained more by the Targum than by the Hebrew text. Recurrent 'Ben Naftali' punctuations are *he* with *mappiq* indicated as הּ; final consonantal *waw* ו—; *qameṣ ḥaṭuph* indicated by ◌ָ◌ְ or ◌ָ◌ְ; כַּל־ instead of כָּל־ consistently in the Targum, a punctuation that reminds us of the use of Palestinian *pataḥ* for *qameṣ* and *ḥolem*.

There are some defective vocalizations and other reminders of the old use of *dagesh lene* and *raphe* on consonants other than *bgdkft*. One can find also remains of the Palestinian confusion of *pataḥ/qameṣ* and *ṣere/segol*.

There are, too, variations in the accentuation, to which the frequent erasures in the accents relate. A great many *maqqeph*s have been omitted. The number of *mĕthāgīm* is very high.

Note the following examples, many of them collated with the corresponding punctuation of MS. 2808—formerly De Rossi 2—edited in facsimile by Sperber: Exod. i. 1 בֵּיתֵיהּ׃; i. 5 יֹצְאֵי (2808 יֹצְאֵי); יַעֲקֹב; (Onqelos) כַּל־; הֲוָה (for הֲ׳); i. 6 אֶחָיו׃ (id. 2808); i. 7 בִּמְאֹד (as B.H.^{3}; 2808 בִּמְאֹד); i. 8 אֲשֶׁר (id. 2808); יָדַע (2808 יָדַע); i. 9 אֶל (2808 אֶל־); i. 10 וְהָיָה (2808 ״); תִקְרֶאנָה (B.H.^{3}, 2808 ׳רֶ׳); i. 13 בְּפָרֶךְ (as 2808 in verse 14); i. 14 בְּפָרֶךְ׃ (as 2808 in verse 13); (Onq.) וּבְכַל פָּלְחָנָה; בְּטִינָא; i. 16 הָאָבְנָיִם (id. 2808); i. 17 הַמְיַלְּדֹת (2808 הַמְיַלְּדֹת); i. 18 לַמְיַלְּדוֹת (2808 לַמְיַלְּדֹת); מַדּוּעַ (2808 מַדּוּעַ); i. 20 אֱלֹהִים; i. 21 הָאֱלֹהִים (2808 הָאֱלֹהִים); vii. 1 מְתֻרְגְּמָנֶךָ׃; vii. 2 כָּל (B.H.^{3} כָּל־);

vii. 3 וָאֲנִי; וְהִרְבֵּיתִי (B.H.³ 'תִי', but Onqelos וְאַסְגֵּי); vii. 4 וְלֹא (B.H.³ וְלֹא־); vii. 4, 5 גְּבָרְתִּי; vii. 10 וַיַּעֲשׂוּ (B.H.³ 'וַיַּעַ'); (Onq.) וְקָדָם; vii. 12 חֲטְרֵיהּ; חֲטְרֵיהוֹן; vi. 12 אֱלָיו; vi. 25 פּוּטִיאֵל; i. 2 יִשָּׂשכָר (= Ben Naftali reading; 2808 יִשָּׂשכָר Ben Asher); iii. 5 שַׁל־ (= Ben Asher); vi. 27 הַמְדַבְּרִים (= Ben Naftali; 'הַמְ' Ben Asher).

12. MS. Heb. b 2 (Cat. 2606), fols. 16–17, Bodleian Library, Oxford

2 fols. Vellum. Three columns per page; 28 lines in each column. Oriental handwriting. According to the Catalogue: 'Karaite square character'. Hebrew text for Joshua xxiv. 6–Judges i. 12 and Judges ix. 1–46. Fol. 16 is dirty and difficult to read. Only in a few cases is the punctuation defective: Judges i. 7 בֶּזק (as compared with בֶּזֶק of i. 6). אשר is given full vocalization.

There is no confusion of vowels; but ix. 14 מְלָךְ־ (for מְלָךְ־).

Ḥăṭephim are written ֲ ֱ ֳ.

There is no *pataḥ gĕnubah*: i. 1 and *passim* יְהוֹשֻׁעַ; ix. 8 לִמְשֹׁח; ix. 9 לָנוּעַ; ix. 13 המשמח; ix. 23 רוּח.

In accordance with Palestinian vocalization, there are such vocalizations as ix. 7 וישמע (B.H.³ 'וַיִּשְׁ'); ix. 19 וְיִשְׂמַח (a small dot under the *yod* seems to be unintentional or second hand); יְרֻבַּעַל (for B.H.³ 'יְרֻ'); Joshua xxiv. 9 בְּיִשְׂרָאֵל (B.H.³ 'בְּיִשְׂ'); but note Judges i. 2 בְּיָדוֹ׃.

Dagesh lene is used with *bgdkft*, but *raphe* is written on other consonants: Judges i. 1 יַעֲלֶה־; i. 2 יְהוּדָה; i. 3 וְנִלָּחֲמָה; ix. 4 אֲנָשִׁים; ix. 9 וַאֲנָשִׁים; ix. 14 הָאָטָד; ix. 16 בֶּאֱמֶת; ix. 2 שִׁכֶם.

We find *raphe* on *yod*, even when *yod* bears explicit or implicit *dagesh forte*: Judges i. 1 וַיְהִי; i. 6 וַיֹּאחֲזוּ; וַיְקַצְּצוּ; ix. 1 וַיְדַבֵּר; ix. 3 וַיְדַבְּרוּ; ix. 8 לַזַּיִת; ix. 15 אַיִן; i. 6 יָדָיו; i. 11 קִרְיַת. Note *dagesh lene* in the *yod*: ix. 5 יוֹתָם. These *raphe*s are small lines. One line is often used as *raphe* for two consonants: ix. 9 יְכַבְּדוּ; ix. 10 לַתְּאֵנָה; ix. 5 עָפְרָתָה.

א̄ is very common, but א does not appear: ix. 5 וַיָּבֹא; נֶחְבָּא; ix. 7 בְּרֹאשׁ.

As far as the accentuation is concerned, there are deviations from B.H.³ accents: postpositive *pashṭa* is often not repeated, a phenomenon we have witnessed several times in the above manuscripts: ix. 1 יְרֻבַּעַל (B.H.³ ירבעל); ix. 11 הֶחֳדַלְתִּי (B.H.³ החדלתי); ix. 15 לְמֶלֶךְ (B.H.³ למלך).

Geresh stands for *gerĕshayim*: ix. 2 דַּבְּרוּ נָא (B.H.³ דַּבְּרוּ־נָא); ix. 5 וַיַּהֲרֹג (B.H.³ ־).

The presence of *gaʿyah* is consistent and this sign is often located under the vowel: Judges i. 1 יַעֲלֶה־; i. 2 יַעֲלֶה; i. 3 בְגוֹרָלִי; i. 7 כַּאֲשֶׁר; i. 3 בַּכְּנַעֲנִי; ix. 2 כָּל־; ix. 8 הָעֵצִים.

Lĕgarmeh is not indicated in the margins.

In the conjunctive accents there are the variations usual in this kind of manuscript: Judges i. 2 ויאמר (B.H.³ ויא׳); ix. 2 בְּאָזְנֵי־ (B.H.³ באזני); כָּל־בַּעֲלֵי (B.H.³ כל־בעלי); ix. 5 בְּנֵי־ (B.H.³ בְּנֵי־); ix. 6 עִם (B.H.³ עם־); ix. 10 לְכִי (B.H.³ לְכִי־); ix. 16 אִם (B.H.³ אם־).

On the margins there are Masoretic notes, less frequently than in B.H.³.

Variant readings in the *matres lectionis*: ix. 7 קלו (B.H.³ קולו); ix. 8 הָלֹךְ (B.H.³ הלוך).

All considered, this manuscript can be placed after the group of early 'Ben Naftali' manuscripts (MSS. 1, 3, 4, 7, 13) and before the more developed ones (MSS. 2, 8, 9, 10, 11).

13. MS. 512, fol. 15, J. Th. S., New York

1 fol. Vellum. Two columns per page; 28 lines in each column. Hebrew text for Isa. xxviii. 29–xxix. 22 (fol. 15b) and xix. 14–23 (fol. 15a, first column; the second column was not available for examination).

The ink is very much faded in the pointing, which makes the study of this manuscript difficult. Yet the punctuation in certain respects is clear enough to indicate the type of manuscript.

Despite the fact that many signs are no longer legible, at least in the photostat, we can still state that the punctuation is sometimes defective; for instance not all the conjunctive *waws* are given *shewa*; xxix. 7 וְהָיָה; xxix. 20 אָוֶן; xxix. 17 הלא (B.H.³ הֲלוֹא־).

'Asher, however, has vocalization: as a rule אֲשֶׁר.

There is regular confusion of *pataḥ/qameṣ* and *ṣere/segol* and some confusion of *o/u*: xxix. 4 וְשִׁפְלַתְ (B.H.³ 'וְשָׁפ); וּמֵעָפָר; xxix. 5 כְּאָבָק; דַּק (B.H.³ דַּק); xxix. 15 בְּמַחְשָׁךְ; xxix. 17 מְעַט (B.H.³ מְעַט); וְהַכַּרְמֶל (B.H.³ והכרמל); xxix. 16 מָעֲשֶׂה (B.H.³ מַעֲשֶׂה).

Gutturals are treated in a very primitive way: xxix. 7 כְּחָלוֹם (B.H.³ כַּחֲלוֹם); xxix. 13 אֲנָשִׁים; xxix. 19 עֲנָוִים; xxix. 16 מָעֲשֶׂה but xxix. 15 מָעֲשֵׂיהֶם, xxix. 21 מַחְטִיאֵי; and אֲשֶׁר *passim*; xxix. 2 כַּאֲרִיאֵל.

It seems that there is no *pataḥ gĕnubah*: xxix. 10 רוּחַ; xxix. 21 וְלַמּוֹכִיחַ.

He with *mappiq* is represented by הּ: xxix. 7 לָהּ; וּמְצֹדָתָהּ (B.H.³ sg. וּמְצֹדָתָהּ).

Note xxix. 5 לְפֶתַע.

Dagesh lene and *raphe* are given to consonants other than *bgdkft*, but not to gutturals: xxix. 1 שָׁנָה; שָׁנָה; xxix. 4 תְּצַפְצֵף; xxix. 5 הֲמוֹן; וּכְמוֹץ (B.H.³ וּכְמֹץ); xxix. 7 לַיְלָה; xxix. 12 לֹא (bis); לֵאמֹר; xxix. 14 יוֹסִיף (B.H.³ יוֹסִף); לְהַפְלִיא; חֲכָמָיו; וּבִינַת; xxix. 15 מִי; xxix. 18 עֵינֵי; xxix. 16 הַיֹּצֵר.

Very often א or אֹ: xxix. 13 אֹתִי; xxix. 16 אִם; אָמַר; xxix. 22 אֶל; xxix. 15 וַיֹּאמְרוּ.

Treatment of final *waw*: xxix. 13 בְּפִיו; ובשפתיו.

In the use of *dagesh* and *raphe* there is little consistency.

One cannot trace any *maqqeph* in the photostat.

Metheg is also very scarce: xxix. 4 וּמֵעָפָר (B.H.³ 'וּמֵ); xxix. 5 עָרִיצִים (B.H.³ 'עָ); xxix. 18 וְשָׁמְעוּ.

There are variations in the accents, but many of them cannot be discovered in the material at our disposal; it seems that the accentuation was also defective: xxix. 19 וְיָסְפוּ (B.H.³ וְיָסְפוּ); xxix. 16 אָמַר (B.H.³ אָמַר).

Apparently there are no double accents: xxix. 15 וַיֹּאמְרוּ (B.H.³ וַיֹּאמְרוּ); xxix. 16 הַפְּכְּכֶם (B.H.³ הַפְכְּכֶם).

The margins are almost completely without Masoretic notes.

The text often differs from B.H.³ concerning the *matres lectionis*: xxix. 4 כְּאֹב (B.H.³ כאוב); xxix. 5 וּכְמוֹץ (B.H.³ וכמץ); xxix. 6 אכלה

(B.H.^{3} אוכ׳); xxix. 7 צבאיה (B.H.^{3} צְבָיהָ); xxix. 8 אכל (B.H.^{3} אוכל); ורקה (B.H.^{3} וריקה); xxix. 13 כִּבְדָנִי (B.H.^{3} כבדוני), &c.

By the handwriting—the *'ayin* and the oblique direction of the vowels, for instance—and from the foregoing analysis, this manuscript may be considered as another example of the early 'Ben Naftali' manuscripts, as MSS. 1, 3, 4, 7.

In xxix. 3 the punctuation seems to be עַלַ֫יִךְ (for B.H.^{3} עָלַ֫יִךְ); in xxix. 16 לְעֹשֵׂ·הוּ (·שׂ instead of שׂ).

14. MS. 558, fol. 2, J. Th. S., New York

1 fol. Fol. 2a is the continuation of 2b; the folio has been pasted in at the wrong end. Vellum 26·7 × 22·5 cm. Three columns per page; 24 lines in each column. Upper edge of one column partly torn out. Hebrew text for Jer. viii. 21–ix. 25. Oriental handwriting. Fragment from the Cairo Geniza.

The manuscript is thoroughly punctuated according to a very elaborate 'Ben Naftali' system of pointing. Vowel signs and accents—both disjunctive and conjunctive—are in almost complete agreement with those of B.H.^{3}. Variations in the consonantal text are practically non-existent: only Jer. ix. 23 וּמִשְׁפָּט with Q^{Or}, LXX, Vet. Lat., Pesh. (B.H.^{3} משפט); ix. 20 מֶרְחוֹבוֹת (B.H.^{3} מרחבות).

Regarding the vocalization, there is no confusion of vowels, only we find ix. 3 יַֽעְקֹב (for יַ־); ix. 6 אֵיךְ (dot in א?).

In some cases the 'segolata' have incomplete vocalization, a feature already observed in many 'Ben Naftali' manuscripts: ix. 1 עֲצֶרֶת; ix. 11 הָאָרץ; ix. 21 כְּדֹמֶן.

In the accents the variations are limited to the use of ֣ instead of ֞: ix. 24 אֱדוֹם (for B.H.^{3} אדוֹם); ix. 14 [אָ]מַר (B.H.^{3} אָמַר). See, however, ix. 9 נִצְּתוּ (B.H.^{3} נצתו).

Yet this so 'Masoretic' manuscript has most of the 'Ben Naftali' characteristics. It is very consistent in the use of *raphe* and *dagesh lene* in all the consonants except gutturals and except—ordinarily but not always—final consonants. Note the following examples: ix. 3 תִּבְטָחוּ; ix. 4 הַעֲוֵה; ix. 5 מֵאֲנוּ; ix. 7 חֵץ; ix. 8 אֶפְקָד־ (dot in א?); ix. 9 הַשָּׁמַיִם;

ix. 11 אֵלָ֣יו; ix. 12 עֲזָבָ֑ם; בָּהּ; ix. 18 נִשְׁמַ֫ע; ix. 23 וַיָּדַ֣ע; ix. 11 וַאֲשֶׁ֣ר; ix. 23 בָּאָ֫רֶץ.

On the margins there are *lĕgarmeh* and a few Masoretic notes not always in agreement with the Masora parva of B.H.³: ix. 3 ל מל עָקוֹב (B.H.³ ב חד מל). One of these Masoretic notes refers to the placing of a *dagesh* in יעקב, a pointing of the real Ben Naftali school: ix. 3 ל דגש יַֽעְקֹּב (B.H.³ ל): Ben Naftali יעקּב; Ben Asher יעקב. ix. 11 ג רפין וַיִּבֶן (B.H.³ ג).

The manuscript is abundant in the use of *metheg*. In ix. 16 לְֽמְקוֹנְנוֹת—note מְֽ—the *metheg* is short and appears to have been written with some hesitation. Ben Naftali לְֽ; Ben Asher לְ.

In conclusion, this manuscript belongs to a developed stage of the 'Ben Naftali' manuscripts, but it is essentially adjusted to the Masoretic tradition as found in B.H.³.

15. MS. 515 (E.N.A. 2589), fols. 70–73, J. Th. S., New York

4 fols. Vellum. Two columns per page; 20 lines in each column. Four lines of the lower part of the second column of fol. 71b are missing. Contents: fol. 70: 2 Chron. xviii. 10–30; fol. 71: xxii. 2–xxiii. 5; fols. 72–73: xxxi. 12–xxxii. 26.

The handwriting is characteristic of the 'Ben Naftali' manuscripts. It is oriental script. The manuscript comes from the Cairo Geniza.

The pointing ordinarily is complete, both in vowels and accents, but in common or proper nouns vowels are missing, although not consistently. Sometimes part of the vowels is not indicated. We find, for instance, אשר and אֲשֶׁר; usually מֶלך, sometimes מֶלֶךְ; often את־, and often אֶת־. In certain cases these words are without accentuation.

There is no *pataḥ gĕnubah* except after long *ḥireq*: xviii. 21 לְר֣וּח; xxxii. 15 אֱלוֹהַ֫ (B.H.³ אֱלוֹהַּ); xxxi. 15 וְיֵשׁ֫וּע; xxii. 3 לְהַרְשִׁ֫יעַ; xxxi. 21 וְהִצְלִ֫יחַ.

Particles with *shewa* before יְ are punctuated לְיְ, וְיְ, בְיְ: xxxi. 13 וִיסְמַכְיָ֫הוּ (B.H.³ וְיִסְ), but there are casual vocalizations in the style of Ben Asher: לִיְ, for instance xxiii. 1 וּלְיִשְׁמָעֵ֫אל.

There is no confusion of vowels.

Ḥăṭephim and *qameṣ ḥaṭuph* are written as in the *textus receptus*: ֲ, ֱ, ֳ, ָ, ָ: xxii. 2 עָמְרִ֫י.

Final *yod*, when a consonant, is written יִ. At the beginning or in the middle of a word יׄ: xxii. 7 יְהוֹרָם 1st time (B.H.[3] יוֹרָם).

א when pronounced, and this is written consistently. Often אֿ when it is not a consonant.

He with *mappiq*: הּ: xxii. 10 בְּנָהּ.

Dagesh lene and *raphe* are found continually with consonants (non-gutturals) other than *bgdkft*.

There are no double accents. There is *geresh*, not *gerĕshayim*; *pashṭa* is postpositive and is not repeated on the stressed syllable: xxxii. 15 אֱלוֹהַּ (B.H.[3] אֱלוֹהַּ).

Lĕgarmeh is noted on the margin.

Metheg is used with more frequency than in B.H.[3].

On the margin there are infrequent Masoretic notes, not always in agreement with the Masora parva of B.H.[3].

There are variations in the *matres lectionis* and variations, too, in the consonantal text, but a second hand—apparently the *naqdan*—corrects them in agreement with the *textus receptus*: xviii. 22 בְּפִי כָל־ (כל erased); xviii. 29 וַיָּבֹא (2 h. and B.H.[3] וַיָּבֹאוּ); xxii. 6 חוֹלֶה (2 h. and B.H.[3] חֹלֶה).

From all this the conclusion may be drawn that this manuscript belongs to the group of developed 'Ben Naftali' manuscripts.

16. MS. 558 (E.N.A. 2640), fol. 11, J. Th. S., New York

1 fol. Vellum. Pss. ix. 10–xi. 7. Sections are missing from the upper middle half of both pages, which is torn out. Twenty-four lines. 25·3 × 21 cm. I describe and publish the more legible lines in my book *La trasmisión del texto bíblico hebreo y arameo* (C.S.I.C., Madrid).

Here it suffices to note that it has a primitive type of punctuation shown both in vocalization and accentuation; for instance x. 16: מֵאַרְצוֹ; ix. 14 עׇנְיִי (B.H.[3] עָנְיִ); xi. 4 קׇדְשׁוֹ (B.H.[3] קָדְשׁוֹ); xi. 1 הַרְכֶם (B.H.[3] הַרְכֶם); x. 18 אֱנוֹשׁ.

The accentuation is quite different from that of B.H.[3]: instead of ֔֗, it uses ֗; instead of ֣֨, the manuscript has ֕; and instead of *ṭiphḥa* (֖) (prepositive), it consistently uses *tĕbir*, as do, too, other 'Ben Naftali' manuscripts of the poetical books: MS. 558, fols. 21–22, which I published in *Estudios bíblicos*, xv, 1956, pp. 187–222; MS. B I 13a of Basel, published by J. Prijs, *Z.A.W.*, N.F., lxix, 1957, pp. 171–84; the manuscript of *M.d.W.* ii, p. 52*, facs. 15; MS. 4083, fols. 13–14, of the University Library, Strasbourg, and the Palestinian MSS. T.-S. 20/58, 20/53, 20/54, which I published in collaboration with N. Allony in *Estudios bíblicos*, xvii, 1958, pp. 83–100, xviii, 1959, pp. 293–8, and *Sefarad*, xviii, 1958, pp. 254–71. There are a few cases of ֥֮ (*ṣinnorit–merka*) instead of ֥ (*merka*), a substitution common to all Ben Naftali manuscripts—genuine or not.[1]

17. MS. 4083, fols. 13–14, University Library, Strasbourg

There is a short description of this manuscript in my article 'Valiosos MSS. bíblicos en la Biblioteca Nacional y Universitaria de Estrasburgo', *Estudios bíblicos*, xvi, 1957, no. 8, p. 78. I published this manuscript in collaboration with Miss Teresa de Jesús Martínez in the aforementioned book. In this manuscript the variation in the accents is very great, and instead of prepositive *ṭiphḥa*, *tĕbir* is used. See the foregoing manuscript. The typical 'Ben Naftali' (and Ben Naftali) schema ֥֮ for ֥ is used in this manuscript.

18. MS. 512, fol. 26, J. Th. S., New York

1 fol. Vellum. Fol. 26a: Hebrew text of Prov. ix. 1–13 (upper and lower part of the text is in very poor condition); fol. 26b: viii. 5–36 (upper part damaged). The fragment comes from the Cairo Geniza. The script is oriental. The vocalization is in accordance with that of B.H.³. There is no confusion of vowels; *ḥăṭephim* are used in the ordinary way, although *ḥaṭeph pataḥ* is written ַ֣. The only variation in vocalization is ix. 14 וְיָשְׁבָ֖ה (B.H.³ וְֽיָשְׁבָ֖ה), an old Palestinian type of vocalizing. In x. 4 we find וְיַ֣ד, but it is impossible to infer from the photostat alone the true character of the dots (namely if the ַ is a second-hand correction; in the *manuscript* there are traces of second-hand corrections). The 'Ben Naftali' characteristics are reduced to the use of *dagesh* and *raphe* with consonants other than *bgdkft* and to the accentuation. But the use of *dagesh* and *raphe* is not consistent. Often a *raphe* line covers two consonants.

[1] Cf. I. Yeivin, 'Qeṭa' Miqrā' . . .', p. 353. This feature occurs too in 'U.M.P.', in the manuscript published by Prijs mentioned above, and in MS. 243 of the Antonin Collection.

Gutturals or final letters—except final *he* or '*aleph*—are not given *dagesh* or *raphe*.

The accentuation is similar to that of the two foregoing manuscripts: there are constant deviations from the accents of B.H.³. Instead of ◌֔◌֗ of B.H.³, the present manuscript has ◌֔. In this manuscript, too, for prepositive *ṭiphḥa*, *tĕbir* is consistently used. Instead of ◌֖, ◌֖֓ is often used, ◌֖ and ◌֥ are interchanged. The accents are on the tone. *Maqqeph* and *metheg* occur with great frequency.

No Masora. There are almost no variants in the *matres lectionis*.

Examples of readings: Prov. viii. 13 יִ֥רְאַ֫ת (B.H.³ יִֽרְאַ֥ת); רָ֑ע 2nd time (B.H.³ רָ֥ע); viii. 15 יִמְֽלֹ֫כוּ; viii. 20 צְדָ֫קָ֥ה; viii. 21 לְהַנְחִ֣יל; viii. 22 קָ֭נָנִי (B.H.³ קָ֭נָנִי); viii. 23 מִקַּ֫דְמֵ֥י [*sic*]; viii. 24 מַעְיָ֫נוֹת (B.H.³ מַ֝עְיָנוֹת); מָ֫יִם; viii. 25 הָטְבָּ֑עוּ; viii. 27 בְּחֻ֫קּוֹ (B.H.³ בְּח֣וּקוֹ); viii. 34 מְ֝זוּזֹ֫ת (B.H.³ ◌֣); viii. 36 אֹהֲ֫בוּ (dot in א?: B.H.³ אֹ֝הֲבוּ); ix. 6 פְּתָאיִ֫ם (B.H.³ ◌֥); ix. 18 בְּעִמְ֫קֵי; x. 2 מִמָּ֫וֶת; x. 7 יִרְקָ֫ב.

19. MS. Heb. c 52, Bodleian Library, Oxford

A small fragment from which only a few lines on both sides can be partially read: Hebrew text for Esther ix. 1, 5–6, 12–13, 15. Although it is on badly damaged and mutilated vellum, one can still see the features of a 'Ben Naftali' manuscript of group ii: always אֽ; אשר (without vowels); שׁ and שׂ; אֿ; הּ; ix. 13 [ו]תֹּ֫אמֶר; לע[שׂ]וֹת֫; ix. 19 כֵּ֫ן (B.H.³ ◌֞); יוֹם֫.

In Esther ix. 8, 9 there is a פֹּס (*paseq*) in the margin.

It is impossible to decide if there is confusion of vowels. The name אסתר and the particle את remain unvocalized. Many occurrences of *metheg*, *raphe*, and *dagesh*. Accents as in B.H.³ except *geresh* for *gerĕshayim*. לֹ in margin.

20. MSS. P 262–4 (Sl. 62. 1, 2), P 451–3 (Sl. 61. 8), P 474 (isolated words from Sl. 62 and 63), John Rylands Library, Manchester

Insignificant vellum fragments from the Cairo Geniza showing 'Ben Naftali' characteristics.

21. MSS. 128, 128a, 129, J. Th. S., New York

MS. 128: part of Exod. MS. 128a: Lev. MS. 129: Num. and Deut. with the Five Scrolls. Exod. is incomplete. MSS. 128a and 129 210 fols. The leaves of Exod. are damaged by water. Vellum. In double columns of 25 lines in square character in a German hand of thirteenth–fourteenth century. Both texts—Hebrew and Targum—are vocalized throughout.

This manuscript is a typical example of a 'Ben Naftali' manuscript thoroughly adjusted to the Ben Asher punctuation, but still preserving different 'Ben Naftali' characteristics.

In the margins there are Masoretic notes.

22. MS. 1031 (2164), Biblioteca Palatina, Parma

Vellum. Gen. and Exod., Hebrew and Onqelos alternating. Without Masora. 'Plures amasoreticae lectiones, quaedam singulares et unicae' (De Rossi). For further description, cf. De Rossi's Catalogue.

In the punctuation of this codex, probably of the fourteenth century, several features of the 'Ben Naftali' manuscripts are preserved. Like MS. 20, it belongs to the 'Ben Naftali' manuscripts, group iii.

23. MS. Digby Or. 3 (*olim* Laud. 269; MS. Heb. Uri 11), Bodleian Library, Oxford

Vellum. Pentateuch: Gen. xxvii. 31 (fol. 1)–end of Deut. (fol. 143). Hebrew without Targum. No Masora. Frequent appearance of 'Ben Naftali' features: שֶׁבַֽע; עֵשָׂו; וַיְשַׁלַּח; final ה consistently, &c.

24. MS. Heb. d 41 (Cat. 2714), fols. 29–32, 39–42, 44–46, 56, Bodleian Library, Oxford

This vellum manuscript contains Qalir *piyyuṭim* vocalized in the developed 'Ben Naftali' pointing of group ii. Both consonantal and vocalic texts belong to the same hand, but now and then a second hand has introduced some corrections, for instance וְצַר (1 h.) > יוֹצֵר (2 h.). Fols. 49, 50–53, and 55a have been partially or completely erased and provided with a different text. The erased text of these folios had the same 'Ben Naftali' pointing as the aforementioned folios. A few examples: נַֽעֲשֶׂה; שְׁמוּעָה; כֶּסֶף; אֱנוֹשׁ; בְּסֵדֶר; וְלָעַד (לַ 1 h.?); כֹּהֲנִים; אֲשֶׁר; וְנִישָׂאִים; לְמִיפְקְדֵיהֶם; וַיַּרְדֵּן (1 h.); שְׁנַיִם; רֹאשׁ; וְשֵׁשׁ.

25. MS. Heb. d 41 (Cat. 2714), fols. 86–87, Bodleian Library, Oxford

Vellum. It contains *piyyuṭim* for the Liturgy of Shabuʿot. The handwriting is that usual in 'Ben Naftali' manuscripts. Pointing as manuscripts of group ii. *Shewa*, even if the following consonant is not a *yod*, is apparently represented sometimes by *ḥireq*, a vocalization often recorded in Palestinian pointing: וְנִהְיֶה, וְאֶהֱיֶה, וְקַרֵב, וְיוֹרְדִים. Examples of pointing: אֱנוֹשׁ, אֵלָיו, לְקַחַת; יָה; וַיִּקָח; נֶחְתָּם; חָכָם; אֵלֶף.

26–31. Other 'Ben Naftali' manuscripts

It is impossible to record in this paper all the manuscripts concerned with 'Ben Naftali' pointing. We may just mention a few more: MS. Heb. d 63 (Cat. 2826), fol. 102, of the Bodleian Library (vellum, 4°, 'Syr. rabb. handwriting'. *Piyyuṭ*; א, שׁ; אשר without vowel signs; ה; ס; ה, &c.).

MS. E.N.A. 1755, p. 3, of the J. Th. S. of New York (9 leaves; אֲשֶׁר, א; see fol. 8); MS. 530, fol. 13, of the same library; MS. 234a, fol. 11 (חֲנֵנִי; fols. 50–59 עָלַי); MS. 236 (E.N.A. 1781, p. 5, fols. 20–23, of the same library) (ה; fol. 5d ה); and MS. Heb. c 20 (Cat. 2736), fols. 25–28, of the Bodleian Library: always ַ (only one ָ) and *ṣere* (no *segol*), no *pataḥ gĕnubah*. 'Segolata' consistently pointed in this way: כֵתֵר (13 times), מֵלֵך, עֵקֵב. Vowelless ע and א are represented by עְ, אְ, or עֲ, עַ, עָ, אַ, אֱ. Some examples: הָאֲדֹנִים, הָאֱלֹהִים, הָעֲרִיצִים. Other readings: חַיֵּ and חַיֵּ; יֵרֵח; וּלְשֵׁבֵח; בְּאַרְבַּע; שַׁדַּי; אֲשֶׁר; שָׁמַיִ; אֲהִיָּה; וְעַרִצִי; כוֹח; בְּרוּח; תַּלוּי; לְיוֹדֵעַ; וְנִהְיָה; consistently כֹּל; וְהַקָּדוֹשׁ; גְּדוֹלָה; טֵפְסְרֵי [*sic*].

Ostracon Clermont-Ganneau n° 44 (grandeur naturelle).
En haut : face concave ; en bas : face convexe

UN OSTRACON ARAMÉEN INÉDIT D'ÉLÉPHANTINE (COLLECTION CLERMONT-GANNEAU N° 44)

Par A. DUPONT-SOMMER, *Paris*

L'OSTRACON ici publié fut recueilli par Ch. Clermont-Ganneau à Éléphantine le 26 mars 1907, lors de sa première campagne de fouilles; Clermont-Ganneau avait quitté le chantier quelques jours auparavant, le 14 mars, en en laissant la direction à son collaborateur Clédat.

Cet ostracon, de couleur brique pâle sur les deux faces, mesure en son état actuel environ 10 cm. de largeur et 7 cm. de hauteur maximum. Il porte cinq lignes d'écriture sur la face concave et cinq sur la face convexe, mais toutes ces lignes, sauf la première de chaque face, sont plus ou moins gravement incomplètes: si, sur la face concave, toutes les fins des lignes se trouvent conservées (et, par suite, sur la face convexe, tous les débuts des lignes), à l'inverse, une malencontreuse cassure a fait disparaître à droite de la face concave les débuts des lignes 2 à 5 (et, par suite, à gauche de la face convexe, les fins des lignes 2 à 5). En outre, si le haut de l'ostracon, et par conséquent le début de l'inscription, est intact, il est possible qu'il manque une ou plusieurs lignes entières au bas de l'ostracon; en tout cas, à cet endroit, d'importants éclats ont sauté, ne laissant subsister que quelques lettres à la ligne 5 de la face concave et aux lignes 4 et 5 de la face convexe.

L'écriture est fine et nette, et, si plusieurs signes, sur la face convexe, sont un peu effacés, ils restent presque tous déchiffrables. Notons que, sur la face concave, subsistent, semble-t-il, quelques traces d'une inscription antérieure, qui aurait été intentionnellement effacée; le présent document serait donc palimpseste.

L'inscription figurant actuellement sur notre ostracon est un message, un billet, adressé à un certain Yedoniah; le nom de l'expéditeur n'est pas connu. Il ne s'agit pas, comme sur la plupart des ostraca d'Éléphantine, de demande d'envois ou d'avis de livraison, mais d'une affaire beaucoup moins banale: l'auteur déclare qu'il a été mis en prison et traité durement. Quel est ce Yedoniah auquel le billet est adressé?

Ce nom était assez courant à Éléphantine, mais il nous semble assez probable, étant donné le caractère du message, qu'il désigne ici le chef même de la colonie juive, ce 'Yedoniah fils de Gemariah' qui se trouve mentionné en plusieurs papyrus (voir notamment Cowley nº 22, col. VII, l. 121); c'est vraisemblablement ce même personnage qui, en 408, adressa à Bagohi, le gouverneur perse de Judée, une missive pour solliciter l'autorisation de reconstruire à Éléphantine le temple de Yahô détruit par les Égyptiens au cours d'un pogrom (Cowley nº 30; cf. nº 33, l. 1). C'est sans doute à ce même Yedoniah qu'un nommé Maʿuziah fait part de ses démêlés avec Widrang, un fonctionnaire perse plus ou moins vendu aux Égyptiens, qui l'a fait emprisonner à Abydos (Cowley nº 38). Nous apprenons encore que 'Yedoniah fils de Gemariah' fut lui-même arrêté et emprisonné à Thèbes, en même temps que quatre autres personnages importants de la colonie d'Éléphantine, et six femmes juives (Cowley nº 34). Notre ostracon, avec son histoire d'emprisonnement, semble appartenir à la même époque troublée, vers la fin de la domination perse en Égypte.

Il présente un autre intérêt: le mot 'Sabbat' (שבה) est à lire, du moins très probablement, sur ce document. Nous avons publié déjà deux ostraca d'Éléphantine où se trouve mentionné le jour sacré des Juifs (le nº 152 de la collection Clermont-Ganneau dans *Semitica*, ii, 1949, pp. 29–39, et le nº 186 de la même collection dans *Rivista degli Studi Orientali*, xxxii, 1957, pp. 403–9). Nous sommes heureux de publier ici le troisième, comme modeste, mais très cordiale participation à l'hommage rendu au Professeur G. R. Driver, l'éminent spécialiste des études orientales et bibliques, par ses collègues et amis.

TRANSCRIPTION

Concave 1 שלם ידניה כען לו

2 [במ]סגרא שימת ופקיד

3 [אמר לם י]כׄלאו מנה לחם ומין

4 [. . . . .] . לי אחוטב להן

5 [. . . . . י]וׄם שבה

Convexe 1 כען הן לא שׄבו לנתן תמה

2 ינפק עלי ואהך אגרס [. . .]

ע̇א אף הושרו לי ל̇ [. . . . .] 3

ואכתב̇ [. . . .] . . [. . . . . . .] 4

ו̇א̇ל [. . . . .] 5

TRADUCTION

Concave 1 *Salut, Yedoniah! Maintenant. Oui,*
2 *[dans] la [p]rison je fus mis, et un officier*
3 *[donna cet ordre: 'Qu']on le prive de pain et d'eau!'*
4 [. . . . .] . *à moi Aḥuṭab, mais*
5 [. . . . . *le j]our du Sabbat*

Convexe 1 *Maintenant. S'ils n'ont pas emmené Natan captif là-bas,*
2 *qu'il parte vers moi, et j'irai, je broierai* [. . .]
3 . . *En outre, envoyez-moi* . [. . . . .]
4 *et j'écrirai* [. . . .] . . [. . . . . . .]
5 *Et que ne...pas* [. . . . .]

NOTES

Face concave. Ligne 1. כען לו. Le mot כען 'maintenant' indique ici simplement le commencement du message, comme il est habituel dans les lettres après la salutation. Ce mot est fréquemment suivi dans les lettres soit de הא soit de הלו soit de חזי (ou חזו), mots qui, pratiquement, signifient tous 'voici'. Dans notre ostracon, la particule לו serait-elle pour הלו, et, par conséquent, à traduire proprement 'voici'? A l'état libre, elle n'est point attestée ailleurs en araméen ancien, du moins à notre connaissance, si ce n'est dans le dialecte spécial des inscriptions de Zencirli (*Panamu*, l. 11 [2 fois]; *Hadad*, ll. 13, 31), où on l'explique généralement comme une conjonction conditionnelle 'si'. En hébreu, לו (aussi לוּא) a ce sens conditionnel, mais aussi celui d'une interjection optative (*utinam!*), comme le syriaque ܠܘܝ. En akkadien, *lû* a également ce sens optatif, mais il a aussi celui d'une simple particule confirmative: 'oui, vraiment, certes' (tel est aussi, selon nous, le sens de לו dans les inscriptions de Zencirli). Dans notre ostracon, le sens optatif n'est guère acceptable; car comment quelqu'un pourrait-il dire: 'Oh! que ne fus-je mis en prison!'? Le sens confirmatif, au contraire, ne présente aucune objection: 'Oui, vraiment, je fus mis en prison'. C'est ce sens que nous adoptons ici. Notons que, dans le mot הלו, l'élément לו vient simplement appuyer la particule הָא 'voici'; mais, que ce soit הא ou הלו, ce 'voici', comme fréquemment הִנֵּה en hébreu, a une valeur faible et surtout stylistique. La particule לו, dans notre ostracon, en est pratiquement l'équivalent.

Ligne 2. [במ]סגרא. Cette reconstitution du mot, étant donné le contexte, nous paraît certaine.—שׂימת. Parfait passif (*peîl*) 1e p. sg. du verbe שׂים: 'je fus mis'; ce ne peut être ici la 3e p. sg. fm., vu qu'il faudrait alors un sujet féminin, ni la 2e p. sg. ms., vu que l'auteur de la lettre n'a vraiment pas à raconter ce qui est arrivé à son correspondant.—פקיד. Ce mot peut être interprété soit comme un parfait ou un participe passif du verbe פקד, au sens impersonnel: 'il a été ordonné' (פְּקִיד)—cf. Cowley, *Aḥiḳar*, l. 103—soit comme un nom ms. sg. à l'état absolu: 'gouverneur, inspecteur, officier' (פָּקִיד); ce nom, bien attesté en hébreu, se rencontre en araméen ancien, dans la stèle III de Sfiré (ll. 4, 10, 13) et aussi probablement à Éléphantine (Cowley no 37, l. 6). Il est difficile, dans notre ostracon, de choisir entre ces deux sens, étant donné la lacune du début de la l. 3. Si l'on adopte le premier sens, on peut compléter ainsi la phrase: ופקיד [עלי לם] 'et on donna cet ordre à mon sujet'; si l'on retient le second sens, on peut supposer ceci: ופקיד [אמר לם] 'et un officier donna cet ordre'. Dans les deux cas, on pourrait même supprimer le mot לם, si l'on jugeait que la lacune, avant [י]כלאו, ne devait comporter qu'un mot de trois lettres.

Ligne 3. [י]כ̇לאו. Il ne reste du כ qu'une partie de la tête, mais la lettre est suffisamment reconnaissable. Étant donné que, dans le complément מנה, le pronom suffixe est à la 3e p. sg. et qu'il ne peut guère se rapporter, vu le contexte, qu'à la personne mise en prison, c'est-à-dire à l'auteur même de la lettre, nous sommes amené à penser que le verbe est au jussif et qu'il exprime en style direct l'ordre donné au sujet du prisonnier, par conséquent à lire [י]כ̇לאו et à compléter la lacune comme nous l'avons exposé plus haut. Noter ici dans יכלאו le maintien du א; le verbe כלא, en effet, est un ל״א primitif. Les verbes de cette catégorie, toutefois, tendent à se confondre, dès cette époque, avec les ל״י: cf. par exemple ostracon Clermont-Ganneau no 152, face concave, l. 4 (*Semitica*, ii, 1949, p. 35): תתכלי, pour תתכלאי; mais, en revanche, אכלאנך (Cowley no 5, l. 6).—מנה לחם ומין. Même construction dans Gen. xxiii. 6: את־קברו לא־יכלה ממך, Ps. xl. 12: לא־תכלא רחמיך ממני. Le pain et l'eau étaient la nourriture habituelle des prisonniers; ici, si nous comprenons bien le passage, l'auteur déclare qu'il fut privé même de ce minimum indispensable à la vie. De ces sévices exercés sur Yedoniah par ses geôliers, on peut rapprocher l'histoire de Jérémie enfermé dans la prison: c'est le roi Sédécias lui-même qui doit donner l'ordre de lui porter chaque jour une miche de pain (Jer. xxxvii. 21).

Ligne 4. לי אחוטב. Le début de la phrase, avec le verbe, a disparu dans la lacune; du mot précédent ne subsiste que la trace du haut de la dernière lettre, pratiquement impossible à identifier. Aḥuṭab est un nom de femme fréquent dans les ostraca d'Éléphantine; voir, par exemple, l'ostracon no 169 de la collection Clermont-Ganneau (publié dans *Revue des Études Sémitiques*, 1945, pp. 65–75). Malheureusement, on ne saurait dire, vu l'état du document, à quel titre cette femme intervient ici.

Ligne 5. שבה. La lecture de ces trois lettres, bien qu'un éclat ait enlevé leur partie inférieure, ne fait pas de doute. Le mot précédent était très probablement יום: les traces qui en subsistent laissent reconnaître le haut d'un ו et d'un מ. Nous proposons donc de lire ici 'le jour du Sabbat', comme sur l'ostracon n° 186 de la collection Clermont-Ganneau, face convexe, l. 1 (voir *Rivista degli Studi Orientali*, xxxii, 1957, p. 407). Sur cette forme araméenne שבה, pour l'hébreu שַׁבָּת, nous nous sommes expliqué tout au long dans notre mémoire intitulé 'Sabbat et Parascève à Éléphantine d'après des ostraca araméens inédits' (*Mémoires présentés par divers savants à l'Académie des Inscriptions et Belles-Lettres*, Paris, Imprimerie Nationale, 1950, pp. 67–88). Malheureusement, tout le début de la ligne a disparu: ces mots 'jour du Sabbat' se trouvent donc privés de contexte. Peut-être formaient-ils la fin d'une phrase, à laquelle aurait fait suite directement la l. 1 de la face convexe; mais il se peut qu'une ou plusieurs lignes aient entièrement disparu au bas de l'ostracon.

Face convexe. Ligne 1. שבו. Le ש est partiellement effacé, mais ce qui reste visible ne permet guère de lire une autre lettre. Le verbe שבה 'emmener captif' est courant en judéo-palestinien (שבא) et en syriaque (ܫܒܐ), de même qu'en hébreu; on le rencontre plusieurs fois sur l'ostracon araméen d'Assour, du VIIe siècle avant J.-C. (ll. 15, 16), aussi sur un papyrus du Ve siècle (*C.I.S.* ii, n° 145 = Cowley n° 71, l. 14).—לנתן. Natan est un nom propre très fréquent à Éléphantine; noter le ל comme signe de l'accusatif.—תמה. Un petit éclat a enlevé une partie du ה, dont la lecture reste certaine. Cet adverbe, 'là-bas', désigne quelque région éloignée d'Éléphantine, par exemple Thèbes; c'est à Thèbes que Yedoniah et ses collègues furent incarcérés (Cowley n° 34). Le cas de ce Natan, s'ajoutant à celui de l'auteur même de notre ostracon, montre à quel point les Juifs d'Éléphantine étaient alors inquiétés et traqués; on ne saurait dire si, en cette période très troublée, les arrestations dont il est ici question étaient faites par les Égyptiens ou par les autorités perses, incertaines de la fidélité des Juifs au régime défaillant.

Ligne 2. ינפק עלי. Si l'auteur invite Natan à venir vers lui, au cas où ce Natan n'aurait pas été emmené 'là-bas', c'est évidemment qu'il a lui-même été relâché; cette libération devait être indiquée sur la face concave, après l'emprisonnement, dans une phrase partiellement ou entièrement disparue.—אהך. Imparfait 1e p. sg. de הלך; c'est, comme on sait, la forme régulière en araméen, cf. תהך (Cowley n° 15, ll. 25, 28; n° 71, ll. 13, 22; *Aḥiḳar*, l. 102), אהך (ibid. n° 8, l. 22), יהכון (ibid. n° 10, l. 19).—אגרס. Du verbe גרס 'broyer' (*pael*); noter l'asyndète, après אהך. Le verbe אגרס appelle un complément: celui-ci a partiellement disparu dans la lacune de la fin de la l. 2, où il y a place pour trois lettres. La fin du mot est conservée au début de la l. 3 (un tel rejet est assez fréquent dans les ostraca): la seconde lettre est clairement un א, marque de l'état emphatique; quant à la première lettre, elle est un peu difficile à reconnaître: nous lirions volontiers un ע, mais peut-être pourrait-on lire un ד (ou ר). De toute manière, cette troisième radicale du nom, seule conservée, ne permet guère de deviner quel était le mot manquant, et nous ignorerons toujours ce que l'auteur de la lettre était si énergiquement disposé à 'broyer', avec l'aide de Natan.

Lignes 3–5. Ces trois lignes, très mutilées, ne laissent pas reconnaître la suite des idées. A la l. 3, le mot הושרו est un impératif *hafel* 2e p. pl. (de la racine ישר) : 'envoyez-moi' ; verbe très fréquent dans les ostraca d'Éléphantine (cf. *Revue des Études Sémitiques*, 1945, p. 70). Mais le complément de ce verbe a disparu : seule, subsiste la trace supérieure de la première lettre, probablement un ל, qui peut être ici ou bien la particule d'accusatif ou bien le début d'un nom (comme לחם ?).—Début de la l. 4 : ואכתב 'et j'écrirai' ; le ב, à la fin du mot, est mutilé, mais pratiquement certain.—Début de la l. 5 : nous lisons d'abord un ו (un éclat a toutefois fait disparaître la queue de ce signe), puis les traces d'un א, enfin le haut d'un ל ; par conséquent, ואל : début d'une proposition négative, au jussif.

THE SECOND LAMENTATION FOR UR

By C. J. GADD, *London*

THE great Sumerian city of Ur was captured and destroyed by enemies in the year 2006 B.C.,[1] at the end of its best-known, if not its most flourishing, age. In the end its destroyers were the Elamites, but the years preceding the disaster were tense with shifting policies and pacts in a supreme effort to stall off hostile pressures both from the east and from the north-west. Ibi-Sin, the last king of the dynasty, long sustained a brave and resourceful struggle to avert his fate, not only by force of arms but by playing off one enemy against the other, a process which can be followed only with great difficulty through the scrappy and indirect evidence which remains to us from this crucial period. But all barriers yielded at last, the city was put to sack and ruin, the inhabitants to the slaughter, and the king himself carried away into captivity.[2]

Material traces of this destruction were found everywhere in the modern excavations of the site, unobliterated by all the population which returned and undoubtedly restored, at different times, many of the public and private buildings, the walls, gates, roads, streets, and waterways of the city. But Ur never truly recovered; it was hardly of the first importance even in the relatively prosperous Old Babylonian period which followed, and it shared the decline of the south through long succeeding ages, with only sporadic attempts by individual rulers to reinstate its structures and its cult.

This disaster evidently created a great sensation, and was long remembered in such historical tradition of that time as Babylonia possessed. It is a literary tradition that concerns us here; the fall of Ur was lamented in at least two long Sumerian dirges, one of which, comprising 436 lines in eleven divisions of very unequal length, has been reconstituted from many partial manuscripts and published in virtual

[1] According to the system calculated by M. B. Rowton for use in the revision of the *Cambridge Ancient History*, I and II.

[2] Recent studies, taking account of accumulating factors, have been contributed by A. Falkenstein in *Z.A.*, N.F., xv, 1950, pp. 59 ff.; T. Jacobsen in *Journ. of Cuneiform Studies*, vii, 1953, pp. 36 ff.; E. Sollberger in *A.f.O.* xvii, 1954–6, pp. 44 ff.; J.-R. Kupper, *Les nomades en Mésopotamie au temps des rois de Mari*, pp. 158 ff.; and D. O. Edzard, *Die 'zweite Zwischenzeit' Babyloniens*, pp. 44 ff.

completeness.[1] The 'second lamentation' is much less known, and only its opening passage has at present been adequately presented.[2] Other parts, too, have been preserved and their texts published, although they could not hitherto be accurately identified. To these must now be added certain tablets found at Ur itself, which both considerably extend the material available and give shape to the whole composition. Since the purpose of the present article is to give only a specimen, albeit ample, of this 'second lamentation', and space is limited, it is not needful here to list and classify all the matter, which will be done elsewhere. The specimen chosen is the 'third division',[3] which exists in full, sixty verses with little damage. These are contained in the following tablets and fragments:

A. U. 16900 B, a complete tablet excavated at Ur by the late Sir Leonard Woolley in 1930–1 from the private house of the Larsa period called 'No. 1, Broad Street' (*Antiquaries Journal*, xi, 1931, pp. 365 ff.).

B. The first 11 lines of the 'third division' (continuing, without a break, from the end of the 'second division') are preserved in E. Chiera, *Sumerian Religious Texts*, no. 51, reverse, 5 ff.

C. Lines 44–59 of this division (beginnings only) are in E. Chiera, *Sumerian Texts of Varied Contents*, no. 26.

D. Ibid., no. 25, obverse, 1–13, has most of lines 52–60 and the concluding 'rubrics' followed by the opening lines of the 'fourth division'.

This composition was listed, by its first line, in three of the 'catalogues' of literary works which have been published hitherto; see recently S. N. Kramer in *Rev. d'Assyriologie*, lv, 1961, p. 172, no. 45.

In purport and language this 'second lamentation' differs little from the 'first', but whereas in the 'first' it is the goddess of the city who appeals to Nanna himself, to An, Enlil, and the Anunna for mercy and

[1] By S. N. Kramer, *Lamentation over the Destruction of Ur* (Oriental Institute, Chicago, Assyriological Studies, no. 12, 1940).

[2] For the texts constituting this, and for a translation and commentary, see A. Falkenstein in *Die Welt des Orients*, i, pp. 377 ff., and also his joint publication (with W. von Soden) *Sumerische und akkadische Hymnen und Gebete*, no. 37, pp. 189 ff. This section is now formally proved to have been the beginning of the composition by a fragment from Ur which ends with the line 60, after which a ruling is drawn followed by DIŠ '60' and [IM-G]ÍD-DA 1-kam-ma.

[3] A neutral word has been chosen to translate the common but still obscure ki-RU-gú, which designates the successive and numbered 'canticles' into which longer Sumerian religious texts are divided; this term has been discussed by A. Falkenstein in *Z.A.*, N.F., xv, 1950, p. 105. According to the literal signification of the signs, this may be a direction for bowing or kneeling at points in the service.

restoration, a distinguishing feature of the 'second' is a dialogue between Nanna and his father Enlil, which begins at line 44 of the third division, while Enlil's reply is contained in the fourth. This reply is to the effect that Ur could not expect to rule for ever—the gods had decreed to it kingship but not eternal kingship ('who ever saw the length of a kingship surpassing all?'[1]), so Nanna must bear with the calamity of his city. Thus a final appeal has been made; the power which has not averted, has even launched, the disaster will not promise restoration of the city's glories, and no hope appears. In these barren polytheistic exchanges and final frustration lies the principal difference between the Sumerian laments and those Biblical passages, especially the Lamentations 'of Jeremiah', which are manifestly under the influence of these.[2] The human note, the sense of personal sin, of retribution and repentance, the hope not all lost of a return and renewal in the end—these are genuine sentiments brought in by the Hebrew writers, and these do something to freshen the aridity of a theme which is deeply tinged with affectation, for there can be little real emotion in literary reminiscences of disaster, composed in subsequent tranquillity and recited (although we know nothing of the circumstances) in a setting of formalism and priestcraft. These studiously, even acrostically, dropped tears savour more of midnight oil than of native salt; the strange Homeric epithet of mourning κρυερός is indeed applicable by metaphor to such frigid performances which pretend to deny that 'time remembered is grief forgotten'. The Biblical Lamentations, owing to the essential lifelessness of this exercise, are no doubt the least appreciated book of the Old Testament, but since nothing therein is alien to the fruitful interest of Professor G. R. Driver a canto from one of its earliest forerunners may not be amiss here as a tribute of admiration and friendship.

[1] The beginnings of these lines are in E. Chiera, *Sumerian Texts of Varied Contents*, no. 25 (that designated D above), obverse, 19–reverse, 2; partially translated by T. Jacobsen in *J.N.E.S.* ii, 1943, p. 171. There is an unflattering allusion to such a dialogue in another hymn to the moon-god published by H. de Genouillac, *Textes religieux sumériens*, ii, plate CLII, recently translated by Åke Sjöberg, *Der Mondgott Nanna-Suen in der sumerischen Überlieferung*, I. Teil, p. 65: there (lines 7, 8) Nanna is said to have wearied Enlil by his importunity.

[2] While the Babylonian inspiration of the Hebrew Lamentations has been observed by several writers, and is so naturally to be looked for in a work which is by its subject exilic, it is surprising to find in a recent book (N. K. Gottwald, *Studies in the Book of Lamentations*, 1954) barely a single remark of alien prompting, amid much discussion of the origin, themes, and theology of the lamentation motif. Certainly not all of the harps were left hanging by the waters of Babylon, and some were attuned to sing at home the songs of a strange land.

TRANSCRIPTION

1. (d)e[n-líl]-li šà-níg-šaga(?) níg-[ḫul] uru(KI)-ta ba-da-tuš
2. níg-uru(KI)-gul-gul nig-é-gul-gul uru(KI)-ta ba-da-tuš
3. níg-igi-bi-šè (giš)tukul-e la-ba-ab-[gi$_4$(?)] uru(KI)-ta ba-da-tuš
4. šà-nu-si-si igi-nigi-nigi-bi uru(KI)-ta ba-da-tuš
5. urí(KI)-ma gi-dili-dù-a-gim sag(?)-gi-nu-gá-gá
6. ukù-bi ku$_6$-túl(?)-a LU-ga-gim × × × mi-ni-ib-túm-túm-mu
7. dumu-maḫ-bi ì-bur$_6$-bur$_6$-ra × × × LÚ(?)-nu-um-zi-zi-zi(?)
8. lugal-bi du-um-lá-a u$_5$-a níg(?) × × × ?-gal
9. lugal-nì-ša$_6$-ga-kú-kú-a × × × ba-an-tuš
10. u$_4$-tu$_{15}$-šú-šú igi-im-lá-e šà-kúš(?)-[ù] [nu-un]-zu-zu
11. é-bappir-na kaš-nu-un-gál bùlug(?)-nu-un-gál
12. é-gal-la-na ninda-kú la-ba-na-gál × × ba-ab-du$_7$
13. gá-nun-maḫ-a-ni še-[nu-u]m-si-si zi-ni(?) × × × túm-mu
14. gur$_7$-du$_6$-gur$_7$-bar-e-(d)nanna-ka (d)ašnan nu-un-gál
15. kin-sig-dingir-re-e-ne-gé RU(?)-SU(?)-e × × -?-lá
16. unu$_6$-gal-kaš-kurun-ta mùš-im-ma-ab-túm
17. gír-pa-a gu$_4$-kú-udu-kú ra ú-šim-e ba-[da]-ná
18. gir$_4$-maḫ-udun(?)-gu$_4$-udu-nu-ag-e ir-nu-mu-un-e$_{11}$-e
19. bur-sag-á-šid-(d)nanna-ka za-pa-ág-bi ba-ra-gul
20. é-gu$_4$-gim(?)-gù-bí-íb-du$_{11}$-ga-a RI(?)-si-ga-bi ba-ir(?)
21. mu-un-du-kù-ga × si(?)-sá-e-gar-ra-bi ba-sù-ud
22. (na$_4$)àra-gaz giš-gan-na ì-dúr-dúr lú-nu-um-ši-gam-e
23. kar-za-gìn-na-(d)nanna-ka a-e ba-da-lá
24. a-má-sag-ga-gé gù-nu-mu-un-gi$_4$-gi$_4$ sil$_6$-lá-nu-mu-un-šub
25. unu$_6$-ri-bàn-da-(d)nanna-ka saḫar-ba-da-dub-dub
26. ú-ú(SAR) ba-da-mú ú-ú(SAR) ba-da-mú kir-ri-e ba-an-mú
27. má-má-gur$_8$-ra kar-za-gìn-na mùš-im-ma-ab-túm
28. íd-má-gur$_8$-ra-ba-ab-du$_7$-a-za á-nu-mu-un-su(d)-sud-e
29. ezen-ki-garza-ka giš-ḫur-bi ba-kúr
30. má-gúg(?)-gá-a-a-ugu-na-ka gúg(?)-nu-mu-un-ab-túm
31. ninda-nidba-bi-(d)en-líl [nibru](KI)-šè(!) nu-mu-un-na-da-an-tu-tu
32. íd-bi šà-sù-ga i-ni-gál má-gur$_8$ nu-mu-un-dib-bi
33. zíg(?)-gur-a-bi-kiš-NU-gál ú-gíd-da ba-àm-mú
34. é-tùr-dagal-la-(d)nanna-ka dub-ba-an-bi ba-si-il

1. B (coll.) šà-níg-LÚ(?) 2. B omits KI and reads -gul-gul-e 3. B omits -šè, -e, and -ab- 4. B nigí-nigí 5. B sag-gi 6. B (coll.) ku$_6$-šu-nigí-na-díb(?)-bi-gim 8. B du-um-lá(!)-e 11. B kaš-bi-nu-un-gál

TRANSLATION

1. Oppression(?) and calamity Enlil has made to abide withal in the city
2. what ruins the city, what ruins the house he has made, &c.
3. what turns not away the weapon before it he has made, &c.
4. a heart unquiet, its eye darting around, he has made, &c.
5. Ur, like a single reed, makes no resistance(?)
6. its people, like fish caught(?) in a pool, [a flood?] has carried away
7. its noble youth, with sprinkled oil [anointed?], goes not forth
8. its king, mounted upon the *dumla* . . . .
9. a king that ate goodly fare sits in . . . .
10. the storm, the destructive wind with uplifted eyes, knows no relenting
11. in the brew-house ale is no more, malt(?) is no more
12. in his palace bread to eat there is none for him, and . . . .(?)
13. his storehouse, barley does not fill it, ... is [not] brought in
14. in the . . . granary, the . . . granary of Nanna, grain there is none
15. the late repast of the gods . . . .
16. in the great vat of ale (and) wine these have failed
17. in the *gir-pa* which pastured oxen and sheep . . . . the grass is(?) laid low
18. the great oven, that made no . . . . of oxen and sheep, no more sends forth an odour
19. the vessel that gathered the dues(?) of Nanna, its resonance is destroyed
20. the 'house' which resounded like a bull, its . . . . . . is taken away
21. the sacred revenue, which made a right . . . ., is removed
22. the grinding mortar, where the pestle rests, no man bends over it
23. at the Blue Quay of Nanna the water has passed away
24. the water at the prow of the boat returns no sound - - - - - -
25. in the great basin of Nanna dust is poured therein
26. grass (and) weeds grow there, grass (and) weeds grow there, young palms(?) grow there
27. boat and barge at the Blue Quay have ceased (to lie)
28. in thy canal (which was) fit for a barge, it is not an arm-[length?]
29. the feast in the place of ritual, its observance is altered
30. the boat of rushes(?) for his father brings rushes(?) no more
31. the food, the sustenance of Enlil, no more goes in to him there [at Nippur]
32. its canal stays bare, it takes no barge
33. its ziggurat Kišnugal grows long grass
34. the spacious cattle-pen of Nanna, its . . . . . is cut off

35. gi-sig-kiri$_6$ × × × × lá geštin-ka$_5$ ba-an-gar-gar
36. áb-tùr-amar-bi-da × × × KU ki-ne-ru-e ba-ab-gin
37. áb-(ú)KI.NANNA-e-edin(KI)-nu-zu-bi gìr-kúr ba-ra-an-díb-bi-eš
38. (d)GAR$_{11}$.A.Ú lú-áb-ki-ág-gá (giš)tukul ganám-ma ba-šub
39. (d)ŠU.NI.DU$_{10}$ ià-ga-àra(ra)-du$_6$-ul-du$_6$-ul-e ià-ga-àra(ra) nu-du$_6$-ul-du$_6$-ul
40. ià-bi lú-ià-nu-zu-ne ì-búr-búr-ne
41. ga-bi lú-ga-nu-zu-ne ì-im-mùš-mùš-ù-ne
42. é-tùr-ri-bi URU×GA-e-búr-búr-e gù-tùr nu-mu-ni-ib-bi
43. izi-ḫur-dugud-bi i-ra-a-ri i-dè-bi ba-gul
44. (d)zuen-e a-a-ni-(d)en-líl-ra ér-mu-un-na-še$_8$-še$_8$
45. a-a-ugu-mu uru(KI)-mu a-na-ra-ab-dù a-na-aš ba-e-da-gur-ri-en
46. (d)en-líl urí(KI)-mu a-na-ra-ab-dù a-na-aš ba-e-da-gur-ri-en
47. má-gúg(?)-gá a-a-ugu-na-šè gúg(?)-nu-mu-un-na-ab-tùm
48. ninda-nidba-zu (d)en-líl nibru(KI)-šè nu-mu-un-na-da-an-tu-tu
49. [é(?)]-uru-bar-ra-en-uru-šà-ga-gé-e ḫa-ba-ab-laḫ$_4$(?)-e-eš
50. urí(KI) uru(KI)-giš-al-e-ri-a-gim du$_6$-du$_6$-da ba-ra
51. [é(?)]-érim-ki-ní-dúb-bu-(d)en-líl-lá èš-líl-lá ba-ab-gar
52. (d)en-líl uru-zu(?) igi-ba(?)-dù(?) é-ri-a-sù-ga
53. urí(KI)-ma UR-bi úr-bàd-da si-im-si-im-nu-mu-un-ag-e
54. TÚL-SAG-bulug-ga malba(ba)-bi-a ki-li-bi-ib-ri-ri-gi
55. a-a-ugu-mu uru(KI)-mu dili-bi-ta da(!)-zu-šè nigín-àm-ši-ib
56. (d)en-líl urí(KI)-mu dili-bi-ta(?) á-zu-šè nigín-àm-ši-ib
57. é-kiš-NU-gál-la-mu dili-bi-da(!) á-zu-šè nigín-àm-ši-ib
58. urí(KI)-ma-mu ḫa-ra-ni-ib-è ukù ḫu-mu-ra-ab-dagal-la
59. me-ki-en-gi-ra ba-da-ḫa-lam-ma ki-ḫa-ra-ab-gi$_4$-gi$_4$

ki-RU-gú III-kam-ma

60. a é-zi é-zi a šaga-bi šaga-bi

iz-gi-gál-bi-im

(d)en-líl-li dumu-ni-(d)zuen-ra mu-un-na-ni-ib-gi$_4$-gi$_4$

I šu-ši

IM.GÍD.DA dam-qi-ì-lí-šu waraḫ ṭebetum ûmu XXI-kam

47. C (coll.) má-nisag-e 52. A repeats(?) igi-ba(?)-dù(?). After this line C and D insert similar line beginning nibru(KI), &c. 54. C and D (coll.) read TUR-SAG-bulug-ga, &c. 55–57. C and D aš-bi á-zu 59. D ḫa-lam-e ki-bi-, &c.

35. within the reed-fences of(?) the garden . . . . . . (and) 'fox-grape' is found
36. the cow from the byre with her calf . . . . . has gone to the enemies' place
37. its cow, which knew not the weeds of the steppe, enemy raids have captured
38. the god [*name*] who loves cows has thrown down the . . . . staff
39. the god [*name*] who pressed(?) butter and cheese, butter and cheese presses(?) no more
40. its butter, those who knew not butter spill
41. its milk, those who knew not milk waste(?)
42. its byre which spilled(?) its milk-churns now utters no sound of the byre
43. its heavy brazier which gave out perfume, its smoke is suppressed
44. Sin to his father Enlil made bitter weeping
45. 'Father, my begetter, what has my city done to thee, why hast thou turned from it?
46. Enlil, what has my Ur done to thee, why hast thou turned from it?
47. the boat of rushes(?) for his father who begot him brings rushes(?) no more
48. the food thy sustenance, O Enlil, it takes not in to thee at Nippur any more
49. from(?) outside the city into the midst of the city they have plundered(?)
50. Ur like a city upturned by the pickaxe has been smitten into mounds (of ruin)
51. the "treasure-house", the resting-place of Enlil, has been made an abode of the wind
52. O Enlil, thy city, which thine eyes beheld, is a lonely waste
53. in Ur, its dogs no longer . . . . (at) the base of the wall
54. ? . . . . ?
55. O father, my begetter, return my city in its unity to thy side again
56. O Enlil, return my Ur in its unity to thy side again
57. my Ekišnugal return in its unity to thy side again
58. may my Ur emerge before thee, may the people be multiplied before thee
59. may the institutions of Sumer, which are forgotten, be restored for thee.'

The third canticle(?)

60. Ah, true house, true house; ah, its oppressed, its oppressed.

Its antiphon

Enlil to his son Sin made answer (thus):

60

. . . . tablet of Damqi-ilišu, 21st of Ṭebet

815427 F

NOTES

1. Both in A and B the third sign of the group šà-níg-? is doubtful. B, in the copy, seems to read LÚ, which is unlikely to be right in itself, although not contradicted by the collation of S. N. Kramer, *Z.A.*, N.F., xviii, 1957, p. 90. In A the sign is not unlike that identified in line 60 below as šaga (LÚ×GÁN-tenû), in which case the meaning would be 'oppression', although the group šà-níg-šaga is not otherwise known. If it were possible to read šà-níg-tuk (but this does not appear likely) we should have a very suitable word *umṣatum, būrum* 'famine'.

4. Translation based upon the equivalences si-si = *šuqammumu* and igi-nigin = *saḫāru ša ēni.*

5. Uncertain; dili-dù-a = *ēdānû* 'single, alone', and for the idea cf. (First) Lamentation over . . . Ur, line 123, also the O.T. book of Lamentations, ii. 6. Another example of this simile is quoted in the Chicago *Assyr. Dict.*, E, p. 27*b* (under *ēdēnû*), and in J. J. A. van Dijk, *Sumerische Götterlieder*, II. Teil, p. 30, both of the phrases in this line are found in different contexts. In the second member of the line B reads sag-gi . . ., less certainly A the same: in B. Landsberger, *Materialien zum sumerischen Lexikon*, v, p. 73, is found sag-gi-gá-gá = *âru*, which does not clearly apply to this passage; the sense may be that given in the proposed translation here.

6. In A the fourth sign is probably túl = *būrtu, ḫirītu,* while B has šu-nigí-na followed by díb(?)-bi, and thus A ought perhaps to be read dib-bi(!), although -ga is clear upon the tablet. In both cases the hapless people are compared with fish caught in a water-hole or in the hand. The figure is found again in the (First) Lamentation, line 229, in view of which the end of the present verse may perhaps be restored as [a] . . . túm-túm-mu.

7. ì-bur$_6$-bur$_6$-ra; cf. A. T. Clay, *Babylonian Records in the Library of J. Pierpont Morgan*, iv, no. 32, obverse, 17, ì-giš-bur: ì-giš-bàr: *bi-'il-ti*, i.e. a pot for oil or fats; see also R. Labat, *Scritti in onore di Giuseppe Furlani*, p. 116, n. 2, 'huile purifiée'. If the idea to be supplied here is 'anointed with', a root šéš(-šéš) must be posited as occurring in the gap. At the end of the line the triple -zi-zi-zi is unknown to me; read possibly -zi-zi-ig.

8. 'its king, mounted upon the . . .'; apparently du-um-lá-a, otherwise unknown. Note that the middle signs alone might be dub-lá, and this the dub-lá-maḫ at Ur, where the king could be described as sitting or even 'mounted' (upon the judgement-seat). There is a puzzling reference to dub-lá in Gudea, Cylinder A, col. 24, lines 18 and 26, 'its dub-lá he set up like a wild-ox' and 'in the temple its dub-lá set up were set up (like) laḫama beside the abzu'. It might seem that the dub-lá was not only a building but also a particular figure.

10. With this phraseology cf. a line in *Cuneiform Texts . . . in the British Museum*, xv, plate 15, obverse, 16: u$_4$-um-me-igi-nigin u$_4$-um-me-igi-lá-lá, referring to the storm-god. There -um-me- of uncertain meaning seems to

be a fuller writing of -im- in the present text. In the (First) Lamentation, line 404, occurs u_4-dam-im-šub-ba-dumu-im-šub-ba, where the force of -im- is also uncertain, but not directly attached to u_4. šà-kúš(?)-[ù?] here in the sense of *nâḫu ša libbi*, *šitūltu*, *mitluku*, &c. 'appeasement, consideration'.

13. gá-(or é-)nun-maḫ was the official storehouse as early as the time of Urukagina; see most recently *Rev. d'Assyriologie*, xlviii, 1954, p. 60. For the excavated gá-nun-maḫ at Ur, see C. L. Woolley, *Antiquaries Journal*, iii, 1924, pp. 319 ff., also B. Landsberger, *O.L.Z.* xxxiv, 1931, p. 134, on no. 123.

14. Upon the gur_7-du_6 'granary, stack', see T. Jacobsen and S. N. Kramer, *J.N.E.S.* xii, 1953, p. 183, n. 60.

16. unu_6, i.e. TU × GUNU+unu (and ùru); the first of these signs is used also in má-gur_8, a boat of great capacity. Here the unu_6 is a container of fluids, probably a great jar or *pithos*: in line 25, below, it is the basin (?) of a canal.

17, 18. A similar phrase occurs in Gudea Cylinder A, col. 28, lines 5 ff. There gír-pa is also described as gu_4-kú-udu-kú, while from line 17 in this present text it would appear that gír-pa was a place of pasture for sheep and oxen. For ra which has no evident connexion with . . . udu-kú I can find no explanation, but I take it as independent (= *miḫṣu*), 'a stroke has laid low the grass'. In line 18 the third sign is plain on the tablet and looks like U+MAŠ, unknown to me, and therefore doubtfully assumed to be meant for U+MU, udun, in apposition to the gir_4-maḫ, *kirmaḫḫu*, upon which, especially that in Ur, see recently A. Falkenstein, *Iraq*, xxii, 1960, pp. 148 f. For ir-(si-im) . . . (nu)-ag, used in connexion with odours, see the Chicago *Assyr. Dict.*, E, p. 345.

19. bur-sag is called by Urukagina (F. Thureau-Dangin, *Die sumerischen und akkadischen Königsinschriften*, p. 46, h. 2) the 'house' of regular offerings (sá-dug_4), and the tenor of lines 19 and 20 here suggests that it was a metal (?) vessel (bur), which resounded as offerings were cast in: á-šid perhaps 'counting the dues'. A building gá-bur occurs several times in the royal inscriptions from Ur (also èš-bur in no. 36 ibid.).

22. For (na_4)àra-gaz, see *A.f.O.* xviii, 1957–8, p. 339, and for giš-gan-na, *bukannu*, B. Landsberger, *Mater. zum sumer. Lex.* v, p. 32. There was found a 'saddle-quern and rubbing-stone' in the kitchen of a house at Ur (C. L. Woolley, *Antiquaries Journal*, vi, 1926, p. 373 and plate XLIX b).

23. The 'Blue Quay' at Ur (also in line 27) is often mentioned, as also the kar-zi-da, but similarly named installations seem to have existed elsewhere; for references, see recently Åke Sjöberg, *Der Mondgott Nanna-Suen in der sumerischen Überlieferung*, p. 103. It is impossible to banish the suspicion that the 'Sumerian' verbal form ba-da-lá is nothing but the (writer's native?) Accadian [*mû*] *baṭlū*, perhaps a sophisticated pun. A description of the ruin of Agade (transl. by I. Bernhardt and S. N. Kramer, 'Sumerische literarische Texte in der Hilprecht-Sammlung', in *Wissens. Zeitschr. der . . . Universität Jena*, v, 1955/6, Heft 6, p. 761) reproduces several of the calamities detailed in lines 23–32 of the Ur lamentation.

24. má-sag, the prow of a boat, see A. Salonen, *Die Wasserfahrzeuge der alten Babylonier*, pp. 75 f.

25. unu_6 here certainly the 'basin' of a canal, as a container (cf. line 16, above). The word has recently been discussed by Åke Sjöberg, op. cit., pp. 93 f.—this is undoubtedly one of the instances noted by him where the sense of 'dining-room' does not fit.

26. ú-sar is explained as = (*šam*)*lišān kalbi* (A. Deimel, *Šumer. Lex.*, no. 318. 84) and = *ur-qi* (*A.f.O.* xviii, 1957–8, p. 238). For a discussion of 'hound's tongue', see R. C. Thompson, *Dict. of Assyrian Botany*, pp. 26 f. The explanation as *urqi* is simply 'grass', but a difference must be intended between ú and ú-sar: kir-ri-e might be Accadian, for in a vocabulary (*Z.A.*, N.F., ix, 1936, p. 250) is found *ki-ir-ru* = *ḫa-ru-ú*, and *ḫarû* is 'young shoot of a date-palm' (Chicago *Assyr. Dict.*, Ḫ, p. 117, *ḫarû* B). Both En-e-du_7-an-na and Nabonidus relate how they had to clear away undergrowth which had sprung up amid the ruins of Ur (*Iraq*, xiii, 1951, p. 37).

28. The first member of this verse appears in the (First) Lamentation, line 367: in view of the conclusion here it must be understood that the canal, once great enough to carry the largest boats, had dwindled to a narrow ditch, 'an arm's length' (wide or deep?). Xenophon (or perhaps an interpolator) in the *Anabasis*, I. vii. 15, gives the interesting intelligence that four canals which the army had to cross after leaving the neighbourhood of Charmande were used for the navigation of grain-ships; these were a plethron (about 100 feet) in width, and of exceeding depth.

30. Uncertainty attaches to the second sign, which, on the Ur tablet, is clearly written, both here and in line 47, below, as bára×EŠ. In line 47 the Philadelphia fragment (C) reads clearly $MURUB_4$, as kindly ascertained for me by Dr. M. Civil, who would read nisag and refers to Ḫḫ. iv. 335 (*Mater. zum sumer. Lex.* v, p. 179) giš-má-$MURUB_4$ = (*elippi*) *nisanni*. The problem is, however, that the boat must have carried a cargo of requisites for the diet of Enlil (lines 31, 48), and in view of this I would propose to read the dubious sign as gúg = *šuppatu*, perhaps the edible roots of the marsh-lands, the γόγγαι described in Berossus fr. 7 (ἰσοδυναμεῖν δὲ . . . κριθαῖς), for which suggestion see R. C. Thompson, *Dict. of Assyrian Botany*, p. 12, and for gúg with other articles of food—grain, oil, butter—cf. L. Matouš, *Archiv Orientální*, xxii, 1954, p. 441. As a favourite dish of Enlil gúg is mentioned again in the poem which has been called 'the journey of Nanna to Nippur'; there (text in S. Langdon, *Babylonian Liturgies*, plate II, lines 49 ff., and E. Chiera, *Sumerian Epics and Myths*, no. 94, obverse, 13 ff.) it is said that Enlil ordered gúg to be served to his visitor, as a food which he particularly fancied. Yet why should Nanna have gone to Nippur for a treat which, it seems, was continually passing through his own city on its way upstream? The translation of gúg as 'cakes' is hardly more than a conjecture *ad sensum*; for an obscure proverb and references see E. I. Gordon, *Sumerian Proverbs*, pp. 66 f. The idea of a god travelling to Nippur in order to provide a feast for his 'father' Enlil and share it with him

reappears with the god Enki as principal actor in the 'Hymn of Eridu', transl. in A. Falkenstein and W. von Soden, *Sumerische und akkadische Hymnen und Gebete*, pp. 136 f.

31. As written on the tablet this line is ungrammatical and beyond translation, but there is an evident scribal omission of [EN.LÍL.]KI (Nippur) after (d)en-líl, and the following sign should be -šè, not (as the tablet) -KU—this is made clear by line 48.

32. For this phrase in the (First) Lamentation, line 346, see the note by S. N. Kramer in his publication of this, p. 94.

34. dub-ba-an here is obscure—it can hardly have anything to do with 'tablets' (cf. *Mater. zum sumer. Lex.* vii, p. 57. 311 and p. 67. 12). si-il is probably best taken as = *dapāru* (*A.f.O.* xiv, 1941–4, p. 121, and the Chicago *Assyr. Dict.*, D, p. 188), 3b, *duppuru* 'to remove (an object)'. The usual equivalent of *duppuru* is sil_6 of line 24, above.

35. Cf. in the (First) Lamentation, line 123, gi-sig-kiri-gim, but probably -gim is not to be read here. gi-sig = *kikkišu* = *ḫuṣṣu*, a reed-fence (*Mater. zum sumer. Lex.* vii, p. 69. 34). geštin-ka_5, *karan šēlabi* 'fox-grape', is suggested to be *solanum nigrum* L. by R. C. Thompson, op. cit., pp. 142 ff.

37. Here it seems to be implied that the sacred cows of the moon-god 'did not know' the kind of herbage which was to be found on the open plain, but were more choicely foddered in the byre. In contrast with this stands a hymn addressed to an unknown temple (for all details, see Å. Sjöberg, op. cit., pp. 140 ff.) where (line 4) the 'sacred byre' itself is described as enclosing(?) 'cows (which feed upon?) the KI-(d)NANNA-herb'; the contradiction, if it exists, is hardly important. Note that there was a 'divine' form of such an animal as occurs in the present text, (d)áb-(ú)KI-(d)NANNA-e-di-nu (K. Tallqvist, *Akkad. Götterepitheta*). A similarly named plant was used in Sumerian medicine; cf. M. Civil in *Rev. d'Assyriologie*, liv, 1960, p. 68.

38 f. Both of these little-known gods are included in the lists as herdsmen of the moon-god; see K. Tallqvist, *Akkad. Götterepitheta*, pp. 308, 466. giš-tukul-ganám-ma is not found in the list of weapons given by ḪAR-ra = *ḫubullu* (*Mater. zum sumer. Lex.* vi, pp. 84 ff.).

40, 41. For the idea in these lines (good things wasted by barbarians unable to appreciate them) cf. the (First) Lamentation, 280 f., and J. J. A. van Dijk, *Sumer. Götterlieder*, II, p. 64. For búr-búr = *pašāru* in the sense of 'get rid of, remove', see A. L. Oppenheim, *The Interpretation of Dreams in the Ancient Near East*, p. 218. In line 41 mùš-mùš-ù seems to have a like sense but is not known to me elsewhere.

42. URU×GA = *šakirum*; cf. *Mater. zum sumer. Lex.* ii, p. 117, translated 'Milchschale', and iii, p. 175, [ša]-ki-ir = URU×GA-gunû. The meaning seems to be that the milk-containers are upset and the cows departed. Cf., however, the passage quoted in I. Bernhardt and S. N. Kramer, *Enki und die Weltordnung* (Jena, 1959–60), p. 247 (from the same composition as this), where the meaning is again very uncertain.

43. i-ra-a-ri: i-ra is probably for ir = *erēšu* 'odour' (cf. the Chicago *Assyr. Dict.*, E, p. 280, quoting *Cuneiform Texts*, xxxix, plate 16, 51 f., the smell of smoke, as here from the brazier). The latter part of the phrase i-ra-a-ri can best be taken as a-ri, for a-ri-a = *riḫû* 'engender'.

45, 46. In both of these lines the scribe has made an alteration of the first verbal form, and both are partly illegible. But they can be restored from a similar passage in H. Zimmern, *Sumer. Kultlieder*, i, no. 5, obverse, ii. 41 ff., uru-zu ta-ra-ab-du_{11}, although the remaining traces here scarcely favour -ab-; dù is certainly a better reading than du_{11}, but one would have expected -ag rather than either of these.

49. First sign uncertain in A, not clear in C: probably é, for which cf. (First) Lamentation, 263 ff., where the phraseology is very similar. en . . . e seems to be for the usual en-na . . . šè (A. Poebel, *Grundzüge der sumer. Gramm.*, p. 140, and see also *Z.A.*, N.F., xviii, 1957, p. 49. As for the verb, transliterate probably $la\underline{h}_4$ = *šalālu* (A. Deimel, *Šumer. Lex.* 206a. 13).

50. Cf. (First) Lamentation, line 258.

51. First sign missing or illegible in both copies—again probably é: second sign is érim (GÁ×ṢAB), for which see *Mater. zum sumer. Lex.* iii, p. 145 = *išittu*, generally translated 'treasury, storehouse' (Chicago *Assyr. Dict.*, I–J, p. 243). ki-ní-dub-ba = *ašar tapšuḫti.*

52. Reading of first part of this verse uncertain and translation similarly. é-ri-a-sù-ga is to be understood as substantive and adjective; for é-ri-a, see A. Deimel, *Šumer. Lex.* 324, no. 46 = *ḫar-bi* 'waste land' (Chicago *Assyr. Dict.*, Ḫ, p. 98, *ḫarbu* B. sù-ga occurs in the phrase šà-sù-ga, for which see I. Bernhardt and S. N. Kramer, op. cit., p. 247: 'der Ausdruck šà-sù-ga . . . gewöhnlich die Bedeutung "Leere, Unfruchtbarkeit" hat.' After line 52 both C and D inserted a line beginning EN.LÍL.KI (Nippur) in place of (d)en-líl, the remainder of which was probably identical.

53. The saying translated by E. I. Gordon, *Sumerian Proverbs*, p. 257 (2. 109), makes it almost certain that UR-bi is to be understood here as 'its dog', not taš-bi = *ištēniš*, as usual. The meaning of simsim is obscure in both places: M. Civil, in *Iraq*, xxiii, 1961, pp. 168 f., 'to sniff'. That dogs do not . . .? at the base of walls at Ur evidently implies that in the desolation neither dogs nor walls were left.

54. According to a collation kindly made by Dr. M. Civil both C and D have clearly TUR as the first sign, while A has clearly TÚL; these must presumably be regarded as phonetic variants. Both these and the following allusions to 'boundary' and 'price' and the concluding verbal form are not intelligible to me.

55. In this and the two succeeding lines the two signs after dili-bi- and before -zu waver between ta, da, and á: presumably dili-bi-ta á-zu-šè is the intended reading. With the final appeal in these lines cf. the similar appeal at the end of the O.T. Lamentations, v. 21.

60. é-zi is found several times in the (First) Lamentation, lines 243, 245,

318 f., and elsewhere; the translation is not easy, for it is uncertain what precise idea was attached to the phrase 'true, firm House' (such as the é-zi-da of Nabu at Borsippa). On a variety of applications, see I. Bernhardt and S. N. Kramer, op. cit., p. 253, n. 119.

There is doubt about the reading of the second member in this line: D reads LÚ, and the sign in A appears to be LÚ with some addition. Moreover, both A and B appear to have the same sign in line 1 of this division. Dr. M. Civil, who again has collated D, thinks the sign intended is most likely LÚ × GÁN-tenû (readings ša-gá, še-e, ḫi-eš), and suggests the Accadian equivalent *ḫablu* 'a person ill-treated, one oppressed' (Chicago *Assyr. Dict.*, Ḫ, pp. 16 f.), which gives an acceptable sense here, although less easy in line 1.

'ROOTS BELOW AND FRUIT ABOVE' AND RELATED MATTERS

By H. L. GINSBERG, *New York*

IN the received text of the Hebrew Bible the two words *šọreš* (or *šorāšīm*, since M.T. always has שׁרשׁיו or שׁרשׁיה where we should expect *šoršō* or *šoršāh*) and *prī* are juxtaposed in the following passages: 2 Kings xix. 30, Isa. xiv. 29, xxxvii. 31, Ezek. xvii. 9, Hos. ix. 16, Amos ii. 9. In all these cases, all modern writers (so far as I know) take *šọreš* to mean 'root' (or—so Koehler—'rootstock') and *prī* to mean 'fruit'. But 'root' (or 'rootstock') is inaccurate in all the passages in question and in some others; while 'fruit' is altogether wrong in all these passages except Hos. ix. 16 (where, moreover, it is right only for the one *prī* that the M.T. has preserved, another which does not mean 'fruit' having suffered corruption—see below) and in a number of additional ones.

Now a *prī* which does not mean 'fruit' is to be restored in parallel with a preserved *šọreš* which does not mean 'root' in Isa. v. 24a. For here, not only must ירפה be emended to שְׂרֵפָה in the light of Isa. xlvii. 14,[1] but also כמק to כַּמֹּץ (contamination by the parallel word *k'bq*) in the light of Isa. xxix. 5 and ופרחם to וּפִרְיָם in the light of the passages enumerated in the preceding paragraph. As emended, our half-verse means: 'Therefore, as straw is consumed by a tongue of fire and hay is licked up by a flame, their *šọreš* shall become like chaff and their *prī* shall go up like dust.'

I have selected just this passage for translation—apart from the two keywords which are left untranslated—because there exists a parallel to it in which one of the keywords is represented by a synonym. In Mal. iii. 19 we read: 'For behold, the day comes, burning like an oven: all godless and evildoers shall be straw, and the day that comes shall burn them up . . . so that it leaves of them neither *šọreš* nor branches (*'ānāp*).'

[1] M. Perles, *Analekten zur Textkritik*, N.F., 1922, 42. [Isa. xxxiii. 11 f. is even stronger evidence, but I too have missed it until now owing to its division into two Masoretic verses. In passing, it may be observed that *šyd* is almost certainly to be emended to *šmyr*; cf. xxxii. 13. This is not the only corruption in Isaiah that is due to the resemblance of *m* to *š* in the Palaeo-Hebraic script.]

And if it is natural to compare Isa. v. 24a with Mal. iii. 19, it is reasonable further to compare both it and the passages cited in the opening paragraph with Job xiv. 9–10, xviii. 16, xxix. 19, where the complement of *šọreš* is again a word meaning 'boughs' (*qāṣīr*).[1] Also to be compared is Isa. x. 33–xi. 1, where the complement of *šorāšīm* is *pūrā* 'crown (of a tree), boughs'.[2] (Kissane is of course right in applying x. 33–34 to Judah, not to the invader.)

By this time the reader may be wondering if the correct meaning of *prī* can have failed to be preserved by any ancient version in any of the *prī–šọreš* passages. As a matter of fact, the Aramaic Targum has preserved it at 2 Kings xix. 30 = Isa. xxxvii. 31, and its treatment of Hos. ix. 16 is of special interest. In this passage, it probably did not read פרים for אפרים but simply rendered the latter word doubly, both as 'Ephraim' and as equivalent to *piryām* 'their boughs',[3] and then took *prī* farther on in its ordinary sense of 'fruit'. It is an excellent idea to take a hint from the Targum and actually emend אפרים to פְּרְיָם, interpreting both this word and the פְּרִי farther on as the Targum does. (In addition, the whole verse has to be relocated between 11 and 12, as has been noted before, but the two changes are mutually independent.) The Targum may have further interpreted *pryh wʿnph*, Ezek. xix. 10, as *piryāh waʿnāp̄āh*; in any case, it connected *pryh* there with *prī* 'boughs', and so do we (see below).

As such, the sense of 'branches' for *prī* was recognized long ago by

[1] As regards Ezek. xvii. 9, a huge bird which is able to tear apart a vine's *šorāšīm* can be credited with doing something equally violent to its twigs. Besides, consuming or destroying the vine's fruit does it no harm: the fruit is there to be disposed of every year. As for Isa. xiv. 29b, the verb there is *yāṣā*, and Isa. xi. 1 shows that what *yāṣā* from a *šọreš* is a shoot. Anyway, fruit does not issue directly from a *šọreš* or *šorāšīm*; certainly not as the word is conventionally rendered in the passages we are considering, and not even as I shall presently interpret it.

[2] Another example of the collocation *šọreš/pūrā* may be Isa. xiv. 30b. As a parallel sequent to שרשך, ופארת(י)ך would certainly make better sense than M.T.'s ושאריתך. It is, however, possible that the Hebrew originally had זרעך for שרשך, and the fact that M.T. has שרש both in verse 29 and in verse 30, while LXX has *sperma* in both, may be due to assimilation having proceeded in opposite directions in M.T. and in LXX. In that case, of course, ושאריתך is original. A decision is not easy. In any case, verse 30a is to be shifted to follow on verse 32, with בכורי emended to בְּכָרוֹ 'in his pasture'; and the first two words of 30b, which will then follow directly on 29b, must be emended in one of two ways: either to וְהֵמִית עַקְרָב (cf. Deut. viii. 15) 'and a scorpion shall kill', if שרשך is retained (and ופארת(י)ך restored); or to וְהֵמִית בְּרֹאשׁוֹ 'and it (the basilisk of verse 29b) shall kill with its venom', if זרעך is adopted (and ושאריתך retained).—בראשו זרעך could have become corrupted—with the help of contamination by verse 29b—to M.T.'s ברעב שרשך.

[3] Cf. the composite rendering ויחל in Pseudo-Jonathan to Num. xxv. 1.

Ehrlich, namely in Lev. xxiii. 40, Ezek. xix. 12, 14.[1] At the time, it was only natural for him to consider it necessary to emend the forms he found there into some forms, or by-forms, of פארה; but now that we know that the passages in which *prī* means 'boughs' include 2 Kings xix. 30 = Isa. xxxvii. 31, Amos ii. 9, where the correctness of the reading is borne out by the famous parallel in the Eshmunʿazor inscription, lines 11 f. (*'l ykn lm šrš lmṭ wpr lmʿl*), Ehrlich's emendations of the words in question are disproved even as his interpretations of them are confirmed.

In connexion with this discovery that *prī*, instead of being occasionally miswritten for, is rather frequently synonymous with, *pūrā/pōrōṯ* 'branches', it is interesting to recall that I pointed out nearly a decade ago that in two passages *prī* is synonymous with and juxtaposed with *tip'ereṯ*, which means 'glory', but is derived from the same root as *pūrā/pōrōṯ*.[2] Probably the Roman Age *pērōṯ*, Aramaic *pērīn*, which shares with *prī* the sense of 'fruit', is also from the root *p'r*. (The Syriac spelling *p'r'*, however, does not prove it.)

It may now fairly be claimed that one of the assertions made in our opening paragraph, namely that in the passages named therein and in some others the rendering 'fruit' for *prī* is altogether wrong, has been proved. The other, that the rendering 'root' (or 'rootstock' or 'rhizome') for *šọreš* is in those and several other passages at least inaccurate, is also true. The *šọreš*, of course, includes the very lowest part of the tree, which divides and subdivides until it ends in threadlike processes which lie well beneath the surface of the ground and extract the tree's nourishment from the soil; but it is not limited to that. It is all that plus the trunk of the tree up to the level at which it branches out into a crown. 'I wiped out their crown above and their *šorāšīm* below' (Amos ii. 9) means 'I wiped out *all* trace of them', and 'so that it leaves of them neither *šọreš*

[1] See A. B. Ehrlich, *Randglossen zur hebr. Bibel*, on these passages.

[2] *Mordecai Kaplan Jubilee Volume*, 1953, English Section, pp. 245 f.—Since *Festschriften* which are not simply special numbers of periodical publications are liable to be inaccessible to many interested persons, I shall repeat the substance of the observation here. In Isa. iv. 2 read *'dny* for *h'rṣ*, and render the verse thus: 'On that day the splendour (Syriac *ṣemḥā*, cf. LXX) of YHWH shall be for beauty and radiance, and the *majesty* of my Lord for proud glory for the escaped of Israel.' And render Isa. x. 12 thus: 'he will requite the *majestic* pride and exalted arrogance of the king of Assyria' (*'pqd* here is only another pronunciation—or maybe only another spelling—of *ypqd*). For the thought of iv. 2 strictly parallels that of xxviii. 5, just as that of iii. 18–iv. 1 parallels that of xxviii. 1–4. [*P'r* and *pry* are, of course, not the only roots which combine the notion of flashing and/or gleaming with that of budding or sprouting; cf. the aforementioned *ṣmḥ*, and see the lexica on *ṣyṣ*, *nṣṣ*, *nbṭ*, *zhr*.]

nor branches' (Mal. iii. 19) means 'so that it leaves *nothing* of them'. Again, new branches are said to sprout from the *šoreš* of cut trees, and, of course, such shoots issue from the part of the stump which is *above* the ground. In Isa. x. 33–xi. 1, Job xiv. 7–9, the cutting is explicit; in 2 Kings xix. 30 = Isa. xxxvii. 31 the reduction of the tree to a mere stump is implied by the expression 'escaped remnant', and in Isa. xiv. 29 f. by 'the staff . . . has been broken'. The refinements of terminology in 2 Kings xix. 30 = Isa. xxxvii. 31 should not be missed. An escaped remnant is like what is left when a tree is cut: it comprises only some of the original tree's *šoreš* and none of its branches. Therefore, to become a great tree again, it must *add to* (*ysp*) its *šoreš* and *produce* (*'śy*) a whole new crown. The nearest English equivalent I can think of for *šoreš* in all the passages that we have discussed is 'stock'.[1] Others may do better.

This, and not 'root', is also the sense of *šoreš* in Deut. xxix. 17b. For just as *prī* means 'branches', so the verb *pārā* means 'to branch out or off'. This passage speaks of 'a stock branching out into (i.e. sprouting) poison weed and wormwood', and Isa. xi. 1b means 'and a shoot shall branch off (sprout) from his stock'. The Masoretic *yprh* in the latter passage is absolutely correct. It does not follow that the *ypr*ḥ of Job xiv. 9 is not; this word means 'it buds', which is quite in order because the new branches of verse 9b have to begin as buds.[2]

'To branch out' is also the sense of the verb *pārā* in the poetic feminine participle *pōriyyā* which serves as a sort of standing epithet of *gepen* 'grapevine', Isa. xxxii. 12, Ezek. xix. 10, Ps. cxxviii. 3. The proof is the Ezekiel passage. For (1) if פֹּרִיָּה meant 'fruitful', וַעֲנֵפָה 'and many-branched' would be an anti-climax;[3] and (2) the whole point of the following verses is that the many branches of the vine in question include a majestic one fit to serve as a ruler's sceptre, which, however, will

[1] Thus *prī* and *šoreš* have in Biblical Hebrew among other meanings those of the pair *nōp* and *'iqqār* in Roman Age Hebrew as defined in E. Ben Iehuda, *Thes. Totius Hebraitatis*; which see for probably exhaustive lists of examples. *Nōp*, by the way, is the very word that the Targum employs in all the four passages in which it recognizes our sense of *prī* (see above).

[2] Similarly, I surmise that Isa. li. 4 originally had להפרח for להפתח. The sense of Isa. li. 13b–14, as I understand it, is this: 'You have always and continually dreaded the fury of the feller (something like הַמְקַצֵּץ ?) who (read אשר) aimed to cut down. Yet what has come of the fury of the feller (?) ? The tree (read הָעֵץ) has quickly burgeoned (read לְהַפְרִחַ): it has not died by cutting down, nor has its sap (Jer. xi. 19; cf. Zeph. i. 17) been lacking.' See Jer. xi. 19 and Job xiv. 9.

[3] This was probably one of the reasons why the Targum, as has already been noted, connected *pryh* in this passage with *prī* 'crown'.

vanish together with the rest of the vine's crown (this being the sense of *prī* in verses 12 and 14, as was pointed out above).[1]

[1] As for Isa. xvii. 6, the fact that in the phrase מסעף פארה, Isa. x. 33, about fifty manuscripts spell the second word פורה shows that the original reading in the first-named passage was בִּסְעִפֵּי הַפּוּרָה 'on the branches of the crown'; which is just what the context requires.

ABRAHAM OF UR

By CYRUS H. GORDON, *Brookline, Mass.*

PROFESSOR G. R. DRIVER has distinguished himself in virtually every main branch of Semitics—an especially remarkable achievement in our age of specialization. This article, offered as a tribute to him, deals with sources in Hebrew, Aramaic, Ugaritic, and Accadian—four of the fields in which Professor Driver has written *magna opera* that have placed us in his debt.

The two Biblical periods that are being conspicuously illuminated by epigraphical discoveries are the Patriarchal Age and the Dawn of Christianity. The importance of the Qumran scrolls is well recognized. What is not so well known is that the Genesis narratives of the Fathers are being revolutionized by cuneiform documents of the Amarna Age (plus or minus about a century)[1] from a number of sites, notably Ugarit and Nuzu.[2] Whenever a large body of new data is brought to bear on an old subject, revaluation is inevitable. This is happening with the Patriarchal Narratives.

In interpreting a text, the comparative method is full of pitfalls for those who read documents into each other. The proper procedure is rather to allow collateral evidence to open our eyes to what the text with which we are specifically concerned actually says. The question arises as to why we need collateral evidence to show what the text plainly states. The answer is simply that we fail to understand even clearly worded statements if we lack the background required for placing them in historic or cultural context. This is particularly so in the case of Biblical or classical texts that we have learned within the framework of a strong tradition that has the effect of telling us what to see and what not to see.

[1] For a critical discussion of some of the literature, see G. E. Wright, 'Modern Issues in Biblical Studies: History and the Patriarchs', reprinted from *The Expository Times*, July 1960, pp. 3–7. The fact that the cuneiform parallels to the Patriarchal Narratives cluster around the fifteenth–thirteenth centuries suggests a date contemporary with the Mycenaean Age; cf. C. H. Gordon, *New Horizons in Old Testament Literature* (Ventnor Publishers, Ventnor, N.J., 1960), pp. 11–19.

[2] See C. H. Gordon, 'Biblical Customs and the Nuzu Tablets', *Biblical Archaeologist*, iii, 1940, pp. 1–12; 'The Patriarchal Age', *Journ. of Bible and Religion*, xxi, 1953, pp. 238–43; 'The Patriarchal Narratives', *J.N.E.S.* xiii, 1954, pp. 56–59; *The World of the Old Testament* (Doubleday, Garden City, N.Y., 1958), pp. 113–33.

The Patriarchal Narratives embody a number of themes including the factor of royal epic.[1] Abraham[2] and Sarah[3] are described as the progenitors of kings. In the Genesis stories, the two ancestors of the royal line deal not with commoners but with royalty such as Pharaoh, Melchisedek the King of Salem, and King Abimelech of Gerar.[4] Abraham, though no mighty emperor, was at least a kinglet (in approximately the Mycenaean sense) with troops of his own, that were combined with the troops of other kinglets, to wage war against a hostile coalition of kings.[5]

Another theme embedded in the Narratives is the commercial interests of the Patriarchs. The first inkling we get of this is the reference to Abraham's payment of 400 shekels of silver as עבר לסחר (Gen. xxiii. 16) 'current for the merchant'. Abraham is repeatedly described as wealthy not only in herds and slaves, but also in gold and silver, which smack of commercial enterprise and prosperity. He had every opportunity to lend precious metal on interest in Canaan in accordance with the methods of *tamkârûtu* 'business enterprise'. Since he travelled between Egypt and the Hittite-dominated province of Paddan-Aram, he could have profited by importing silver into Egypt and gold into the Hittite realm.[6]

Genesis confirms (xxxiv. 10, 21) and reconfirms (xlii. 34) the commercial interests of the Patriarchs suggested by xxiii. 16. When the Prince of Shechem invites Jacob and the latter's sons to join the Shechem community, he offers as inducements the rights of permanent domicile, of trading, and of acquiring real estate: ואתנו תשבו והארץ תהיה לפניכם שבו וסחרוה והאחזו בה (Gen. xxxiv. 10) 'And with us you may dwell; and the land will be before you; dwell, trade, and acquire real estate therein.' Later, Joseph offers his brothers trading rights in Egypt: ואת־הארץ תסחרו (Gen. xlii. 34) 'and you may trade throughout the land'. The thread of business enterprise is thus unmistakably woven into the fabric of the Patriarchal Narratives. This now obvious

[1] This is now clear in the light of the royal Ugaritic epics of Krît and of Aqhat.

[2] ומלכים ממך יצאו (Gen. xvii. 6) 'and kings shall go forth from you' (said to Abraham).

[3] מלכי עמים ממנה יהיו (Gen. xvii. 16) 'there shall be kings of nations from her' (said of Sarah).

[4] Gen. xii. 15–20, xiv. 18, xx. 2–18.

[5] Gen. xiv.

[6] I am at a loss to understand H. W. F. Saggs, 'Ur of the Chaldees: A Problem of Identification', *Iraq*, xxii, 1960, pp. 200–9, who states (p. 203) that the Patriarchs could not have traded in metals because their property consisted in something 'quite different', to wit, animals, 'silver and gold'.

fact might have remained unobserved were it not for the following tablet of Hattusili III (*c.* 1282–1250 B.C.) found at Ugarit:[1]

^{aban}*kunukku-ma* ^{m}*ta-ba-ar-na*
The seal of the Emperor,

^{m}*ḫa-at-tu-ši-li šarri rabî*
Hattusili the Great King,

š[à]r ^{mât}*ḫa-at-ti a-na* ^{m}*níq-mu-pa*
King of Hittite Land. To Niqme/upaʿ

qí-bi-ma
speak!

ša a-kán-na táq-te-bi a-na pa-ni-ia
Thus have you said in my presence:

ma-a mârū^{meš} ^{âl}*ú-ra awîlū*^{meš} *tamkârū*
'The Ur(a) merchants

elī mât ardi-ka ka-ab-tù dan-níš
are very burdensome to the land of your vassal.'[2]

ù ^{il}*šamšu*^{šu} *šarru rabû ri-kíl-ta*
So the Sun-god, the Great King, has established

a-na mârī^{meš} ^{âl}*ú-ra it-ti mârī*^{meš} ^{âl}*ú-ga-ri-it*
the following regulation for the

a-kán-na ir-ku-us-šu-nu
people of Ur(a) with the people of Ugarit:

ma-a mârū^{meš} ^{âl}*ú-ra i-na e-bu-ri*
Let the men of Ur(a) ply

i-na libbi^{bi} ^{mât}*ú-ga-ri-it tám-kà-ru-ta-šu-nu*
their trade during the harvest

li-i-pu-šu ù i-na ûmîti^{mi-ti}
in the midst of Ugarit, but in the days

ku-uṣ-ṣi iš-tu libbi^{bi}
of winter they shall send (them) out

[1] Published by J. Nougayrol, *P.R.U.* (*Le Palais royal d'Ugarit*) iv (Paris, 1956), pp. 103–5, plate XV. For the Genesis connexions, see C. H. Gordon, 'Abraham and the Merchants of Ura', *J.N.E.S.* xvii, 1958, pp. 28–31.

[2] This complaint of Niqme/upaʿ, King of Ugarit, is mistakenly attributed to me in *Iraq*, xxii, 1960, p. 203, n. 15. So as not to waste time and space, I refrain from listing exhaustively all the statements falsely attributed to me ibid., pp. 200–9.

^{mât}ú-ga-ri-it u-še-ṣu-ni a-na mâti-šu-nu
of Ugarit to their (own) country.

ù mârū^{meš} ^{âl}ú-ra i-na ku-uṣ-ṣi
Yea, the people of Ur(a) in the winter

i-na libbi^{bi} ^{mât}ú-ga-ri-it
shall not dwell in the midst of

la-a uš-ša-bu ù bîtâti^{ḫá}
Ugarit nor shall they

eqlâti^{meš} i-na kaspi^{meš}-šu-nu la-a i-ṣa-ba-[t]u_4
get real estate with their silver.

ù šum-ma awîlu tamkâru awîl ^{âl}ú-ra
And if (any) merchant of Ur(a)

kaspa^{meš} ša ma-an-da-at-ti-šu
has caused the loss of the silver

i-na libbi^{bi} ^{mât}ú-ga-ri-it ú-ḫal-liq
of his tribute in the midst of Ugarit,

ù šàr ^{mât}ú-ga-ri-it a-na a-ša-bi
the King of Ugarit shall not let

i-na libbi^{bi} mâti-šu la-a ú-maš-šar-šú
him dwell in the midst of his land.

ù šum-ma kaspu^{meš} ša mârī^{meš} ^{âl}ú-ra
And if anyone cannot repay

it-ti mârī^{meš} ^{âl}ú-ga-ri-it
the silver of the people of Ur(a)

ù a-na šu-lu-mi-šu la-a i-li-ú
lent to the people of Ugarit,

ù šàr ^{mât}ú-ga-ri-it awîlam^{lim} ša-a-šu
the King of Ugarit shall deliver that man (the debtor)

qa-du aššati-šu qa-du mâ[r]ī^{meš}-šu
together with his wife and children

i-na qâti^{ti} mârī^{meš} ^{âl}ú-ra
into the hand(s) of the

awîlī^{meš} tamkârī i-na-an-di-nu-šu-nu-ti
Ur(a) merchants.

ù mârū^{meš} ^{âl}*ú-ra awîlū*^{meš} *tamkârū*
But the merchants of Ur(a)

a-na bîtâti^{há} *a-na eqlâti*^{meš} *ša šàr* ^{mât}*ú-ga-ri-it*
shall not draw near the real estate of the King of

la-a i-qa-ru-bu-nim anumma^{ma} ^{il}*šamšu*^{šu} *šarru rabû*
Ugarit. Lo, thus has the Sun-god, the Great King,

ri-kíl-ta i-na be-ri mârī^{meš} ^{âl}*ú-ra*
established a regulation between

awîlī^{meš} *tamkârī ù i-na be-ri mârī*^{meš} ^{mât}*ú-ga-ri-it*
the merchants of Ur(a) and the people

a-kán-na ir-ku-us-šu-nu-ti
of Ugarit.

There is much that we could say about this important document. For present purposes suffice it to note that the Hittite monarch sponsored merchants from Ur(a) in Canaan, and that while he protected (1) their transaction of business, he prohibited (2) their settling permanently in their theatre of operations and (3) their purchasing of real estate there. These three items are precisely those covered in Gen. xxxiv. 10, 21, where the Prince of Shechem offers Jacob's family the right to transact business, to settle permanently, and to acquire real estate.

Abraham had at his disposal a company of 318[1] troops. The *tamkârū* often had troops assigned or attached to them. The statement that Abraham's troops show that he was definitely not a merchant but a sheikh[2] is wrong. Alphabetic texts from Ugarit mention *bdl ar dt inn mhr lhm!* 'merchants of Ar who have no troops'[3] in contradistinction to merchants who have troops. Moreover, merchants were assigned to military personnel such as those of the *mryn* and *mḏrǵl* classes: *bdl mrynm* (400 : III : 6) and *bdl mḏrǵlm* (400 : VI : 17).[4] Merchants were thus assigned to troops, or troops to merchants, probably because the commanders of the outposts had to look after their sovereign's trading interests as well

[1] Not '314' (*Iraq*, xxii, 1960, p. 203); see Gen. xiv. 14 for the number '318', and cf. *The World of the Old Testament*, p. 87, n. 1, for the bevy of 318 maidens on the Giluḫepa scarab of Amenophis III.

[2] *Iraq*, xxii, 1960, pp. 203 f.

[3] Published by Ch. Virolleaud, *P.R.U.* ii, text 35 : 4–5. For *bdl* = *tamkâru*, see C. H. Gordon, *Ugaritic Manual* (1955), p. 245, no. 312.

[4] *Ugaritic Manual*, pp. 178 f.

as defence. Cf. the colony at Elephantine, which was at once military and mercantile.

Against the above background it appears that Abraham, the merchant prince, may well have come from the Ur whence other merchants came into Canaan under Hittite sponsorship.[1] In other words, Abraham (*qua* immigrant from Ur) need not be a unique phenomenon in cultural history, but rather part of a movement for which we have authentic documentation.[2] This gives point to the words wherewith the Hittites of Hebron address Abraham: נשיא אלהים אתה בתוכנו (Gen. xxiii. 6) 'You are a prince of God in our midst'. The Septuagint translates נשיא as βασιλεύς 'king' (with more or less Homeric rather than Ptolemaic kingship in mind). 'In our midst' suggests that Abraham may have enjoyed the role of נשיא specifically in the Hittite enclave around Hebron because the enclave owed allegiance to the Hittite sovereign.[3] Furthermore, it is possible that when the Hittites speak of 'God' in Gen. xxiii. 6 they have in mind the reigning Hittite monarch, who had the divine title of ^{il}*šamšu*^{šu} 'sun-god' as we have noted above.

The concept of merchant princes was quite familiar in Old Testament Canaan; e.g. Isa. xxiii. 8 speaks of Tyre אשר סחריה שרים כנעניה נכבדי־ארץ 'whose princes are merchants, whose traders are the honoured of the land'. In fact the very word 'Canaan(ite)' is a well-known synonym of 'merchant'.[4]

The affinities of the Patriarchal Narratives are with the north, not with Sumer in the south. The tablets that illuminate the Narratives at every turn come from northern sites such as Nuzu, Ugarit, and Hattusa. In the texts of Sumer and Accad, Sumerian Ur is never called 'Ur of the Chaldees'. The latter is rather some northern Ur (of which there are quite a few—probably named after the mother city of Ur in Sumer).

[1] Note also *P.R.U.* iv, pp. 190 and 203, for the personal names of some of the Ur(a) merchants named in tablets found at Ugarit.

[2] Ur(a) may have been founded by the Third Dynasty of Ur around 2000 B.C. and, after the collapse of the homeland, persisted as a trading colony down into late Hittite times. Ur(a) may thus have been a centre of mercantile activity throughout the Middle and Late Bronze Age.

[3] Canaan was the scene of interpenetrating commercial empires. Thus the Egyptians had personnel in Ugarit (*Ugaritic Manual*, p. 291, no. 1151) within the Hittite sphere of influence, while the Hittite enclave at Hebron lay close to, if not actually within, the Egyptian sphere of influence.

[4] It is often asked why the Chosen People got their Promised Land in a location so conducive to instability and war. The advantage that Palestine used to have for international trade is as good an answer as any to this question. Palestine is the Land Bridge between the two largest continents with access also by water to the west via the Mediterranean and to the east via the Red Sea.

In the Nuzu tablets, there are 'Great Ur'[1] and 'Small Ur'.[2] One or more towns called Ur appear in the Alalaḫ tablets.[3] Orrhai (the Syriac form of modern Urfa) probably reflects the same name, and prior to the days of Assyriology was generally (and perhaps rightly) held to be Abraham's Ur of the Chaldees. There is still another Ur(a) said to be about 200 miles north of Harran.[4]

That the Chaldeans did not reach Babylonia until the end of the second millennium is another reason for not locating 'Ur of the Chaldees' in Sumer. Of all the Urs that 'Ur of the Chaldees' might be, it is not likely to be one that involves us in an anachronism.[5] Moreover, the designation of the Harran–Urfa area as Aramean and Chaldean[6] is appropriate not only in the Patriarchal Narratives[7] but throughout Old Testament times down through the Achaemenian Age (e.g. in Xenophon) and long thereafter.[8]

The material in the Patriarchal Narratives is ancient. We can control its authenticity in texts of the second millennium at several levels: sociological,[9] literary,[10] onomastic,[11] &c. We can now state that the

1 $^{\bar{a}l}$*ú-ri GAL* (E. R. Lacheman, *Harvard Semitic Series*, xiv (Cambridge, Mass., 1950), text 75:3), $^{\bar{a}l}$*ur-ra GAL* (ibid. xv (1955), text 72:13).

2 $^{\bar{a}l}$*ú-ri TUR* (ibid. xiv, text 195:2).

3 D. J. Wiseman, *The Alalakh Tablets* (London, 1953), p. 157. The forms are *ú-ra*, *ú-ri-e*, and *ú-ur-ri*.

4 *Iraq*, xxii, 1960, p. 202, n. 13.

5 The anachronism is pointed out ibid., p. 205. For the demise of another widely held 'anachronism' in the Patriarchal Narratives, see W. G. Lambert, 'The Domesticated Camel in the Second Millennium—Evidence from Alalakh and Ugarit', *B.A.S.O.R.*, no. 160, 1960, pp. 42 f.

6 The Biblical tradition is clear about the Aramaic origin of the Fathers. Their land is called פדן ארם (e.g. Gen. xxv. 20) or ארם נהרים (e.g. Gen. xxiv. 10); and both Bethuel and Laban are described as הארמי (Gen. xxv. 20) 'the Aramean'. Gen. xxxi. 47 represents Laban as speaking Aramaic, and accordingly referring to גַּלְעֵד in Aramaic as יגר שהדותא 'a heap of testimony'. Every Israelite was to declare before Yahweh: ארמי אבד אבי (Deut. xxvi. 5) 'my Father (was) a wandering Aramean'. There is no reason for questioning the appropriateness of the 'Chaldeans' in אור כשדים located in the old stamping grounds of the Arameans. Xenophon mentions the northern Chaldeans in connexion with the Kurds and Armenians (cf. *J.N.E.S.* xvii, 1958, p. 30). In Isa. xxiii. 13 the Land of the Chaldeans is mentioned between Mediterranean areas and Assyria, suggesting a northern location somewhere in between (the further implications falsely ascribed to me constitute the strawman knocked down in *Iraq*, xxii, 1960, pp. 205–8). The name כשד (directly following ארם), related to כשדים, is furthermore built into the Patriarchal genealogies (Gen. xxii. 22). The confusion between eponymous ancestors and personal names in the old genealogies is not in my mind (*Iraq*, xxii, 1960, pp. 208 f.), but constitutes a feature of the literature; cf. the Twelve Sons of Israel = the Twelve Tribes of Israel.

7 Admitted in *Iraq*, xxii, 1960, p. 208.

8 Orrhai (= Edessa, now Urfa) long remained a bulwark of Aramaism, becoming as it did the centre of Syrian Christianity.

9 Especially through the Nuzu tablets.

10 The Ugaritic epics are the main source.

11 Ugaritic administrative texts tell of two Abrams (*abrm*) and one Israel (*yšril*); they will be published by Ch. Virolleaud.

milieu of the Narratives is genuine, and not contrived by first-millennium authors. This does not mean that the Narratives were not used, and retouched, tendentiously by later generations. The Patriarchal Narratives, *qua* the Hebrew Epic of Kings, were doubtless used to celebrate and legitimize the royal line. Nor is it out of the question that specifically Solomon—the most famous of Israel's merchant kings—gloried in tracing his lineage back to Abraham, the merchant prince who, in theory at least, founded the dynasty.

ON THE SO-CALLED *INFINITIVUS ABSOLUTUS* IN HEBREW

By E. HAMMERSHAIMB, *Aarhus*

WITHIN the Semitic group of languages the infinitives exhibit a vast number of syntactical peculiarities, which, however, early caught the attention of various medieval grammarians.[1] Some of these peculiarities, it will be remembered, belong to the common property of the entire Semitic group of languages, whereas others are characteristic of one language only, making due allowances for our often very limited knowledge of those languages and dialects which are now extinct. The most important common feature is that of the infinitives taking up a position intermediate between verbs and nouns—belonging, according to their formal structure, to nouns, even though functionally they often, yet not always, betray their verbal character. It remains to add, however, that the formal structure is capable of great variation within the respective languages, and it also differs widely according to whether the infinitives functionally approach verbs or nouns. In Arabic the structure of the infinitives in the simple stem of the verb shows the most pronounced variation. Some fifty different forms[2] here indicate that in the cognate languages, besides the ordinary infinitives, one can expect to find nominal types which, sporadically, may adopt infinitival function. As far as the function of the infinitives is concerned, there are also marked divergences within the respective languages. It naturally follows that rules can be laid down with some degree of clarity only in such languages as have retained their case-endings, whereas obscurity prevails in languages with no case-endings in the script, or with no reliable tradition as to the pronunciation of the language in former times.

Hebrew here occupies an exceptional position. It is true that the case-endings have been dropped except for some few isolated instances, which are insignificant here, but, on the other hand, the accusative sign

[1] Sibawaihi, Zamaḫshari, Qimḥi, and others.

[2] W. Wright, *A Grammar of the Arabic Language*[3], i (1933), § 196, mentions forty-four forms. Zamaḫshari enumerates 'only' thirty-two instances; see *Mufaṣṣal*, p. 97 (J. P. Broch's ed., 1879).

־אֶת greatly helps towards ascertaining the verbal function of the infinitives in many cases, whereas in others the question must be left undecided.

The fact that the current treatments of the Hebrew infinitives operate with two sorts of infinitives, of which one is termed *infinitivus constructus* (כְּתֹב < *kŭtŭb*), and the other *infinitivus absolutus* (כָּתֹב < *kătāb*), is due not only to a distinction in the Masoretic vocalization of the two types of infinitives, but also to a realization of their different functions. In addition, the correctness of the Masoretic distinction in the vocalization of the two infinitives remains indirectly but firmly supported since the occurrence of roughly the same types in the cognate languages has been substantiated by comparative Semitic philology. Only a partisan judgement on Hebrew alone combined with profound scepticism as to the Masoretic vocalization can lead to a repudiation of the functional difference between the two infinitives.[1] Admittedly the two terms, inf. constr. and inf. abs., are not altogether appropriate, because they involuntarily put one in mind of the difference between stat. constr. and stat. abs.[2]

In what follows I shall not undertake an exhaustive treatment of the use of the two infinitives in general, but confine myself to inquiring into the inf. abs. and some of its principal fields of application.

If the Semitic infinitives are looked upon as a means of denoting in the abstract the verbal action or the state or quality inherent in the verb without any regard to circumstances of agent, number, and gender,[3] it is apparent that they are employed mainly in sentences expressing command, but also, it is to be noticed, in hurried or otherwise excited speech. Arabic employs the indeclinable forms with imperative force, such as نزالِ 'alight!', حضارِ 'be present!', حذارِ 'beware!', &c.[4] This is analogous to the employment of the inf. abs. in Hebrew in such examples

[1] This is the view adopted by A. Sperber, though he does not define his position explicitly. He wants to discard the term inf. constr. and maintains that the inf. abs. also can be joined with a suffix, e.g. בְּבָרְחֲךָ Gen. xxxv. 1, where he reads the *qameṣ*-sign under the first radical as *ā*, and not as *å*; see his *Biblical Exegesis* (1945), §§ 69–70. Cf. *The Pre-Masoretic Bible I. The Codex Reuchlinianus* (Copenhagen, 1956), p. xvi, § 14, and p. xxvi, § 62a.

[2] Some scholars, however, have suggested the term 'rigid infinitive' for inf. abs. and simply 'infinitive' for inf. constr. So H. Bauer and P. Leander, *Hist. Gramm. der hebr. Sprache* (Halle, 1922), p. 317, following Stade.

[3] So already to some extent G. H. A. Ewald, *Krit. Gramm. d. hebr. Sprache* (Leipzig, 1827), § 293.

[4] The same examples often recur in the more exhaustive grammars; see Wright, op. cit. i, p. 62B. Cf. already *Mufaṣṣal*, p. 61, § 187.

as שָׁמוֹר Deut. v. 12, זָכוֹר Exod. xx. 8. According to Hebrew speech instinct these forms have been felt as containing a subject in the plural wherever such was made necessary by the context, e.g. זָכוֹר occurred in addressing a plurality, Exod. xiii. 3, Joshua i. 13. The early translations of the Old Testament (the Arabic, Syriac, Aramaic, LXX) in such cases render the meaning correctly by the imperative. Here the inf. abs. possesses a function which is lacking in the inf. constr. As the inf. constr. is indistinguishable from the imperative in the sing. masc. of most verbs in the simple stem, the inf. constr. could not have been employed if the point was to show that the command was addressed to a plurality.

Both in the cases where the inf. abs. has imperative force and where it is employed in excited and abrupt speech to describe a number of actions (e.g. Hos. iv. 2), it is self-evident that it must have verbal regimen (זכור את־היום Exod. xiii. 3).

By far the most frequent use of the inf. abs. in Hebrew is its substantival employment as the object of a verb derived from the same stem or of a verb of kindred meaning. Here, again, it is noticeable that the inf. abs. is alone in possessing this function. This is the more remarkable since the internal object can be another noun frequently determined by an attributive adjective.[1] No matter whether the infinitive stood before or after the verb, this construction was originally intended to intensify the idea of the verb, and we need not enter further into the modifications and shades of meaning that can be rendered by the infinitive[2] preceding the verb. Nor shall we dwell on the fact that the infinitive, when placed after the verb, can have partly the same meaning as when preceding it, and can partly express the continuing or continued action.

Identical features are exhibited by all branches within the Semitic family of languages, but they differ, however, in the mutual position of infinitive and verb. In Accadian the strengthened infinitive precedes the finite verb.[3] Infinitives following the verb are instanced notably in Mari texts in connexion with the verb *ratāb/pum* 'continue doing something'. This syntactical peculiarity must probably be ascribed to Canaanite influence.[4] In the Tell-el-Amarna letters the strengthened

[1] In this way the Semitic languages circumvent their paucity of adverbs compared with the Indo-European languages, where, however, constructions with internal object, also called paronomasia or figura etymologica, are not infrequently met with.

[2] Cf. P. Joüon, *Grammaire de l'hébreu biblique*[2] (Rome, 1947), pp. 349 ff.

[3] W. von Soden, *Grundr. d. akkad. Gramm.* (Rome, 1952), § 150, uses the term 'the paronomastic infinitive construction'.

[4] See von Soden, op. cit., § 130d.

infinitive is placed before the finite verb.[1] In Ugaritic the prepositive use is the most common,[2] but a single instance of postpositive infinitive, however, is substantiated.[3] From the North-western Semitic branch it remains to mention the Old Aramaic inscriptions from Sfire (probably dating back to the middle of the eighth century B.C.); examples are הסכר תהסכרם 'thou shalt surely hand them over' (inf. abs. Haf'el + impf. Haf'el) III. 2 and רקה תרקה III. 18 (cf. with suffix III. 6, where the meaning is doubtful).[4] A similar succession is seen in Phoenician ואם פתח תפתח (Tabnit, lines 6 f.).[5] To this corresponds in Moabite וישראל אבד אבד (inscription of Meša, line 7), where the first אבד is supposed to be the inf. abs. The later Aramaic dialects being strongly influenced by Old Testament Hebrew, it is difficult to establish whether the prevailing prepositive inf. abs. reflects genuine Aramaic usage.

It is probably accidental that there are no instances of the infinitive used as internal object in Biblical Aramaic and in Egyptian Aramaic. In the Targums, on the other hand, it is a frequent occurrence and follows the Hebrew pattern in the Old Testament.[6] It is likewise very common in the Babylonian Talmud,[7] whereas it appears only sporadically in the dialect of Galilee.[8] Syriac and Mandaic generally put the infinitive before the verb.[9] As far as quotations from the Bible are concerned, Ethiopic seems to correspond to the usage of Old Testament Hebrew in generally placing the infinitive before the verb, though instances of postpositive infinitive are also known.[10] In classical Arabic the place of

[1] Cf. the examples adduced by F. M. Th. Böhl in *Die Sprache der Amarnabriefe mit besonderer Berücksichtigung der Kanaanismen* (Leipzig, 1909), p. 63.

[2] See the examples enumerated by the present writer in *Das Verbum im Dialekt von Ras Schamra* (Copenhagen, 1941), pp. 127–33.

[3] *yspi spu* R I II. 10.

[4] See A. Dupont-Sommer, *Les Inscriptions araméennes de Sfiré* (Paris, 1958), pp. 127 f.

[5] See also additional examples in J. Friedrich, *Phönizisch-punische Gramm.* (Rome, 1951), §§ 137 and 267; cf. Z. S. Harris, *A Grammar of the Phoenician Language* (New Haven, 1936), p. 41.

[6] W. B. Stevenson, *Grammar of Palestinian Jewish Aramaic* (Oxford, 1924), § 20.

[7] According to M. L. Margolis, *Lehrb. d. aram. Sprache d. babyl. Talmuds* (Munich, 1910), § 61g, it is most commonly placed before the verb, rarely after.

[8] See G. Dalman, *Gramm. d. jüd.-pal. Aramäisch* (Leipzig, 1905), p. 280. According to M. H. Segal, *A Grammar of Mishnaic Hebrew* (Oxford, 1927), p. 165, it is never employed in the Mishna except in liturgical passages with allusion to the Old Testament.

[9] See Th. Nöldeke, *Kurzgef. syr. Gramm.*[2] (Leipzig, 1898), §§ 295–6, and his *Mand. Gramm.* (Halle, 1875), § 271.

[10] See A. Dillmann, *Gramm. d. äthiop. Sprache*[2] (Leipzig, 1899), §§ 174 and 181. It is worthy of notice that the Ethiopic translation has an infinitival construction after the verb in its rendering of לַעֲבֹד אֶת־עֲבֹדַת יהוה Joshua xxii. 27. Ethiopic, it may further be remarked, has other substantives than the infinitives proper as internal object. In such cases the object is most frequently placed after the verb; see Dillmann, op. cit., § 175.

the infinitive as the object of a verb is naturally after it,[1] and this succession is retained in translations of the Old Testament, even in cases where in Hebrew the infinitive precedes the verb (e.g. Gen. xv. 3, xxviii. 22, Deut. vi. 17, 2 Sam. xix. 43, according to the London Polyglot). The few exceptions I have adduced must very probably be ascribed to the influence of the Hebrew pattern (e.g. Gen. xxxvii. 8). The Arabic translation very frequently omits the infinitive or renders the meaning in another way.[2]

The above statements necessarily imply that the infinitive, whether it precedes or follows the verb, is its object. The Arabic construction thus clearly establishes that the infinitive after the verb is its object, but the matter is not quite so simple when the infinitive precedes it. Ugaritic shows, at all events, two instances where the prepositive infinitive can be regarded as in the nominative, viz. *ġmu ġmit* 'thou art surely thirsty' II AB IV. 34, and *bu tbu* 'she surely enters'. The ending *-u* in these examples might be regarded as a fossilized nominative ending.[3] We are faced with the same problem in Accadian, in so far as the prepositive infinitive here often appears with the ending *-um* (*ḫadûm-ma ḫadi* 'he is very happy', *alākum-ma ula nittalak* 'we have not at all departed'), and, as far as I can see, von Soden has convincingly shown that it is an adverbial ending, which has nothing to do with the nominative ending.[4] Therefore it is preferable to explain the Ugaritic ending *-u* in a similar way, and also the Hebrew inf. abs. must in that case most naturally be explained as the object of the verb, when it stands before it, the departure from the normal word order of the verbal clause being due to the express emphasis which is given to the object in this prominent position.

Widely different from this field of application is the employment of the inf. abs. instead of a finite verb. Even in the more exhaustive works

[1] See Wright, op. cit. ii, pp. 53–56; cf. H. L. Fleischer, *Kleinere Schriften 1* (Leipzig, 1886), pp. 92 and 184, and the instances adduced by H. Reckendorf in *Die syntakt. Verhältnisse d. Arabischen* (Leiden, 1898), § 56, and his *Arabische Syntax* (Heidelberg, 1921), § 48.

[2] It is interesting to notice that the LXX prefers a participle or an adverb or some other construction; see H. Kaupel, *Z.A.W.*, N.F., xx, 1945–8, pp. 191 f.

[3] See E. Hammershaimb, op. cit., pp. 128 f. The nominative might then be due to the fact that the prepositive infinitive originally was an independent nominal clause, the contents of which were expressed in action in the following verbal clause, or an independent nominal clause with exclamatory force; see G. R. Driver, *Canaanite Myths and Legends* (Edinburgh, 1956), p. 132, n. 3.

[4] See von Soden, op. cit., §§ 150 and 66b; cf. J. Lewy, 'Paronomastic Infinitives in Classic Akkadian', *Orientalia*, xv, 1946, pp. 410–15. An adverbial ending *-u*, by the way, also appears in many Arabic words, see Wright, op. cit. i, § 363.

on Hebrew grammar little attention has been paid to the problem whether there exists a connexion between this use and the intensifying use, or what shades of meaning this employment might convey as compared with the finite forms.

Before we turn our attention to this problem, it is important to bear in mind that this construction occurs only rarely in the Old Testament. The number of instances totals about 45–58, according to whether textual errors are taken into consideration or not.[1] Compared with the whole of the Old Testament the instances are so strikingly few that it is hardly advisable to attach too much weight to their proportion within the various parts of the Old Testament.[2]

A careful examination of these instances will reveal how difficult, almost impossible, it is to detect a shade of meaning common to all of them. In some of the passages a contrast between the finite verb and the infinitive might be implied (e.g. Exod. viii. 11, Hag. i. 6), or a change of subject might be indicated (e.g. Gen. xli. 43) as a finite verb as well as an infinitive admits of an implicit subject, or, on the other hand, special emphasis might be given to the infinitive (e.g. Isa. v. 5). If the explanation is true that the infinitive has a special emphasis, there is a strong presumption that the infinitive was originally connected with a finite verb as its internal object, and that gradually the practice was adopted of using the infinitive alone;[3] but in many other passages it is impossible

[1] A. Rubinstein, in his recent investigation of the problem, lists forty-five certain instances, see his article 'A Finite Verb Continued by an Infinitive Absolute in Biblical Hebrew', *Vet. Test.* ii, 1952, pp. 362–7. B. L. Goddard, *The Origin of the Hebrew Infinitive Absolute in the Light of Infinitive Uses in Related Languages and its Use in the O.T.* (Diss. Harvard University, 1950), has not been available to me.

Among the earlier treatments of the problem E. Sellin's work *Die verbal-nominale Doppelnatur d. hebr. Participien u. Infinitive* (Leipzig, 1889) especially deserves notice. T. W. Davies's paper 'The Infinitive, especially the Infinitive Absolute in Hebrew and its Cognates. A Study in Comparative Philology and Translation' (*J. of the Manchester Egypt. and Orient. Soc.*, 1918–19, pp. 55–69) aims further, but is not nearly so incisive in its details as Sellin's work.

[2] According to Rubinstein, loc. cit., p. 363, the incidence is high in Zechariah, Esther, and Nehemiah, and there is a comparatively large number of instances in Jeremiah, but few in the Pentateuch and the Former Prophets. Further, it is worth noticing that the Samaritan text of the Pentateuch seems to avoid the construction wherever possible (loc. cit., p. 364, n. 1; cf. Sperber, 'Hebrew Based upon Biblical Passages in Parallel Transmission', *H.U.C.A.* xiv, 1939, §§ 98 and 101). It must be added, however, that the defective spelling in the Samaritan text can be ambiguous. It is still too early to use the material from the DSS with certainty. That the inf. abs. also here has been employed in some cases instead of a finite verb is probably shown by the form הלוך in DSIa in Isa. xx. 2, where the M.T. has *scriptio defectiva*. This example is not listed by Rubinstein.

[3] Cf. Sellin, op. cit., pp. 70 f. The infinitive, in that case, must originally be the object.

to see why the infinitive is employed instead of a finite form (e.g. Judges vii. 19, Neh. ix. 8, Isa. xxxvii. 19, where the M.T. has וְנָתֹן; but DSIa ויתנו). This could only be understood on the assumption that the original meaning had undergone a process of weakening because Hebrew speech instinct had gradually ceased to distinguish between them. This would explain why the same text has sometimes been transmitted partly with the inf. abs. and partly with a finite form.[1]

Since the discovery of the Ugaritic texts at Ras Shamra and of the North Phoenician inscriptions in Karatepe many scholars have contended that the use of the inf. abs. in Hebrew reflects a usage which was common both in Canaanite and Phoenician. Thus the Ugaritic phrases *wʿn rbt aṯrt ym* 'and the mistress the Aṯirat from the sea answered' I AB I. 25, and *wʿn aliyn bʿl* 'and Aliyan Baʿl answered' II AB VI. 7, have led to the assumption that the form *ʿn* cannot in both cases be the perf. but must be the inf. abs. (read *waʿanô* < *waʿanâwu*),[2] and this explanation has been extended to cover many other cases.[3] The discussion about the correct interpretation of these forms was further invigorated at the end of the 1940's when the Karatepe inscriptions (probably from about 800–750 B.C.) contributed fresh material with such constructions as מלא אנך 'I filled' I. 6, ען אנך 'I humiliated' I. 18, בן אנך 'I built' I. 13, 17, II. 9, 17, cf. בני אנך 'I built it' II. 11, שת אנך 'I placed' I. 11, II. 9 f., 17 f., תרק אנך 'I destroyed' I. 9, ישב אנך 'I sat down' I. 11, &c. Some of these forms may formally be regarded as participles,[4] but not in the case of the intensive form מלא אנך and ען אנך, where the participle requires a prefixed *m*. The explanation is equally untenable in a number of forms with the prefix *y*, יחו אנך 'I revived' I. 3, ירחב אנך 'I expanded' I. 4, ירדם אנך 'I made them descend' I. 20. These forms must be causal forms, but not participles. Many have regarded them as Yifʿil-forms in the inf. abs. (with a transition in the prefix similar to that in the Phoenician perf. caus.),[5] and as for the following pronoun in the

[1] On the other hand, I regard as doubtful the view that later scribes employed the infinitive in cases where different transmissions of the text made them uncertain as to which finite form to choose (thus Rubinstein, loc. cit., p. 365). According to the old principle of always preferring the more complicated reading, I consider the infinitive to be the original form, and the fact that this old construction gradually fell into desuetude must then have influenced later transmissions of the text.

[2] Thus Ginsberg, *J.P.O.S.* xv, 1935, p. 331, n. 8; *Orientalia*, N.S., v, pp. 176 and 177, n. 3.

[3] See C. H. Gordon, *Ugaritic Manual*, §§ 9. 25 and 13. 52.

[4] Thus by J. Obermann, *Discoveries at Karatepe. A Phoenician Royal Inscription from Cilicia* (Supplement to *J.A.O.S.*, 1948, p. 16).

[5] So A. Dupont-Sommer, *Comptes rendus de l'académie des inscriptions et belles-lettres*,

above-mentioned instances, it has been pointed out that such a construction occurs sporadically in the Old Testament, e.g. וְשַׁבֵּחַ אֲנִי Eccles. iv. 2 and וְנַהֲפוֹךְ הוּא Esther ix. 1. It must, however, be considered highly confusing when such forms as ירדם אנך 'I made them descend' and ישבם אנך 'I made them dwell' (Karatepe I. 20) are called inf. abs., though the verbal form has an appended object suffix. If we add to this that the Karatepe inscriptions employ quite regular perfects in the 1st pers., שברת I. 8 and ישבת II. 1 after preceding אנך, it is indeed tempting to assume that in that particular dialect the sentence might have been introduced by the 3rd pers. perf. regardless of the continuation, but that, on the other hand, the 1st pers. perf. had to be employed where the pronoun headed the sentence.[1] If this explanation is correct as far as the Karatepe inscriptions are concerned, the same must be true of other Phoenician inscriptions such as the Kilamuwa inscription,[2] and very probably also of many of the examples which have been regarded by Gordon and others as inf. abs. in the Ugaritic texts.[3]

If the correctness of the text in Eccles. iv. 2 and Esther ix. 1 is maintained—which I consider advisable—we have here a syntactical phenomenon which is well known in other Semitic languages. According to what has been stated above, it was alleged to have been found again in the Karatepe inscriptions and in the Ugaritic texts, but without sufficient

1948, p. 254, n. 3, and *Rev. d'Assyriologie*, xlii, 1948, p. 182; R. T. O'Callaghan, *Orientalia*, N.S., xviii, 1949, pp. 184 and 189; C. H. Gordon, *J.Q.R.*, N.S., xxxix, 1948, p. 42, and *Orientalia*, N.S., xx, 1951, p. 499; A. M. Honeyman, *Muséon*, lxi, 1948, pp. 49 f., and *P.E.Q.*, 1949, p. 31; A. Herdner, *Syria*, xxix, 1952, pp. 170 f., in her review of Johs. Pedersen's article in *Act. Orient.* xxi, 1950, pp. 33–56, where he holds (p. 48) that such forms as *yrḥb* are the 1st pers. sing. 'Yif'il', where *y* represents an *i*- or an *e*-sound.

[1] Thus J. Friedrich, *Forschungen und Fortschritte*, xxiv, 1948, pp. 76–79, *Orientalia*, N.S., xx, 1951, p. 203, and *Phön.-pun. Gramm.* (Rome, 1951), § 286, n. 1, and G. R. Driver, *J.B.L.* lxxiii, 1954, pp. 128–30.

[2] Which runs (l. 7) ושכר אנך עלי מלכאשר 'and I hired against him the King of Assur'. Quite impossible is Lidzbarski's translation 'denn er hatte den Assyrerkönig gegen mich gedungen' (*Ephem. für sem. Epigraphik*, iii, 1915, pp. 218–38). Equally improbable is Smend's proposal, according to which שכר is part. active (ibid., pp. 230 and 237 n.). Also in this inscription the 1st pers. perf. is employed after a preceding pronoun; see ll. 4, 6, 9, 11, and 13.

[3] G. R. Driver has here been clear and outspoken in his view; cf. *J.B.L.* lxxiii, 1954, pp. 128–30, and *Can. Myths and Leg.*, pp. 131 f., where he gives a discussion of all the relevant instances, which are regarded either as participial constructions or as verbal nouns, imperatives, or a tense form without congruence between verb and subject according to the rule stated above. An incontestable proof of the validity of this rule in Ugaritic is seen from the sentence *yṣḥ aṯrt wbnh* 'Aṯirat and her sons cried out' II AB IV. 48 f. In this case *yṣḥ* cannot be the inf. abs.; cf. Driver, *J.B.L.* lxxiii, 1954, p. 129, and *Can. Myths and Leg.*, pp. 130 f., with reference to Gen. i. 14. While the present writer does not fully share Professor Driver's view in all particulars, he is firmly convinced of the correctness of his fundamental attitude towards the problem.

evidence. The phenomenon is due to the fact that the Semitic infinitives, by virtue of their original, neutral position, intermediate between nouns and verbs, show a marked tendency to take the logical subject in the nominative and not in the genitive case.[1] This applies to the inf. constr. as well as to the inf. abs. in Hebrew, and both infinitives may have a verbal regimen like the finite verbs in verbal clauses.[2] It has been mentioned above that this was true of the inf. abs. when it had imperative force, but it is also conspicuous in such an example as יָדֹעַ אוֹתִי 'to know me' (Jer. ix. 23) and in a whole sentence רָגוֹם אֹתוֹ בָאֲבָנִים כָּל־הָעֵדָה 'all the congregation shall stone him' (Num. xv. 35; the Samaritan text reads רגמו, Targum רגומו). The last-mentioned example is especially instructive as it shows, simultaneously, both the verbal regimen of the infinitive and the resemblance of the whole sentence to the normal verbal clause. This might serve to point out the danger of defining too narrowly and one-sidedly the syntactical rules in Hebrew, for living language does not admit of the strait jacket of grammar. Analogous instances might be adduced from Syriac, Targum-Aramaic, and Mandaic.[3] Though this construction is uncommon in Arabic,[4]

[1] See C. Brockelmann, *G.V.G.* ii, § 87, with examples from Arabic, Ethiopic, Hebrew, Aramaic, and Accadian, and his *Hebr. Syntax* (1956), § 45. Basically, however, the clash between the two above explanations of the problem in the Karatepe texts is not irreconcilable if support is given to the theory that historically the perf. has arisen from a nominal form **qatāl*+appended pronoun. It is a necessary condition, however, that the pronoun follows immediately after the nominal form, and not as in ירדם אנך and similar cases. The rule about incongruence has the advantage of holding good in all the instances adduced and of being applicable at all stages in the development of the language.

[2] The definition of the verbal clause is often a disputed point. H. S. Nyberg, *Hebr. Gramm.* (Uppsala, 1952), § 85, claims that the verbal clause as predicate must have a finite verb, and that the sequence must be predicate–subject. If the subject precedes the predicate, he, like the Arab grammarians, regards the construction as a compound nominal clause whose predicate is constituted by a verbal clause. Johannes Pedersen, *Hebr. Gramm.* (Copenhagen, 1926), § 120b, defines a verbal clause as a sentence containing a finite verb. But he expressly emphasizes that the limit between the verbal and the nominal clause is often vague; see especially § 122r. In their concept of the word order in a verbal clause Johannes Pedersen and C. Brockelmann are in complete agreement; see the latter's *Hebr. Synt.*, § 48. Cf. also, concerning the whole problem, K. Schlesinger, 'Zur Wortfolge im hebr. Verbalsatz', *Vet. Test.* iii, 1953, pp. 381–90.

[3] As regards Syriac, Nöldeke refers to the translation of 2 Chron. iv. 6 ܠܡܥܡܕܘ ܒܗܘܢ ܟܗ̈ܢܐ ܐܝܬܝܗܘܢ ('Zur Gramm. des class. Arabisch', *Denkschriften der kais. Akad. der Wiss.*, Phil.-hist. Classe, Bd. xlv, II (Vienna, 1897), § 61a, n. 3). This example is exceedingly appropriate, as the M.T. in that place has no infinitival construction, which might very well induce a verbatim translation. In his *Mand. Gramm.*, pp. 387 f., Nöldeke adduces, besides this example, others from the Targum and characteristic examples from Mandaic, where the infinitive with ל after ד appears with the same meaning as a finite verb in verbal clauses.

[4] See Nöldeke, loc. cit., § 61a. It is peculiar that South Arabic in this case differs from

there are instances which establish that the infinitive may have an object exactly as in a verbal clause. Sibawaihi[1] lists some very instructive instances of the verbal function of the infinitive, e.g. عجبتُ مِن ضَرْبٍ زيدٌ عمرا. The above example shows how freely the infinitive, even in Arabic, appears with a verbal function. If the above view is maintained it will solve many of the difficulties that have hitherto obscured a clear understanding of the Hebrew inf. abs. All sentences, where the inf. abs. continues or replaces a finite verb, ought to be viewed in the light of what has been elaborated above, and ought to afford grounds for an extension of the limits of the Hebrew or the Semitic verbal clause. Therefore the definition of verbal clauses should not, in principle, exclude the sentences described above, where the inf. abs. replaces a finite verb.

I prefer to halt my inquiry into the facts at this point, and thus refrain from developing results into theories about the ancient history of the Semitic verbal system.

North Arabic and exhibits constructions that are in many respects suggestive of the Hebrew inf. abs.; see Maria Höfner, *Altsüdarab. Gramm.* (Leipzig, 1943), § 54, which lists other examples illustrating the inf. interchanging with the finite forms.

[1] H. Derenbourg, *Le Livre de Sîbawaihi*, i (Paris, 1881), § 40 (p. 79); cf. *Mufaṣṣal*, p. 99 (§ 339).

שַׁחַל

By SIGMUND MOWINCKEL, *Oslo*

IN my Norwegian translation of the Psalms (1923) and of Job (1924), I translated this word by 'ögle' = 'lizard', especially in the folkloristic sense of the word = 'worm-dragon, wyvern', having already written briefly on the word in *Gamle spor og nye veier* (Oslo, 1922, pp. 7 ff.). As this, however, seems to have been 'written in water', I should like to give my reasons for that translation, submitting them to the judgement of our esteemed colleague, whom we are honouring in these pages.

1. According to Ges.–Buhl[16] שחל is a poetical word for 'lion'. Koehler has 'Löwenjunges, young lion'; for the shade of meaning 'young' he refers to Arab. *ḥislun* 'young one'. None of the O.T. passages, however, gives any indication as to whether the animal in question is a young one or an old one.

The meaning 'lion' seems unquestionable in (*a*) Job iv. 10 f. || אריה, כפיר, ליש, לביא, (*b*) Hos. v. 14 || כפיר, (*c*) Hos. xiii. 7 || נמר, (*d*) Prov. xxvi. 13 || ארי. For (*c*) and (*d*) see below.

There is, however, at least one passage where 'lion' seems impossible, viz. Job xxviii. 8. The context speaks about man breaking through the rocks, 'putting forth his hand upon the rock, overturning the mountains by the roots', 'searching the darkness to the depth, and the pitchy gloom for (precious) stones' and metals, 'on paths which the עיט ("eagle"? A.V. "fowl") does not know and even the איה ("black kite"; A.V. "vulture") has not seen, where בני שחץ have not trodden, nor the שחל has passed', i.e. the narrowest and most inaccessible rocks and crevices, through which no living animal can pass, into which, however, man is able to break his way. In this context the lion does not fit in at all; the lion is not an animal which can find its way or live in such places. Here we must think of some animal of the serpent species, whether a real or a fabulous one. From popular tales, folk-lore, and myths the idea is well known that the serpent is able to find its way through rocks and crevices, where no other being can manage to do so. It suffices to refer to the old Norse myth of Odin, who changed himself into a serpent in order to slip into the hidden chamber in the mountains and seize Suttungr's mead.

שחל seems to have the sense of 'serpent' in Ps. xci. 13 as well. The god-fearing and pious man is able to 'walk over שחל and פתן ("horned snake") and trample on lion and dragon (תנין)'. Here Moffatt translates 'walk over reptiles and cobras', and his interpretation fits in with the parallelism שחל || פתן. Moffatt here probably follows LXX and Pesh. ἀσπίδα. B.H.[3] suggests זֹחֵל (?). However, it is not necessary to think that they had any other text than that of M.T.; LXX and Pesh. may have known—or felt—that here the lion is out of place. But it is possible that we have here a double parallelism, one dangerous beast of prey and one reptile in the two hemistichs respectively, and that שחל here corresponds to כפיר.

Job x. 16 also points to some kind of serpent. God is here compared to a שחל who 'rises up' (יגאה) and makes Job his prey. The venomous serpent 'raises' its head and the front part of its body to attack, whereas the lion crouches before it jumps upon its prey.

It is also more probable that the pretext of the lazy man in Prov. xxvi. 13 means that a serpent (שחל) may be lying in the road, whereas the lion (ארי) can be expected to turn up in the narrow passages 'between the open places' (of the farms). Then here too we have the two most dangerous kinds of animals—reptiles and beasts of prey. The same interpretation would then be possible in Hos. xiii. 7 as well.

2. Parallel to שחל in Job xxviii. 8 is בני שחץ. Etymologically שחץ, according to the other Semitic dialects, means something like 'pride, haughtiness, insolence'. The word is found only here and in Job xli. 26. The context in both places shows that we have to do with some kind of 'haughty' and terrible animals. In xli. 26 it is said about Leviathan that 'all that is high has fear of him (read אֹתוֹ and יִירָא), he is king of all בני שחץ'. In this context Leviathan means the crocodile. That Leviathan, however, is originally a mythical being, representing and 'symbolizing' the primeval sea, the pre-creation chaos, needs no further proof since H. Gunkel's *Schöpfung und Chaos in Urzeit und Endzeit*. Since then we have also met it in the Ugaritic mythology as לותן. This mythical Leviathan is shaped like a terrible dragon (cf. Ps. lxxiv. 13 f. לויתן || תנינים). Another name of the arch-dragon is רהב || תנין (Isa. li. 9).[1] As a

[1] O. Kaiser, 'Die mythische Bedeutung des Meeres in Ägypten, Ugarit und Israel' (*B.Z.A.W.* lxxviii, 1959, pp. 143 ff.), is inclined to take רהב in Job xxvi. 12 f. as identical with נחש בריח and to explain it as a monster in the heavens, of the same sort as the Egyptian Apophis. The connexion of רהב with the sea is, however, in other places evident, and in Isa. xxvii. 1 נחש בריח is identical with Leviathan. On the meaning of בריח, which is likewise found in Ugarit, see W. F. Albright, *B.A.S.O.R.* lxxxiii, 1941, p. 39, n. 5.

dragon Leviathan has become the name of the crocodile; in popular fancy the crocodile is a kind of dragon, an empirical proof that such beings really exist. Together with the name the crocodile in Job xli has taken over many of the mythical features of Leviathan.[1] And vice versa the dragon in ancient pictures of the Dragon-Killer (St. George); the dragon often has features borrowed from the crocodile or is depicted as a crocodile.

The context of Job xli. 26 then seems to indicate that the בני שחץ, whose king is Leviathan, are beings of the same kind as himself, i.e. serpent-like and dragon-like beings, primarily conceived of as living in the sea.[2]

As a close parallel to Leviathan as the king of the בני שחץ, we have the idea of Rahab and her helpers (Job ix. 13). The two conceptions are in fact identical. רהב is another name for the primeval monster of the sea, which Yahweh conquered before the creation (Ps. lxxxix. 11, Job xxvi. 12, Isa. li. 9), and as Leviathan has become the (Egyptian) crocodile, Rahab has become the symbolic name of Egypt (Isa. xxx. 7, Ps. lxxxvii. 4). The etymological meaning of רהב is nearly the same as that of שחץ: 'pride, haughtiness, rebelliousness',[3] and that is just the quality which the mythopoetical mind has found in the primeval sea (Ps. lxxxix. 10, Ezek. xxix. 3, Pss. of Sol. ii. 29).[4] This Rahab has her helpers, whom Yahweh has crushed together with her (Job ix. 13).

Thus the idea of Leviathan as king of בני שחץ is no free invention of the poet in Job, but belongs to the mythical features of the tradition. The *benē šaḥaṣ* do not so much belong to zoology as to mythology. Of course, the old Israelites thought that they really existed, but they conceived of them as monsters, on which perhaps no living man had ever set eyes. It would therefore fit in much better with the idea if our translations did not rationalize with phrases like 'fierce lion' or 'children of pride' (A.V. Job xxviii. 8, xli. 26 respectively), but found a 'non-realistic' word like the heraldic 'wyvern' or the German 'Lindwurm', Norw.–Dan. 'lindorm'.[5]

[1] See Gunkel, op. cit., pp. 48 ff. On Leviathan and the sea-dragon in Ugarit and Israel, see A. Kaiser, op. cit., pp. 74 ff., 140 ff.

[2] Gunkel has already touched upon the connexion between בני שחץ and the mythical beings of the sea, op. cit., p. 53, n. 5.

[3] Cf. Kaiser, op. cit., p. 143.

[4] See further Gunkel, op. cit., p. 84.

[5] Is there, perhaps, some connexion between the בני שחץ and the γεννήματα ἐχιδνῶν, Matt. iii. 7, xii. 34, xxiii. 33? The expression then has been interpreted of, or transferred to, the ungodly, including a certain idea of their 'demoniac' quality. As an analogy may be mentioned the plur. רהבים (Ps. xl. 5), used of the heathen gods or/and the

So this nature and quality of the בני שחץ corroborates our interpretation of שׁחל. They are all of them originally mythical beings having the shape of a serpent or a dragon. They are connected with the sea as well as with the hidden ravines and grottos in the mountains, with the 'inner parts of the earth', where the serpent shape of שׁחל normally makes it possible for it to creep in.

In Job xxviii. 8 we hear that it is when searching for precious stones and gold and silver that man intrudes into the hidden regions of שׁחל, and owing to his intelligence he is able to break his way in even where שׁחל cannot creep in. This very connexion between שׁחל and the metals and treasures of the mountains is important and belongs to its nature. Here we are reminded of the widespread popular belief in myths and legends that dragons and wyverns are owners of immense treasures. It suffices to refer to Favnir and the Favnir-treasure in 'Nibelungenlied' and in the Nordic saga, or to the wyvern in the saga of Ragnar Lodbrok, lying on an immense plate of gold. In Job xxviii. 8 we are certainly not concerned with any lion. שׁחל is a fabulous beast of the serpent (dragon) type, an animal that the poets would only know from the poetical tradition.

3. We here face the fact that the same word means both 'lion'—certainly only in highly poetical texts—and the fabulous 'wyvern'. How is this to be explained?

First we have to mention an analogy. The Hebr. נָחָשׁ = 'serpent' is also found in Accadian *nêšu*, but here it means 'lion'.[1] Curiously enough, the Accadian word shows something of the same double meaning as Hebr. שׁחל. In the Gilgamesh Epic (xi. 287 f.) we are told of a *nêš ḳaḳḳari*, literally an 'earth lion', that 'snuffs the fragrance of the plant (of life) and comes up (from the water) and carries off the plant'. This 'earth lion' can mean nothing else than a serpent, and we have the same combination of ideas in the Greek *χαμαιλεῶν*, as Professor P. Jensen pointed out in his seminar in 1912. To non-scientific zoology, chameleon, serpent, and dragon belong to the same class of animals.

Another analogy is the Ethiopic *'arwē* 'serpent', surely the same word as Hebr. *'aryēh*, *'arī*.

demoniac powers. On the same lines is the interpretation of the serpent (Gen. iii) as Belial, or the medieval interpretation of Leviathan as the Devil (already in the soteriology of St. Gregor).

[1] C. Brockelmann, *Kurzgef. vergleich. Gramm. der sem. Sprachen* (Porta Ling. Or. xxi, Berlin, 1908), § 47 f., takes *nêšu* as originating from *laiš*, Hebr. = 'lion', through reciprocal dissimilation of the sonant sounds. The analogy with שׁחל (see below), however, indicates that *nêšu* = נחשׁ.

A point of departure for answering the above question may be provided by נָחָשׁ and the root נחשׁ. Ges.–Buhl[16] gives five different roots נחשׁ. It may, however, be duly supposed that they all ultimately belong together. As for נחשׁ^III, the supposed root of נְחֻשְׁתּ^II (Ezek. xvi. 36), Accad. *naḫšatu* 'menstruation' (see Koehler s.v.), even Ges.–Buhl is inclined to identify the root with נחשׁ^V, found in the Accadian *naḫāšu* 'have abundance', *nuḫšu* 'abundance, abundant force' ('Kraftfülle, Machtfülle'); the abundant force especially is seen in sexual forces and functions.

Even the four roots נחשׁ must be reduced. There is no reason to separate נחשׁ^II, from which נְחֻשְׁתּ^I 'copper', and at least according to Hebrew etymology נְחֻשְׁתָּן, the copper serpent in the temple of Jerusalem, are derived, from נחשׁ^V (see above). There was a time when copper was considered *the* metal, at the same time indicative of riches and of 'abundant might', both as to material wealth and mysterious 'mana'. That metals have their respective special 'force' is an idea common to the 'folk-lore' of most 'primitive cultures'. Thus the five roots are reduced to three.

It seems undeniable that there is a connexion between Ges.–Buhl's נחשׁ^I, Piʿel נִחֵשׁ = 'look for an omen; take for a (lucky) omen; divine' (the same in New Hebr. and Aram.), Arab. *naḥasa* = *infaustus fuit* (of bad omens), from which Hebr. נַחַשׁ = 'spell; (unlucky) omen' = Arab. *niḥsatu* '(unlucky) omen' is derived, and נחשׁ^IV, from which נָחָשׁ 'serpent', Arab. *ḥanaš* = 'serpent'. A connexion between these words has long been supposed.[1] Some scholars derive נָחָשׁ 'serpent' from Arab. *naḥus* = *augurium*. Even the reverse might be supposed: the meaning 'divine, look for an omen', &c., might be derived from 'serpent', as this animal often plays an important part as oracle medium (cf. Python in Delphi). To me, however, a derivation of both these roots from a common original root ('Urwurzel') seems more likely to be the right one. The relatively most 'original' meaning of this common root would then be represented by the Accadian *naḫāšu* (see above) 'have abundance of force'. The five roots should then be reduced to one only. The 'original' meaning would then be something like 'have abundance of the mysterious (life) force', the 'mana' of religious phenomenology.

This force is active in the powers and functions of sexual life. It is found in the metal, it is presupposed and used at omen-taking and divination. It is found in special 'mana animals' as well. And among

[1] See W. von Baudissin, *Studien zur sem. Religionsgeschichte*, i (Leipzig, 1876), p. 287.

the latter the serpent has always played an important part as bearer of mysterious (supernatural) forces, as is well known from folk-tales, myths, and folk-lore of all peoples. It suffices here to refer to the above-mentioned connexion between serpents and dragons and the gold and other precious treasures of the nether world. In Gen. iii the serpent is the possessor of superhuman 'wisdom', just as in the Gilgamesh Epic it has stolen the 'eternal life' that man has been seeking in vain: all the serpents of myth and folk-lore are 'of old'; serpents are believed to have a very long life.

The wisdom of the serpent is, of course, the reason why it plays such a great part in divination and seeking omens. In this connexion the close relations between serpents and the spirits of the deceased and the demons of the nether world[1] are important. The spirits of the deceased are also known for their superhuman wisdom; in Hebrew they are called יִדְּעֹנִים 'knowing ones', and may also be called אֱלֹהִים 'gods' (1 Sam. xxviii. 13). And these spirits and demons are often conceived of in the shape of serpents; thus, for example, in Babylonia.[2] Even gods are conceived of as serpents. In Dêr they worshipped a serpent goddess.[3] A serpent god Sir is often sculptured on the *kudurrus*.[4] Nergal is described as the great dragon Tiâmat;[5] *ušûmgallu* 'the great serpent' (dragon) is not infrequently met with as a divine epithet. From the shoulders of the god Ningišzida two serpents grow out, and his emblem is the caduceus, the serpent staff with two winding serpents.[6] Between Eriškigal, the goddess of the nether world, and serpents there are close connexions; she is 'the mother of the demons'[7] and is sculptured with serpents in her hands.[8] Especially chthonic deities often have the shape and nature of the serpent. This idea is found not only among the Babylonians (see above), but also among other Semitic peoples,[9] and among the Greeks[10] and other nations.[11] In Israel we hear of the divine copper serpent, the Neḥuštān (2 Kings xviii. 4), the serpent-shaped

[1] Cf. H. Gressmann, 'Die Paradiessage', *Festgabe für Dr. Adolf von Harnack zum siebzigsten Geburtstag* (Tübingen, 1921), pp. 33 f.

[2] M. Jastrow, *Die Religion Babyloniens und Assyriens*, i (Giessen, 1905), p. 281; Gressmann, op. cit., p. 36.

[3] *Beitr. z. Assyr.* iii. 238, 42, quoted from Gressmann, op. cit., p. 37.

[4] Jastrow, op. cit. i, pp. 166, 189, 195, &c.

[5] Ibid., p. 468.

[6] B. Meissner, *Babylonien und Assyrien*, ii (Heidelberg, 1925), p. 35.

[7] Jastrow, op. cit. i, p. 360.

[8] See for example Jastrow, *Bildermappe zur Religion Babyloniens u. Assyriens*, no. 100.

[9] So von Baudissin, *Adonis und Ešmun* (Leipzig, 1911), pp. 325 ff.

[10] See for example O. Gruppe, *Griechische Mythologie*, ii, p. 807.

[11] See Hopf, *Tierorakel und Orakeltiere*, pp. 182 ff.

שחל
19892

seraphs,[1] and the cult places 'Serpent stone' (1 Kings i. 9) and 'Dragon well' (Neh. ii. 13).

The connexion between the forces of sexuality and fertility was hinted at above. No wonder then that the great Mother and fertility goddess of the ancient Near East is often conceived of as a serpent goddess[2] and that we meet her in this form in Palestine as well; thus, for example, at Beth-shean.[3] We have good reason to believe that even the serpent of the Paradise myth was originally a chthonic deity endowed with both wisdom and creative forces.[4] A variant upon the same idea is reflected in the name of Adam's wife חַוָּה.[5] The name occurs only once in the tale (Gen. iii. 20), and it is probably a later element in the transmitted form of the myth; originally the persons may only have been called 'Man' (*'ādhām*) and 'Woman' (*'iššāh*). In a Punic inscription we meet with a 'חות Lady, Goddess, and Queen'.[6] We are here concerned with the old Mother Goddess of fertility and procreation, and we may accordingly think that the interpretation of the name in Gen. iii. 20 'Mother of all living' is not invented by the 'Author' of Gen. iii (J), but has been taken over from older tradition. The interpretation is etymologically wrong; for the nature of the old goddess, however, correct enough. Now, as חוה is obviously the same word as Aram. חִוְיָא = 'serpent',[7] Nöldeke, Lidzbarski, Gressmann, Gunkel, Dietrich,[8] and others are quite right in finding the serpent-shaped mother goddess in the name of the first woman.

As for the etymology of the name it seems justifiable to connect it with Hebrew and Aramaic 'make known, tell, interpret'. If that be so, the serpent mother goddess has also been an oracle and omen goddess and has obtained her name from that function—another indication of the connexion between serpent deities and oracles and divination.

This role of omen mediator may also be traced in the Jerusalem

[1] Isa. vi. 2 ff.; cf. Num. xxi. 6 ff., Deut. viii. 15, Isa. xiv. 29, xxx. 6.

[2] See von Baudissin, *Adonis und Ešmun*, pp. 203 ff.; S. A. Cook, *The Religion of Ancient Palestine in the Light of Archaeology* (Schweich Lectures 1925, London, 1930), pp. 98 f.; cf. pp. 117, n. 1, 193, n. 5, 220, n. 3, 82, 130, 106 f., 147; W. F. Albright, *Archaeology and the Religion of Israel* (Baltimore, 1953), p. 189; K. Galling, *Bibl. Reallexikon*, 1937, s.v. 'Schlange'; P. Thomsen, *Reallexicon der Vorgeschichte*, s.v. 'Schlange'.

[3] See Albright, op. cit., p. 189; J. N. Schofield, *The Religious Background of the Bible* (1944), p. 55. See also Galling, op. cit.

[4] See Gressmann, op. cit., pp. 32 ff.; H. Gunkel, *Genesis* (1917), p. 15, with literature.

[5] See the references in n. 4.

[6] See M. Lidzbarski, *Ephem. für sem. Epigraphik*, i, p. 34.

[7] See Nöldeke, *Z.D.M.G.* xlii, 1888, p. 487; Gressmann, *A.R.W.* x, 1907, pp. 359 f.

[8] A. Dietrich, *A.R.W.* viii, 1905, pp. 20 ff.

Lincoln Christian College

neḥuštān. In the legend (Num. xxi. 6 ff.) we are told that Moses 'made a serpent of brass and set it upon a pole', and if anyone had been bitten by a serpent, 'when he beheld the serpent of brass he lived'. The verb used here (הביט) means more than merely 'look at' or 'behold'. It means 'glance towards, regard', with attention. Is it too daring to suppose that the original meaning was: to look for a sign, an omen of some sort, imparted in some way or other by the copper serpent?

4. In this roundabout way, through our study of נָחָשׁ we again arrive at שחל. Beside the verb נִחֵשׁ and the noun נַחַשׁ, we also have the root לחשׁ (only in Piʿel ptcp. plur. מְלַחֲשִׁים 'whisperers, charmers', Ps. lviii. 6, where it is used of the serpent charmers), Hithp. הִתְלַחֵשׁ 'whisper, charm'[1] (cf. Accad. *luḫḫušu* with the same meaning), and the noun לַחַשׁ 'serpent-charming' (Isa. iii. 3; Jer. viii. 17). So beside the root נחשׁ there existed a root לחשׁ with the same meaning. No doubt the two roots were originally identical. Through dissimilation the sonant sound *n* has become *l* because of the influence of the sibilant *š*.[2] To this root לחשׁ, שחל also must be related. We have to do with a reciprocal dissimilation of the sonant sound and an apparent metathesis.

This means in fact that שַׁחַל is fundamentally the same as נָחָשׁ. The fundamental meaning of שַׁחַל also is a being 'endowed' with supernormal and mysterious force, with 'mana'. The word may have been used both of serpents and dragons—there is no essential difference between the two as to nature and forces; even Leviathan is called a נָחָשׁ (Isa. xxvii. 1).

5. How did the word come to be used of the lion as well? To a certain degree even the lion was a demonic beast. The Babylonians especially imagined demons in the shape of lions, wild bulls, and wild dogs.[3] Dragons and lions are mentioned together as the two most terrible beasts known to the ancient east (cf. Ps. xci. 13). In Babylonian palaces and temples we find lions (and bulls) along with dragons (*mušruššu*) as guardian 'spirits' at the gates or on the walls (see the dragons on the gates of the Ishtar temple, M. Jastrow, *Bildermappe*, no. 53; the lions

[1] This latter meaning the word undoubtedly has in Ps. xli. 8. In 2 Sam. xii. 19 the meaning is more neutral; it must, however, be remembered that to the primitive mind 'whisper' always implies some evil-working spell and magic; whispering and whistling as well as blowing are well-known magical practices in many lands. The magical words, the spells, have as a rule to be whispered.

[2] Brockelmann, op. cit., § 47. Theoretically a change from *l* to *n* is possible, cf. נִשְׁכָּה>לִשְׁכָּה; see, however, below.

[3] See O. Weber, 'Dämonenbeschwörung bei den Babyloniern und Assyrern', *A.O.* vii. 4 (Leipzig, 1905), pp. 11 ff.; S. Mowinckel, *Psalmenstudien*, i (Kristiania [= Oslo], 1921), p. 75.

along the processional way in Babylon, ibid., no. 54; for bulls and dragons before the city gates of Babylon, see the Nabukudurriuṣur inscr. no. 13 in S. Langdon, *Die neubabylon. Königsinschriften*,[1] &c.).

I think, however, that we may put the question in another way, and ask: where above all do lion and dragon, or serpent, meet? Answer: in the figure of the griffin, which was very popular in the fancy and art of the ancient Near East. The oriental griffin can be defined as a combination of dragon and lion. This is quite obvious with regard to the two serpent griffins in Jastrow's *Bildermappe*, nos. 52 and 53. The former, the above-mentioned *mušruššu* at the Ishtar gate in Babylon, has the trunk, the forelegs, and the tail of a lion; the body, however, is covered with scales like the body of a serpent. Very similar is no. 53 from the Marduk temple in Babylon. (See also the serpent griffin from the temple of Marduk at Nippur.[2]) The two figures flanking the caduceus on the famous vase of Gudea are curious.[3] They are standing upright on their hind legs, the feet being those of an eagle; from the eagle they also get their wings. The body is a lion's body, likewise neck, head, and forelegs, but body and tail are winding and marked like the body of many serpents. (See also the close relation between the serpent griffin, Jastrow, no. 92, and the lion griffin, no. 120.) Very likely the *mušruššu*s and griffins from the temples of Marduk represent the Tiâmat dragon, or her helpers, the dragons of the original chaos. Their main nature is that of a dragon, but they have also taken over important features from the lion.

Against the background of these considerations it seems reasonable to suppose that we meet with the same word as the name of a serpent-like dragon, a 'wyvern', and as a poetical term for the lion. Originally שחל may have meant the serpent dragon, the mythical wyvern or 'Lindwurm'.[4] Because of the combination of serpent (dragon) and lion in mythopoetical and artistic fancy, it has also been adopted as a term for the lion.

As a rule the O.T. poets may have meant 'lion'. But at least in one passage, Job xxviii. 8, this sense is impossible: here the poet must have known what שַׁחַל originally meant.

[1] *Vorderasiatische Bibliothek*, 4 (Leipzig, 1912).

[2] H. Gressmann, *Altorient. Texte und Bilder z. A.T.* (Tübingen, 1909), ii, p. 92, no. 167.

[3] Jastrow, *Bildermappe*, no. 92; Gressmann, op. cit., no. 170. See above, p. 100.

[4] Even the Accadian *nêšu* may originally have meant 'serpent', as the poetical compound *nêš ḳaḳḳari* proves (see above, p. 98).

THE ORIGIN OF THE SUBDIVISIONS OF SEMITIC

By C. RABIN, *Jerusalem*

THE 60–70 identifiable Semitic dialects are normally grouped into five 'languages', Accadian, Aramaic, Canaanite, Arabic, and South Arabian–Ethiopic, and these again into three subgroups, East Semitic, North-west Semitic (Aramaic and Canaanite), and South Semitic (Arabic and South Arabian–Ethiopic); the last two, finally, are mostly opposed as West Semitic to the East Semitic Accadian. The 'languages' are supposed to have come into being by ethnic 'waves' of emigrants from the original home of the Semites, mostly thought to have been the Arabian Peninsula. This 'classical' view is expounded most clearly by Brockelmann.[1]

The concept of a Canaanite 'language' was first called into doubt by H. Bauer and P. Leander in 1922,[2] who proposed a new division, cutting right across Canaanite, between 'older' and 'younger' Semitic languages, though they still explicitly acknowledge the idea of ethnic movements from a common home.[3] When Ugaritic was discovered in 1930, it was at first taken to be a Canaanite dialect,[4] but it was soon realized that a 'proto-Canaanite', to be the ancestor of both Hebrew–Phoenician and of Ugaritic, must have had so few distinguishing marks as to be identical with proto-Semitic. It was claimed that Ugaritic formed a separate 'language' or subgroup with 'Amorite',[5] a language which had been taken to be 'East Canaanite' by its discoverer.[6] Others[7] attempted to connect it with Arabic, which, of course, is widely thought

[1] *Grundriss der vergl. Gramm.* i (1908), pp. 7, 8, 13, 21.

[2] *Historische Gramm. d. hebr. Spr.* i (1922), p. 8.

[3] 'Semitische Bewegungen', ibid., p. 10.

[4] e.g. J. A. Montgomery and Z. S. Harris, *The Ras Shamra Mythological Texts* (1935), p. 16; Z. S. Harris in his *Development of the Canaanite Dialects* (1939)—more cautiously 'Ras Shamra: Canaanite Civilization and Language', *Smithsonian Report* for 1937, p. 501; C. Virolleaud, H. L. Ginsberg, *Orientalia*, v, 1936, pp. 179 f.; H. Cazelles, *R.B.* liv, 1947, p. 388, &c.

[5] A. Goetze, 'Is Ugaritic a Canaanite Dialect?', *Language*, xvii, 1941, pp. 127–38. The name 'Amorite', though its justification has never been proved, is a useful one. J. Cantineau, and C. H. Gordon from 1947 onwards, claim that Ugaritic belongs to a hitherto unknown 'language'.

[6] T. Bauer, *Die Ostkanaanäer* (1926).

[7] N. H. Tur-Sinai, *Ha-lashon veha-sefer*, i (1948), p. 269, and *Tarbiṣ*, xxiii, 1951–2,

to be particularly close to proto-Semitic. J. Friedrich brought into the discussion another unplaceable language, the Ya'udic of Zinjirli in northern Syria,[1] and suggested that all these Canaanite and near-Canaanite dialects went back to proto-North-west Semitic without any intermediate link. To express this in terms of geographical linguistics: these dialects were not due to migrations, but arose in their known locations by the normal process of the spread of linguistic innovations and formation of isoglosses.

In 1956 S. Moscati[2] demonstrated that early Aramaic dialects lacked typically 'Aramaic' features and that important isoglosses ran impartially across the 'Aramaic' and 'Canaanite' areas. He therefore suggested replacing the genealogical theory of the origin of Aramaic by one based on geographical linguistics, with northern Mesopotamia as the centre of radiation of 'Aramaic' features over an area divided by previous isoglosses. The negation of the existence of an Aramaic ethnic wave has in fact deprived the migration theory of one of its mainstays, as—apart from the spread of Arabic in the mid-first millennium A.D.—the spread of Aramaean tribesmen was one of the few identifiable ethnic movements in Semitic history.

There were, of course, some cases of Semitic languages spreading by ethnic movements: Arabic before and after Islam, Ethiopic in Africa,[3] and Aramaic during the late Assyrian and neo-Babylonian periods.[4] We are not concerned with these late alterations in the geographical pattern of Semitic, but with the genesis of the great 'languages', for which the classical theory assumed original migrations on linguistic grounds alone. Our task will be to examine whether the linguistic evidence does in fact require such migrations, or whether the distribution of typical linguistic features can be explained as well or better by purely linguistic diffusion.

pp. 143–5; I. Al-Yasin, *The Lexical Relation between Ugaritic and Arabic* (1952); connexion with South Arabian was claimed by T. H. Gaster, 'The Beth Shemesh Tablet and the Origins of Ras Shamra Culture', *P.E.F.Q.S.*, 1934, pp. 94–96.

[1] 'Kanaanäisch und westsemitisch', *Scientia*, lxxxiv, 1949, pp. 220–3.

[2] 'Il Semitico di nord-ovest', in *Studi Orient. in onore di G. Levi della Vida*, ii (1956), pp. 202–21.

[3] Note, however, that it has never been shown that Geʿez stands in a particularly close relation to any specific branch of South Arabian.

[4] The role of the ethnic movements in the spread of either Aramaic or Arabic should, however, not be overstressed. Aramaic owes much of its expansion to its being an administrative language in the Persian empire and a means of intercommunication between populations displaced by Assyrian and Babylonian transplantations. The Jews of Judaea went over to Aramaic centuries after any possible Aramaean migration. Arabic, too, became dominant outside Arabia long after the migration wave of the conquests, mainly as a result of conversions and of its official use.

In a situation created by ethnic migration we should expect sharp limits between the languages of the various 'waves', and a distribution of features unrelated to the geography of the area: no clear distinction between centre and margins, and the recurrence of genetically related features in disconnected areas. In a dialect geography created by the diffusion of linguistic features we should, on the other hand, find consistent isoglosses, recognizable centres of diffusion, and some distinction between dialects lying in the centre and those on the margin.

A diffusional distribution of features does not exclude the possibility that the populations forming the area migrated to their actual habitats in waves. It may well be that all the ethnic waves arrived at a time when proto-Semitic was still undifferentiated. But then the connexion between migrations and language formation would dissolve into nothing. The migrations, if provable by other means, would be part of the prehistory of Semitic, not of its history as a group of individual dialects.

One of the difficulties in dealing with Semitic linguistic features geographically is that we get our first glimpse of the different language units at such widely different times, ranging from the third millennium B.C. for Accadian to the first half of the first millennium A.D. for Ethiopia and the centre of the Arabian Peninsula. However, though this cannot be demonstrated in the course of this brief preliminary study, it seems to me that we get good results by ignoring the time factor and treating the various dialects as coexisting each in the location in which we first encounter it, on condition that we also try to take into account for each dialect mainly the earliest evidence, and not only the later standardized forms, such as the Classical Arabic of the grammarians. We shall see later that on the assumption of such a homogeneous field we can also make good use of the time factor.

Another principle which ought to be self-evident is that conservative features are in themselves of no value[1] for determining dialect connexions. For instance, the preservation of most of the proto-Semitic sound-system by Ugaritic, Classical Arabic, and Old South Arabian does not provide any proof that these languages were more closely related to each other than to other dialects. The preservation of case-endings for a longer time does not give us any information about the genetic relationships of the languages which did so. Every Semitic dialect is conservative in some respects and has developed away from Com-

[1] They may be of value as a negative criterion, showing which areas remained unaffected by certain developments.

mon Semitic in others. Some of these developments cover larger areas, while others are restricted. It is not claimed that we can say with confidence in all instances which of two existing alternative phenomena is the older one. On the other hand, if the thesis put forward in this paper should be acceptable, it would help us to determine the direction of development, since a feature found in disconnected and distant areas—unless it can be shown to be the result of a tendency inherent in the language—is likely to be an indication of 'islands' as against an innovatory feature which spread over the continuous intervening territory.

We shall be able in what follows to distinguish between a central part of the Semitic area, consisting mainly of the Arabian Peninsula, but in some cases also including the Syrian home of Aramaic, and two marginal regions: one extending from Palestine via Ugarit to Mesopotamia, the other the Ethiopian group on the African mainland. The concepts of centre and margin play an important role in geographical linguistics. In many cases the marginal dialects are more conservative than the centre. One of the reasons for this is no doubt that the central area of a language territory is also culturally and economically the most active part. In our case we shall find that the margins, especially the culturally highly advanced northern margin, were the least conservative part, and that especially the strip along the Mediterranean seaboard was the apparent centre of radiation for a number of innovations.

Just as there are innumerable isoglosses enclosing parts of 'language' areas, and isoglosses marking off the different 'languages' from each other, so there are, of course, bundles of isoglosses marking off the subgroups against each other, although it should be noted that the number of these 'group isoglosses' has somewhat diminished by new discoveries since the time when scholars established the threefold division now commonly accepted. It is the contention of this paper that there are also a number of 'cross-group isoglosses', no less important than the group isoglosses, which, however, unlike the former, cannot be explained except on the assumption that from the Common Semitic period onwards the dialects affected were in the geographical locations they later occupied. The following are only instances.

A. PHONOLOGY

1. Reduction of the ternary opposition *s*/*š*/*ś* (ס, שׁ, שׂ) to a binary opposition. This took place everywhere except in Modern South

Arabian,[1] but in Accadian, Hebrew, and Old South Arabian the reduction took place within the observable history of the language.[2] In later Hebrew[3] and in all modern Ethiopian languages (i.e. in two markedly 'marginal' areas) the binary opposition was neutralized. The point which here interests us is the geographical distribution of the three mathematically possible types of binary reduction. The opposition *ś*/*š* was neutralized in the marginal area Phoenician[4]–Ugaritic–Amorite[5]–Accadian; the opposition *s*/*ś* in Hebrew and Aramaic; and the opposition *s*/*š* in Arabic, later Old South Arabian, and Geʿez. The dates of the reduction in the different languages, as far as observable, give the impression that the *tendency* to reduce advanced from a radiation centre in the north-west corner of the Semitic area, reached southern Arabia by the end of the first millennium B.C., and stopped short at the isolated Hadramaut, but the *realizations* of the tendency were different in the various areas. The remarkable thing is that the final result both in Hebrew–Aramaic and in Arabic of all types was an opposition [s]/[ʃ].[6]

2. Another instance of the reduction of a ternary opposition is offered by the emphatic fricative series S(ibilant) = ص/L(ateral) = ض/I(nterdental) = ظ, which will in the following be indicated by the initials of their names so as to avoid complicated signs and dubious phonetic fixations.[7] Again the full series has been preserved only in Modern South Arabian.[8] However, the three have also been kept quite distinct in

[1] The reflection of *s*/*š* is somewhat erratic, and in Mehri *š* tends to become *h*. Note that Modern South Arabian is not descended from Old South Arabian. Except for the little-known Hadramitic, no ancient inscriptional language was used in the areas where South Arabian is now spoken.

[2] For the history of the distinction *s*/*š* (𐩪/𐩦) in Old South Arabian, see A. F. L. Beeston, *J.S.S.* vii, 1962, pp. 222 ff.

[3] See Y. F. Gumpertz, *Mivṭa'ē śefatenu* (1953), pp. 33–50. The coalescence persists in Lithuania and part of Morocco, but elsewhere the opposition has long been restored. Curiously enough it tends again to get lost in the speech of the younger generation in Israel.

[4] As early as the Tell-Amarna age, cf. Z. S. Harris, *Development of the Canaanite Dialects* (1939), pp. 33 f.

[5] Where the *Z*-signs represent *s*, the *S*-signs *ś*, *š*, and the *Š*-signs *th*, cf. I. J. Gelb, 'La lingua degli Amoriti', *Rendiconti Acc. dei Lincei*, Cl. di sc. morali, &c., VIII. xiii, pp. 150 f.

[6] In older loanwords and transliterations (from *šārōthayikh* Ezek. xxvii. 25 onwards, and probably until the Islamic period) Arabic س corresponds to Hebrew–Aramaic *š*; this may have something to do with the different method of reduction.

[7] The exact phonetic nature of both L and I is doubtful; nor is it known whether the three were voiced, voiceless, or neutral.

[8] In Soqotri I has coalesced with *ṭ*, and there seems to be a tendency for this in Mehri (cf. V. Christian, 'Die Stellung des Mehri innerhalb der sem. Sprachen', *Sitzb. Ak. d. W. in Wien*, Phil.-hist. Kl., ccxxii. 3, 1944, p. 4). Note the similarity to Aramaic, but also to South Ethiopian.

Aramaic by the fact that L and I coalesced with different phonemes outside the series (L > ʿ; I > ṭ). Here the binary reductions follow a north–south axis: in Ugaritic the opposition S/L was neutralized;[1] in Arabia (where Classical Arabic still has the ternary series) the opposition I/L; in Geʿez the opposition S/I. The two marginal areas have effected further simplification: the northern margin this time consisting of Hebrew–Phoenician–Amorite[2]–Accadian, the southern one of Tigre, Tigriña, and northern Amharic, while in the rest of modern Ethiopic the whole series has coalesced with ṭ.

3. The pronunciation of *ā* as [o:] (and its eventual coalescence with *o: < au*) is a feature typical at an early stage of a belt stretching from Hadramaut via Yemen, western Arabia, Nabataean Arabic, Hebrew, Phoenician, to Western Syriac.[3] The fact that Egyptian, which is contiguous to this area, had the same feature suggests that it is an archaism dating from some stage of Hamito-Semitic development, and that the realization [a:] (æ:) is the innovation, contrary to the substrate theory propounded by Praetorius[4] for the explanation of the phenomenon in North-west Semitic. The innovation took place in two marginal areas: Ugaritic–Amorite–Eastern Aramaic–Accadian–Eastern and Central Arabic in the north, Ethiopic in the south, with a 'conservative axis' lying rather askew to that in no. 2 above.

There are, however, cases of innovation along the central axis, with the marginal areas remaining partly unaffected. The following two examples will be dealt with briefly, to avoid repetition of fuller discussions elsewhere.

4. In an area including Ugarit,[5] Western Syriac (in traces), Tell-Amarna Canaanite, Hebrew, and Early Arabic dialects of the Syrian Desert, the north-east, and the centre,[6] the opposition *i/a* is neutralized in the prefixes of the imperfect, so that *i* precedes *a*-stems and *a* other stems. In one form of Hebrew, represented by the Tiberian pointing of our Bibles, this neutralization is not morphophonemically restricted,

[1] In the Hadad text (Gordon, no. 75), L is written with the sign for I; cf. also G. R. Driver, *Canaanite Myths and Legends* (1956), p. 128.

[2] Gelb (loc. cit., par. 2. 7. 7) assumes here 'fonemi' not expressed in writing.

[3] Cf. C. Rabin, *Ancient West-Arabian* (1951), map 12 (p. 108); also his reappraisal of the sound-law in Hebrew, '*ā* shemit ve-hishtaqfuyoteha be-ʿIvrit', *Tarbiṣ*, xxxiii, 1960–1, pp. 99–111.

[4] *Z.D.M.G.* liv, 1900, p. 369.

[5] H. L. Ginsberg, *Tarbiṣ*, iv, 1932–3, p. 182; E. Hammershaimb, *Das Verbum im Dialekt von Ras Schamra* (1941), pp. 175–85.

[6] J. Barth, *Z.D.M.G.* xlviii, 1894, p. 4; C. Rabin, *J.J.S.* i, 1948, pp. 22–26.

but general.[1] On the general experience in geographical linguistics, it would be reasonable to assume that the area of maximum effect of a tendency is also the focus of radiation.

5. The change of *iya* > *a:* exists in a number of dialects stretching from Hebrew (where this *a:* did not become *o:*) via Tayyi' in north-west Arabia and Ghanī in the centre to the northern Yemen, with gaps in our information for the intervening areas.[2] This axis lies just south of the one described in no. 4.

B. MORPHOLOGY

6. Perhaps the clearest example of cross-group innovation is the replacement of the ternary tense opposition *yaqtul* / $yaqat(t)^{a}/_{i}l$ / *qatal(a)*[3] by a binary opposition. The following is in essentials a restatement in terms of geographical linguistics of Driver's results in his *Problems of the Hebrew Verbal System* (1936). In this case Accadian is the conservative area. The entire Semitic area has preserved (in the north-west in traces, in the south-east in a highly developed form) the employment of *yaqtul* as a modal form ('jussive'). Ugaritic currently uses a prefix tense in perfective sense, though because of the lack of vocalization we cannot say whether it was *yqtl* or *yqatl*;[4] this tense can in some cases be shown to have had a final *-u*, but also to have ended in zero or *-i* in non-jussive as well as jussive use. The oldest stage of Hebrew, as exhibited in Judges v and Deut. xxxii, still used free *yqtl* perfectively, while at the next stage, until the First Exile, perfective *yqtl* became bound to copulative *wa(n?)-*;[5] though it is often identical in form with imperfective *yqtl*, some thirteen sets of forms with either shortening or retraction of stress prove that *wayyaqtul* continues *yaqtul*, while the imperfective form represents a prefix tense with final vowel, presumably *yaqtulu*.[6] In Arabic the perfective use of *yaqtul* is even more narrowly bound, and

[1] Philippi's Law+Law of Attenuation, cf. C. Rabin, 'Ha-tenuʿot ha-qeṭannot ba-ʿIvrit ha-Ṭabranit', *Sefer Ṭur-Sinai* (1960), pp. 169–206.

[2] Cf. *Ancient West-Arabian*, map 18 (p. 198). Tayyi' was formerly contiguous to the Fertile Crescent (ibid., p. 193).

[3] For simplicity's sake these three will in the following be referred to as *yqtl, yqatl,* and *qtl,* while *yaqtulu* will appear as *yqtlu*.

[4] Cf. Hammershaimb, op. cit., pp. 105–10.

[5] In Deut. xxxii, where copulative *w-* is required by the context before perfective *yqtl,* it is pointed like *waw* consecutive, but this may be later standardization. On the other hand, it may be that the doubling of the following consonant was from the beginning associated with *wa-* before perfective *yqtl.*

[6] Since in the first person it is opposed to modal ('cohortative') *'aqtula*.

the imperfective is *yaqtulu*. In Phoenician and in Aramaic no traces of perfective *yqtl* appear. In Middle Aramaic, Mishnaic Hebrew (except with 'to be'), and colloquial Arabic, the modal use of *yaqtul* disappears, and *yaqtul*(*u*), with its final vowel lost,[1] takes over its functions, too. We may thus state for the area Phoenician–Hebrew–Aramaic–Arabic three distinct events, which appear to have taken place in this chronological order: (1) replacement of *yqatl* by *yqtlu*;[2] (2) loss of the perfective use of *yqtl*; (3) loss of the modal use of *yqtl*.

A closer look at Hebrew shows us that between (1) and (2) another event must have taken place, namely the coalescence in temporal meaning between perfective *yqtl* and perfective *qtl*, thus creating a binary opposition only, with the perfective *Zeitstufe* represented by two syntactically conditioned alloforms—indeed with the specific Hebrew use of *w-qtl* each *Zeitstufe* was doubly represented. This was not the case in Arabic, where *lam yaqtul* kept an aspectual function distinct from *mā qatala*. The binary reduction in Arabic was thus completed only after stage (2).

In Modern South Arabian and in Geʿez the binary reduction is completed, but in a manner different from the group described hitherto: *yqatl* fills its original function and is opposed to *qtl*, *yqtl* being restricted to modal functions.[3]

We have here the geographical and the historical factors closely interwoven. The binary reduction is most completely effected in Phoenician and Aramaic, from *c.* 1200 and 900 onwards; in Hebrew it is partly effected by *c.* 900 (formation of prose style?) but completed only about the middle of the first millennium B.C.; in Arabic the completion dates from the rise of the colloquials, some time after the middle of the first millennium A.D., though the process must have begun before the formation of Classical Arabic some centuries earlier. The facts are thus consistent with—though they do not absolutely demand—the assumption that the reduction of the ternary system spread gradually along an axis north-west–south-east. On the other hand, this innovation crossed in its advance a previous isogloss, dividing an area where *yqatl* had been replaced by *yqtlu* from one where *yqatl* had been preserved. Since *yqtlu*

[1] We might say that Aramaic and colloquial Arabic continued the jussive rather than the indicative as far as the forms with *-ī* and *-ū* suffixes are concerned, but I do not think far-reaching conclusions should be drawn from this.

[2] The alternative assumption, that 'proto-North-west Semitic' and 'proto-Arabic' had from the beginning a ternary opposition *yqtl*/*yqtlu*/*qtl*, seems to me improbable.

[3] Indicatives such as *yqm* from *qwm* and *yzʿ* from *wzʿ*, as against Geʿez *yeqawwem*, *yewalled*, suggest that the *yqtlu* isogloss included Old South Arabian.

exists also in an area where (and when) the binary reduction did not exist, we may assume further that it, too, spread along the same axis, but came to a stop earlier. Since the loss of modal *yqtl* covers exactly the same area as *yqtlu* + reduction, it is impossible to say whether it represents a further radiation or resulted from the structure of the *yqtlu*/*qtl* opposition with subsequent loss of final vowels.

7. If the verbal form *qātala* is an innovation, and if the apparent remnants of Hebrew *qōṭēl* are accepted as a reflection of **qātala*,[1] we would have another instance of a cross-group feature along the same axis, this time, however, reaching as far as Ethiopic.

8. Innovation can consist in the rejection of one of previously existing synonymous forms, i.e. in the reduction of an alternance rather than of an opposition.[2] It seems probable that Common Semitic possessed both a *h*- (ʾ-) prefix for the causative and a *š*- prefix, the latter existing also in Egyptian. Both coexist in Modern South Arabian, which thus proves again to be the most archaic branch of Semitic. The *š*- type alone exists in Accadian, on the one hand, and in Old South Arabian, excluding Sabaean, on the other. However, the occurrence of the name-types *hqtl*, *yhqtl*, in the 'S-languages'[3] suggests that in the not too distant past they, too, possessed a *h*- causative; as is well known, personal names often preserve obsolete grammatical features. In Ugaritic the *š*- type is dominant, but there are clear traces of ʾ-.[4] Hebrew has *h*-, but a number of secondary roots formed by means of initial *š* from weak roots[5] proves that *š*- was used at an earlier stage of the language. A few autochthonous *š*- formations seem to exist in Mishnaic Hebrew.[6] Amorite, Arabic, Sabaean, and Ethiopic have the *h*- (ʾ-) type, but all of them bear evidence of former possession of *š*- in the reflexive–causative **št*- (Arabic X form).[7]

[1] Cf. Dhorme, *R.B.*, N.S., xi, 1914, pp. 37 ff.; Perles, *Analekten*, N.F., p. 69; Z. Har-Zahav, *Diqduq ha-lashon ha-ʿIvrit*, iii, 1956, pp. 505 ff.

[2] We cannot be quite sure, though, that *šqtl* and *hqtl* were not originally in opposition, and only subsequently became alloforms (cf. Hebrew *qtl* and *wyqtl* in no. 6).

[3] Collected by the present author in a note to I. Ben-Zvi, 'Le-qadmut yishshuvam shel shivṭē Yisra'el ba-ʿArav', *Ereṣ-Yisraʾel*, vi, 1960, p. 144, transl. *Le Muséon*, lxxiv, 1961, pp. 175–7 (with additions by G. Ryckmans). There are no *ysqtl* names, and instances of *sqtl* names are very doubtful.

[4] See S. Moscati, 'Sulla più antica storia delle lingue semitiche', *Rendiconti Acc. dei Lincei*, Cl. di sc. morali, &c., VIII. xv, 1960, p. 95, and literature cited there.

[5] Cf. W. F. Albright, 'The Old Testament and Canaanite Language', *C.B.Q.* vii, 1945, p. 18, and literature cited there.

[6] See M. H. Segal, *Mishnaic Hebrew Grammar* (1927), p. 70. Most of these forms also exist in Jewish Palestinian Aramaic, and it is difficult to say which way the borrowing went.

[7] I do not feel qualified to judge whether Amharic *as*- is a survival or a re-formation from *asta*-.

Though matters are by no means as clear as in the cases we have discussed hitherto, it is worth pointing out that the dialects which in the end chose *h*- ('-) lie along the same axis as those which reduced the ternary tense system, and that Modern South Arabian, this time in common with the eastern part of the Old South Arabian area, was left out of the development. Interesting is also that the '- area is, so to say, geographically embedded in the *h*- area. I would suggest that '- is not an independent original alloform of the morpheme, but a re-formation from *yaqtilu*, which arose through phonetic causes from $y^{a}/_{i}$*haqtilu*. This type of imperfect is found in combination with *h*- perfect in Hebrew, Ya'udic, Biblical Aramaic (together with *yhqm* and one instance of perf. *'qtl* and one of inf. *'qtlt*), and Amorite. It would be consistent with the chronology of the appearances of perf. *'qtl* that it arose first in Phoenician (written *yqtl*[1]) and spread thence across Aramaic, Early Arabic (Old Arabic had *h*-), and Ethiopic.

CONCLUSIONS

Each of the cases of cross-group isoglosses discussed above has to be judged on its own merits. Some may turn out to be incorrect, but there are others which I believe to be demonstrable as belonging to this class.[2] However, even a very few cross-group isoglosses call into question the entire theory of ethnic-migration origin of the various 'languages', even outside the North-west Semitic area, where it seems to have been conclusively disproved. The ethnic-migration theory presupposes that the bearers of the various 'languages' arrived in their later locations as colonizers, i.e. groups with some consciousness of their difference from other groups, whom they either partly or wholly displaced or with whom they established common frontiers. Now we have, indeed, some instances of diffusion of linguistic features across established language borders, such as the Balkan languages and the Germanic influences in Hungarian and Estonian. These, however, mostly concern matters on the surface of language structure. Extensive and repeated diffusion of innovations like the ones here discussed seem to me inherently improbable in a social situation such as envisaged by the ethnic-wave theory. There are two other possibilities, unconnected with the ethnic-migration

[1] I would suggest that the spelling indicates nothing more than that this form was felt to begin with the vowel *i*, and not with a glottal stop.

[2] Such as the definite article, the distribution of the third person pronouns *hū* and *šū* and of the first person pronouns *'n* and *'nk*, the internal passive, &c.

theory, of explaining these and similar phenomena. One is the substrate theory; but this would in our case involve a substrate population stretching from Phoenicia to central Arabia and across into Ethiopia, on the one hand, and another occupying most of the Fertile Crescent. This seems hardly likely. The other possible explanation presupposes parallel developments caused by factors inherent in the phonological and morphological structure of Semitic. Such parallel developments there were, no doubt; we may mention the loss of final vowels and the tendency towards a more analytical structure. Some of the examples cited in our paper may in fact represent such common tendencies, but then it still seems curious that different possible results of these tendencies should be grouped in such clear geographical fashion. On the other hand, it may be argued that innovations which are likely to spread are those which correspond to inherent tendencies of change. If correct, this would make it rather difficult to distinguish between inherent tendencies and linguistic diffusion, but would not exclude linguistic diffusion as such.

Linguistic diffusion does not work in a vacuum, but, as has frequently been shown, follows axes of social contact, i.e. trade routes, pilgrimage roads, influence of cultural or administrative centres, &c. The three areas we have established fit into this picture. The northern marginal area roughly corresponds to the Fertile Crescent, in which there were, of course, constant political, cultural, and religious currents of influence in all directions, as well as trade. The southern marginal area represents the sphere of influence of Aksum, with both its cultural isolation as a Christian state and its trade and political ties with Arabia. The central axis represents the caravan routes, which brought Arabian tribesmen into contact with the sophisticated and luxurious Mediterranean sea-coast, which thus played a similar role as Antwerp in the *locus classicus* of geographical linguistics, the distribution of the vowels in 'house' and 'mouse' in Dutch.[1] There were no doubt linguistic diffusions also from the opposite end of the caravan route, the South Arabian cities. These features, notably the spread of the broken plural, may well be the factor which is responsible for the apparent genetic unity of South Semitic.

Since the two North-west Semitic 'languages' have been proved to be comparatively late phenomena due to secondary linguistic diffusion,

[1] G. G. Kloeke, *De hollandsche expansie in de 16e en 17e eeuw* (1927), quoted in L. Bloomfield, *Language* (1933), p. 328, and in other standard works on linguistics.

we may well apply similar tests to the remaining three 'languages'.[1] Babylonian and Assyrian are set apart from the other languages of the Fertile Crescent margin primarily through their common conservativism and their treatment of the laryngeals, which is likely to be due to substrate; for the rest there was the strong influence of certain centres, notably Babylon. The South Arabian–Ethiopic group is such a loose conglomeration that the question of a 'proto-South Arabian' could hardly be seriously discussed. The common features are evidently due to the cultural and trade influence of the Minaean and Sabaean centres. For Arabic the present writer has attempted to show[2] that Classical Arabic resulted from the contact of two originally distinct dialect groups, neither of which was sufficiently unified to be called a language. However, even if this thesis is not accepted, a consideration of the various dialects of Old Arabic (Ancient North Arabian, also called 'proto-Arabic'), the early dialects, and Classical Arabic shows that there were deep-rooted differences preceding the apparent homogeneity created by the adoption of Classical Arabic as the language of culture and administration, and its subsequent profound influence upon the colloquials.

It thus becomes clear that the trend of evolution within each 'language' was not from a unified speech imported by a wave of immigrants towards later diversification, but from a dialect cluster towards more or less pronounced common features. As the existence of transition dialects on the border between North-west Semitic and Arabic and on the border between Arabic and South Arabian shows, these dialect clusters at first shaded imperceptibly into each other, or in other words, the Semitic area was a homogeneous whole, the divisions in which are due to subsequent linguistic diffusion.

[1] None of these Semitic 'languages', of course, was in historical times a language in the ordinary sense of the word, except perhaps for post-Islamic Arabic. They were what is called 'dialect clusters', a term usually reserved in Semitic philology for the Gurage group of Ethiopic.

[2] In *Ancient West-Arabian*.

NOTES ON THE ARAMAIC OF THE *GENESIS APOCRYPHON*

By H. H. ROWLEY, *Manchester*

THE last of the major scrolls from Qumran Cave I to be unrolled was the text which had previously been thought to be the lost Lamech work, but which proved to be the Aramaic work now called the *Genesis Apocryphon*.[1] Five columns of this have been published by N. Avigad and Y. Yadin,[2] and it is reported that parts of eight more columns have been deciphered.[3] An important and valuable study of its language in relation to older and younger forms of Aramaic has been published by E. Y. Kutscher,[4] who has been criticized for attempting this study by P. Kahle[5] on what seems to the present writer doubtful grounds.[6] Various other studies of this scroll have been made,[7] but none on the scale of

[1] In character it is a sort of Targum of the book of Genesis, but with Midrashic additions in places. Cf. P. Kahle, *The Cairo Geniza* (2nd edn., 1959), p. 198. It is described as a Midrash by R. de Vaux, *R.B.* lxiv, 1957, p. 624, M. R. Lehmann, *R.Q.* i, 1958–9, p. 251, G. Lambert, *La Secte de Qumran* (Recherches Bibliques IV, 1959), p. 105, and A. Dupont-Sommer, *Les Écrits esséniens* (1959), p. 293.

[2] *A Genesis Apocryphon* (1956).

[3] Cf. R. North, *C.B.Q.* xxi, 1959, p. 342.

[4] 'The Language of the "Genesis Apocryphon": a preliminary study', in *Aspects of the Dead Sea Scrolls* (Studia Hierosolymitana IV, ed. by C. Rabin and Y. Yadin, 1958), pp. 1–35.

[5] Op. cit., p. 199.

[6] Kahle objects that it is more important to utilize other Aramaic fragments found in the Qumran caves than the inscriptional texts of the Nabataeans and Palmyrenes, and that new critical editions of Jewish, Samaritan, and Christian texts are needed before they can be used. So far as Nabataean and Palmyrene are concerned, we can only use the texts that have survived, and they have been used hitherto by S. R. Driver (*Introduction to the Literature of the Old Testament*, 9th edn., 1913); W. Baumgartner (*Z.A.W.* xlv, 1927, pp. 81–133; reprinted in *Zum Alten Testament und seiner Umwelt* (1959)); and the present writer (*The Aramaic of the Old Testament* (1929)—referred to below as *A.O.T.*) in discussions of the place of Biblical Aramaic in the pre-Targumic Aramaic dialects. So far as the critical edition of Jewish, Samaritan, and Christian texts is concerned, it can scarcely be thought that Kutscher should have prepared these critical editions before undertaking a preliminary survey of the language of the *Genesis Apocryphon*, or all discussion of the language of this text would be precluded for many years. So far as the other Aramaic fragments from Qumran are concerned, they are not all published yet, and while they may throw additional light on the language of the *Genesis Apocryphon*, their study may be helped by the study of this larger text, so far as it is yet published.

[7] Studies dealing with aspects of the language of the scroll have been made by S. Zeitlin, *J.Q.R.*, N.S., xlvii, 1956–7, pp. 245 ff.; E. Y. Kutscher, *J.B.L.* lxxvi, 1957,

Kutscher's. In the present essay I wish to limit myself to a comparison between the Aramaic of the scroll and that of the book of Daniel, though reference will be made to other texts, albeit on a lesser scale than Kutscher's.

I

In the matter of consonantal changes which took place within Aramaic, the scroll aligns itself closely with the Aramaic of Daniel.

(1) Whereas in surviving older Aramaic texts Hebrew ז, when it corresponds to Arabic ذ, is represented by ז, and in the fifth-century texts from Egypt is normally represented by ז but sometimes by ד as in later Aramaic,[1] the scroll uniformly has ד, as in the Aramaic of Daniel, e.g. אדין II. 8, 11, XXI. 20; דכר II. 9; דנא II. 2, 17, XX. 28 (?); כדבין II. 6 f.; דא XIX. 10, 19; דרעיהא XX. 4; דהב XX. 33; מדבח XXI. 20; מדבחא X. 15, XXI. 1, 9.

(2) Whereas in older Aramaic Hebrew צ, when it corresponds to Arabic ض, is represented by ק, and in the fifth-century texts from Egypt is represented sometimes by ק and sometimes by ע as in later Aramaic,[2] the scroll uniformly has ע as in the Aramaic of Daniel, e.g. ארעא XIX. 10, XX. 13, 16, XXI. 10, 12 f., 15 f.; עובע XX. 9;[3] ענה XXII. 2; לעורעון XXI. 31.[4]

(3) Whereas in older Aramaic Hebrew שׁ, when it corresponds to Arabic ث, is represented by שׁ, the scroll uniformly has ת as in the

pp. 288 ff.; M. R. Lehmann, *R.Q.* i, 1958–9, pp. 249 ff.; P. Grelot, ibid., pp. 273 ff.; A. Dupont-Sommer, op. cit., pp. 291 ff.; and J. A. Fitzmyer, *C.B.Q.* xxii, 1960, pp. 277 ff. A Concordance to the scroll marked by a number of errors and omissions has been published by H. Lignée, *R.Q.* i, 1958–9, pp. 163 ff.

[1] Cf. *A.O.T.*, pp. 16 ff. Since the publication of this work the Brooklyn Papyri (referred to below as B.A.P.) have been published by E. G. Kraeling in *The Brooklyn Museum Aramaic Papyri* (1953), and a collection of Aramaic documents on leather from Egypt (referred to below as A.D.) by G. R. Driver in *Aramaic Documents of the Fifth Century B.C.* (1954) (an abridged and revised edition appeared in 1957). These bring much additional evidence, but rarely divergent evidence on the points here discussed. It may be added that in the Qumran Aramaic fragment of the *Testament of Levi*, published by J. T. Milik in *R.B.* lxii, 1955, p. 400, we find אדין col. II. 15, and באדין, line 11.

[2] Cf. *A.O.T.*, pp. 30 ff. In the Aramaic *Prayer of Nabonidus* from Qumran, published by Milik in *R.B.* lxiii, 1956, p. 408, we find אעא, line 8.

[3] This word now supplies the missing link between עבק (A.P. XXVI. 6, 22, XLII. 7 f., 13, Aḥ 103; A.D. IX. 3) and Targumic אבע (A.P. = the Aramaic Papyri published in A. Cowley, *Aramaic Papyri of the Fifth Century B.C.*, 1923). It was already postulated by P. Grelot (*J.S.S.* i, 1956, 202 ff.) before the publication of the scroll (cf. *J.S.S.* ii, 1957, p. 195).

[4] This word is not found in Biblical Hebrew, where it would be ערץ, but it is found in Egyptian Aramaic (cf. *A.O.T.*, p. 30). In the Targum of Onkelos the same form is found, but in the Targum of Jonathan we find the dissimilated form ארע, which is found also in Syriac.

Aramaic texts from Egypt (save in the word שקל[1]) and in the Aramaic of Daniel,[2] e.g. תרין XX. 8; תרתין XX. 18; תלת XXI. 27, XXII. 6; תלתהון XX. 8; תבת XXI. 19; תמן XXI. 1 ff., 20; יתב XXI. 5; תורא XXI. 16.

(4) Whereas Hebrew שׂ is represented in older Aramaic by שׂ, and so still in the Egyptian Aramaic texts, save in a few doubtful cases, in the scrolls we also find שׂ uniformly, while in the Aramaic of Daniel we find שׂ, with a few exceptions where ס is found,[3] as in later Aramaic,[4] e.g. שגי XIX. 27, XX. 8, XXII. 32; שגיא XX. 7; שער XX. 3; שמאל XXI. 8, XXII. 10; עשרה XXI. 26 f.; מעשר XXII. 17; שנאיך XXII. 17.

In all these respects the language of the scroll belongs to the same broad period of development as the Aramaic of Daniel. This period lies somewhere between that represented by the fifth-century Egyptian Aramaic texts and that represented by the Targums.[5] As the Palmyrene texts of the first to third centuries A.D., which share the first three of these usages with the Aramaic of Daniel and the scroll, in the fourth show a preference for ס as against שׂ,[6] we may perhaps conclude that the scroll seems to lie between the period of the Papyri and that of the Palmyrene texts.

II

In the matter of terminal ה or א, the scroll appears to be somewhat later in its usage than the book of Daniel.[7]

(1) The termination of the feminine singular absolute in Daniel is predominantly ה, as in older Aramaic, including the texts from Egypt.[8] There are, however, some exceptions, both in Daniel and in the older texts. In the scroll א is usually found, e.g. חדא XII. 16, XIX. 15; קדישא XIX. 8; חכמא XX. 7; אנתא XX. 9; באישא XX. 17; עלא XXI. 20; מנחא XXI. 20. ה is found, however, in אנתה XX. 27, 34; מנחה XXI. 2.

(2) Similarly for the termination of the emphatic state, Daniel usually

[1] This appears as תקל in A.P. X. 5, and in B.A.P. II. 8.

[2] Cf. *A.O.T.*, pp. 28 ff. So also we find תרתי in the Qumran Aramaic fragment published by M. Baillet in *R.B.* lxii, 1955, p. 223, line 14.

[3] In Dan. iii. 27, the Qumran Daniel fragment published by D. Barthélemy in *Qumran Cave I* (1955), p. 151, reads שרבל[יהון] for M.T. סרבליהון. But this word is probably a loanword, and not quite in the category here referred to. In the Qumran Aramaic fragment published by Baillet, loc. cit., we find עשר, line 13.

[4] Cf. *A.O.T.*, pp. 33 ff. [5] Cf. ibid., pp. 155 f. [6] Cf. ibid., pp. 34 ff.

[7] Cf. Kutscher, *Aspects of the Dead Sea Scrolls*, pp. 26 ff.

[8] Cf. *A.O.T.*, pp. 41 f.

has א, as throughout the Aramaic dialects, but with a number of exceptions.[1] In the scroll א is found in almost all instances, e.g. הריאתא II. 1, 15; עולימא II. 2; בעליא II. 4; רבותא II. 4; קושטא II. 5; ענתא II. 10; קדישא II. 14; רבא II. 14; זרעא II. 15; מדבחא X. 15; שתא XII. 15; כפנא XIX. 10; רבתא XX. 14; רוחא XX. 20, 28; נכסיא XXI. 3. ה is found, however, in חלמה XIX. 18; ענה XXII. 2; מרה XX. 15.

(3) Daniel uses מה = *what?*, and this is the common usage throughout the older texts, where the word is found.[2] Here the scroll has מא, as in the Targum of Onkelos, viz. XX. 3 ff., 26. It is to be observed, however, that we already find מא in Ezra vi. 8, and that מה is found in the Targum of pseudo-Jonathan. Moreover, in the scroll we find כמה, XX. 2, beside כמא, XX. 2 ff., and למה, XX. 32, beside דלמא, XXII. 22.

(4) For the first personal pronoun singular Daniel normally has אנה, as in older Aramaic, including the Egyptian texts, but once has אנא,[3] the form found in the Targums. The scroll has אנה, e.g. II. 3, 10, 14, 19, 24, XIX. 14, XX. 10 f., 33, XXI. 6 f., 10, 21.

(5) For the demonstrative pronoun Daniel uses the form דנה, which agrees so far as the termination is concerned with the form זנה, used in older Aramaic, including the Egyptian Aramaic texts.[4] Here the scroll prefers the form דן, which is close to the Targumic form דין (see below, III (6)). The form דנא, also found in the Targums, is found occasionally, e.g. II. 2, 17, XX. 28 (?).

(6) For the termination of verbs with weak third radical Daniel uses ה or א without any consistent distinction, whereas the Egyptian texts discriminate between words originally ל״א, which have א, and verbs originally ל״ו and ל״י, which have ה.[5] The scroll normally has א,[6] e.g. הוא XIX. 10, XX. 20, XXII. 2, 15; בעא XX. 9, 24; יאא XX. 4, 8; שרא XXII. 13; ימא XX. 30. Forms with ה, however, are also found, e.g. אתה XX. 21, XXI. 23, XXII. 1, 13; רמה XXII. 8; קנה XX. 34; אצלה XX. 21; יצלה XX. 23; יחה XX. 22 f.; תהוה XXII. 22; אהוה XXII. 30.

[1] Cf. ibid.
[2] Cf. ibid., p. 41.
[3] Dan. ii. 8. So also Ezra vi. 12, but elsewhere in Ezra אנה; cf. *A.O.T.*, p. 40. In the fragment of the *Testament of Levi* published by J. T. Milik in *R.B.* lxii, 1955, p. 400, we find אנה, I. 6, II. 14. For the first personal pronoun plural, cf. below, III (3).
[4] Cf. *A.O.T.*, p. 40. The form זנא is found in one passage in the Elephantine Papyri, in B.A.P. IX. 16.
[5] Cf. *A.O.T.*, pp. 43 ff.
[6] In the Qumran Aramaic fragment published by Baillet in *R.B.* lxii, 1955, p. 227, we find יתכלא, line 6, and in the *Prayer of Nabonidus*, published by Milik, ibid. lxiii, 1956, p. 409, we find דמא, line 4.

(7) Daniel has the form כחדה, which is found also in Egyptian Aramaic.[1] Here the scroll has כחדה, e.g. XXI. 21, 25, XXII. 1; cf. also חדא[2] XIX. 15, and לחדא XX. 33.

(8) The form דלמא is found in the scroll in XXII. 22. This form approximates closely to the Targumic form דילמא. The corresponding form is not found in the Aramaic of Daniel, but in Ezra vii. 23 we find די למה.

(9) For the proper name Shaveh (Gen. xiv. 5, 17) we find in the scroll both שוה, XXI. 29, and שוא, XXII. 14.

(10) The numeral מאה is found in Dan. vi. 1. In the scroll we find the form מאא, XXII. 6.[3]

It will be seen that while there is no uniform usage in the scroll, there is a stronger preference for א than is found in Daniel, and this would suggest that the usage of the scroll is somewhat later than that of Daniel. Since Nabataean and Palmyrene still employ some forms with ה, there is no need for us to presume any long interval between Daniel and the scroll.

Here it may be noted that J. A. Montgomery attributes the inconsistencies in this respect in Daniel to scribal confusion.[4] It is, of course, certain that there was sometimes such confusion, since the manuscripts are not always in agreement.[5] But the fact that no manuscript has any consistent usage strongly suggests that the original text was without consistency, and that the Aramaic of Daniel, like that of the scroll and the Nabataean and Palmyrene inscriptions, comes from a time when usage was fluid.

III

In the pronominal forms, again, the scroll stands very close to Daniel.

(1) With Daniel it uses הוא and היא, as against הו and הי of the Egyptian Aramaic texts and of Nabataean and Palmyrene,[6] e.g. הוא XIX. 7, 20, XX. 10; היא XX. 27, XXII. 13.

[1] Cf. *A.O.T.*, p. 67.

[2] In the Qumran Aramaic fragment published by Baillet, loc. cit., p. 223, we find חדא, line 15.

[3] In the Qumran Aramaic fragment published by Milik, loc. cit., p. 412, we find מאה, B 2; so in that published by Baillet, loc. cit., p. 227, line 8.

[4] Cf. *Daniel* (1927), p. 18.

[5] It may be noted that in the Qumran Daniel fragments published by Barthélemy in *Qumran Cave I*, pp. 150 ff., נחוה is found for M.T. נחוא in Dan. ii. 4, ענא for M.T. ענה in ii. 5, and דמא for M.T. דמה in iii. 25.

[6] Cf. *A.O.T.*, p. 51. It should be noted that the Palmyrene Tariff has הא also, and this form is found in the Zenjirli inscriptions (cf. *A.O.T.*, ibid.).

(2) In the *k^ethîbh* of Daniel we find the form אנתה = *thou*, as against אנת of the Egyptian Aramaic texts and of Palmyrene.[1] Here the scroll has אנתה, e.g. XIX. 7, XX. 12 f., 15, XXI. 9.

(3) Daniel has the form אנחנא, as against אנחנה and אנחן[2] of the Egyptian Aramaic texts,[3] and אנחנה of Ezra.[4] The scroll has the Targumic form אנחנא, XIX. 12.

(4) Daniel employs the form אלן = *these*,[5] as against אלה of the Egyptian texts and of Ezra.[6] In agreement with Daniel the scroll has אלן, e.g. XIX. 23, XX. 25, XXI. 23, 25, XXII. 27. This form is found in Palmyrene.

(5) For the relative pronoun Daniel has די, as against the older זי, found still in the Egyptian Aramaic texts.[7] The scroll has די, but with the occasional use of ד, as in later Aramaic, not found in Daniel, e.g. די in XX. 6, 8, 15, 21, 27, XXI. 1, 8; בדי II. 20; כדי II. 12, 21, XX. 8, 10, 11, 24; but ד in XX. 27, XXI. 29, XXII. 14, 21 f.

(6) For the demonstrative pronoun Daniel uses דנה, as against זנה in older Aramaic.[8] The Egyptian Aramaic texts normally have זנה, but occasionally דנה.[9] The scroll has דנא in II. 2, 17, XX. 28 (?), and elsewhere דן, e.g. II. 15, XVI. 12, XVII. 16, XIX. 17 f., 21, XX. 9, 12, 15 f., 19, 26, XXI. 4, 16, XXII. 21, 34. This approximates to the Targumic form דין.

(7) Daniel employs the demonstrative דכן, which is peculiar to it, and hence not found in the scroll or elsewhere.[10]

(8) For the prepositional suffixes the usage agrees with that of Daniel, save that

(*a*) in the scroll we find לכא, V. 9, as against לך in Daniel, and

[1] Cf. *A.O.T.*, p. 50. אנת is found also in the Targum of pseudo-Jonathan. The Targum of Onkelos has את, which is the form found in the older Aramaic texts (cf. *A.O.T.*, ibid.). In the fragment of the *Testament of Levi* published by Milik in *R.B.* lxii, 1955, p. 400, we find אנתה, I. 10, and so in the *Prayer of Nabonidus*, ibid. lxiii, 1956, p. 409, line 4.

[2] When *A.O.T.* was published, only a few occurrences of אנחן were known in the Aramaic Papyri. Now many further examples are known, viz. B.A.P. III. 3, 5, 7, 10, 12 f., 15, 20 f., V. 11, 13 f., XII. 12.

[3] Cf. *A.O.T.*, p. 51.

[4] In Ezra v. 11 אנחנא stands. For the interchange of ה and א, cf. also above, II.

[5] In Dan. ii. 40, vi. 3, vii. 17 we find אלין. In the Qumran fragment published by Milik in *R.B.* lxiii, 1956, p. 414, אלן occurs, Fc 2.

[6] Cf. *A.O.T.*, p. 56.

[7] Cf. ibid., p. 57.

[8] Cf. ibid., p. 56.

[9] Cf. ibid., p. 21. To the single reference there given we may now add B.A.P. V. 3, X. 3.

[10] This word appears in one Palmyrene inscription (*C.I.S.* ii. 4174, line 6, and *P.E.F.Q.S.*, 1928, p. 101; a good facsimile of the text is given in J.-B. Chabot, *Choix d'inscriptions de Palmyre* (1922), plate XXV, no. 3, but Chabot is doubtful if it is to be identified with the pronoun found in Daniel (cf. *C.I.S.* ad loc.).

מנכה, XX. 26, as against מנך in Daniel. Elsewhere the scroll has the same form as in Daniel, e.g. לך II. 14, XX. 27, XXI. 8, מנך II. 15, XXII. 31.

(*b*) in the scroll וי— is found once, in אחוי, XXI. 34, instead of והי—, as in Daniel, which stands elsewhere, e.g. אבוהי II. 20, 22, 24; עלוהי XX. 18, 22 f., XXI. 2; אחוהי XXII. 3; קודמוהי XXII. 9; חברוהי XX. 8.

(*c*) in the scroll הא— is found for the third person singular feminine,[1] as against ה— in Daniel, e.g. עליהא VII. 1; אנפהא XX. 3; אנפיהא XX. 2; מנהא XX. 6; שפרהא XX. 7; עמהא XX. 7; נסבהא XX. 9; דילהא XX. 10; דרעיהא XX. 4; ידיהא XX. 4 f., 7; רגליהא XX. 5; בעלהא XX. 23. A few examples of ה—, however, are found in the scroll, e.g. ראישה XX. 3; חדיה XX. 4; כפיה XX. 5.

(9) Daniel inserts *nun energicum* before the verbal suffixes with the imperfect, save in יבהלך, Dan. iv. 16, where the jussive is employed. This usage is found in the Egyptian Aramaic texts alongside forms without the *nun*. Palmyrene also has forms with and without the *nun*.[2] The scroll uses forms with the *nun*, e.g. תחוינני II. 5 f.; יחזנה XIX. 23; ירתנני XXII. 33.

In all these respects we have a usage in the scrolls little different from that in Daniel, save in (7) and (8) (*c*), but with a tendency to show later usage.

IV

In verbal forms the scroll shows a slightly more marked tendency to reflect a usage later than that of Daniel.

(1) For the second person masculine singular of the perfect Daniel always has ת, except in Dan. ii. 41, where we twice find חזיתה, and Dan. v. 27, where we find תקלתא. In the scroll we have עבדתה XX. 26; עברתה (or עבדתה) XXII. 28; נפקתה XXII. 28; אצלתה XXII. 19.

(2) For the third person masculine plural of the perfect the scroll normally has forms in ו—, in agreement with the usage of Daniel, e.g. תקפו XX. 18; גברו XX. 18; יכלו[3] XX. 20; עקרו XX. 21; אכלו XXI. 21, XXII. 23; אשתיו[4] XXI. 22; עבדו XXI. 24; מחו XXI. 28;

[1] Similar forms are found in the Hebrew text of 1QIs[a].

[2] Cf. *A.O.T.*, pp. 64 f.

[3] The imperfect form יכולון XX. 19 is to be compared with יְכֻל in Dan. iii. 29.

[4] With prosthetic א, exactly as in Dan. v. 3 f.

דבקו XXI. 29, XXII. 10; נפקו XXII. 30. Two forms in ון— are found in the scrolls, viz. אתון XIX. 26; בעון[1] XIX. 15. More anomalous is the form הווא = *they were*[2] in XIX. 24, XXI. 26, 28, with which may be compared שבוא[3] XXII. 10.

(3) For the third person feminine plural of the perfect we find in the scroll the form שלמא XXII. 28.[4] This is the Targumic form. In Daniel the termination ו— is found in the *k^etĥibh*, but the *ḳ^erê* has ה—.[5]

(4) In the causative of verbs[6] Daniel usually prefixes ה—, in agreement with the usage of older Aramaic, including the Egyptian Aramaic texts, but three times has א—, as in later Aramaic.[7] The scroll here aligns itself with later usage and uniformly has א—, e.g. אשכח[8] XXII. 7; אצל[9] XXII. 10; אתיב XXII. 12, 24; אתיבני XXI. 3; אכליאת XIX. 16; אקרבת XXI. 2; אוספת XXI. 6; אסקת XXI. 20.

Similarly, for the prefix of the reflexive stems Daniel normally has הת—, but occasionally את—, as in later Aramaic.[10] Here the scroll has את—, e.g. אשתעי XIX. 18; אתפלי XX. 29; אתחזי XXI. 8; אתחלם XXII. 5; אתבניאת XIX. 9; אתעירת XIX. 17; אתחננת XX. 12; אתחזיו XXII. 27; אזדמנו XXI. 25; אתכנשנא XII. 16; לאשתעיא XIX. 18; באתעצבא XX. 12. It is to be noted, however, that here the Egyptian Aramaic texts already use the prefix את—.[11]

[1] In אתו ובעון, where both terminations stand side by side.

[2] The same form is found for the singular in XXII. 8 f.

[3] Cf. שבאו XXII. 12.

[4] H. L. Ginsberg (*J.N.E.S.* xviii, 1959, p. 146) argues that אשתני II. 12 is third person feminine plural.

[5] Cf. *A.O.T.*, pp. 77 f.

[6] A Shaph'el form was found by Avigad and Yadin in שחלנפא XX. 26, but P. Grelot (*R.Q.* i, 1958–9, pp. 273 ff.) proposed to read שחלניא and to derive from the root שחן. He has been followed by A. Dupont-Sommer (op. cit., p. 301) and J. A. Fitzmyer (*C.B.Q.* xxii, 1960, p. 289). H. Lignée (*R.Q.* i, 1958–9, p. 184) reads שתלניא, but offers no explanation of the form.

[7] Cf. *A.O.T.*, pp. 80 f. For the interchange of ה and א in terminations, cf. above, II. In the Qumran fragment of the *Testament of Levi*, *R.B.* lxii, 1955, p. 400, we find ארחק, I. 12, and in the Qumran fragment published by Milik in *R.B.* lxiii, 1956, p. 414, we find אטעו, Fa 1, while in the *Prayer of Nabonidus*, ibid., p. 408, we find החוי, line 5.

[8] Here this word has its usual Aramaic meaning *find.* In XXI. 13, however, it has the meaning *be able*, a Syriac sense not hitherto exampled in Palestinian Aramaic; cf. Fitzmyer, loc. cit., p. 283.

[9] On the meaning of this word and אצלתה XXII. 19, cf. M. R. Lehmann, *R.Q.* i, 1958–9, p. 262, where it is observed that it does not mean *rescued*, as Avigad and Yadin render, but *took away*, as Cowley renders A.P. VIII. 18, XVIII. 3 (cf. IX. 10), and as Kraeling renders B.A.P. II. 13, IV. 20, VI. 15, X. 10.

[10] Cf. *A.O.T.*, pp. 79 f. In Dan. iii. 24 the Qumran Daniel fragment published by Barthélemy in *Qumran Cave I*, p. 151, reads באת[בהלה] for M.T. בהתבהלה.

[11] Cf. *A.O.T.*, p. 80. Further examples are now provided by A.D. IV. 3 (אשתמעו), VIII. 3 (אתעשת), VIII. 4 (אשתבק), XIII. 1 (אתנצח), and by B.A.P. XII. 6 (אשתאר).

(5) In the imperfect of the causative of verbs, Daniel usually retains the preformative —ה—, in agreement with the usage of older Aramaic, including the Egyptian texts. There are, however, some examples of the omission of this —ה— in both Daniel and the Egyptian texts.[1] In the scroll this —ה— is omitted, e.g. אשגה XXI. 13; יתיבו XX. 25. In Nabataean and Palmyrene and in later Aramaic this —ה— is similarly omitted.

(6) The passive of Peʿal, or Peʿil, is found in Daniel and in the scroll, e.g. קטיל XXII. 3; קטילת XX. 10; שביק XIX. 16; שביקת XX. 10; דבירת XX. 11; שימא XXII. 10. This usage is found in Nabataean and Palmyrene,[2] but not in later Aramaic.

(7) In פ״ן verbs the first radical is usually unassimilated in Daniel, in agreement with the usage of the Egyptian Aramaic texts and also of Nabataean, whereas in Palmyrene and in later Aramaic it is normally assimilated.[3] There are a few cases of assimilation in Daniel, however. In the scroll we find both usages, e.g. אנפק XXII. 14; למנתן XXII. 24; אנתננה XXI. 14; but יפוק XXII. 34; מפקך XXII. 30; אסב XX. 22; אצל XXII. 10.

(8) In the Peʿal imperfect of ידע Daniel inserts —נ—, whereas in the Egyptian texts this is not done.[4] The scroll follows the usage of Daniel, e.g. ינדע II. 20; אנדע XIX. 18; cf. וינדעון XX. 15. So also with the infinitive, למנדע[5] II. 22.

(9) In the causative of עלל Daniel sometimes introduces —נ—, as the Egyptian Aramaic texts almost always do, and sometimes does not, in agreement with Palmyrene and later Aramaic usage.[6] The only occurrences in the scroll are without this —נ—, viz. יעלן XX. 6; מעלנא XIX. 14.

In all these respects there is little to distinguish the usage of the scroll from that of Daniel, but such evidence as there is points to a slightly later stage of development for the language of the scroll.

[1] Cf. *A.O.T.*, pp. 83 f. Further examples of the omission of —ה— in the Aramaic Papyri are now known, e.g. B.A.P. IX. 21, X. 15 (ינפקון); B.A.P. II. 13 (אנצל); B.A.P. IX. 21 (יכהילוו).

[2] Cf. *A.O.T.*, p. 84. In the Qumran Aramaic fragment published by Baillet in *R.B.* lxii, 1955, pp. 223 f., we find יהיב, line 17, and יהיבת, lines 15 f.

[3] Cf. *A.O.T.*, pp. 86 f. In the Qumran Aramaic fragment published by Milik in *R.B.* lxiii, 1956, p. 413, we find למנתן, C 2, while in that published by Baillet, ibid. lxii, 1955, p. 223, we find ויסבון, line 9. In the text published by M. Testuz in *Semitica*, v, 1955, p. 38, we find סב, line 3.

[4] Cf. *A.O.T.*, p. 88.

[5] Cf. the noun מנדע, which stands in the fragment of the *Testament of Levi*, *R.B.* lxii, 1955, p. 400, I. 14.

[6] Cf. *A.O.T.*, p. 90.

V

A few particular words call for notice.

(1) In Daniel we find the word אנפוהי, with unassimilated *nun*. Similar forms are found in the Egyptian Aramaic texts, whereas the *nun* is assimilated in Palmyrene.[1] In the scroll the *nun* is unassimilated, as in Daniel, e.g. אנפי II. 12; אנפיך II. 17; אנפיהא XX. 2, 4; אנפהא XX. 3. It is to be noted, however, that similar forms are found in the Targum of pseudo-Jonathan, whereas in the Targum of Onkelos the assimilated forms are found.

(2) In the scroll we find *nun* unassimilated or intrusive in certain words which are not found in Daniel:

(*a*) ענתא = *time*, II. 10. In Egyptian Aramaic this word is found both with and without the *nun* in כענת and כעת, both of which are found also in Ezra.[2]

(*b*) אנתא = *woman*, XX. 9; אנתה XX. 27, 34; אנתת XX. 25; אנתתי XIX. 17, 24, XX. 14 f.; אנתתך XX. 27; אנתתה XX. 23. In Egyptian Aramaic this form is frequently found, but in one passage the form without the *nun* stands.[3] The normal Targumic form is איתא or אתא, but in the Targum of pseudo-Jonathan the form אנתא is found.

On the other hand, whereas in the Egyptian Aramaic texts we find שנתא = *year*, in the scroll we have the assimilated form, which is found in the Targums, שתא XII. 15.

(3) In Daniel we find the form באתר[4] = *after*, alongside בתר, which is found in later Aramaic.[5] In the scroll we find only the form בתר, e.g. בתר XII. 10, XXI. 5, XXII. 27; לבתר XIX. 23; בתרהון XXII. 7. This word is not found in the Egyptian Aramaic texts, which use אחרי. This is found also in Daniel and in the scroll, in אחריך XXI. 14.

(4) The form לות, which is found in the Egyptian Aramaic texts and in Ezra, is not found in Daniel,[6] but is found in the scroll in the form לואת, e.g. לואתי XXI. 5, 7. Later Aramaic knows the form לות.

(5) The word הן = *if* is found in Daniel. This is found also in older Aramaic, including the Egyptian Aramaic texts, and in Nabataean and Palmyrene.[7] Palmyrene has also אן, which is found in later Aramaic texts

[1] Cf. ibid., p. 110. In the Qumran Aramaic fragment published by Milik in *R.B.* lxiii, 1956, p. 413, we find אנפיהון, C 1.

[2] Cf. *A.O.T.*, p. 67.

[3] A.P. XXXIV. 3 (*ter*).

[4] Cf. Zenjirli באשר.

[5] Cf. *A.O.T.*, p. 71. In the Qumran Aramaic fragment published by Milik, loc. cit., p. 412, בתר stands, A 2.

[6] Cf. *A.O.T.*, p. 71.

[7] Cf. ibid., pp. 71 f.

(also written אין). The scroll has both forms, e.g. הן II. 5, XX. 19; אן XXII. 21 f.

(6) The word אדין is found in Daniel, as in the Egyptian Aramaic texts,[1] but not in later Aramaic. It is found also in the scroll, e.g. אדין II. 8, 11, XXII. 20; באדין II. 1, 3, 13, XX. 21, XXII. 2, 18.

(7) The particle איתי = *there is* is found in Daniel, as also in the Egyptian Aramaic texts.[2] It is found also in the scroll in XXII. 19, 22, 29. Here it should be noted that Nabataean provides many occurrences of the same form, whereas Palmyrene has אית, in agreement with the Targumic form. It is to be noted, however, that the form אית is found once in Egyptian Aramaic.[3]

(8) The form מרא = *lord* is found in Daniel and in some older Aramaic texts, including the texts from Egypt. The same form is found also in Nabataean and Palmyrene, while Palmyrene has also the form מר. In a few instances, mostly doubtful, the form without the א is found in Egyptian Aramaic texts.[4] In the scroll we normally have the form without the א, e.g. מרי II. 9, XX. 12, 14 f., 25, XXII. 18, 32. Here we should note the occasional use in the scroll of the construct form מרה, e.g. מרה שמיא VII. 7, XII. 17, XXII. 16, 21; מרה רבותא II. 4; מרה עלמיא XXI. 2.

(9) Daniel uses the form גוא in בגוא, לגוא,[5] מן־גוא, whereas the Egyptian Aramaic texts have בגו.[6] Here the scroll has לגו, II. 10.

(10) The prohibitive particle אל is found in Daniel, as in older Aramaic, including the Egyptian texts.[7] It is also found in the scroll, e.g. אל תקוצו XIX. 16; אל ישלט XX. 15; אל תדחל XXII. 30.

(11) תניאני = *again* is found in the scroll in XXI. 1, whereas Daniel has תנינות in Dan. ii. 7. Here Kutscher notes[8] that the form found in the scroll is found in Samaritan Aramaic.

(12) למחרתו כן, which stands in the scroll in XXI. 10, is rendered by Avigad and Yadin 'on the morrow'. No word for *tomorrow* is found

[1] Cf. *A.O.T.*, p. 67. In the Qumran fragment of the *Testament of Levi*, *R.B.* lxii, 1955, p. 400, we find אדין, II. 15, and באדין, II. 11.

[2] Cf. *A.O.T.*, pp. 75 f. Further examples in Egyptian Aramaic are now known in A.D. V. 2, VIII. 1, XII. 9, B.A.P. VII. 29, 35 f.

[3] B.A.P. VII. 31.

[4] Cf. *A.O.T.*, pp. 111 f.

[5] In Dan. iii. 24 the Qumran Daniel fragment published by Barthélemy in *Qumran Cave I*, p. 151, has [ל]גו for M.T. לגוא. So also has the text with superlinear pointing published by H. L. Strack in *Gramm. des Biblisch-Aramäischen* (6th edn., 1921), p. 33*, in Dan. iii. 15, 21, 23, 24. In the Qumran Aramaic fragment published by Milik in *R.B.* lxiii, 1956, p. 412, we find גוא, B 2.

[6] In the Egyptian texts it has the meaning *therewith*.

[7] Cf. *A.O.T.*, p. 68.

[8] Cf. *Aspects of the Dead Sea Scrolls*, p. 13.

in the Aramaic of Daniel, but this word would seem to connect with the Hebrew מחרת. H. L. Ginsberg proposes[1] to read למחרתי כן and to render 'on the morrow of that'.

(13) בטלל, which is found in the scroll in XIX. 16, is rendered by Avigad and Yadin 'for the sake of'; cf. בטליכי XIX. 20 'for thy sake'. This word is not found in Daniel, but is found in the Aramaic Papyri; cf. בטלל A.P. XXXVIII. 5 (Cowley 'with the help of'), בטלה Beh. 5, 13, 28 (Cowley 'by the protection of'), מן טלא ל B.A.P. V. 9 (Kraeling 'before'). Kraeling suggests[2] that the root may be נטל, but this seems unlikely. If Kraeling is right in taking the following word, סמשא, to mean 'the sun-god' (written unusually with ס), the meaning 'under the protection of' would be appropriate. It is to be noted that in the scroll, as in the papyri, there is a single ל when there is an addition at the end of the word.[3] In the Aramaic texts on leather לטלא is found in A.D. XIII. 3. Here Driver connects[4] it with טלאי = *patch* and renders 'all right'. In that case it is quite unconnected with the other words here referred to. It is possible, however, that it is to be connected with them, and that it should be rendered 'under protection', i.e. *safely*.

In all these cases we find little to distinguish the usage of the scroll from that of Daniel. Such evidence as there is points to a slightly later date, since where a difference can be found it is usually in the direction of the later usage, save in the case of לואת, where we may have merely a *plene* spelling, such as can be paralleled in the Hebrew text of 1QIs[a]. A number of similar *plene* spellings can be found in the scroll,[5] e.g. אתבניאת XIX. 9; אכליאת XIX. 6; ראישה XX. 3; הואת XX. 17, 27, XXII. 25; ארגואן XX. 31; תניאני XXI. 1; משריאתי XXI. 1; עלואן XXI. 2; תמניאת XXII. 6.[6]

VI

In Daniel we find a number of Hebraisms, such as אלפים, אנשים, מלכים. As Hebraisms are also found in the Egyptian Aramaic Papyri, where we are certainly dealing with original documents, we do not need

[1] Cf. *J.N.E.S.* xviii, 1959, p. 148.
[2] Op. cit., pp. 185 f.
[3] Cf. Fitzmyer, loc. cit., pp. 287 f.
[4] Cf. *Aramaic Documents of the Fifth Century B.C.* (1954), p. 36.
[5] Cf. יתאעל, which stands in the Qumran Aramaic text published by M. Testuz in *Semitica*, v, 1955, p. 38, line 4.
[6] Cf. also קושט II. 7, 10, 18, and תוקף XX. 14, which can be similarly paralleled from 1QIs[a]. In the fragment of the *Testament of Levi*, *R.B.* lxii, 1955, p. 400, we find קשט, I. 12, II. 9.

to regard these as scribal errors in the text of Daniel. In the scroll we find similar Hebraisms in עלמים II. 4, 7, XX. 13, XXI. 10, 12, beside עלמיא XXI. 2, 14.

The causative of the verb נצל in Daniel has sometimes been regarded as a Hebraism. This is probably incorrect.[1] It is found in Egyptian Aramaic, and also in the scroll, e.g. אצל XXII. 10; אצלתה XXII. 19.[2]

VII

Finally, we may note a few expressions which are common to the scroll and the book of Daniel. Here it is possible that the scroll has been influenced by the Biblical text, though it is equally possible that both were reflecting the idiom of their age.

(1) In the scroll we find לבי עלי משתני II. 2 and לבי עלי אשתני II. 11. With this may be compared the expression צלם אנפוהי אשתנו in Dan. iii. 19.

(2) In the scroll we find ביצבא = *of a surety* in II. 20. With this may be compared מן־יציב Dan. ii. 8; cf. also iii. 24, vi. 13, vii. 16.

(3) In the scroll we find באש עלי in XXI. 7. With this may be compared באש עלוהי in Dan. vi. 15.

(4) In the scroll we find נשמתי לגו נדנהא in II. 10. With this may be compared אתכרית רוחי בגוא נדנה in Dan. vii. 15. Many modern editors have emended the Biblical text to read for the last two words בגין דנה[3] or בגו דנה,[4] on the basis of the LXX[5] and Vulgate.[6] It is now clear that this is unnecessary, and the meaning 'within its sheath',[7] i.e. *within the body*, is quite satisfactory.[8]

(5) In the scroll we find צלם אנפיהא in XX. 2. The same expression is found in צלם אנפוהי in Dan. iii. 19.

[1] Cf. *A.O.T.*, p. 131.

[2] Avigad and Yadin found *waw* consecutive in ויבן XXI. 6, but Ginsberg (*J.N.E.S.* xviii, 1959, p. 148) reads ובן, and so Kutscher (*Aspects of the Dead Sea Scrolls*, p. 15).

[3] So K. Marti, *Daniel* (1901), p. 53; B.D.B., p. 1102; Ges.–Buhl (17th edn., 1921), p. 915; J. A. Montgomery, *Daniel* (1927), p. 306; Bauer–Leander, *Kurzgef. Bibl.-Aram. Gramm.* (1929), p. 62; A. Bentzen, *Daniel* (1937), p. 32; Koehler–Baumgartner (1953), p. 1098.

[4] So R. H. Charles, *Daniel* (1929), pp. 188 f.

[5] *ἐν τούτοις*.

[6] *in his*.

[7] So A.V. marg. So also M. Stuart, *Daniel* (1850), p. 217; S. Oettli and J. Meinhold, *Die geschichtlichen Hagiographen und das Buch Daniel* (1889), p. 302; Fabre d'Envieu, *Le Livre du Prophète Daniel*, II. i (1890), p. 601; A. A. Bevan, *Daniel* (1892), p. 124; H. L. Strack, op. cit., p. 52*.

[8] Cf. Fitzmyer, loc. cit., pp. 282 f. On the equivalence of בגו and לגו, cf. Kutscher, *Aspects of the Dead Sea Scrolls*, pp. 29 f.

(6) In the scroll we find לעלא מן in XX. 7. With this may be compared עלא מנהון in Dan. vi. 3.

(7) In the scroll we find בחזוא די ליליא in XXI. 8. The same expression is found in Dan. ii. 19 (cf. vii. 2, 7, 13).

Little can be based on these expressions, save that they emphasize the closeness of the links between the language of the scroll and the Aramaic of Daniel.

VIII

While most of the points that have been examined could singly sustain no firm argument, their cumulative weight makes it clear that the language of the scroll is very close to that of the Aramaic parts of the book of Daniel, though slightly later. To define with precision how much later is less easy. Avigad and Yadin[1] think that the present copy of the scroll was made at the end of the first century B.C. or in the first half of the first century A.D. S. Birnbaum would date this copy on palaeographical grounds in the third quarter of the first century A.D.,[2] while on the same grounds Avigad would date it very close to 1QIs^{a},[3] which he ascribes to the second half of the second century B.C.[4] Unless there is evidence that we have the author's autograph copy, we can only suppose that the composition of the work is older than the present copy.[5] Kutscher would place the composition of the work on linguistic grounds in the first century A.D. or possibly the first century B.C.,[6] but Kahle thinks[7] it was older than the first century B.C. On linguistic grounds there is nothing to preclude a date in the second century B.C., since there is nothing that would require any long interval between the date of the Aramaic of Daniel and the language of the *Genesis Apocryphon*.[8]

[1] Op. cit., p. 38.

[2] Cf. *B.S.O.A.S.* xxi, 1958, p. 185.

[3] Cf. *Aspects of the Dead Sea Scrolls*, p. 74.

[4] Ibid., p. 69.

[5] Cf. Kahle, op. cit., p. 199.

[6] Cf. *J.B.L.* lxxvi, 1957, pp. 288 ff.; also *Aspects of the Dead Sea Scrolls*, p. 20.

[7] Op. cit., p. 199.

[8] It lies outside my purpose to discuss other evidence relative to the dating of the composition. Fitzmyer (loc. cit., p. 277) thinks it is dependent on the book of Jubilees, while R. de Vaux (*R.B.* lxiv, 1957, p. 624) is less sure as to which is the earlier work. Several writers have discussed the reference to Pharaoh's courtier, who is apparently given the name Hyrcanus, as a possible indication of the age of the work (cf. F. Altheim and R. Stiehl, *Philologia Sacra* (1958), pp. 54 f., where the work is dated in the early part of the first century B.C.; G. Lambert, *La Secte de Qumran*, pp. 95, 106 f.; J. Coppens, ibid., pp. 109 ff.), but this seems to me highly doubtful.

JESAJA XV–XVI

Von WILHELM RUDOLPH, *Münster/Westf.*

DASS in das Moaborakel Jeremias (Jer. xlviii) nachträglich größere Stücke aus Jes. xv–xvi eingeschoben sind, ist heute weithin anerkannt. Da es aber nicht die Pflicht des Erklärers des Jeremia-Buches sein kann, zugleich eine Exegese von Jes. xv–xvi mitzuliefern, habe ich mich in meinem Jeremia-Kommentar (2. Aufl., 1958, 261) mit dem Satz begnügt, daß 'Jes 15, 1–16, 12 nach Ausscheidung des Orakels 15, 9; 16, 2. 12 eine elegische Darstellung des durch den Angriff Jerobeams II. heraufbeschworenen Schicksals Moabs in klarer Ordnung gibt, was hier freilich nicht bewiesen werden kann'. Dieser Beweis soll hier nachgeholt werden. Ich hoffe, dafür auch das Ohr des Jubilars zu gewinnen, der schon mehrfach zu einzelnen Versen des Stückes das Wort genommen hat (s. u.).[1]

ÜBERSETZUNG

xv. 1 Ausspruch über Moab.
Es ist so: in der Nacht, da Ar überfallen wurde,
ward Moab vernichtet,
es ist so: in der Nacht, da Kir überfallen wurde,
ward Moab vernichtet.
2 Hinaufstieg die Tochter Dibon
auf die Opferhöhen zum Weinen,
auf Nebo und (in) Medeba
muß Moab heulen,
jedes Haupt ist kahlgeschoren,
jeder Bart gestutzt.
3 Auf seinen Straßen geht man im Trauergewand,
auf seinen Dächern herrscht Klage,
auf seinen Plätzen heulen sie alle,
in Tränen zerfließend.

[1] Von der Identifizierung der vielen Ortsnamen soll nur dann die Rede sein, wenn diese nicht in Jer. xlviii vorkommen. Ich verweise auf die Ortsliste in meinem Kommentar, S. 263–5.

4 Aufschreit Cheschbon und Eleale,
daß es bis Jahaz vernehmbar ist.
Darum zittern die Lenden Moabs,
die Seele zittert ihm.

5 Mein Herz schreit um Moab,
geht doch sein Fluchtweg bis Zoar [zum dritten Eglat],
ja, die Steige von Luchit
steigen sie weinend hinauf,
ja, am Wege nach Choronaim
erheben sie Geschrei über den Zusammenbruch,
6 ja, die Wasser von Nimrim
werden zur Öde,
denn verdorrt ist das Gras, verschwunden das Kraut,
kein Grün mehr zu sehen.
7 Darum: das Letzte, das sie erworben,
und was ihnen blieb —
über den Pappelbach
nehmen sie's mit sich.
8 Denn das Geschrei erfüllt ringsum
Moabs Gebiet;
bis Eglaim geht sein Heulen,
bis Beer Elim sein Heulen.

xvi. 1 'Sendet Lämmer
dem Landesfürsten
aus der felsigen Wüste
zum Berg der Tochter Zion:
3 schaffe doch Rat,
wirke Entscheidung,
mach gleich (dem Dunkel) der Nacht die Schatten
am hellen Mittag,
beschirme die Flüchtlinge,
den Fliehenden verrate nicht!
4 Laß meine Flüchtlinge [Moab] bei dir zu Gaste sein,
sei ihnen Schutz vor dem Verwüster!
Ist's dann vorbei mit dem Bedrücker, zu Ende mit dem Verwüster,
sind die Zertreter aus dem Lande verschwunden,
5 dann werde in Gnaden ein Thron aufgerichtet,
und auf ihm sitze in Treue

in Davids Zelt ein Richter,
der nach Recht fragt und im Richten erfahren ist.'

6 Wir haben Kunde vom Stolze Moabs,
des gar stolzen,
von seinem Hochmut und Stolz und hochfahrenden Sinn,
und wie unwahr sein Gerede ist.

7 Darum muß Moab heulen,
ganz Moab heulen;
um die Traubenkuchen von Kir Chareset
klagt man, völlig niedergeschlagen.
8 Denn verwüstet sind die Fluren von Cheschbon,
verschmachtet der Weinstock von Sibma,
von dessen Edeltrauben bezwungen wurden
die Herren der Völker,
der bis Jaeser drang,
in die Wüste sich verlor,
dessen Ranken sich ausbreiteten,
hinüberdrangen zum Meer.

9 Drum weine ich mit Jaesers Weinen
um den Weinstock von Sibma,
ich netze dich mit meinen Tränen,
Cheschbon und Eleale;
denn auf deinen Herbst und deine Lese
ist ein Hussa gefallen.
10 Es schwindet Freude und Wonne aus dem Fruchtgefild,
und in den Weinbergen fehlt Jubel, fehlt Freudenschrei.
Kein Kelterer keltert Wein in den Kufen,
das Jauchzen ist still geworden.
11 Darum klagt mein Herz um Moab wie Zitherklang
und mein Inneres um Kir Cheres.

* * *

xv. 9 Ja, die Wasser von Dimon sind voll Blut,
doch ich füge zu Dimon noch Weiteres hinzu:
für die Geretteten Moabs Angst
und für seinen Rest Schrecken,
xvi. 2 und so soll's geschehen: gleich flatternden Vögeln beim aufgestörten Nest

werden die Töchter Moabs an den Furten des Arnon.
12 Und mag auch erscheinen, mag auch sich abmühen
Moab auf der Opferhöhe,
mag es zu seinem Heiligtum kommen, um zu beten —
es richtet nichts aus.

* * *

13 Das ist das Wort, das Jahwe vormals über Moab geredet hat.
14 Aber nun hat Jahwe also geredet: in drei Jahren — gleich den
Jahren eines Taglöhners — wird die Herrlichkeit Moabs trotz
all der großen Menge verächtlich sein und der Rest arg gering,
nur ganz winzig.

TEXTKRITISCHE UND ANDERE EINZELBEMERKUNGEN

xv. 1. כי am Anfang kann nur afformativ sein (ebenso 5 f., 8 f.).—לֵיל, verglichen mit לֵיל xvi. 3, ist von 𝔐 trotz xxi. 11 als st. cstr. gedacht (Kittel[1]), muß es aber nicht sein (König, § 337y). Also entweder: 'in der Nacht, da Ar Moab verwüstet wurde, wurde es vernichtet' (was, weil fast tautologisch, wenig sinnvoll), oder: 'bei Nacht (vgl. D.S. בלילה) wurde Ar Moab verwüstet, vernichtet' (wobei das Asyndeton sehr hart ist). Besser die Trennung von Ar (Kir) und Moab und dann am einfachsten und sinngemäßesten ליל st. cstr. (Procksch, Scott). Dadurch wird nicht nur das Metrum gut, sondern auch der Sinn: die Eroberung der Hauptstädte bedeutet die Vernichtung des Landes (zu der Konjektur von Ehrlich כְּלִיל ist kein Anlaß). עָר sucht man in Muḥaṭṭat el-ḥağğ am südlichen Arnonufer oder wegen der Lautähnlichkeit in *Αρεοπολις* (nach Euseb = Rabbat Moab, heute Rabba), mehr als 20 km südlich vom Arnon; auf jeden Fall also lag die Stadt an der großen Nord-Süd-Straße, an der auch קיר liegt, das sicher = el-kerak, dem heutigen Hauptort im Süden von Jordanien, wohl identisch mit קיר חרשׂ(ת) xvi. 7, 11; 2 Reg. iii. 25 f. Die Parallelität von ער und קיר widerrät, ער hier für einen Landschaftsnamen zu halten (gegen Gazov-Ginsberg in: *Palestinskij sbornik*, 1959, Nr. 67, S. 12 ff.; vgl. *Z.A.W.* lxxii, 1960, 84). Daß Ar und Kir identisch seien (Buhl), braucht nicht angenommen zu werden (Procksch), obwohl D.S. beidemal עיר hat. Unmöglich ist es, in קיר ein kollektives Appellativ ('jede Stadt') zu sehen (gegen König).

2. 𝔐 'es (Moab) stieg hinauf zum Hause (= zum Zentralheiligtum) und Dibon auf die Höhen' (so König) ist unmöglich, da die Hervorhebung von Dibon trotz Power (*Biblica*, xiii, 1932, 437 ff.) nicht recht verständlich ist. Entweder steckt in הבית ein verstümmelter Ortsname (Kittel, Oort u. a.),

[1] Bloße Autorennamen beziehen sich auf die Verfasser der betreffenden Jesaja-Kommentare.

oder man liest mit Duhm עָלְתָה בַּת דִּיבֹן.—עַל־ hier 'auf', nicht 'über' (Procksch).—יְיֵלִיל abnorm für יְיֵלִיל (vgl. D.S. יליל); auch ראשיו mit *ô* ist abnorm (aber wohl nicht 'dialektisch', Kittel), l nur ראשׁ parallel זקן; D.S. hat ראשׁו.—'Gestutzt' kann sowohl גרועה als auch גדועה heißen (Driver, in *Die Welt des Orients*, i, 1947, 29, hält גד׳ für die ursprüngliche Form).

3. Die ungleichen Suffixe sind wohl kaum ursprünglich. L c B.H.³ Maskulinsuffixe (D.S. stellt überall Femininsuffixe her). Am Schluß der ersten Zeile fehlt ein Wort (vgl. B.H.³), aber nicht מִסְפֵּד o. ä., weil sonst der Ausfall unerklärlich wäre, sondern am ehesten יְנֹהוּ oder נָהוּ.—ירד ב׳ heißt nicht 'hinabsteigend (auf die Plätze) unter Weinen' (Procksch; vgl. auch Driver: *Z.A.W.* lxix, 1957, 77), sondern ist prägnante Ausdrucksweise: während sonst das 'Hinabsteigen im Weinen' vom Auge ausgesagt wird, ist es hier direkt auf die Person bezogen, also: 'zerfließend in Tränen'.

4. 𝔐 'die Gerüsteten Moabs erheben Kriegsgeschrei' paßt nicht, l c B.H.³ חֲלָצָיו, und nicht יָרִיעוּ, sondern יָרֵעוּ (Wurzel ירע, wie gleich nachher: hap leg, aber durch arab. *wr'* 'schwach, furchtsam sein' in seiner Bedeutung bestimmt). Daß D.S. mit ירע (statt ירעה) das Imperfekt von רעע meine (יֵרַע: 'es ist ihm in der Seele übel': Nötscher in *Vet. Test.* i, 1951, 299), ist unwahrscheinlich. Man würde das Femininum תרע erwarten.

5. In לבי ist die 1. Person zu belassen (vgl. xvi. 9, 11), da die 3. Person, auf Moab bezüglich, neben dem Namen Moab selbst eine ganz unbeholfene Ausdrucksweise wäre.—In בריחה ist zunächst das richtige Suffix herzustellen: ה֫– (= וֹ), auf Moab bezüglich, aber auch das Wort selbst ('Riegel') gibt keinen Sinn, kann auch nicht für 'Fürsten' stehen (König), sondern ist (vgl. 𝔗 'um zu fliehen'; D.S. ברחוה = בְּרָחוּ?) בְּרִיחֹה zu vokalisieren: 'seine Flüchtlinge' (koll.) (𝔊 ἐν (ἑ)αυτῇ = בְּרוּחָהּ, ebenso Θ συν τῳ πνευματι αυτης und 𝔖).—Während man den Ortsnamen ע׳ שׁ׳ heute meist als 'das dritte Egla(t)' deutet (= einem von Josephus genannten Αγαλλα?), hält Hvidberg (*Graad og Latter in det Gamle Testamente*, 1938, 108 f.) eine Ableitung für möglich, die in עגלת den Namen der Göttin Anat und in שׁלשׁ einen ugaritischen Verbalstamm findet, der irgendwelche rituellen Handlungen ausdrückt. Procksch denkt an eine falsch in den Text geratene Glosse zu אגלים 8; Glosse ist es auf alle Fälle.—יעערו: l c B.H.³ יְעַרְעֵרוּ (Pilpel von עור).

6. היה: D.S. falsch אהיא (wohl nicht Dittogr. von א, da לוא auf der vorhergehenden Zeile steht).

7. יתרה 'Erübrigtes'; dazu ist עשׂה Relativsatz (in Jer. xlviii. 36 steht deshalb der st. cstr. יתרת), doch ist wegen der folgenden Suffixe besser עשׂוֹ zu lesen. Während ופקדתם zweihebig gelesen werden kann (oder פְּקֻדַּת יָדָם ?), ist ישׂאום zu kurz für den Vers; add אִתָּם (Haplogr.).—Der 'Pappelbach' (nicht 'Weidenbach') ist der sel el-ḳurāḥī, der Unterlauf des Wadi el-ḥesā, die alte Grenze zwischen Moab und Edom (identisch mit dem Steppenbach Amos vi. 14?; s. Kittel). Warum D.S. ערבי statt הערבים hat, ist so wenig zu erklären wie sein תישׂאום statt יש׳.

8. אגלים ? Vielleicht das Αγαλλα des Josephus (s. 5)? Oder Αιγαλειμ des

Onomast. (8 Milien südlich von Areopolis)? Wegen 8a erwartet man Grenzorte, was von *Αιγαλειμ* nicht zutrifft; die Lage von *Αγαλλα* ist unbekannt.— באר אילים 'Terebinthenbrunnen'; man denkt an בְּאֵר Num. xxi. 16, also an der Nordgrenze Moabs, so daß in 8b Nord- und Südpunkt zur Beschreibung der gesamten Ausdehnung gegeben wäre (vgl. 'von Dan bis Beerseba').— יללתה 'das Geheul davon', auf זעקה bezüglich; besser תֹה– mit Bezug auf Moab. Zur Streichung des zweiten 'יל ist kein Anlaß, vgl. V. 1 und xvi. 7.

9. Bei dem häufigen Wechsel von *m* und *b* kann kaum bezweifelt werden, daß Dimon = Dibon (so D.S.) wegen des Wortspiels mit דם. An den namenlosen Bach von 2 Reg. iii. 21 f. zu denken, weil er auch rot ist wie Blut, ist unbegründet (gegen Procksch). Das Wasser von Dimon könnte ganz wohl der Arnon sein (gegen Kittel), vgl. xvi. 2 (andere denken an den Teich von Dimon). Freilich fällt auf, daß hier nun plötzlich wieder ein Ort im Norden kommt, der außerdem in V. 2 schon genannt war. Die Bedenken gegen V. 9 werden bestärkt durch die Fortsetzung, wo plötzlich Jahwe das Wort ergreift (das einzige Mal in xv. 1–xvi. 12; zu xvi. 10 s. u.); auch der Ausdruck 'ich bringe zu Dimon Hinzugefügtes (= Hinzuzufügendes)' ist in einem Zusatz, der wirklich noch etwas hinzubringt, am ehesten verständlich. Dieses 'Weitere' wäre nach V. 9b ein Löwe ('den Geretteten Moabs einen Löwen und dem Rest des Bodens'), aber 9b mit der sonderbaren Stellung von אריה ist kaum richtig. Dem könnte zwar durch die Anfügung von שַׁחַל am Schluß des Verses (Haplogr. wegen des folgenden שלח) abgeholfen werden (so Reider in *H.U.C.A.* xxiv, 1953, 87 f.). Aber was soll hier überhaupt ein Löwe (trotz 2 Reg. xvii. 25 f.)? Eine 'ironische' Auffassung des Verses (Power in *Biblica*, xiii, 1932, 435 ff.) ist ausgeschlossen. Es gibt viele Konjekturen. Ich lese יִרְאָה (oder mit Kissane אֲנִיָּה Trauer) statt אריה und אֵימָה (so auch Kissane) statt אדמה, dazu שְׁאֵרִיתוֹ.

xvi. 1. Der Imperativ שלחו ist nicht zu korrigieren, auch nicht nach 𝔊 𝔖 (gegen Procksch), da beide in V. 1 gänzlich abweichen (zu 𝔊 s. B.H.[3]; 𝔖, der den Schluß von xv. 9 herübernimmt, hat hier offenbar eine messianische Weissagung gefunden: 'über die übrige Erde sende ich den Sohn des Herrschers der Erde'; eine solche Deutung liegt sicher vor in 𝔙: *emitte agnum, domine, dominatorem terrae* [vgl. dazu Grill in: *Bibel und Liturgie*, 1955, 85 ff.], ähnlich 𝔗: 'sie werden Abgaben bringen dem Messias Israels'). 'Bringt das Lamm des Landesfürsten' ist schließlich verständlich, aber besser כָּרִים לְמ' (Procksch): *aberratio oculi* von einem מ zum anderen.—'Vom Fels in die Wüste' stimmt nicht, da ja nicht die Wüste, sondern der Zion das Ziel ist ('durch die Wüste' kann מדברה nicht heißen), l c 𝔊 𝔖 הַמִּדְבָּר 'vom Wüstenfels', d. h. aus der felsigen Wüste Edoms, in die sie xv. 7 übergetreten sind (an den Ortsnamen Selaʿ ist nicht zu denken, da dieses viel zu weit südlich liegt, auch wenn man es nicht mit Petra gleichsetzt, s. Procksch); vgl. noch Jer. xlviii. 28. D.S. hat מסלה = ?

2. V. 2 unterbricht den Zusammenhang, da das Bild von den umherflatternden Vögeln und dem aufgestörten Nest nicht auf die emsige Rührigkeit

zur Beschaffung des in V. 1 genannten Tributs (Kittel) oder gar als Aufforderung der Edomiter zur Verjagung der Moabiter (gegen Power in *Biblica*, xiii, 1932, 440 f.) gedeutet werden kann, sondern selbstverständlich ein angstvolles Umherrennen bedeutet. Zudem ist V. 2 ein Orakel, das hier völlig aus dem Rahmen fällt, da überdies die in V. 1 Angeredeten sich ganz im Süden befinden, während hier plötzlich wieder der Arnon genannt wird. Dagegen paßt formal (Orakel) und inhaltlich (Arnon) xvi. 2 hinter xv. 9: xvi. 1 und xvi. 2 sind also umzustellen (Duhm, König, Feldmann, Kissane), und xvi. 2 bildet die Fortsetzung des Zusatzes xv. 9.—'Die Töchter Moabs' sind die moabitischen Städte und ihre Bewohner (vgl. Ps. xlviii. 12).—l 'בְּמַעְ; ב Haplogr. (Procksch u. a.).

3. Wegen aβ.b l in aα auch Singular (B.H.[3]).—Für הביאי 'bringe' einfacher הָבִי 'gib', vgl. D.S. הביו.—פלילה hap leg 'Entscheidung, Urteil'; פליטה (Ehrlich, B.H.[3]) ist unnötig.—גלה hier: verraten.

4. יגורו 'es mögen weilen dürfen'.—Dem vereinfachenden Vorschlag von B.H.[3] ist doch wohl 𝔐 vorzuziehen, wobei מואב richtige Glosse ist. Dann läßt sich V. 4a als 3+4 lesen wie V. 4b als 4+3.—כי 4b ist Vordersatz zu 5 (Duhm, Procksch, Scott).—המץ: מץ hap leg, Part. von מיץ 'pressen', weshalb man 'Erpresser' übersetzt; da das zweifelhaft ist und auch der Artikel, der in den parallelen Subjekten fehlt, auffällt, l c B.H.[3] חֹמֵץ oder c D.S. חָמוֹץ (Jes. i. 17, vgl. *Vet. Test.* i, 1951, 228 und 301); ebenso l c B.H.[3 d] (persönliches Subjekt wie vorher und nachher) und B.H.[3 e] (מ Haplogr.).

5. באהל דוד gehört aus metrischen Gründen zu 5b. Das Zelt muß hier ein Bild sein für den Schutz, den der fremde Gast im Zelt des Gastgebers genießt (vgl. die phönizischen Eigennamen אהלבעל und אהלמלך), deshalb wird es nicht notwendig sein, באהל nach V. 3 in בְּצֵל zu verwandeln; dazu darf auch nicht die Übersetzung *εν σκεπη* in 𝔊[v] verführen, weil dort offenbar nur ein Schreibfehler für *εν σκηνη* vorliegt. Immerhin ist die Verschreibung sachlich bemerkenswert.—Man kann das ו vor דרש mit B.H.[3] streichen oder ו . . . ו als 'sowohl . . . als auch' auffassen.—Zu מְהִר = 'Experte, Fachmann', vgl. Ullendorff: *Vet. Test.* vi, 1956, 195; es bedarf also nicht der Änderung in שֹׁחֵר (Prov. xi. 27): 'der auf Gerechtigkeit aus ist' (gegen Ginsberg: *J.B.L.* lxix, 1950, 54 f.).

6. גא Verkürzung von גֵּאֶה, falls nicht wirklich so zu lesen ist (= D.S.). Das Adjektiv kann von גאון oder von מואב abhängen (Procksch).—'Die Unechtheit seines Geschwätzes' (Kittel u. a.) ist dem Sinn nach richtig, aber grammatisch kann לא־כן nicht als Substantiv gefaßt werden, von dem ein Genitiv abhängt, sondern das Ganze ist ein Satz: 'daß unwahr ist sein Geschwätz' (D.S. לכן statt לא־כן, aber nachher das unmögliche ולכן לוא statt לכן).

7. למואב kann heißen 'über Moab' (xv. 5) oder 'gegen Moab' (also die Moabiter gegen einander); das Metrum würde besser, wenn man ל striche und מואב zum Folgenden zöge (Ehrlich). Procksch streicht למואב ganz.—Die 'Traubenkuchen' passen gut in den Zusammenhang (8 ff.), deshalb ist

nicht Jer. xlviii. 31 אנשי vorzuziehen (gegen Ehrlich und Driver in: *Von Ugarit nach Qumran*, 1958, 43).—l c B.H.[3] הָגוּ, da die 2. Person überrascht (ת Dittogr.).

8. Auffallend der sing. masc. nach שדמות und das nachhinkende 2. Subjekt: füge vor שד׳ nach 𝔗 שֻׁדַּד ein, so daß אמלל zum Folgenden gehört (*vor* femininem Subjekt kann ja das Verbum im Maskulinum stehen; auch גפן ist Femininum, wie das Folgende zeigt; D.S. hat אמללה).—Der Rest von V. 8, der in D.S. zusammen mit V. 9a*α* wegen Homoioteleuton weggefallen ist, enthält lauter Relativsätze zu גפן. שרוקיה 'dessen Edeltrauben' (eigentlich 'rote Trauben', von שרק, der Edelrebe) ist Subjekt, בעלי ג׳ Objekt, nicht umgekehrt, da הלם auch in xxviii. 1 vom Wein ausgesagt wird (vgl. 3 Esra iii. 17–24).—יעזר: Zu dem in meinem Kommentar, S. 264, über Jaeser Gesagten ist hinzuzufügen, daß nach den Untersuchungen Gese's (*Z.D.P.V.* lxxiv, 1958, 20, 63 f.) der archäologische Befund gegen chirbet es-sīre spricht. Noth (*Z.D.P.V.* lxxv, 1959, 62 ff., bes. 69 ff.) hat die ganze Jaeser-Frage erneut gründlich geprüft mit dem Ergebnis: 'Nach wie vor bleibt die Lage von Jaeser unbekannt' (70). Doch hat inzwischen Rendtorff (*Z.D.P.V.* lxxvi, 1960, 124 ff.) einen neuen Vorschlag gemacht: tell ʿarēme südlich von es-sīre.—תעו 'verloren sich' nach Osten in die Wüste.—ים ist das Tote Meer.

9. 'Mit dem Weinen von Jaeser', d. h.: so, wie die Leute von Jaeser ihn beweinen. Vielleicht ist ב Haplogr., die Änderung in B.H.[3] ist unnötig; zu dem Änderungsvorschlag von Landes (*B.A.S.O.R.* cxliv, 1956, 31 ff.) vgl. meinen Jeremia-Kommentar, S. 260.—l c B.H.[3] und D.S. אֲרַוֶּךְ (𝔐 Schreibfehler). —Die Lesung von B.H.[3] בְּצִ׳ ist zwar sachlich richtig, trotzdem ist 𝔐 zu belassen, weil ein Wortspiel mit קיץ beabsichtigt ist.—הידד 'das Juchzen' hier vom Geschrei der Feinde, in V. 10b wie sonst vom Jauchzen bei der Weinlese; שֹׁדֵד Jer. xlviii. 32 ist viel matter.

10. V. 10a ist nur eine Zeile (4+3).—ירעע Poʿlal von der Wurzel רוע.—השבתי: das hier plötzlich auftauchende göttliche Ich ist nicht am Platze, l c B.H.[3] הָשְׁבָּת (𝔐 aus Jer. xlviii. 33?).

11. V. 11 umfaßt auch nur eine Zeile (3+4), deshalb braucht er keine Ergänzung nach Jer. xlviii. 36.

12. Hier kommt plötzlich wieder ein einzelner Vers, der ein Orakel enthält und mit seiner Umgebung in keinem erkennbaren Zusammenhang steht; dagegen gehört er mit xv. 9, xvi. 2 zusammen (vgl. Duhm).—Über die konzessive Bedeutung von כי s. Vriezen in: *Von Ugarit nach Qumran*, 1958, 272.—כי־נלאה könnte Dittogr. sein (s. B.H.[3]), könnte aber auch auf die krampfhaften kultischen Anstrengungen gehen (vgl. 1 Reg. xviii. 26 ff.); falls man es streicht, ist hinter מואב aus metrischen Gründen וְעָלָה einzufügen (Haplogr.), vgl. Ehrlich; בא statt נלאה in D.S. ist falsche Vorwegnahme aus b*α*.—ולא יוכל: 'wird nichts erreichen'; Änderungen sind unnötig.

14. שכיר eher 'Taglöhner' als 'Söldner', s. xxi. 16.—Ob כבוד und המון hier den Gegensatz von Adel und Plebs darstellen (Procksch), ist doch fraglich; der Vergleich mit V. 14b führt vielmehr auf den Gegensatz 'viel . . .

wenig' (vgl. Ehrlich).—ושאר braucht nicht geändert zu werden, die Versionen glätten.—לוא כביר: Litotes; כבוד statt כביר in D.S. (vgl. 𝕲 εντιμος) ist Verschreibung unter dem Einfluß des vorausgehenden כבוד.

AUFBAU

(*a*) Auszugehen ist von xvi. 13 f., wo das Vorangehende deutlich als eine frühere Weissagung bezeichnet wird, die jetzt wieder aufgenommen wird. Daß 'früher' 13 und 'jetzt' 14 einen *sachlichen* Gegensatz bedeute, daß also eine *Verheißung* für Moab vorausgegangen sein müsse, die jetzt widerrufen werde (Procksch), ist ganz unbegründet: der zeitliche Gegensatz braucht kein sachlicher zu sein: eine frühere Bedrohung Moabs soll sich jetzt erfüllen, offenbar weil sie sich seither nicht erfüllt hat.

(*b*) Der Nachtrag faßt also das Vorausgehende als unerfüllte Weissagung. Liegt aber in xv. 1–xvi. 12 wirklich Weissagung vor? Nur in xv. 9, xvi. 2, 12 (in xv. 9 die einzige Jahwe-Rede, s. o.), das Übrige ist teils Klage (xv. 1–8, xvi. 7–11), teils Mahnung (xvi. 1, 3–5) mit einem Bericht über die Wirkung ihrer Befolgung (xvi. 6). Nun könnte das prophetische Vorausdarstellung sein, also in Wirklichkeit doch Prophetie trotz der andersartigen Form (vgl. Kap. xxiii). Aber hier geht die Schilderung so ins Einzelne (Übertritt der Moabiter auf edomitisches Gebiet, Gesandtschaft an Juda, abschlägige Antwort), daß das nicht nur Weissagung sein kann, sondern konkrete Tatsachen voraussetzt. Also liegt abgesehen von den drei genannten Versen, die unter sich gut zusammenpassen, die aber Zusatz sind (s. o. bei xv. 9), keine Weissagung vor.

(*c*) Ist diese elegische Darstellung des Schicksals Moabs einheitlich? xv. 1–8 gehört zweifellos zur Klage über das Schicksal Moabs. Wir haben zwei Abschnitte: 1–4 der Norden, 5–8 der Süden (je 9 Zeilen; die Zäsur liegt nicht zwischen 5a und 5b, gegen Procksch und Scott, da 5a auch schon vom Süden spricht). Mit xvi. 1 kommt formell etwas Neues: Aufforderung zu einem Bittgesuch an Juda, aber inhaltlich ist dabei xv. 1–8 vorausgesetzt: xv. 7 Übertritt auf edomitisches Gebiet, von dem in xvi. 1b die Gesandtschaft ausgehen soll. xvi. 3–5 ist der Wortlaut des Bittgesuches, xvi. 6 die abschlägige Antwort. Warum diese Zuordnung sekundär sein soll (Hertzberg), ist nicht einzusehen. (xvi. 1, 3–5 hat ebenfalls 9 Zeilen, die Antwort xvi. 6 steht strophisch für sich.) Darauf bleibt den Moabitern nichts übrig als weiterhin zu klagen: xvi. 7–11 (zweimal 6 Zeilen). Freilich fällt auf, daß sich hier die Klage fast nur um den Weinbau dreht, aber wenn schon dem Ganzen historische Tatsachen zugrunde liegen, wird auch das einen konkreten Grund gehabt haben. Also handelt es sich hier um eine einheitliche Komposition. Procksch will freilich xvi. 6 ff. einer anderen Hand aus anderer Zeit zuweisen: xvi. 6 könne nicht mit dem Vorhergehenden zusammengehören, weil bisher nicht von der Hoffart Moabs die Rede gewesen sei, aber das ist keineswegs nötig (s. u.) und befremdet nur, wenn man wie Procksch Kap. xv fälschlich den Moabitern in den Mund legt (s. u.). Umgekehrt setzt der Satz, ihr Gerede sei unwahr, voraus, daß vorher, d. h. in xvi. 3–5, die Moabiter geredet haben. Auch die anderen von Procksch behaupteten Unterschiede treffen nicht zu: das Mitgefühl xvi. 9, 11 kommt ebenso in xv. 5 zum Ausdruck; auf feindlichen Einfall weist wie Kap. xv auch xvi. 8a*α*, 9b.

ERKLÄRUNG

(*a*) xv. 1–8.—Die Klage beginnt mit dem Wichtigsten, der nächtlichen Eroberung der beiden Hauptstädte und Hauptfestungen, die für das ganze Land den Ruin bedeutet. Man darf deshalb aus der Vorausstellung dieses Ereignisses nicht schließen, daß es *zeitlich* das erste gewesen sei, und daraus einen Angriff von Osten (Araber) ableiten (Marti u. a.). Der Angriff kam vielmehr von Norden, wie die Flucht nach Süden (5 ff.) zeigt. (Die Meinung von Power in *Biblica*, xi, 1930, 30 ff., und xiii, 1932, 443 ff., daß der Angriff von Süden nach Norden gegangen sei, beruht in erster Linie auf seiner These, daß Zoar im Norden des Toten Meeres liege, wogegen Abel in *Revue Biblique*, xl, 1931, 388 ff., bes. 398, zu vergleichen ist.) V. 2–4 schildern nun die Wirkung der Eroberungen von V. 1 im Norden: Klagen und Jammern (V. 2b*β*, 3 Trauerbräuche, V. 2 Anrufung der Gottheit). Daß diese Bezirke im Norden selbst verwüstet seien, wird nicht direkt gesagt (höchstens in 2b*α*, wenn man על mit ‘über’ übersetzt), ergibt sich aber aus xvi. 7 ff. und aus der Tatsache, daß der Feind von Norden kam. Die 2. Strophe (5 ff.) beginnt der Verfasser mit der Bekundung seines persönlichen Mitgefühls mit Moab, weil es die Heimat lassen und unter Weinen und Klagen mit der ihm verbliebenen Habe auf edomitisches Gebiet (7) übertreten muß. In diesem Zusammenhang kann V. 6 nicht eine Naturkatastrophe (Dürre) bedeuten (gegen König), sondern das hier Geschilderte ist auf menschliche Einwirkung zurückzuführen (Verwüstung des Landes und Verstopfung der Quellen durch den Feind; vgl. 2 Reg. iii. 25, Marti, Procksch). V. 8 faßt zum Schluß noch einmal alles Vorausgehende zusammen: innerhalb des ganzen moabitischen Gebietes herrscht Wehklage.—Die Meinung von Procksch (209, 214 f.), Kap. xv sei die Klage der moabitischen Gesandten, die sie in Jerusalem vorbringen, scheitert schon daran, daß die Aufforderung zu dieser Gesandtschaft erst in xvi. 1 ergeht (die dortige Textänderung Procksch’s ist willkürlich, da sie deutlich auf der vorgefaßten Meinung beruht), ganz abgesehen davon, daß dann Kap. xv irgendwo etwas davon verraten müßte, daß es Zuhörer voraussetzt, auf die doch Eindruck gemacht werden soll (kein ‘du’, kein ‘wir’, nur ein spärliches ‘ich’ in 5). Der Redende ist selbstverständlich der Prophet, der freilich mit Moab Mitleid hat (5).

(*b*) xvi. 1, 3–6.—Von Haus und Heimat vertrieben, suchen die Moabiter in Jerusalem Hilfe, werden aber abgewiesen. ‘Das wird hier dramatisch lebendig in Rede und Gegenrede der Beteiligten . . . ausgeführt’ (Kittel). V. 1 ist

Anrede Moabs an die Moabiter (also sachlich eine Selbstaufforderung, doch ist die 2. Person lebendiger). Sie wollen Lämmer als Tribut (vgl. den Tribut Mesas an Israel 2 Reg. iii. 4) an den Landesherrn senden 'vom Fels der (edomitischen) Wüste zum Berg Zion'. Daraus folgt mit Sicherheit, daß Edom damals unter judäischer Hoheit stand ('Landesherrscher'), nicht dagegen, daß *Moab* zu Juda in freundschaftlichem Verhältnis stand (gegen Procksch), vgl. V. 6. V. 3–5 ist der Hilferuf an Juda; sie bitten um Rat und Schutz (3a, 4aβ), um Nichtauslieferung (3b) und um Aufnahme als gērīm (4aα); für die Zeit, wo ihr Land wieder vom Feinde frei ist (4b), geloben sie Unterstellung unter die Herrschaft des davidischen Königtums: '. . . so möge in Gnaden ein Thron aufgerichtet werden, auf dem in (Vasallen-)Treue im Schutze Davids ein Richter (= König) sitzen soll, der das Recht sucht und sich auf Gerechtigkeit versteht'. Diese Auffassung fügt sich am leichtesten in den Zusammenhang; die Annahme, daß V. 5 nur ein Segenswunsch der Moabiter für das davidische Königtum sei (Kittel), ist zu schwach. Unnatürlich ist es auch, nicht bloß V. 5, sondern schon V. 4b auf Juda zu beziehen, so daß 'ein den Judäern schmeichelnder Hinweis auf die in Juda eingetretenen glücklichen Verhältnisse' die Bitte um Hilfe motiviere (König). Andere (auch noch J. Fischer, Hertzberg, Scott und Fohrer) sehen in V. 4b–5 eine messianische Weissagung, und da diese nicht von den Moabitern gesprochen sein kann, wird sie entweder als Einschub gestrichen (Marti) oder dem Propheten in den Mund gelegt, entweder als Begründung für die Hilfebitte der Moabiter (Orelli, Feldmann) — aber er kann die Moabiter nicht gut für messiasgläubig gehalten haben — oder als Antwort auf den Hilferuf (Procksch). Aber es ist nicht zu erkennen, inwiefern darin eine Antwort für sie liegen soll, es sei denn, daß ihnen die Gedankengänge der messianischen Dogmatik geläufig gewesen wären. (Vollends aus der Verwandtschaft von V. 4b mit x. 5 ff., von V. 5 mit ix. 5 f. auf Jesaja als Verfasser zu schließen, ist ganz unberechtigt, da diese Verwandtschaft nicht über Allgemeinheiten hinausgeht, die in der Sache liegen; gegen Procksch.)—V. 6 gibt die ablehnende Antwort Judas: Juda kennt den unerträglichen Hochmut Moabs von jeher (z. B. Mesa-Zeit; von diesem Hochmut im Bisherigen zu reden, war gar keine Gelegenheit, gegen Procksch), deshalb kann es das Versprechen V. 4b–5 nur als ein von der Not erpreßtes unwahres Gerede ansehen. (Der Rückverweis von 6bβ auf 4b–5 beweist für Zusammengehörigkeit, gegen Procksch.)

(*c*) xvi. 7–11.—Damit bleibt Moab nichts anderes übrig als weiter zu klagen, und zwar nun speziell über die Verheerung des Weinbaus, dessen Zentrum Kir Chareset (7, 11) und Cheschbon (8 f.) gewesen zu sein scheint (aus V. 8 geht eine weite Verbreitung des Weins von Sibma hervor, er wird 'dichterisch dargestellt als ein großer Weinstock, der sich nach allen Seiten hin weit ausbreitete' [Knobel bei Kittel]; Buhl und Procksch denken weniger gut an Traubenhandel). Diese ganze Weinkultur mit ihrem frohen Treiben (10) ist nun durch den feindlichen Überfall zugrunde gegangen (9b). Darüber klagt auch der Dichter selbst (9a, 11, vgl. xv. 5), der demnach wohl mit der brüsken Abweisung (6) nicht einverstanden war, vielleicht weil ihn irgendwelche persönliche Beziehungen mit Moab verbanden (vgl. Buch Ruth).

(*d*) xv. 9, xvi. 2, 12.—Diese drei Verse (dreimal 2 Zeilen), die formal dadurch zusammengehören, daß sie allein Orakel sind, schließen sich auch inhaltlich gut zusammen. Es handelt sich offenbar um einen Kampf am und in der Nähe des Arnon, der vor allem um die Furten geht, an denen sich die Bewohner der moabitischen Ortschaften wie aufgescheuchte Vögel drängen (xv. 9, xvi. 2; oder sind die 'Töchter Moabs' doch die Frauen [vgl. Baudissin: *Th.St.Kr.* lx, 1888, 518], die nach ihren gefallenen Männern [xv. 9aα] suchen?). Da die Katastrophe von Jahwe verhängt ist (אשית xv. 9), ist es zwecklos, wenn sich die Moabiter hilfeflehend an ihre Götter wenden (xvi. 12; der Vers setzt natürlich nicht voraus, daß es nur *eine* bāmā und *einen* miqdāš in Moab gab: 'Der Singular genügt, weil Moab einheitlich aufgefaßt ist' [Kittel]; 𝔊 mit ihrem Plural ist also sachlich im Recht). Da nun dieses Unheil in xv. 9 als '*Hinzukommendes*' bezeichnet wird, das zudem nur den Rest Moabs trifft, so geht daraus deutlich hervor, daß es sich auf ein späteres Ereignis bezieht als die übrigen Abschnitte. Wir haben es also mit einem *Zusatz* zu tun, ohne angeben zu können, was für ein Ereignis gemeint ist (wegen der speziellen Lokalisierung dürfte es sich nur scheinbar um Weissagung handeln); vielleicht hat 𝔊 recht, wo נוספות mit *Αραβες* wiedergegeben wird, daß es sich um einen Beduinenüberfall handelt. Warum die Verse jetzt auseinandergerissen sind, läßt sich nicht sagen.

(*e*) Der Nachtrag xvi. 13 f. kündet schwerste Dezimierung der Moabiter innerhalb von drei knappen Jahren als Jahwes Willen an, indem er ausdrücklich auf das vorhergehende Stück Bezug nimmt. Man braucht nicht anzunehmen, daß er sich dabei nur auf xv. 9, xvi. 2, 12 beziehe, obwohl nur hier ein Wort Jahwes (xvi. 13) im engsten Sinn vorliegt, während sonst der Prophet spricht; denn auch Propheten-Wort ist Jahwe-Wort, und daß die Klage eines Propheten über Gegenwärtiges als Weissagung gedeutet wird, ist naheliegend (vgl. König, 193).

ECHTHEIT UND ENTSTEHUNGSZEIT

(*a*) Daß das Hauptstück xv. 1–8, xvi. 1, 3–11 vorexilisch ist, folgt mit Bestimmtheit aus xvi. 5 (die davidische Dynastie regiert). Zur näheren Datierung ist zu beachten: 1. daß edomitisches Gebiet unter judäischer Oberhoheit steht (xvi. 1, 4a), 2. daß Moab Juda die Fähigkeit zutraut, ihm zu helfen, daß dieses also von dem Feind, der Moab verheert, nicht bedroht ist (xvi. 3–5), 3. daß dieser Feind von Norden kommt, weil die Flucht der Moabiter nach Süden geht (xv. 5 ff.), 4. daß das Gebiet Moabs damals über den Arnon ziemlich weit nach Norden reichte (xv. 2–4, xvi. 8 f.). Damit ist die Deutung des Feindes auf Assyrien ausgeschlossen, da hier Punkt 2 zu keiner Zeit zutraf. Die beste Lösung ist nach wie vor die Deutung auf Jerobeam II., der

Israels Grenze bis zum 'Steppenbach' ausdehnte (2 Reg. xiv. 25), also auch Moab sich einverleibte, während gleichzeitig in Juda Ussia kraftvoll regierte und auch in Edom gebot (2 Reg. xiv. 22). Daß in diesem Fall 'doch wohl Efraim als Moabs Zerstörer mit Namen genannt sein würde' (Baudissin: *Einleitung in die Bücher des Alten Testaments*, 1901, 358), ist eine unbeweisbare Behauptung. Beweisen läßt sich aber auch nicht, daß der unter Jerobeam II. lebende Prophet Jona b. Amittai (2 Reg. xiv. 25) der Verfasser sei, da ja das Stück gar keine Weissagung ist und somit das in 2 Reg. xiv. 25 über Jona Gesagte darauf nicht zutrifft. Wegen xvi. 1, 3–6 wird man eher an einen judäischen Verfasser denken, der aber vielleicht persönliche Beziehungen zu Moab hatte. König's Datierung in die Zeit des Vorvorgängers Ussias, Joas, beruht auf falscher Exegese von xvi. 4b, 5, 8a.

Ist aber das Stück älter als Jesaja, so scheidet er natürlich als Verfasser aus. Dem entspricht auch der andersartige Sprachgebrauch und die manchmal unbeholfene Darstellung (König), vor allem aber der völlige Mangel an religiösen Gedanken. Der neueste Versuch von Procksch, wenigstens xv. 1–xvi. 5 für Jesaja zu retten, ist nicht gelungen: 1. läßt sich xvi. 6 ff. nicht abtrennen (s. o.), 2. läßt sich der auffallende Stil von Kap. xv nicht damit erklären, daß Jesaja diese Worte den Moabitern in den Mund lege und sich ihrer Redeweise anbequeme (s. o.), 3. xvi. 4b–5 sind keine Worte Jesajas, sondern der Moabiter, womit der Hauptbeweisgrund entfällt, 4. im Jahre 715, in dem Procksch das Stück ansetzen möchte, war Juda von Assur nicht weniger bedroht als Moab, war also eine zweifelhafte Hilfe; auch hatte es in Edom nichts mehr zu sagen (2 Reg. xvi. 6).

Somit haben wir hier *die älteste Schriftprophetie* des Alten Testamentes vor uns.

(*b*) Diese älteste Prophetie wäre uns wohl nicht erhalten, wenn nicht ein späterer Prophet auf sie Bezug genommen hätte (xvi. 13 f.). Die nächstliegende Annahme, daß dieser Prophet Jesaja sei, läßt sich nicht damit widerlegen, daß ein Mann wie Jesaja keine fremde Weissagung übernehme. Es wird hier ja nur geweissagt, daß ein früheres Wort über Moab demnächst in Erfüllung gehen werde, ohne daß sich der Prophet mit dem ganzen Inhalt dieses Wortes identifiziert. Das verstößt keineswegs gegen die Würde Jesajas. Aber freilich: irgendeine Sicherheit ist nicht zu gewinnen.—Der Nachtrag kann ebensogut älter oder jünger als die Zeit Jesajas sein. Für die Zeit Jesajas könnte man anführen, daß 732 unter Tiglatpileser und wieder 701 unter Sanherib der König von Moab als assyrischer Vasall erscheint (Kittel 146), oder man könnte an die Verschwörung gegen Sargon um 711 denken, an der auch Moab beteiligt war (Procksch 226). Worauf sich die Voraussage der drei Jahre (xvi. 14) gründet, ist nicht zu sagen.

(*c*) Der Zusatz xv. 9, xvi. 2, 12 war wohl schon eingefügt, als der Nachtrag xvi. 13 f. dazukam. Da aber der Nachtrag keinen sicheren Terminus ad quem gibt (s. o.), läßt sich auch der Zusatz nicht datieren. Beduinenüberfälle mögen oft vorgekommen sein.

RELIGIÖSER GEHALT

(*a*) In dem Hauptstück fehlt er völlig, das ist für dieses älteste 'prophetische' Stück interessant genug. Wie ganz anders der fast zeitgenössische Amos! Bemerkenswert ist, daß kein Haß gegen Moab vorliegt, beim Propheten sogar Mitleid, das man nicht für scheinheilig und ironisch halten darf (gegen Greßmann).

(*b*) Der Zusatz und der Nachtrag enthalten den religiösen Gedanken, daß Jahwe auch Moabs Geschicke lenkt und daß (xvi. 12) Moabs Gottheit dagegen machtlos ist.

LE *QAYL* EN ARABIE MÉRIDIONALE PRÉISLAMIQUE

Par G. RYCKMANS, *Louvain*

L'HISTOIRE des institutions des États sud-arabes préislamiques n'a été entreprise qu'au cours de ces dernières années. On en trouve une première esquisse dans la contribution de N. Rhodokanakis au *Handb. der altarab. Altertumskunde* de D. Nielsen.[1] L'attention de Rhodokanakis s'est portée surtout sur l'organisation économique des diverses nations de l'Arabie du sud-ouest et des groupements dont la hiérarchie formait la structure de l'État. Cette étude est l'œuvre d'un pionnier qui a frayé la voie en un domaine presque inexploré jusque là. La chronologie sud-arabe n'en était qu'à ses débuts. Aussi ne s'étonnera-t-on pas du caractère descriptif de la contribution de Rhodokanakis.

Les institutions religieuses ont fait successivement l'objet de deux exposés dans des ouvrages encyclopédiques.[2] A part la dernière période de Saba, dont les inscriptions datées permettaient d'établir la chronologie, le reste de l'histoire religieuse des anciens États arabes ne se prêtait qu'à un exposé descriptif.

Le premier ouvrage fournissant un exposé exhaustif en matière d'institutions sud-arabes a été publié, il y a une dizaine d'années, par Jacques Ryckmans sur l'institution monarchique.[3] On y trouve, non seulement l'histoire de l'institution monarchique sous le régime des *mukarribs* et des rois, mais un aperçu sur l'organisation de la société et de sa hiérarchie politique et sociale. L'auteur a aussi le mérite de présenter son étude dans un cadre chronologique, et de frayer ainsi la voie aux

[1] 'Das öffentliche Leben in den alten südarab. Staaten', dans *Handb.* i (Copenhague, 1927), pp. 109–42.

[2] G. Ryckmans, 'Les Religions arabes préislamiques', dans M. Gorce et R. Mortier, *Histoire générale des religions*, iv (Paris, 1947), pp. 307–32, 526–34; la 2e édition a été publiée sous le même titre en volume séparé dans Bibliothèque du Muséon, xxvi (Louvain, 1951); la 3e édition, revue et corrigée, a paru dans *Histoire générale des religions*, ii (Paris, 1960), pp. 200–28, 593–607. A. Jamme, 'La Religion sud-arabe préislamique', dans *Histoire des religions* (publiée sous la direction de M. Brillant et R. Aigrain, Paris, 1956), pp. 239–307.

[3] *L'Institution monarchique en Arabie méridionale avant l'Islam* (*Ma'în et Saba*) (Bibliothèque du Muséon, xxviii, Louvain, 1951).

recherches que Mlle Pirenne a poussées plus loin en ce domaine en se basant sur la paléographie des inscriptions.

Il faut enfin signaler le travail qui se poursuit en Union Soviétique à l'initiative de Mme N. Pigulevskaja. Dans son volume *Byzance sur les routes de l'Inde*[1] aux IVe–VIe siècles de notre ère, elle a consacré un chapitre à la structure sociale du Nejran au cours du siècle qui a précédé l'hégire. Cette province était le carrefour des grandes voies caravanières de l'Arabie. Or il se fait que les sources littéraires fournissent de nombreux renseignements sur l'organisation de la société dans cette province. Confrontées avec les inscriptions, elles permettent de se faire une idée des relations entre les diverses classes sociales et entre clans et tribus, ainsi que de la condition libre et servile, et de la hiérarchie des pouvoirs.[2]

Le Dr A. G. Lundin s'est engagé, lui aussi, dans cette voie. L'examen de la terminologie sociale dans les inscriptions sud-arabes du VIe siècle l'amène à conclure à des modifications de la structure sociale de Saba, et cela notamment en ce qui concerne le *kabîr* et le *qayl*.[3] Il dégage, du sens de ces deux termes dans le contexte des inscriptions de cette période, les attributions de ceux qui étaient ainsi qualifiés.

Cet article du Dr Lundin retiendra à juste titre l'attention des historiens des institutions. Peut-être certaines conclusions paraîtront-elles trop tranchées. Ainsi l'esclavage fait-il l'objet de diverses considérations fondées sur l'interprétation de *hgn* dans Ry 512. 1 et *R.E.S.* 3904. 15.[4] Il ne faut pas, en outre, perdre de vue que l'enquête du Dr Lundin porte sur une période de temps limitée: le siècle qui précède l'hégire, période au cours de laquelle les inscriptions attribuent

[1] *Vizantija na putjach v Indiju* (Akademija Nauk S.S.S.R., Institut vostokovedenija, Moscou–Leningrad, 1951).

[2] Voir notre compte rendu de ce volume dans *Le Muséon*, lxvi, 1953, pp. 197–9.

[3] A. G. Lundin, 'Socialnoie rassloenie v južnoii Aravii, VI v. n.e.', dans *Palestinskii Sbornik*, iv (67), 1959, pp. 97–111.

[4] *Le Muséon*, lix, 1946, pp. 165–72: Istanbul 7608 bis, que j'ai publiée d'après une photographie de cette inscription, connue seulement par des extraits lorsque je l'avais publiée dans *R.E.S.* 3904. Cette inscription est mutilée: le fragment de droite de la pierre a disparu, et le début de chaque ligne manque. C'est ainsi que le sens de *hgn* à la l. 15 (. . . *hgn/'bhw*) ne peut être précisé. Dans Ry 512. 1, la construction exige que *hgn* soit interprété comme un verbe: *ḥgy/'yhr/hgn/qyln* (2) *šrḥb'l/ykml/kq*(3)*rn/'m/'ḫhw/ wmr'h* (4) *w/šrḥ'l/ḏyz'n*; la proposition introduite par *kqrn* (ll. 2 s.), 'lorsqu'il combattit', dépend d'une proposition principale qui réclame un verbe. Ce verbe ne peut être que *hgn*. Le même terme se retrouve dans *C.I.H.* 541. 23 dans un contexte mutilé. Il s'agit vraisemblablement là, comme dans *R.E.S.* 3904, d'un n. pr. ou d'une épithète d'homme. Voir aussi plus loin, pp. 153 s.

aux *qayls* un pouvoir que la tradition islamique a assimilé au pouvoir royal.[1]

Je me propose de relever dans la présente contribution les différents contextes dans lesquels les inscriptions font mention des *qayls*, afin de préciser la qualité et les attributions de ceux qui portaient ce titre.

Voyons d'abord comment se présente ce terme, et les formes sous lesquelles il est usité.

On connaît les graphies *qyl*, *qwl* et, en *scriptio defectiva*, *ql*. L'alternance des consonnes faibles *w* et *y* est bien connue.[2] L'alternance *w* et *y* est attestée également au duel: *qylyhmw*, Ry 538. 30–31; *qwlnhn*, *R.E.S.* 4176. 5. Quant au pluriel, il est connu sous les formes *'qwl* et *'ql* (*'qlhmw*, Ry 507. 1). M. Hartmann rattache ce terme à l'arabe *qâla* 'parler'.[3] Le *qawl* est 'celui qui parle, qui ordonne'. On pourrait rapprocher ce sens de celui de *'amîr* en arabe: 'celui qui ordonne, qui commande'; en hébreu, *'âmar* signifie simplement 'parler'; en arabe, *'amara* s'est sémantiquement spécifié en 'ordonner'. On verra plus loin que l'émir arabe présente certaines analogies avec le *qawl* de l'Arabie antique.

A part quelques inscriptions de la dernière période de Saba, les textes épigraphiques qui font mention de *qayls* signalent généralement à la suite de cette qualification la tribu sur laquelle ils exercent leur pouvoir.[4]

Certains *qayls* exercent leur fonction dans la tribu à laquelle ils

[1] Voir chez Lundin (p. 110) les 'huit rois de Ḥimyar' dont parle la qaṣîda ḥimyarite. Notons que Ṭabarî raconte que la reine Bilqîs, lorsqu'elle fit visite à Salomon, était, selon Ibn 'Abbâs, escortée de 'mille chefs. Ibn 'Abbâs', poursuit Ṭabarî, 'dit que les gens du Yemen nomment le chef *Qayl*, et qu'avec chaque *Qayl* il y a dix mille (hommes)' (Ṭabarî, *Annales*, éd. de Goeje, i. 2, p. 580). Après que Bilqîs se fut convertie à l'Islam, Salomon lui fait épouser un homme de sa nation, 'Ḏū-Bata', roi de Hamdân' (op. cit., p. 585). Selon Našwân ibn Sa'îd (s.v. *Bilqîs*), les principaux conseillers de Bilqîs 'étaient mille chefs dont chacun avait mille guerriers sous son commandement'. On voit que dans la tradition islamique les *qayls* sont tantôt des chefs, tantôt des rois. (Mlle J. Pirenne a réuni, sur Bilqîs, une abondante documentation tirée des sources littéraires islamiques. Ces textes ont été traduits par le regretté Philby et revus par Pirenne, qui a bien voulu les mettre à ma disposition.)

[2] Cf. A. F. L. Beeston, *Le Muséon*, lxv, 1952, p. 147; voir aussi M. Höfner, *Altsüdarab. Gramm.* (Leipzig, 1943), p. 26, § 24; pp. 93 s., §§ 77–78.

[3] '« Der Sprecher », « der sagen kann », der durch sein Wort die Masse des Volkes zum Handeln bestimmt.' M. Hartmann, *Die arabische Frage* (Leipzig, 1909), p. 445.

[4] Nous n'entendons pas par 'tribu' un groupement de nomades. Le terms *š'b* désigne, chez les populations sédentaires du Yemen, une communauté rurale ou citadine d'hommes libres, astreints toutefois à fournir certaines prestations (cf. A. G. Lundin, loc. cit., pp. 104 s.). Ces communautés n'avaient plus de tribal que le nom; mais sauf à la dernière période, elles gardaient le patronyme ancestral des éléments prépondérants du groupe. Il en était ainsi en Israël: les patronymes des tribus survécurent après leur passage à l'état sédentaire, bien que, dans l'organisation sédentaire, 'le clan, représenté par le village', vienne souvent s'y substituer (cf. R. de Vaux, *Les Institutions de l'Ancien Testament*, i (Paris, 1958), p. 29).

appartiennent. Une statue est offerte à Hawbas, à 'Almaqah et à Ḏât-Ḥimyam par des *bny/ḏyqnʿm/'qwl/šʿbn/yqnʿm/wšʿbn/yqnʿm/ḏhgrn/ʿlbm* 'banû ḏî-Yaqnaʿum, *qawls* de la tribu Yaqnaʿum, et la tribu Yaqnaʿum de la ville ʿAlabum' (il s'agit de la fraction de la tribu composée d'habitants de cette ville) (*R.E.S.* 4677). Il en est de même dans la tribu de Ma'ḏin.[1] Sous le roi 'Ilšaraḥ Yaḥḍub, des travaux sont exécutés par *'lw/m'ḏnm/'qwl/šʿbn/m'ḏnm* 'ceux de Ma'ḏinum, *qawls* de la tribu Ma'ḏinum', pour le bien-être de leur seigneur, 'Ilšaraḥ, &c. (Fakhry 95 et 94. 1). Dans *C.I.H.* 587. 2 et Ry 404. 2–3, il est question aussi de *qawls* de Ma'ḏin; mais ces deux inscriptions sont des fragments dont les noms des auteurs ont disparu. Il est peut-être question de *qayls* de Hamdân appartenant à cette tribu dans Nami 15. 4: *bny/hmdn/qyly/h*[*mdn*](?) 'banû Hamdân, les deux *qayls*, de H[amdân](?)'. La restitution est proposée par Nami. Les *qayls* de la tribu Bakîl sont mentionnés dans plusieurs inscriptions, comme on le verra plus loin. Il en est une, sous 'Ilšaraḥ Yaḥḍub, dans laquelle les *qayls*, exerçant leur autorité sur Bakîl, pourraient appartenir à cette tribu. Le roi promulgue un décret concernant les *'qwl/šʿbn/bklm/w . . . /šʿbhmw/bklm* 'les *qawls* de la tribu Bakîlum, et . . . leur tribu Bakîlum' (*C.I.H.* 599. 2).

Mais il est des cas où le *qayl* appartient à une tribu différente de celle qui lui est soumise. Sous le roi Rabbšamsum Nimrum, des travaux sont exécutés par des [*bnw/ḏ*]*nʿmt/wlḥmm/'qwl/šʿbn/shmn* '[banû ḏî]-Naʿmat et Laḥmim, *qawls* de la tribu Suhmân' (Nami 70. 1). La restitution [*bnw/ḏ*]*nʿmt* est fondée sur Nami 69. 3: *bnw/ḏnʿmt/'qwl/šʿbn/s*[*hmn*]. Quant à *lḥmm*, cette lecture correspond à la copie de Nami, tandis que la photographie de Schlobies suggérerait *lzmm*.[2] Sous le règne de Laʿzum Nawfân Yuhaṣdiq, des travaux sont exécutés par des *bnw/mḏrḥm/ . . . /'qwl/šʿbynhn/mh'nfm/wbkylm* 'banû Maḏraḥim, . . . *qawls* des deux tribus Muha'nifum et Bakîlum' (*C.I.H.* 40. 1). On constate qu'ici les *qayls* sont étrangers à l'une et à l'autre tribu chez lesquelles ils sont en exercice. On peut conclure de l'examen de ce texte que le *qayl* ne peut être assimilé au *šayḫ* issu de la tribu ou du groupe dont il est élu chef par ses contribules. Il a déjà été question plus haut de Bakîlum, sous l'autorité de *qayls* appartenant à la même tribu.[3] Une inscription commémorant des campagnes de 'Ilšaraḥ Yaḥḍub et Ya'zil Bayyin a pour auteur un *qayl* de Bakîl dont la tribu n'est pas nommée: *qyl/bklm/rbʿn/ḏrydt* (*C.I.H.*

[1] Cf. G. Ryckmans, *Les Noms propres sud-sémitiques*, i (Louvain, 1934), p. 285. (Nous citons cet ouvrage sous le sigle *R.N.P.*)

[2] Jamme lit *yḥšm* (*Le Muséon*, lxxii, 1954, p. 332, nº 496).

[3] Cf. supra.

314. 2). Le *Corpus* traduit *rb'n* par *incolae*. Il faut traduire par 'quart de Raydat', une fraction de cette tribu, fixée à Raydat.[1] Quant à Muha'nifum, cette tribu avait, sous le roi Yasirum Yuhaṣdiq, des *qayls*, des prêtres de 'Alam, vraisemblablement un sanctuaire de 'Aṯtar à Maḏab:[2] *'ršw/'lm/'qwl/š'bn/mh'nfm* 'prêtres de 'Alam, *qawls* de la tribu Muha'nifum'. Notons que cette inscription est la seule qui fasse mention de prêtres-*qayls*.

La tribu Radmân[3] est associée à la tribu Ḫawlân sous la conduite de *qayls* de la tribu de Mu'âhir,[4] qualifiés de 'seigneurs de Ḫawlân': *bn/m'hr/wḏḫwln/qyl/rdmn/wḫwln* 'bin Mu'âhir, et seigneur de Ḫawlân, *qayl* de Radmân et Ḫawlân' (*R.E.S.* 3958. 1; voir aussi *C.I.H.* 658. 1 s.; *R.E.S.* 4100. 3, que nous restituons d'après les deux inscriptions précédentes). Différents personnages, dont le dernier est Naš'ân, de la tribu Śayrum, sont qualifiés dans *C.I.H.* 648. 2 de *qayls* d'une fraction de la tribu Radmân, appelée Salfân (mentionnée comme tribu indépendante dans *C.I.H.* 621. 5): *wnš'n/ḏśyrm/[']qwl/š'bn/rdmn/ḏslfn* 'et Naš'ân, ḏû-Śayrum, *qayls* de la tribu Radmân ḏû-Salfân'. D'autre part, le roi Naša'karib Ya'man Yuharḥib promulgue un décret concernant des *qayls* de la tribu 'banû ḏû-Ḥabîb, *qayls* de la tribu Ṣirwâḥ et Ḫawlân' *bny/ḏḥbb/'qwl/š'bn/ṣrwḥ/wḫwln* (Fakhry 3. 1–2).

Des personnages appartenant à la tribu Suḫaym sont attestés sous le roi Yarîm 'Ayman en qualité de *qayls* de la tribu Sum'ay, dont un tiers est Hagarum: *b[nw]/sḫymm/'qwl/š'bn/sm'y/[š]lṯn/ḏhgrm* 'ba[nû] Suḫaymim, *qawls* de la tribu Sum'ay, tiers ḏû-Hagarim' (*R.E.S.* 4190. 2–4). Dans la même inscription sont mentionnés *qlhmw/wš'bhmw/yrsm/šlṯn/ḏhgrm* 'leurs *qayls* et leur tribu Yarsum, tiers ḏû-Hagarim'.[5]

D'autres *qayls*, de la même tribu Suḫaym, exercent le pouvoir sous le règne des fils de 'Ilšaraḥ Yaḥḏub dans la tribu de Sum'ay: *bnw/sḫymm/'b'l/bytn/rymn/'qwl/š'bn/yrsm/ḏsm'y/ṯlṯn/ḏhgrm* 'banû Suḫaymim, seigneurs de la maison Raymân, *qayls* de la tribu Yarsum ḏû-Sum'ay, tiers ḏû-Hagarim' (*C.I.H.* 538. 3–5, sous le roi Naša'karib Ya'man Yuharḥib; voir aussi Nami, *N.A.G.* 8. 4–6, sous le même roi). Des *qayls* de Sum'ay, sans mention d'appartenance tribale, sont en exercice sous le règne de 'Ilšaraḥ: *'q[wl/š]'bn/sm'y/ṯlṯn/ḏhgrm* (*R.E.S.* 3990. 3). Des hamdânites, *qayls* d'un autre tiers de Sum'ay, sont les auteurs d'une dédicace à

[1] Voir à ce sujet Ry 533. 17: *rb'n/rydt*, avec les références à cette fraction; l'inscription Ry 533 provient de Rayda. Voir infra, *ṯlṯn ḏhgrm*.

[2] Cf. *R.N.P.* i, p. 357.

[3] Cf. ibid. i, pp. 315 et 368.

[4] Cf. ibid. i, p. 368. Au sujet de Ḫawlân, cf. ibid. i, pp. 298 et 339.

[5] Pour *yrsm*, cf. ibid. i, pp. 316 s.; pour *hgrm*, cf. ibid. i, p. 298.

Ta'lab: [*bnw/rfšn/bn/h*]*mdn/'qwl/š'bn/sm'y/ṯlṯn/ḏḥšdm* '[banû Rafšân, bin Ha]mdân, *qawls* de la tribu Sum'ay, tiers ḏû-Ḥašidim' (*C.I.H.* 315. 12; à la l. 5, il est question des 'rois de Saba et ḏû-Raydân', et à la l. 19, des 'rois de Saba' sans autre précision). Les hamdânites de la tribu Bata',[1] parmi lesquels 'Alhân Nahfân, exécutent des travaux sous l'égide de Ta'lab: *'lhn/nhfn/bn/bt'/whmdn/ ... /w'wslt/rfšn/wbnyhw/bnw/hmdn/ ... / 'qwl/š'bn/sm'y/ṯlṯn/ḏḥšdm* ''Alhân Nahfân, bin Bata' et Hamdân, ... et 'Awslât Rafšân et ses fils, banû Hamdân, ... *qawls* de la tribu Sum'ay, tiers ḏû-Ḥašidim' (*C.I.H.* 305; voir aussi des banû Bata', *qayls* de la tribu Sum'ay, *C.I.H.* 181. 2 s.). Signalons enfin des *qayls* de Sum'ay, attestés sans autre précision dans *R.E.S.* 4624. 6 s.: *q*[*yl/s*]*m'y* sous Karib'il, roi de Saba.[2]

Terminons cette série de *qayls* de Sum'ay et Yarsum par les textes où ne sont mentionnés que des *qayls* de la seule tribu Yarsum: *bn/sẖ*[*ym*]*m/ 'qwl/š'bn/yrsm* 'ban[û] Suẖa[ymi]m, *qawls* de la tribu Yarsum' (*C.I.H.* 24. 3 s.); on connaît enfin un *qayl* de Yarsum sous le règne d'un roi de Sum'ay: *'mšfq/bn/srwm/qwl/yrsm* ''Ammšafaq, bin Sarwim, *qawl* de Yarsum' (*C.I.H.* 37. 5 s., sous le règne de Yuhâ'in Ḏubyân, roi de Sum'ay).

Plusieurs inscriptions font enfin mention de *qayls* de diverses tribus sans indication de leur tribu d'origine. Dans Ry 497. 5, est cité un *qylqm/ḏrḥn/m'd'/wḏ'bkrb* '*qayl* de groupe de Ḏarḥân, Ma'da' et ḏû-'Abkarib'. Le terme *qylqm* ne se présente que dans cette inscription; notons qu'il s'agit d'un texte qatabanite. On pourrait en conclure qu'en Qatabân le *qayl* était ainsi désigné, à moins que ce terme ne qualifie une catégorie spéciale de *qayls*. Nous avons traduit *qm* par 'groupe' dans Ry 497, en arabe *qawm*. Le safaïtique connaît la divinité Šay-ha-Qawm 'celui qui conduit, qui groupe le clan',[3] en arabe *qawm* 'troupe'.

Le fragment Nami 39. 2 porte *qwl/mbnḥn*; dans *R.E.S.* 4176, décret émanant de Ta'lab, il est question des *qwlnhn/ḏyhybb/wḏ/mḏnḥn* 'les deux *qawls* de Yuhaybib et de Maḏnaḥân' (l. 5); peut-être faut-il lire aussi, dans Nami 39. 2, *mḏnḥn* au lieu de *mbnḥn*. Quant aux *qayls* de Yuhaybib, *'qwl/yhybb*, ils sont qualifiés dans *C.I.H.* 37. 6 d'ancêtres du roi Yuhâ'in Ḏubyan, de Sum'ay (voir plus haut l'inscription de

[1] Cf. ibid. i, p. 289.

[2] *C.I.H.* 358. 1 fait allusion à un *qwl/sm'y* d'après Mordtmann–Mittwoch, *Sabäische Inschriften* (Hambourg, 1932), p. 14, n. 3; *C.I.H.* lit: *qwl/mrṯdm*. Dans *R.E.S.* 4712 on lit *'qwl/š'bn/s*[*m'y*]; la restitution est plausible, bien que non assurée.

[3] Cf. G. Ryckmans, 'Les Religions arabes préislamiques', 3e éd., dans *Histoire générale des religions*, ii (Paris, 1960), p. 208.

ʿAmmšafaq, *qawl* de Yarsum). Il est encore question d'un *qwl/yhybb* dans *R.E.S.* 4231, inscription qui commémore la construction d'une sépulture.

Des travaux sont exécutés par trois personnages, dont l'un est *qayl* de deux tribus: *qyl/šʿbnhn/qšmm/wmdḥym* '*qayl* des deux tribus Qašamum et Maḏḥîyum', sous le roi Yasîrum Yuhanʿim et Šamîr Yuharʿiš, son fils, en l'année 316 de l'ère de Nabaṭ.[1]

Une autre inscription datée de 574 de l'ère sabéenne (environ 450 après J.-C.) traite de la restauration d'un sanctuaire de Raḥmanân (le Miséricordieux) par des *qayls* judaïsants de six tribus différentes: *'qwl/šʿbn/tnʿbm/wwmʿm/wmd'l/wnymn/wyṯʿn/wḥlmlm* '*qawls* de la tribu de Tanʿabum, et Wamuʿum, et Madd'il, et Naymân, et Yaṯʿân, et Ḥalmalum' (Ry 520). Ces noms sont inconnus; les cinq derniers pourraient désigner des fractions de *šʿbn/tnʿbm* 'la tribu Tanʿabum'.

Un fragment cite un *qwl/yhzḥm* '*qawl* de Yuhazḥim' (*R.E.S.* 4638).

Nous avons dit déjà au début de cette enquête que l'importance des *qayls* tend à s'affirmer nettement à la dernière période de l'histoire de Saba; c'est ce que A. G. Lundin a bien mis en lumière, comme nous l'avons signalé. L'inscription chrétienne d'Abraha *C.I.H.* 541. 14–17 cite des *qayls* 'de Saba', Saḥarites et Yaz'anites, exerçant leur autorité sur des tribus vassales. Ils sont ligués contre les Éthiopiens: *'qwl/sb'/'sḥrn/mrt/wṯmmt/wḥnšm/wmrṯdm/wḥnfm/ḏḫll/w'z'nn/'qwln/mʿdkrb/bn/smyfʿ*, &c. '*qawls* de Saba: Saḥarites, Murrat, et Ṯumâmat, et Ḥanašum, et Marṯadum, et Ḥanîfum ḏû-Ḫalîl; et les Yaz'anites, les *qawls* Maʿadkarib, fils de Sumyafaʿ, &c.'. On constatera que les *qayls* appartenant à la grande tribu Yaz'ân portent simplement le titre, sans qu'il soit fait mention d'une tribu qui leur est soumise. Il en est de même dans Ry 507–9: *qyln/šrḥ'l/ḏyz'n* 'le *qayl* Šaraḥ'il ḏû-Yaz'ân'; dans Ry 508: *qyln/šrḥ'l/.../bnw/yz'n/wḥbm/wns'n/wġb'* 'le *qayl* Šaraḥ'il..., banû Yaz'ân, et Ḥabbum, et Nas'ân, et Ġaba'' (l. 1); *'qwln/.../'lht/yz'n* 'les *qawls*..., ceux de (la tribu) Yaz'ân' (l. 9). Ces deux inscriptions datent du règne de *mlkn/ysf/'s'r* 'le roi Yûsuf 'As'ar' = ḏû-Nuwâs. Une autre inscription, contemporaine des deux précédentes, est du *qyln/šrḥ'l/ḏyz'n* 'le *qayl* Šaraḥ'il ḏû-Yaz'ân'. La formule n'est plus 'X, de la tribu Y, *qayl* de la

[1] Selon A. F. L. Beeston, l'ère de Nabaṭ devait être antérieure de 50 à 75 ans à l'ère sabéenne qui date d'environ 118–110 avant J.-C. (A. F. L. Beeston, *Epigraphic South Arabian Calendars* (Londres, 1956) (en dactylographie), pp. 36 s.). Voir aussi J. Ryckmans, *La persécution des chrétiens himyarites au sixième siècle* (Publications de l'Institut historique et archéologique néerlandais d'Istanbul I, Istanbul, 1956), pp. 1–4.

tribu Z', mais 'le *qayl* X, de la tribu Y'. Le terme *qayl* semble être non plus une fonction, mais un titre, une dignité.

C'est ce qu'on constate aussi dans *C.I.H.* 621. 9, la fameuse inscription de Ḥuṣn al-Ġurâb, qui date de 640 de l'ère sabéenne = environ 525 après J.-C. On y voit cités *mlk/ḥmyrm/w'qwlhw/'ḥmrn/w'rḥbn* 'le roi de Ḥimyarum, et ses *qawls* ḥimyarites et raḥabites'.[1] Les *qayls* sont qualifiés par leur tribu d'origine; il n'est pas fait mention d'une tribu qui leur fût subordonnée. Ces *qayls* étaient des adhérents du roi judaïsant, et ils périrent avec lui dans le combat que commémore l'inscription.[2]

Il nous reste à signaler des inscriptions découvertes par le Dr B. Maisler (Mazar) au cours des fouilles de 1936–40 dans la nécropole souterraine de la ville talmudique de Beth She'arim à 20 km. au sud-est de Haifa. Beth She'arim fut, du IIe au IVe siècle de notre ère, le siège du Sanhédrin, après le transfert du foyer national et religieux de Judée en Galilée. La nécropole est établie dans plusieurs catacombes dont les entrées sont pourvues de façades monumentales, taillées dans le rocher. Les dépouilles des rabbins illustres étaient déposées dans d'énormes sarcophages qui encombrent littéralement certains de ces hypogées. Des centaines d'inscriptions et de graffites, grecs, araméens, palmyréniens, attestent que des Juifs originaires de nombreux établissements de la Dispersion dorment de leur dernier sommeil dans cette nécropole.

Un graffite grec, *OMHPITΩN*, permet de conclure que 'des Ḥimyarites' ont été transportés à Beth She'arim. Un monogramme a été lu par le Dr Ch. Z. Hirschberg: *mnḥm qwl ḥmyr* 'Menaḥem, *qawl* de Ḥimyar'; ce monogramme serait à rapprocher d'inscriptions grecques: *Μεναὴ πρεσβύτερος (τῶν) Ὁμηριτῶν*.[3] Les sarcophages des salles où furent relevés ces graffites datent du IIIe siècle de notre ère.

Il y a, me semble-t-il, deux observations à faire au sujet du monogramme. J'ai pu en examiner la photographie que M. Izhak Ben-Zvi a eu l'obligeance de me faire parvenir. Elle est moins claire que le facsimilé; si celui-ci correspond à l'original (Hirschberg décompose les lettres dans l'ordre *rmyḥwqln*), le *n* est sans emploi, de même qu'une

[1] Cf. *R.N.P.* i, pp. 315 et 369, sous *rḥb*.

[2] Cf. J. Ryckmans, *La persécution*, pp. 7–12.

[3] חיים זאב הירשברג, יִשְׂרָאֵל בַּעֲרָב (Tel Aviv, 1946), pp. 53–57 et 283 s. Voir pl. ב׳ le fac-similé stylisé du monogramme et la photographie du graffite *OMHPITΩN*. Hirschberg s'y réfère à sa première publication de la découverte, dans *Bull. of the Pal. Expl. Soc.* xi, 1944, pp. 25–34. Le Dr P. Bar Adon a traité du même sujet, ibid. xiii, 1946–7, p. 172. M. Izhak Ben-Zvi a eu l'obligeance de me signaler ce dernier article, dont il m'a fait parvenir un exemplaire. Cf. J.-B. Frey, *Corpus inscriptionum iudaicarum* (Pont. Ist. di Archeol. Crist.) ii (Città del Vaticano, 1952), p. 207, nº 1137: *MENAHΠATPOCΠPEC* (*Μεναὴ πατρὸς πρεσ[βυτέρου]*).

autre lettre, à droite, qui pourrait être aussi un *n*. Je lirais *qwln ḥmyrn* 'le *qawl* ḥimyarite' (comme plus haut '*qwln*/*ḥmrn*) au lieu de '*qawl* de Ḥimyar', ce qui supposerait *ḥmyrm*, le *m* ayant, comme en d'autres monogrammes, une double utilisation.

Ce monogramme, ainsi lu, apparaîtrait comme un anachronisme: les *qayls* du IIIe siècle sont des *qayls* exerçant leur pouvoir sur des tribus. Peut-être l'usage du terme dans les communautés juives a-t-il été à l'origine d'un changement dans l'usage de ce terme, changement que nous avons relevé chez les *qayls* judaïsants du VIe siècle.

La lecture du Dr Hirschberg soulève une autre difficulté. Les monogrammes ḥimyarites ne sont formés que de noms propres.[1] Nous aurions ici une véritable épitaphe, faite d'un composé de noms propres et d'un substantif. Faudrait-il attribuer aussi cette anomalie au caractère erratique de ce monogramme?

Dans une étude sur 'Les Origines de l'établissement des tribus d'Israël en Arabie'[2] M. Izhak Ben-Zvi, l'historien bien connu des communautés juives dans le Proche Orient, conclut de la signification du nom grec 'presbyteros', זקן, 'vieillard', qu' 'il désigne un chef d'une tribu ḥimyarite. Si nous le rapprochons de "*qawl*" ou قول sa signification sera "le Prince de Ḥimyar".'[3]

Il semble toutefois que le rôle des *πρεσβύτεροι* ne soit pas aussi considérable dans les communautés de la Dispersion. Selon J.-B. Frey, ce titre 'était sans doute conféré aux chefs des familles les plus considérées';[4] et il cite E. Schürer, qui estime que 'les *πρεσβύτεροι*, les membres de la *gerousia*, n'étaient pas des magistrats proprement dits'.[5] Dans l'inscription de Beth She'arim (Frey 1137, citée plus haut, p. 151, n. 3) *ΜΕΝΑΗΠΑΤΡΟCΠΡΕC*, le titre *πατρός* précède celui de *πρεσβυτέρου*, sans qu'il soit fait mention de dénomination ethnique. Il semble en résulter que l'appellation *Ὁμηριτῶν* dans l'autre inscription de Menaḥem indique simplement son appartenance ethnique. Nous disions que la qualification de 'père' précède celle de '*presbyter*'. Or, d'après Frey, les 'pères' peuvent avoir été chargés de 'la direction des œuvres de bienfaisance et d'assistance dans la communauté';[6] mais dans cer-

[1] Cf. J. Pirenne, *Syria*, xxxiv, 1957, pp. 210–13 (compte rendu de A. M. Honeyman, 'The Hombrechtikon Plate', *Iraq*, xvi, 1954, pp. 23–28).

[2] ארץ־ישראל, vi, 1960, pp. 130–48, dont la traduction a paru dans *Le Muséon*, lxxiv, 1961, pp. 143–90.

[3] Art. cit., traduction, p. 161.

[4] Op. cit. i, 1936, p. lxxxvi.

[5] *Die Gemeindeverfassung der Juden in der Kaiserzeit nach den Inschriften dargestellt* (Leipzig, 1879), p. 19.

[6] Op. cit. i, p. xcvi.

taines inscriptions, ce titre, et d'autres, lui 'paraissent être purement honorifiques'.[1]

Il reste à traiter brièvement de quelques contextes qui permettent de situer approximativement le *qayl* dans la hiérarchie des fonctions et des emplois en Arabie du Sud.

Le roi est qualifié de 'seigneur' (*mr'*) par le *qayl*, lorsque celui-ci cite nommément son souverain,[2] et cela même à la dernière période de l'histoire de Saba, sous le roi judaïsant Yûsuf 'As'ar = D̲û-Nuwâs: *qyln/šrḥ'l* 'le *qayl* Šaraḥ'il' et d'autres personnages commémorent les expéditions entreprises par *mr'hmw/mlkn/ysf/'s'r* 'leur seigneur, le roi Yûsuf 'As'ar' (Ry 507. 1, 2). D'autre part, le roi qualifie les *qayls* de *'dmhw* 'ses gens', 'ses sujets'; le roi Naša'karib Ya'min Yuharḥib ordonne *l'dmhw/ . . . /'qwl/š'bn/ṣrwḥ/wḫwln* 'à ses gens . . ., les *qawls* de la tribu Ṣirwâḥ et H̲awlân' (Fakhry 3. 1 s.).

Dans l'inscription Glaser 1220 publiée par G. J. Botterweck,[3] il est fait mention de deux *qayls* dont l'un serait le seigneur du dédicant. Un certain Ṣabḥhumû commémore des travaux de construction, *bt'lb/wb/r'shmw/wb/yhyf'/qwlnhn/mr'hw.* Botterweck traduit les deux derniers mots: 'den beiden Vögten ihres Herrn'. Cette traduction se heurte à deux difficultés: *qwlnhn* est à l'état absolu et ne peut admettre un génitif; le pronom suffixe de *mr'hw* est au singulier. Je traduirais: 'par Ta'lab, et par Ra'shumû, et par Yuhayfi', les deux *qayls*, son seigneur' (de Ṣabḥhumû, le dédicant). Le suffixe de *mr'hw* se rapporte à Ṣabḥhumû; *mr'* se rapporte au second des deux *qayls*, Yuhayfi', qui est qualifié de 'seigneur'.

Ainsi le *qayl* est sujet du roi, qu'il qualifie 'son seigneur'; mais il peut être qualifié du même titre par des personnages de rang inférieur.

Dans une inscription datant du règne de Yûsuf 'As'ar, *ḥgy/'yhr/hgn/qyln/šrḥb'l/ykml/kqrn/'m/'ḫhw/wmr'hw/qyln/šrḥ'l/d̲yz'n* 'Ḥaggay 'Ayhar a prêté main-forte au *qayl* Šaraḥbi'il Yakmul, lorsqu'il a combattu avec son frère et son seigneur, le *qayl* Šaraḥ'il d̲û-Yaz'ân' (Ry 512).

Le Dr A. G. Lundin[4] conclut de ce texte que Ḥaggay est le frère de Šaraḥ'il et, par conséquent, le fils de Šaraḥbi'il, d'après Ry 508. 1.[5] Lundin le tient pour un fils de femme esclave (*hgn*), ce qui explique qu'il

[1] Ibid. i, p. xcv.
[2] Cf. *R.E.S.* 4190. 2–4; Nami 70. 2, &c.
[3] *Orientalia*, xvi, 1950, p. 439.
[4] Art. cit., p. 107; voir plus haut, pp. 145 s.
[5] *qyln/šrḥ'l/yqbl/bn/šrḥb'l/ykml/bnw/yz'n.*

ne porte pas le titre de *qayl* comme son père et son frère. J'ai déjà dit plus haut que le terme *hgn* me semble, eu égard à la construction, s'entendre comme un verbe; d'autre part *'ḫhw*, de même que *'ḫwthw* dans les textes apparentés Ry 507. 10 et 508. 8, signifie 'allié'. Le tributaire Ḥaggay prête, évidemment avec des troupes dont il a le commandement, main-forte à Šaraḥbi'il dans les campagnes que celui-ci mène avec le *qayl* Šaraḥ'il, allié et seigneur de Ḥaggay. Lundin observe avec raison 'qu'au ve–vi^{e} siècle, le fils d'une esclave, reconnu par son père, entrait dans la tribu comme membre égal en droits, et occupait la même situation que son père'. Mais il estime qu'il n'en était pas de même chez les sédentaires de l'Arabie du Sud, 'où existait une gradation sociale plus fractionnée'. Cette opinion devrait être fondée sur des données plus précises. On ne trouve pas, croyons-nous, dans les textes épigraphiques, de distinction entre la situation sociale du fils de femme libre et celle du fils de femme esclave dans la famille d'un homme libre. D'autre part, l'inscription Gl 1220 citée plus haut nous apprend, comme Ry 512, que le *qayl* peut être qualifié de 'seigneur' (*mr'*) par des gens de condition inférieure.

Le *qayl* remplit parfois les fonctions de *mqtwy* (*muqtawî*) du roi. Dans Ry 538. 3–7 les *qawls* sont *mqtt* (pluriel) du roi Naša'karib Ya'man Yuharḥib, au cours des campagnes menées par le roi. Il en est de même de deux *qayls*, qui prennent part en qualité de *mqtwyy* aux expéditions militaires du roi 'Ilšaraḥ Yaḥḍub (*C.I.H.* 314. 1–4). Le roi 'Alhân Nahfân et ses fils rendent grâces à Ta'lab pour la protection dont il a entouré *kl/'qwl/wmqtt/nblw* 'tous les *qawls* et les *muqtawîs* qu'ils avaient envoyés' pour combattre l'ennemi (*C.I.H.* 308. 1 s., 16 s.). Le *muqtawî* est un 'officier', dans le sens qu'avait ce terme sous l'ancien régime. Il est le plus souvent un officier dans l'armée; mais il peut aussi remplir une charge dans la vie civile. Une *muqtawîyat* d'un bin Hamdân est chargée de percevoir la dîme pour le dieu 'Aṯtar de Bana' (Nami 14). Nous traduisons *mqtwy* par 'fonctionnaire'.[1] Ce fonctionnaire exerce un commandement sous le contrôle du pouvoir royal.

Un autre *qayl* cumule sa fonction avec celle de *mḥrg*. Le *maḥrag* est un chef de groupe; il commande, semble-t-il, à ceux qui sont chargés de faire fournir des prestations; il est souvent associé au *kbr* (p. ex.

[1] Cf. G. Ryckmans, *Le Muséon*, lx, 1947, pp. 161 s.; J. Ryckmans, *L'institution monarchique*, pp. 145 s.; Sidney Smith, *Vet. Test.* ii, 1952, p. 286, y voit 'something like "famulus"'; et en byzantin, *δομέστικος*, qui est devenu un terme militaire. A propos de la *muqtawîyat* C. Conti Rossini m'a signalé 'une *caporala*, ayant la direction et la surveillance des femmes ayant un travail commun' (lettre du 11 septembre 1947).

dans *C.I.H.* 621. 6), chargé plutôt de la direction de certains travaux.[1] Il est fait mention d'un *qwl/wmḥrg/rdmn* '*qawl* et chef de Radmân' (*C.I.H.* 648. 2).

Le *qayl* semble avoir un rang supérieur à celui des *'b'l/bytn* 'seigneurs de la maison, du clan': *lwfyhmw/wwfy/bytn/rymn/w'b'lhw/wqlhmw* 'pour le bien-être de leur maison Raymân, et de ses seigneurs, et de leur *qayl*' (*R.E.S.* 3990. 7–9). Les *'b'l* sont en relation avec Raymân, tandis que le *qayl* exerce son pouvoir sur tous ceux qui sont nommés.

Signalons enfin un texte selon lequel le *qayl*, tout en exerçant le pouvoir sur une tribu, et tout en étant un *kbr 'qynm*, un 'kabîr des 'Aqyan', personnage revêtu d'une dignité héréditaire appartenant à une ou plusieurs familles,[2] reste un 'protégé' (*'ḏr*).

Dans *C.I.H.* 599, le roi fait bénéficier des sujets d'une concession qui s'étend aux bénéficiaires: *[w'wld]hmw/wḏ''ḏrhmw/'kbrw'qynm/'qyl/s̀'bn/bklm* '[et] leurs [enfants], et leurs affiliés, les *kabîr* de 'Aqyanum, *qawls* de la tribu Bakîlum'. Selon A. F. L. Beeston *ḏ'ḏr* signifie celui qui est 'connected with protection', en hébreu, *'zr* 'défendre, protéger'.[3]

De tout ceci il ressort que le *qayl* est un sujet du roi; il exerce son pouvoir sur une tribu; il peut être investi d'une dignité héréditaire ou d'une fonction telle que celle de chef dans l'armée, de chef d'un groupe. Son importance varie avec l'importance de la tribu qui lui est soumise, et à laquelle il n'est pas requis qu'il appartienne. Il appartient souvent lui-même à une tribu illustre. A la dernière période de l'histoire de Saba, la qualité de *qayl* pourrait n'être parfois qu'un titre honorifique porté par les membres des grandes familles des tribus prépondérantes, comme le sont les émirs en Arabie sa'udite. Les membres de la famille royale y portent ce titre qui n'implique aucun exercice du pouvoir, bien que les hautes fonctions dans l'État soient assumées par ces princes. Les gouverneurs de province, issus des familles de haut rang, les chefs de certaines tribus bédouines et des chefs de localités plus ou moins importantes sont appelés émirs. Le pouvoir du *qayl* pourrait être comparé à celui d'un 'préfet'. Nous traduisons le terme *qayl* par 'préposé'.

[1] Cf. A. G. Lundin, art. cit., pp. 103 s.; N. Pigulevskaja, *Vizantija na putjach v Indiju* (Moscou–Leningrad, 1951), p. 366.

[2] Cf. N. Rhodokanakis, *Studien*, ii, p. 149; J. Ryckmans, *L'institution monarchique*, p. 180.

[3] *B.S.O.A.S.* xiii, 1949, p. 308.

COMPOUND TENSES CONTAINING THE VERB 'BE' IN SEMITIC AND EGYPTIAN

By T. W. THACKER, *Durham*

ONE of Professor G. R. Driver's greatest contributions to Hebrew and Semitic scholarship is his book *Problems of the Hebrew Verbal System*, a work which repays constant reference and study. It illuminates the early history and development of the Semitic verb and it explains phenomena in Hebrew, Accadian, and the other Semitic languages which were hitherto unclear. The present essay, stimulated by this great book, deals with certain compound verb-forms, relatively late developments, which are found in the West Semitic languages and which have their counterparts in ancient Egyptian. The significance and function of some of these Egyptian forms have not been fully appreciated and it is hoped to elucidate them with the aid of their Semitic parallels.

In historic times the West Semitic verb has two finite indicative forms which describe action. One of them is the perfect, **qatala*, formed by postfixing the pronominal elements to the stem of the verb: the other is the imperfect, **yáqtul* (Eth. *yeqáttel*), formed by prefixing the pronominal elements to the stem of the verb. There have been various attempts to define the functions of the perfect and the imperfect, both by grammarians of the individual languages and also by scholars studying the languages as a group.[1] As yet there is no consensus of opinion, but perhaps the most satisfactory and the most widely held view is that these two forms are subjective aspects. The perfect narrates an action which is completed at the moment of speaking, while the imperfect describes an action which is regarded by the speaker as incomplete or in progress. Each language has employments of the two forms which appear to conflict with this definition, but as Professor G. R. Driver has shown, such exceptions can nearly always be explained on an historical basis. They are primitive survivals which go back to the earliest stages of the Semitic languages or to the parent language whence

[1] See especially Driver, *Problems*, pp. 9 ff.; Gesenius–Bergsträsser, *Hebr. Gr.*, ii, § 3.

they were all derived, when **qatala* and **yáqtul* had wider and less clearly defined uses.

If this view of the functions of the West Semitic perfect and imperfect is accepted, it follows that these forms have no temporal connotation and that they do not correspond, for example, with any of the tenses of Latin and the modern Western European languages. They do not describe an action as occurring in past, present, or future time and the time-sphere must be inferred from the context.

There is, however, a verb in the West Semitic languages which in one of its employments is treated differently from all others, in that the choice of its perfect or imperfect is mainly dictated not by subjective aspect, but by considerations of time. This verb is the verb 'be' (Heb. הָיָה; Aram. הֲוָה, ܗܘܳܐ; Arab. كَانَ; Eth. ኮነ), when employed as the copula.[1] In Hebrew,[2] Aramaic,[3] and Arabic[4] the perfect of the verb 'be', when it has the functions of a copula, normally has reference to past time and its imperfect normally has reference to future time.[5] These forms are used when the speaker wishes to define with accuracy the time-sphere of his statement. In Ethiopic[6] the usage is less widespread and not so fixed, but there is the same general trend.

This use of the verb 'be' is well known and the following examples will be sufficient to illustrate it.

Hebrew. And the earth was (הָיְתָה) without form and void.[7]
Thou shalt be (תִּהְיֶה) over my house.[8]

Aramaic. It was (הות) no longer the land of Dargman.[9]
And Joseph was (ܗܘܳܐ) in Egypt.[10]
And the fourth kingdom shall be (תֶּהֱוֵה) as strong as iron.[11]
Thou shalt be (ܬܗܘܶܐ) blind.[12]

Arabic. And how the beginning of God's creating it was (كَانَ) and how its end will be (يَكُونُ).[13]

[1] In general, see M. Cohen, *Le Système verbal sémitique* (Paris, 1924), pp. 107–38; Brockelmann, *Grundriss*, ii, § 55.

[2] Gesenius–Kautzsch, *Hebr. Gr.*, § 141, *g–i*.

[3] Bauer–Leander, *Gr. d. Bibl.-Aram.*, § 98, *x*; Nöldeke, *Syr. Gr.*, §§ 299, 300; Duval, *Gr. syr.*, §§ 334, 336.

[4] Wright, *Ar. Gr.* ii, § 131; Reckendorf, *Synt. Verh.*, § 63.

[5] Exceptions are mainly after certain particles, in certain types of clauses, and in a few idiomatic uses.

[6] Dillmann–Crichton, *Eth. Gr.*, pp. 499 f.

[7] Gen. i. 2.

[8] Gen. xli. 40.

[9] Cowley, *Aram. Pap.* 6. 7.

[10] Exod. i. 5.

[11] Dan. ii. 40.

[12] Acts xiii. 11.

[13] Quoted in Reckendorf, *Synt. Verh.*, p. 105, n. 1.

In Egyptian the position is similar. Old Egyptian, the earliest phase of the language, possesses three primary finite narrative verb-forms (by 'primary verb-forms' are understood those which do not have the elements *n*, *ỉn*, *ḫr*, and *kꜣ* attached to the stem of the verb). The first of these is the old perfective, corresponding closely in form and function with the Accadian permansive: as an active narrative verb-form in main clauses it was already obsolescent and need not be considered further here. The other two, known as the perfective and imperfective *sḏm·f* forms, seem broadly speaking to correspond in function with the West Semitic perfect and imperfect. The perfective *sḏm·f* form, which must be carefully distinguished from the prospective *sḏm·f* form which has a jussive–optative meaning, expresses a single action or what is complete, and is often used in narrating past events.[1] The imperfective *sḏm·f* form expresses what is repeated, continuous, or incomplete, regardless of the time-sphere.[2] According to the context it may be rendered by an English past, present, or future tense.

In Middle Egyptian, the phase of the language which succeeded Old Egyptian, the position is substantially the same, except that the perfective *sḏm·f* form as a form narrating past events has been almost entirely replaced by the *sḏm·n·f* form, a form which has the preposition *n* 'to, for' in its composition.

Both Old and Middle Egyptian employ the verb 𓃹𓈖𓈖 *wnn* 'be' as copula. The perfective *sḏm·f* form 𓃹𓈖𓆑 *wn·f* has past meaning, 'he was',[3] and the imperfective *sḏm·f* 𓃹𓈖𓈖𓆑 *wnn·f* has future meaning, 'he will be'.[4] They were used when it was felt necessary to specify the time-sphere. The perfective *sḏm·f* form *wn·f* as copula is not common in Old and Middle Egyptian, but the imperfective *sḏm·f* form is much more frequently encountered:

> (When) I was (𓃹𓈖 *wn*(·*ỉ*)) a palace official . . . king M. appointed me prince and governor of Upper Egypt.[5]

[1] Gardiner, *Eg. Gr.*, § 449 (for Middle Egyptian); Thacker, *Semitic and Egyptian Verbal Systems*, p. 213.

[2] Gardiner, op. cit., § 438; Thacker, op. cit., p. 209.

[3] There is no need to assume that *wn·f* is a *sḏm·n·f* form, though there is clear evidence that Old Egyptian possessed a relative *sḏm·n·f* form from *wnn* (see Edel, *Altäg. Gr.* i, §§ 676–7; Gardiner, op. cit., p. xxxii, *addendum* to p. 94). Note that the prospective *sḏm·f* form of *wnn* is not differentiated in writing from the perfective *sḏm·f* form.

[4] Gardiner, op. cit., § 118. 2. The few examples of *wnn·f* with past meaning may well be *sḏm·n·f* forms.

[5] *Urk.* i. 105. 11. Sim. l. 17.

When I was a child, I was (*wn·i*) a Friend.[1]
I have been (*wn*(·*i*)) in the mine country and I have seen it.[2]
My wife shall be (*wnn*) there.[3]
He shall be (*wnn·f*) in the disfavour of Rēʿ.[4]

The ability of the verb 'be' to indicate time led to its employment in a number of compound verb-forms in the West Semitic and Egyptian languages in order to express various temporal nuances or to define the time-sphere of the verbal action with precision.

Let us first consider the West Semitic languages. When the verb 'be' is compounded with another verb the compounds fall into two groups:

(i) 'be' compounded with a finite form,
(ii) 'be' compounded with an infinite form.

Leaving out of account cases where the verb 'be' may be in the imperative, jussive, subjunctive, or the participle, as sometimes happens when the compound is given a modal force or when it appears in a construction where one or other of these forms is required, four combinations are possible when it is compounded with a finite form: the perfect of the verb 'be' may be compounded with (*a*) a perfect or (*b*) an imperfect, or the imperfect of the verb 'be' may be compounded with (*c*) a perfect or (*d*) an imperfect. All these four compounds do, in fact, occur in one or more of the West Semitic languages to a greater or lesser degree of frequency.

(*a*) The perfect of the verb 'be' compounded with the perfect of another verb is very commonly found in Arabic[5] and Syriac,[6] and is often best rendered by an English pluperfect tense. In Arabic كَانَ precedes the other verb, while in Syriac ܗܘܐ follows it enclitically.

Arabic. Al-Rashīd died at Ṭūs, after he had set out (وَكَانَ خَرَجَ) for Khurāsān.

The Apostle of God . . . said to ʿĀ'isha, after she had vowed (كَانَتْ نَذَرَتْ).

Syriac. They had been taught (ܐܬܬܠܡܕܘ ܗܘܘ) together. Herod had seized (ܐܚܕ ܗܘܐ) John.

This compound is occasionally found in Ethiopic.[7] It has apparently

[1] Anthes, *Hatnub.* 22. 2–3.
[2] *J.E.A.* iv, 1917, plate 9. 2.
[3] *P. Kah.* 12. 13.
[4] *J.E.A.* ii, 1915, plate ii. 6.
[5] Wright, *Ar. Gr.* ii, p. 5c; Reckendorf, *Ar. Synt.*, § 154. 6, *b.*
[6] Nöldeke, *Syr. Gr.*, § 263.
[7] Chaine, *Gr. éth.*, § 200. 5.

pluperfect meaning, but it is perhaps to be regarded as late and probably due to Arabic influence.[1]

(*b*) The perfect of the verb 'be' compounded with the imperfect of another verb is very common in Arabic, where it expresses a continuous or repeated action in the past:[2]

Men who used to be (كَانُوا يَكُونُونَ) with the princes.

He used to ride out (كَانَ يَرْكَبُ) every day several times.

In Syriac the perfect of ܗܘܐ used enclitically with another verb in the imperfect is sometimes found in conditional clauses and the like, and denotes an action repeated in the past:[3]

If anyone used to say (ܢܐܡܪ ܗܘܐ).
Whenever he was angry (ܢܪܓܙ ܗܘܐ).

This employment is very close to the Arabic, but there are two others of a different kind. The combination is commoner in deliberative questions of the type:[3]

Why should he have fled (ܢܥܪܘܩ ܗܘܐ)?
How should he not have been handsome (ܢܫܦܪ ܗܘܐ)?

It is very common in dependent clauses when the verb in the main clause is in the perfect:[3]

He gave them life that they might be moved (ܘܢܬܬܙܝܥܘܢ ܗܘܘ).
And thou besoughtest that thine offerings might be accepted (ܘܢܬܩܒܠܢ ܗܘܝ).

Ethiopic frequently compounds the perfect of ኮነ with the imperfect of another verb to express repeated or continuous action:[4]

He used to fabricate (ኮነ፡ይገብር) implements of brass.
I was praising (ኮንኩ፡እሴብሕ) God.

(*c*) The imperfect of the verb 'be' followed by the perfect of another verb occurs only in Arabic, and the resulting compound has the force of a future-perfect:[5]

And there shall not have been left (لَا يَكُونُ بَقِيَ) behind me anything.

[1] Cohen, op. cit., § 104.
[2] Wright, *Ar. Gr.* ii, § 9; Reckendorf, *Ar. Synt.*, § 154. 6, *a*.
[3] Nöldeke, *Syr. Gr.*, § 268.
[4] Dillmann–Crichton, *Eth. Gr.*, p. 172.
[5] Wright, *Ar. Gr.* ii, § 10; Reckendorf, *Ar. Synt.*, § 154. 6, *c*.

(*d*) The imperfect of 'be' compounded with the imperfect of another verb occurs very rarely in Classical Arabic.[1] On the analogy of كَانَ يَقْتُلُ one would expect it to denote a continuous or repeated action in the future. In modern literary Arabic the imperfect of كَانَ with prefixed سَـ- followed by another imperfect could be employed for this purpose.[2] Again, the combination seems not to occur in any of the other languages.

The only infinite forms with which the verb 'be' is compounded in the West Semitic languages are the active and passive participles. For the moment we will concern ourselves only with the compounds containing the active participle.

The perfect of the verb 'be' with the active participle is a common combination. It portrays an action which extended over a more or less prolonged period or which was repeated in past time. It is employed instead of the simple participle when the speaker wishes to make clear that the action occurred in past time. Hebrew, Aramaic, and Arabic all possess this compound.

It is already found in the early books of the O.T. and becomes increasingly common in the later books,[3] while in Post-Biblical Hebrew it is the normal way of expressing prolonged or repeated action in the past.[4] Early examples from Biblical Hebrew are:

Joseph was tending (הָיָה רֹעֶה) the flock.[5]
And the child used to minister (הָיָה מְשָׁרֵת) unto the Lord.[6]
And he used to grind (וַיְהִי טוֹחֵן) in the prison house.[7]

The perfect of the verb 'be' with the active participle is very common in the Aramaic dialects, especially Biblical Aramaic:[8]

Three times a day he used to kneel (הֲוָא בָּרֵךְ) and pray (וּמְצַלֵּא), and thank (וּמוֹדֵא) God, as he had been wont to do (הֲוָא עָבֵד) aforetime.[9]

All peoples and nations used to tremble and fear (הֲווֹ זָאֲעִין וְדָחֲלִין) before him.[10]

[1] Reckendorf, *Ar. Synt.*, § 154. 6, *f*.
[2] I am indebted to my Arab colleague, Mr. H. M. A. Dabbagh, for this information.
[3] Gesenius–Kautzsch, *Hebr. Gr.*, § 116, *r*; Driver, *Tenses*, § 135. 5.
[4] Segal, *Gr. Mishn. Hebr.*, § 324.
[5] Gen. xxxvii. 2.
[6] 1 Sam. ii. 11.
[7] Judges xvi. 21. In this example and others quoted later, the imperfect with *wāw* consecutive is regarded as equivalent to the perfect and the perfect with *wāw* consecutive is regarded as equivalent to the imperfect.
[8] Bauer–Leander, *Gr. d. Bibl.-Aram.*, § 81, *p–q*.
[9] Dan. vi. 11 (M.T. הוּא ברך).
[10] Dan. v. 19.

We were wearing (לבשן הוין) sack-cloth.[1]

Each item month by month they used to send (הוו שלחן) to me.[2]

And he used to light (ܘܡܫܒ ܗܘܐ) a fire and place (ܘܣܐܡ) on it incense.[3]

In Arabic the combination كَانَ قَاتِلًا is sometimes encountered:

He was dwelling (كَانَ نَازِلًا).[4]

The imperfect of the verb 'be' with the active participle expresses prolonged or repeated action in future time. It is not so common as the combination with the perfect, and a few examples from Biblical Hebrew[5] and some early dialects of Aramaic[6] will suffice to illustrate its meaning:

And thou shalt be groping (וְהָיִיתָ מְמַשֵּׁשׁ) at noonday.[7]

And thine eyes shall be beholding (וְהָיוּ . . . רֹאוֹת) thy teachers.[8]

And they shall not be cleaving (וְלָא־לֶהֱוֺן דָּבְקִין) one to another.[9]

All money and interest that I shall be paying (אהוה משלם) you.[10]

They will continue to drink (יהוון . . . שתין) water from this well.[11]

If the uses of all these compounds are analysed, it will be found that they fall into two categories.

First, the perfect of the verb 'be' adds a temporal nuance to the perfect or the imperfect with which it is compounded, producing the equivalent of a pluperfect (Arab. كَانَ قَتَلَ, Syr. ܩܛܠ ܗܘܐ) or a future-perfect (Arab. يَكُونُ يَقْتُلُ), or it forms the equivalent of the Latin imperfect subjunctive (Syr. ܢܩܛܘܠ ܗܘܐ in deliberate questions and dependent clauses).

Second, the perfect or the imperfect of the verb 'be' turns the compound into a form expressing duration or repetition, the perfect limiting the action to the past and the imperfect limiting it to the future. Here the verb 'be' is compounded with a finite form, the imperfect (Arab. كَانَ يَقْتُلُ, Syr. ܢܩܛܘܠ ܗܘܐ, Eth. ከነ፡ይቀትል), or it is compounded with an infinite form, the active participle (Heb. הָיָה קוֹטֵל, Arab. كَانَ قَاتِلًا,

[1] Cowley, *Aram. Pap.* 30. 15.
[2] Ibid. 17. 3.
[3] Quoted in Nöldeke, *Syr. Gr.*, § 277.
[4] Wright, *Ar. Gr.* ii, § 74 Rem.
[5] Gesenius–Kautzsch, *Hebr. Gr.*, § 116, *r*; Driver, *Tenses*, § 135. 5.
[6] Bauer–Leander, *Gr. d. Bibl.-Aram.*, § 81, *i*.
[7] Deut. xxviii. 29.
[8] Isa. xxx. 20.
[9] Dan. ii. 43.
[10] Cowley, *Aram. Pap.* 11. 7.
[11] Ibid. 27. 7–8.

Aram. הֲוָא קָטֵל, Heb. יִהְיֶה קוֹטֵל, &c.). It will be observed that Arabic and the Aramaic dialects employ both methods.

When the perfect or the imperfect of the verb 'be' adds a temporal nuance to the form with which it is compounded (the perfect, or imperfect, or active participle), it acts as a time-indicator. In the case of the Syriac ܗܘܳܐ ܢܶܩܛܘܿܠ it has a similar function: when this compound is used as a past continuous tense ܗܘܳܐ restricts the continuous meaning inherent in the imperfect ܢܶܩܛܘܿܠ to past time. The Arabic كَانَ يَقْتُلُ 'he was killing, he used to kill' might be explained in the same way, but it is also possible to regard this compound as originally meaning 'he was, he killing', where يَقْتُلُ is equivalent to a circumstantial clause. The latter seems the more likely view.

It is instructive to compare the constructions employed by the various languages in circumstantial clauses with the compound forms expressing duration or repetition. The verb in a circumstantial clause describes an action which is in progress at the same time as that of the main verb. The verb-form selected for the circumstantial clause must therefore be one which is capable of denoting continuous or prolonged action. Thus in Arabic the verb of a circumstantial clause may be the imperfect,[1] e.g. 'Zaid came laughing (يَضْحَكُ)', or a participle,[2] e.g. 'I met the sultan in his house weeping (بَاكِيًا)', 'Zaid rose up weeping (وَهُوَ بَاكٍ)'. Both the imperfect and the active participle are used with كَانَ to express continuous or repeated action in the past. In Syriac the verb of a circumstantial clause may sometimes be the imperfect, e.g. 'while thinking (ܟܰܕ ܐܶܬܪܰܟܰܫ)', or, more commonly, the participle, e.g. 'while praying (ܟܰܕ ܡܨܰܠܶܐ)'. Again both the imperfect and the active participle[3] are employed with ܗܘܳܐ to denote continuous or repeated action in the past. In Hebrew the participle, usually with ו, is the normal construction in circumstantial clauses,[4] e.g. 'and the two angels came to Sodom at even, while Lot was sitting (וְלוֹט יֹשֵׁב) at the gate'.[5] It is the participle that is compounded with הָיָה or יִהְיֶה to express continuous or repeated action in the past or future. In Ethiopic the participles are not fully developed and the imperfect is the verb-form

[1] Wright, *Ar. Gr.* ii, §§ 8, *e*, 183, *b*.

[2] Ibid., §§ 74, 183, *a*.

[3] Nöldeke, *Syr. Gr.*, § 275.

[4] Gesenius–Kautzsch, *Hebr. Gr.*, §§ 116, *a*, 141, *e*.

[5] Gen. xix. 1.

found both in circumstantial clauses[1] and the compound ኮነ፡ይቀትል 'he was killing, he used to kill'.

Before leaving the Semitic languages it is interesting to note that Hebrew alone has no compound verb-form consisting of the verb 'be' with the perfect or imperfect of another verb. Why this should be is difficult to see, unless the existence of the common idioms וַיְהִי 'and it came to pass' and וְהָיָה 'and it shall come to pass' hindered such a development.

Let us now turn to the compound verb-forms in Old and Middle Egyptian. Already in these early stages of the Egyptian language there is a wealth of such forms, but we must confine ourselves to those which have the verb 𓃹𓈖 *wnn* 'be' as the first member of the compound. Detailed analysis of them is more difficult than in the case of the Semitic forms for two reasons. First, the fact that the script does not indicate vowels prevents the three *sḏm·f* forms from being distinguished, except with verbs whose second and third radicals are identical (*2ae gem.*), verbs whose third radical is *y* (*3ae inf.*), and several anomalous verbs. Second, the amount of textual material which has survived is far smaller than that of the classical Semitic literatures and consequently there are far fewer examples of the compound forms available for study.

Each *sḏm·f* form has developed its own active and passive participles and its own relative form (a form which means 'whom/what he hears/heard, &c.' and agrees in number and gender with its antecedent as well as being inflected for person). It will sometimes be necessary to cite examples of compounds where the first member, *wnn*, is in one of these forms when there are no others available. In the case of this verb the perfect participle and the perfective relative form seem to refer to past time, like the perfective *sḏm·f* form *wn·f*, but the imperfective participle and the imperfective relative form seem to be usually present or relatively present in meaning, like all other imperfective participial and relative forms. The form *wnnty·fy* serves as the future participle active, as does the *sḏmty·fy* form of all verbs.

Egyptian also possesses three secondary forms *sḏm·in·f*, *sḏm·kꜣ·f*, and *sḏm·ḫr·f*, which are employed as narrative forms in main clauses and which denote the result or sequel of what precedes. The verb *wnn*, and perhaps other verbs, seems to have developed a set of these forms corresponding in meaning with the perfective and imperfective *sḏm·f* forms: where the stem of the verb is *wnn* the meaning is future and

[1] Dillmann–Crichton, *Eth. Gr.*, p. 172.

where it is *wn* the meaning is usually past.[1] Compounds in which *wn·in·f*, *wnn·ḫr·f*, &c., occur as the first element will therefore have to be taken into account.

Like the West Semitic compound verb-forms, the Old and Middle Egyptian compound verb-forms with *wnn* as first element fall into two classes:

(i) the verb *wnn* compounded with a finite form,
(ii) the verb *wnn* compounded with an infinite form.

In the first category the finite form with which *wnn* is compounded may be a *sḏm·f* form or it may be the old perfective. For the moment only compounds with a *sḏm·f* form will be considered, since the old perfective has come to be virtually an inflected perfective passive participle, like the Accadian permansive, and compounds containing it are better treated with the second category.

The only compounds of the first category known to Old and Middle Egyptian have a perfective or imperfective form of *wnn* followed by another verb in a *sḏm·f* form and they express continuous or repeated action, as modern grammarians have all recognized.

The perfective *sḏm·f* form  *wn·f* compounded with another *sḏm·f* form is of very rare occurrence and describes continuous action in past time:[2]

I kept on addressing ( *wn·i wšd·i*) the workmen.[3]

The form 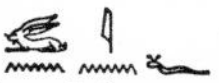 *wn·in·f*, where the stem of the verb is perfective, compounded with another *sḏm·f* form, is also rarely encountered. It narrates an action repeated in the past, the result or sequel of what preceded:[4]

Thereupon His Majesty kept sending ( . . .  *wn·in* . . . *hꜣb·f*) me presents.[5]

In this example the nominal subject goes with the first verb *wn·in* and is caught up by the pronominal suffix *·f* of the second verb *hꜣb·f*. There are several examples where the subject goes with the second verb of the compound and the first verb is without an expressed subject.[6] One such clearly refers to past habit:

The children of the vizier read his advice and found it good, so

[1] Thacker, op. cit., pp. 137 ff.
[2] Gardiner, op. cit., § 474. 2.
[3] *Sinai*, 90. 8.
[4] Gardiner, op. cit., § 473.
[5] *Sin*. B 174–5.
[6] Gardiner, op. cit., § 472.

they proceeded to live ( *wn·ỉn ꜥḥꜥ·sn ḥms·sn*, lit. stand up and sit down) accordingly.[1]

The compound  *wnn·ḫr·f sḏm·f*, where the stem of the verb *wnn* is imperfective, describes repeated or continuous action in future times resulting from a previous action:[2]

> Then the gods shall look upon ( *wnn·ḫr mꜣꜣ*) him as one of themselves.[3]

This category of compounds, *wnn* followed by a *sḏm·f* form, is infrequent in Old and Middle Egyptian. It never took firm root in the language and by the time of Late Egyptian it had disappeared altogether.

In which of the *sḏm·f* forms is the second verb of the compound? In the last example quoted above, the second verb is *mꜣꜣ* from the root *mꜣꜣ* (*2ae gem.* class): this is an imperfective *sḏm·f* form. There are, however, examples of the *wn·f sḏm·f* form in Old and Middle Egyptian in which *wnn* is followed by a perfective *sḏm·f* form. (In these examples *wnn* is in the perfective relative form or the perfective participle active.)

> Thou doest what thou wert accustomed to do ( *wnt·k ỉr·k*) before.[4]
>
> What I used to do ( *wnt ỉr·ỉ*) was my (real) character.[5]

The *sḏm·f* form in both these examples is from the root *ỉry* (*3ae inf.* class), which distinguishes its perfective and imperfective *sḏm·f* forms in writing. The evidence is too scanty to admit of any firm conclusions about the identity of the *sḏm·f* form in the compounds under discussion. It would appear to be an imperfective *sḏm·f* form when the verb belongs to the *2ae gem.* class and a perfective *sḏm·f* form when it belongs to the *3ae inf.* class. This would not be the only case where verbs belonging to the *3ae inf.* class employ a perfective *sḏm·f* form when verbs of the *2ae gem.* class, and perhaps others, employ an imperfective *sḏm·f* form.[6]

Little can be said about the origin of these compounds. The verb *wnn* in its various forms may perhaps be acting as a time-indicator. Alternatively, the second member of the compound, the *sḏm·f* form, could constitute a circumstantial clause 'he was/will be, he hearing': both the perfective and the imperfective *sḏm·f* forms can function in this way.[7]

[1] *Pr.* 2. 7.
[2] Gardiner, op. cit., § 473.
[3] *Nu* 133. 20–21.
[4] *Pyr.* 623, *c.*
[5] *Urk.* iv. 973. 14.
[6] Cf. Thacker, op. cit., pp. 211 ff.
[7] Gardiner, op. cit., §§ 454. 1, 444, 213.

These compounds may be compared with the Arabic كَانَ يَقْتُلُ 'he was killing' and the modern literary Arabic سَيَكُونُ يَقْتُلُ 'he will be killing'. There is, however, nothing in Old and Middle Egyptian comparable with كَانَ قَتَلَ 'he had killed' and يَكُونُ قَتَلَ 'he will have killed'. In the latest phases of the language *wn*, used impersonally, may be prefixed to certain verb-forms to give them a past nuance[1] and in Coptic ⲛⲉ, derived from this *wn*, may be employed in the same way, e.g. ⲁϥⲥⲱⲧⲙ̄ 'he heard', ⲛⲉ ⲁϥⲥⲱⲧⲙ̄ 'he had heard'.[2]

The second category of compounds, where *wnn* is followed by an infinite form, contains the infinitive preceded by the preposition *ḥr* 'upon' as the second element, 'he was/will be upon hearing'. It is here suggested that such compounds denote prolonged, continuous, or repeated action in past or future time, according to the form of *wnn* employed, and that they are analogous to the Hebrew, Aramaic, and Arabic compounds made up of the verb 'be' and the active participle.

The perfective forms of *wnn* followed by *ḥr* and the infinitive have reference to past time. The compound *wn·in·f ḥr sḏm* is fairly common:[3]

> Then this prince kept sending (. . . *wn·in . . . ḥr sbt*).[4]
>
> Then this peasant wept (. . . *wn·in . . . ḥr rmyt*) greatly.[5]
>
> Then one gave (*wn·in·tw ḥr rdt*) him 10 loaves of bread and 2 jugs of beer every day.[6]

The compound *wn·ḫr·f ḥr sḏm* is also found in the texts with similar meaning, but it is very uncommon:[7]

> Then I accompanied (*wn·ḫr·i ḥr šms*) the sovereign on my feet.[8]

The imperfective *sḏm·f* form of *wnn* followed by *ḥr* and the infinitive expresses a prolonged or repeated action in the future:[9]

> In truth I shall spread (. . . *wnn(·i) ḥr sṯp*) my protection round my daughter.[10]

[1] Erman, *Neuäg. Gr.*, §§ 534–8.
[2] See Polotsky, *Orientalia*, xxix, 1960, p. 400.
[3] Gardiner, op. cit., § 470.
[4] *Urk.* i. 127. 7.
[5] *Peas.* B1, 24.
[6] Ibid. 84.
[7] Gardiner, op. cit., § 471.
[8] *Urk.* iv. 3. 5.
[9] This has been recognized by N. S. Petrovsky (Египетский язык, Leningrad, 1958, p. 286), who, however, wrongly attributes the ability of the compound to express prolonged action to the imperfective *sḏm·f* form of *wnn*. See also Gardiner, op. cit., § 326.
[10] *Urk.* iv. 225. 13.

Thou shalt cause (*wnn·k ḥr rdt*) provisions to be given to him.[1]

As remarked earlier, the imperfective participle of *wnn* does not have future meaning, but the form *wnnty·fy* is used for this purpose:

These spirits which are wont to go in and out (*wnnyw ḥr ʿk prt*) of Rostjaw.[2]

He who will accompany (*wnnty·fy ḥr šms*) the king.[3]

The construction *ḥr* plus the infinitive is very commonly employed in circumstantial clauses when the portrayal of action rather than state is uppermost in the speaker's mind.[4] When the subject of the clause is pronominal it often appears as a suffixed pronoun attached to the word *iw*:[5]

He found him going out (*ḥr prt*) from the door of his house.[6]

I heard his voice, as he was speaking (*iw·f ḥr mdt*).[7]

As the Semitic compounds with the participle may be compared with the participial construction in circumstantial clauses, so the Egyptian compounds with *ḥr* plus the infinitive may be compared with *ḥr* plus the infinitive in circumstantial clauses. In the one case the participle conveys the idea of prolonged, continuous action, in the other case *ḥr* with the infinitive does so.

As well as in the compounds just discussed and in circumstantial clauses, *ḥr* plus the infinitive is very commonly employed as a narrative verb-form. When the subject is pronominal it must be introduced by the word *iw*[8] or by a particle such as *mk* 'behold'.[9] When the subject is nominal it may stand alone or be preceded by *iw* or particles like *mk*.[10] It is further suggested that, like *wn·in·f ḥr sḏm*, *wnn·f ḥr sḏm*, &c., these constructions were selected when the speaker wished to draw attention to the prolonged or continuous nature of the action, but unlike the compound forms, they were used when it was not felt necessary to specify the time-sphere of the action.

[1] *Peas.* B1, 83. Compare this example with the example in past time, *wn·in·tw ḥr rdt*, &c., quoted above, which follows in the next line of the papyrus.

[2] Budge, *The Book of the Dead*, 1898, Text volume, p. 270. 2–3.

[3] *P. Pet.* 1116 B, 70 (restored from Cairo tablet 25224, B11).

[4] Gardiner, op. cit., § 304. 1.

[5] Ibid., § 323.

[6] *Peas.* B1, 34–35.

[7] *Sin.* B 2.

[8] Gardiner, op. cit., § 323.

[9] Ibid., § 324.

[10] Ibid., §§ 322, 323.

Examples of *ḥr* with the infinitive plus a nominal subject without any introductory word abound in descriptive and narrative passages. The action may lie in the present or the past:

> Behold, we have reached home . . . every man is embracing (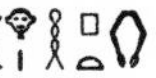 *ḥr ḥpt*) his fellow.[1]
>
> The strength is perishing ( *ḥr ȝk*) through weariness of heart.[2]
>
> Women and men murmured ( *ḥr ‘‘i*).[3]

Examples when the subject is introduced by  *iw* are also very common and refer to present or past time:

> The nobles give ( . . .  *iw* . . . *ḥr rdt*) to thee.[4]
>
> This army of the king looked on ( . . .  *iw* . . . *ḥr mȝȝ*).[5]

The preposition *ḥr* with the infinitive was, then, preceded by a form of *wnn* 'be' only when it was desired to make clear the time-sphere of the prolonged or continuous action and to limit it to the past or future. Usually the context was felt to be sufficient guide to the time. This usage finds an exact parallel, for example, in Biblical Hebrew, where the participle was similarly employed:[6]

> Tell me where they are shepherding (הֵם רֹעִים).[7]
>
> I am fleeing (אָנֹכִי בֹּרַחַת) from my mistress Sarai.[8]
>
> And David danced (מְכַרְכֵּר) before the Lord with all his might . . . so David and all the house of Israel brought up (מַעֲלִים) the ark of the Lord with shouting and the sound of the horn.[9]

It is highly probable that in the later stages of Middle Egyptian some of the forms containing *ḥr* with the infinitive had lost their implication of duration, repetition, and the like, and had weakened to mere past narrative forms. Late Egyptian abandoned the simple verb-forms in favour of compound forms and in the literary texts of the period *wn·in·f* (*ḥr*) *sḏm* and *iw·f* (*ḥr*) *sḏm*, where the preposition *ḥr* is sometimes written and sometimes omitted, are the staple forms of past narrative.[10] Here they certainly do not denote continuous or repeated action. The orthography of Late Egyptian is notoriously unreliable and erratic, and

[1] *Sh. S.* 1–5. [2] *Pt.* 12. [3] *Sin.* B 131–2.
[4] *Peas.* B1, 301. [5] *Hamm.* 100. 5–6.
[6] Gesenius–Kautzsch, *Hebr. Gr.*, § 116, *n–p;* Driver, *Tenses*, pp. 166 ff.
[7] Gen. xxxvii. 16. [8] Gen. xvi. 8. [9] 2 Sam. vi. 14 f.
[10] Erman, *Neuäg. Gr.*, § 513.

it is impossible to be sure whether these forms really are what they appear to be, or whether the scribes, as so often, were attempting to write some other forms which had arisen in the spoken language in what they thought was the correct historical spelling. In particular, *iw·f ḥr sḏm* is already common in the historical texts of the Eighteenth Dynasty as a past narrative form. If it is identical with the earlier *iw·f ḥr sḏm* 'he is/was hearing', is it used as an historic present, as was the participle in Biblical Aramaic,[1] or is it an attempt to write the form which was the ancestor of the Coptic ⲁϥⲥⲱⲧⲙ̄ 'he heard'?

Finally, closely allied with the compounds and constructions containing *ḥr* with the infinitive are compounds and constructions containing the old perfective. The old perfective may be preceded by the various forms of *wnn*,[2] when there is the wish to restrict the time-sphere to the past or future, or by *iw* and particles like *mk*,[3] or, if the subject is nominal, it may have no introductory word.[4] It may also be used in a circumstantial clause.[5] In fact, every construction containing *ḥr* with the infinitive has a corresponding one with the old perfective. In all of them the old perfective expresses state or passivity, in contrast to *ḥr* with the infinitive which denotes action:

Thereupon the heart of His Majesty was refreshed (. . . *wn·in . . . ḳbḥ*).[6]

Nay, but he who is yonder shall stand (. . . *wnn . . . ꜥḥꜥ*) in the bark.[7]

King Sehetepibre has gone (*wḏꜣw*) to the horizon.[8]

Nay, but thou art sated (. . . *iw·k . . . sꜣ·t*) with thy bread.[9]

Then His Majesty fared downstream, his heart rejoicing (*ꜣw*).[10]

These constructions also have their parallels in the Semitic languages, where the passive participles may be similarly employed.[11] In Biblical Hebrew, for example, we find passages such as the following:

And his carcase was cast (וַתְּהִי . . . מֻשְׁלֶכֶת) in the way.[12]

[1] Bauer–Leander, *Gr. d. Bibl.-Aram.*, § 81, *s*.
[2] Gardiner, op. cit., §§ 470–1.
[3] Ibid., §§ 323–4.
[4] Ibid., § 322.
[5] Ibid., § 314.
[6] *Westc.* 6. 1.
[7] *Leb.* 14. 3–4.
[8] *Sin.* B 36.
[9] *Peas.* B1, 124–5.
[10] *Urk.* iv. 5. 13.
[11] Gesenius–Kautzsch, *Hebr. Gr.*, § 116, *r*; Driver, *Tenses*, pp. 170 ff.
[12] 1 Kings xiii. 24.

And the people to whom they are prophesying shall be cast out (יִהְיוּ מֻשְׁלָכִים).[1]
And David was girded (חָגוּר) with a linen ephod.[2]
Your country lies desolate, your cities are burned (שְׂרֻפוֹת) with fire.[3]
We did esteem him stricken (נָגוּעַ), smitten of (מֻכֵּה) God, and afflicted (וּמְעֻנֶּה).[4]

Thus the Egyptian constructions with *ḥr* plus the infinitive, expressing prolonged, continuous, or repeated action, and plus the old perfective, expressing state or passivity, together known to grammarians of Egyptian as the pseudo-verbal construction, have their counterparts in the Semitic constructions with the active participle and with the passive participle.

The comparison of the various compound verb-forms containing the verb 'be' in the West Semitic languages with analogous compounds in Old and Middle Egyptian containing *wnn* 'be' has shown that both West Semitic and Egyptian followed the same broad lines of development. The Semitic languages can often throw light on problems of Egyptian grammar and syntax, and their use as a means of increasing our understanding of Egyptian is still far from exhausted.

[1] Jer. xiv. 16. [2] 2 Sam. vi. 14. [3] Isa. i. 7. [4] Isa. liii. 4.

DIE VOKABEL-VARIANTEN DER *O*-REZENSION IM GRIECHISCHEN SIRACH

Von JOSEPH ZIEGLER, *Würzburg*

VOKABEL-VARIANTEN (Wortlautänderungen) in Übersetzungen verdanken ihre Entstehung vor allem der Einsicht in die Vorlage. Bei allen Büchern der LXX, wo ein hebr. Urtext vorlag, wurde dieser immer wieder eingesehen; an solchen Stellen, wo die Wiedergabe fehlte oder von ihm abwich, wurde der griech. Text gewöhnlich ergänzt oder oftmals korrigiert. Dies ist auch in Sir. geschehen, dessen vollständiger hebr. Text (H)[1] in den ersten christlichen Jahrhunderten noch vorhanden war. Gewöhnlich ist bei dieser Revision die alte griech. Vokabel durch die neue Wiedergabe verdrängt worden. In einzelnen Fällen blieb jedoch die alte Vokabel stehen, so daß Dubletten vorliegen.

[1] Sigel und Abkürzungen

H	= Hebräischer Text nach der Ausgabe von Israel Lévi, *The Hebrew Text of the Book of Ecclesiasticus.* First published Leiden, 1904, reprinted 1951.
G	= Griechischer Text (Übersetzung des Enkels).
GrII	= Zweite griechische Übersetzung.
Syr	= Syrische Übersetzung (Peschitta) nach der Ausgabe von P. A. de Lagarde, *Libri VT apocryphi syriace*, Lipsiae–Londinii, 1861.
La	= Vetus Latina (Vulgata); die von G abweichende Kapitel- und Verszählung von La ist in Klammern beigegeben.
O	= 253-Syh (origeneische oder hexaplarische Rezension).
L	= 248–493–637 (Hauptgruppe der lukianischen Rezension).
l	= 106–130–545–705 (Untergruppe der lukianischen Rezension).
a	= 149–260–606.
b	= 249–254–603–754.
c	= 296–311–548–706.
Smend	= Rudolf Smend, *Die Weisheit des Jesus Sirach*, Berlin, 1906.
Smend, *Index*	= R. Smend, *Griechisch-Syrisch-Hebräischer Index zur Weisheit des Jesus Sirach*, Berlin, 1907.
Pe.	= Norbert Peters, *Das Buch Jesus Sirach oder Ecclesiasticus* (Exeget. Handbuch z. AT 25), Münster i. Westf., 1913.
Herk.	= Henr. Herkenne, *De Veteris Latinae Ecclesiastici capitibus I–XLIII*, Leipzig, 1899.
Hart	= J. H. A. Hart, *Ecclesiasticus. The Greek Text of Codex 248*, Cambridge, 1909.
Marcus	= Joseph Marcus, *The Newly Discovered Original Hebrew of Ben Sira* (*Ecclesiasticus XXXII*, 16–*XXXIV*, 1), Philadelphia, 1931.

In der *O*-Rezension sind nur zwei gleichlautende Dubletten in zwei benachbarten Versen festzustellen:

x. 14 (17) ἀρχόντων] *superborum* Arm = גאים H; + υπερηφανων *O*-V La (*ducum superborum*).

x. 15 (18) ἐθνῶν גוים H] + υπερηφανων *O*-V *L* La (*gentium superbarum*).

An beiden Stellen hat GrII in seiner Vorlage גאים gelesen. Smend 95 meint, daß so V. 14–16 überall stand.

In meinem Aufsatz 'Die hexaplarische Bearbeitung des griechischen Sirach' (*Bibl. Zeitschr.*, N.F., iv, 1960, 174–85) habe ich zum Abschluß geschrieben: 'Erst eine genaue Untersuchung des Wortschatzes von GrII, die in einem eigenen Aufsatz gemacht werden soll, kann die Vorlage von *O* (und *L*) näher charakterisieren und sie vielleicht auch zeitlich genauer festlegen.'

In diesem Beitrag soll ein Teil des Wortschatzes von GrII, und zwar die von *O* überlieferten Wortlautänderungen, über die in Abschnitt III (S. 179 f.) des oben genannten Aufsatzes kurz gesprochen wurde, ausführlich behandelt werden. Man kann die Vokabel-Varianten von *O* in fünf Abschnitte einteilen:

I. Neue Wiedergaben von Vokabeln, die mit H übereinstimmen.
II. Synonyma an solchen Stellen, wo H vorhanden ist.
III. Neue mit Syr übereinstimmende Wiedergaben an solchen Stellen, wo H nicht vorhanden ist.
IV. Synonyma (oder parallele Wörter) an solchen Stellen, wo H fehlt.
V. Vokabeln, die nicht mit H übereinstimmen.

I

Die folgenden Stellen sind Korrekturen nach der hebr. Vorlage; sie sind am leichtesten zu beurteilen.

(1) iv. 9 καὶ μὴ ὀλιγοψυχήσῃς] και μη ολιγωρησης τη ψυχη *O*; ואל תקוץ רוחך.

ὀλιγοψυχεῖν nur 2mal bei Sir., hier und vii. 10 (= התקצר); in der LXX selten; 3mal = קצר נפש, so auch Symmachus Zach. xi. 8 καὶ ὠλιγοψύχησα (LXX καὶ βαρυνθήσεται ἡ ψυχή μου).

ὀλιγωρεῖν steht nur noch Prov. iii. 11 für מאס. Die hebr. Vorlage mit Verbum und getrenntem Substantiv war wohl entscheidend für die Übersetzung in *O*. La *non acide feras* geht auf *μὴ ἀκηδιάσῃς* = H zurück, vgl. xxii. 13 (16) *οὐ μὴ ἀκηδιάσῃς non acediaberis* La.

(2) xii. 8 *ἐκδικηθήσεται*] *επιγνωσθησεται O*-S[c] (*γνωσθ.*) *l* La (*agnoscetur*) = יודע.

ἐκδικεῖν bei Sir. 6mal, 2mal = נקם.

ἐπιγιγνώσκειν bei Sir. 14mal.

Pe. 108: 'Das vielbesprochene rätselhafte *οὐκ ἐκδικηθήσεται* des Gr entpuppt sich als ein alter durch das ursprünglich unmittelbar vorhergehende *ἐκδίκησιν* (V. 6) veranlaßter Schreibfehler.' Dies ist nicht anzunehmen; *ἐκδικηθήσεται* ist ursprünglich (so auch Herk. 132), *ἐπιγνωσθήσεται* stammt aus GrII als Neuübersetzung von H.

(3) xii. 17 *ὑποσχάσει* (*πτέρναν σου*) יחפש] *υποσκαψει O*-V La (*suffodiet*).

ὑποσχάζειν ist Hapaxleg. der LXX; im N.T. fehlt es.

ὑποσκάπτειν fehlt in der LXX und im N.T.

Schleusner III. 354 und Smend 120 möchten *ὑποσκάψει* als ursprünglich annehmen. Dies ist nicht zuläßig, da es eine Neuübersetzung von יחפש ist, das vom Stamm חפס, der im Jüd.-Aram. und im Christl.-Pal. 'graben' heißt, abgeleitet wurde.

(4) xiv. 5 *ἐν τοῖς χρήμασιν αὐτοῦ*] *εν τοις αγαθοις αυτου O*-V La (*in bonis suis*) Arm = בטובתו.

Vgl. xiv. 4 *καὶ ἐν τοῖς ἀγαθοῖς αὐτοῦ* = ובטובתו.

χρήματα Lieblingswort bei Sir. (15mal).

ἀγαθά 'Güter' bei Sir. sehr häufig (31mal), = immer טוב oder טובה. G hat mit *χρήμασιν* das Ursprüngliche bewahrt, und wahrscheinlich in der Vorlage חיל wie v. 1, xl. 13, xl. 26, oder נכסים wie v. 8, oder הון wie xxxiv. 3 gelesen: und seines Besitzes wird er sich nicht mehr freuen. Dagegen stammt בטובתו aus xiv. 4b (ist also sekundär), das in GrII wörtlich wiedergegeben wurde.

(5) xiv. 20 (22) *τελευτήσει*] *μελετησει O*-S[c] *L* = יהגה; *meditabitur* La V. 22b, *morabitur* La[V] V. 22a, *morietur* La[pl] V. 22a.

τελευτᾶν bei Sir. 7mal.

μελετᾶν bei Sir. nur vi. 37 = הגה (so gewöhnlich in der LXX).

Herk. 144, Smend 137, Pe. 127 sehen richtig in *τελευτήσει* einen Fehler oder eine Korrektur, die 'durch mißverständliche Beziehung der Worte auf das Vorhergehende' (Smend 137) entstanden sei.

(6) xiv. 27 (*σκεπασθήσεται*) *ὑπ' αὐτῆς*] *εν τη σκεπη αυτης O*-V La (*sub tegmine illius*) = בצלה.

Vgl. xiv. 26 *ἐν τῇ σκέπῃ αὐτῆς* בעופיה.

σκέπη bei Sir. 6mal; in der LXX 15mal für צל.

Smend 139 möchte *ἐν τῇ σκέπῃ αὐτῆς* als Textlesart aufnehmen (der Art. *τῇ* fehlt versehentlich bei Smend). Es ist jedoch nicht anzunehmen, daß ursprünglich zweimal (in 26a und 27a) *σκέπη* stand, zumal in 27a bereits das Verbum *σκεπάζειν* verwendet ist; man würde *σκιά* erwarten, vgl. xxxi (xxxiv) 2 *σκιᾶς* = טללא Syr (H fehlt). Smend verweist auf Koh. vii. 12 LXX: *ὅτι ἐν σκιᾷ αὐτῆς* (בצל) *ἡ σοφία, σ' ὅτι ὡς σκέπει σοφία.*

Es ist somit deutlich, daß *ἐν τῇ σκέπῃ αὐτῆς* von GrII stammt, das *O* und La übernommen haben. Vielleicht ist *ὑπὸ σκιὰν αὐτῆς* als ursprünglich anzunehmen.

(7) xxxvi. 9 (xxxiii. 10) *ἀνύψωσεν καὶ ἡγίασεν* ברך והקדישו] *ηυλογησεν και ανυψωσεν* *O*-V.

Vgl. xxxvi (xxxiii) 12 *εὐλόγησεν καὶ ἀνύψωσεν . . . ἡγίασεν* (deest H).

ηὐλόγησεν ist deutlich Korrektur nach H. Auffallend ist, daß *O* *ἡγίασεν* (= H) nicht belassen hat; dies kommt daher, daß in der Vorlage והרים stand, das auch an der Parallele xxxvi (xxxiii) 12 wahrscheinlich vorlag (von Marcus 16 so rekonstruiert). *ἀνυψοῦν* ist Lieblingsverbum des griech. Sirach (es kommt 22mal vor). Smend 298 zieht *ηὐλόγησεν* wegen Gen. ii. 3 vor und meint, daß *ἀνύψωσεν* aus V. 12 eingedrungen ist. Gewiß ist im Anschluß an H *ηὐλόγησεν* vorzuziehen, aber *ἀνύψωσεν* hat seinen festen Platz in G.

(8) xxxviii. 2 *δόμα* משאות] *δοξαν* *O*-V 248 Sa.

δόμα selten (3mal) bei Sir. (häufiger *δόσις* 18mal, gewöhnlich für מתן o. ä.).

δόξα häufig (über 50mal) bei Sir., gewöhnlich für כבוד.

In der LXX steht *δόμα* für משא Par. II xvii. 11 und *δόξα* für משא Is. xxii. 25. GrII hebt die Stellung des Arztes höher, indem er ihn von den Königen geehrt sein läßt, anstatt daß er ihn nur Geschenke empfangen läßt.

(9) xlii. 8 *πρὸς νέους*] *περι πορνειας* *O*-V *L a* Sa Aeth Arm = בזנות.

Vgl. Sir. xli. 17 *αἰσχύνεσθε . . . περὶ πορνείας* אל זנות.

νέος Sir. ix. 10 (2mal) = חדש und li. 13 *νεώτερος* = נער.

πορνεία Sir. 3mal; LXX oft, immer = זנה o. ä.

Smend 391 und Pe. 354 sehen richtig in *πρὸς νέους* eine Verderbnis aus *περὶ πορνείας*. Herk. 262 möchte verbessern: *κρινομένου πορνείας* = '*qui respondet* (עֹנֶה) *crimini scortationis*'.

(10) xlvi. 7 (9) (ἔναντι) ἐχθροῦ] εκκλησιας *O*-V 248 = קהל.

Nach Smend 442 ist ἐχθροῦ 'ohne Zweifel' Korrektur, ebenso nach Pe. 396: 'sicher Fehler' für ἐκκλησίας. Es ist jedoch schwer verständlich, wie aus ἐκκλησίας phonetisch oder graphisch ἐχθροῦ werden konnte. Die Lösung ist anders: ἐχθροῦ ist sekundär, geht auf den Plur. ἐχθρῶν (so L^{-248} *a* alii) zurück, und dieser ist aus ἐθνῶν verderbt. ἐθνῶν ist Wiedergabe von קהל, wie die beiden Parallelverse xxxix. 10 und xliv. 15 zeigen:

xxxix. 10 ἔθνη עדה . . . ἐκκλησία קהל;
xliv. 15 λαοί עדה . . . ἐκκλησία קהל.

ἐκκλησίας stammt von GrII als genaue Wiedergabe von קהל.

(11) xlix. 9 (11) καὶ ἀγαθῶσαι המכלכל] και κατωρθωσεν *O*-V *L'*.

Beide Verba finden sich bei Sir. nur hier. Smend 472 und Pe. 421 halten κατορθῶσαι (Inf.) für ursprünglich. Dies ist nicht richtig; κατώρθωσεν ist Neuübersetzung nach H.

Die Wiedergabe mit ἀγαθῶσαι erschien dem Rezensor nicht als richtig, da dieses gewöhnlich הטיב entspricht.

II

An verschiedenen Stellen stehen in *O* Synonyma, die zwar mit H übereinstimmen, aber nicht allein durch die hebr. Vorlage, sondern durch die Wahl des zweiten Übersetzers (oder des Rezensors) bedingt waren, weil sie ihm persönlich geeigneter erschienen und zu seiner Zeit geläufig waren.

(1) iii. 16 (18) ὑπὸ κυρίου] υπο θεου *O l* La (*a deo*); בוראו.

v. 4 ὁ γὰρ κύριος = ייי H^D] ο γαρ υψιστος *O* La (*altissimus enim*) = אל H^A.

xii. 2 παρὰ (τοῦ) ὑψίστου] παρα του κυριου *O* La (*a domino*) = מייי.

Vgl. xi. 4 κυρίου = H] *altissimi* La (+*solius*) Syh.

xxxviii. 1b (ὁ) κύριος אל] ο υψιστος Clem. La (*altissimus*).

xxxviii. 2a παρὰ γὰρ ὑψίστου] παρα δε κυριου Clem. La (*a deo enim*); π. γαρ κυριου υψιστου 613; *a deo domino enim* Sa.

xliii. 2 ὑψίστου] κυριου PsAth. IV. 381 = ייי; ισχυρον PsChr. VIII. 630.

xlviii. 5 ὑψίστου] *domini dei* La; *domini* La^X = ייי.

vii. 9 (11) θεῷ ὑψίστῳ] κυριω υψιστω S* *l* La^Q (*domino altissimo*) Aeth; υψιστω *O* = Syr.

xli. 8 (11) *θεοῦ ὑψίστου*] *υψιστου* S 248 543* La$^{\Omega M}$ Aeth = עליון; *domini altissimi* La; *κυριου* Dam. p. 1157; *θεου* Anton. p. 777; *υψιστου θεου* 155.

xxxix. 35 (*τὸ ὄνομα*) *κυρίου* הקדוש.

xlvii. 18 (19) (*ἐν ὀνόματι*) *κυρίου τοῦ θεοῦ* הנכבד.

xlvi. 13 (16) *ὑπὸ κυρίου αὐτοῦ* עושהו.

l. 17c *τῷ κυρίῳ* (*θεω* S* 315–672 = Syr) *αὐτῶν* לפני עליון.

l. 17d *παντοκράτορι θεῷ* (*τῷ*) *ὑψίστῳ* לפני קדוש ישראל.

Die angeführten Beispiele zeigen, daß sowohl der Übersetzer als auch der Rezensor mit den Gottesnamen frei umging. Die hebr. Vorlage war zwar für beide richtunggebend, aber nicht bindend. Dies zeigt auch die Statistik der Wiedergabe mit *κύριος* in Sir.: = יהוה 35mal, = אל 30mal, = אלהים 14mal.

(2) iii. 21 (22) *μὴ ἐξέταζε* אל תחקור] *μη ερευνα O* Or. IV. 230 La (*ne scrutatus fueris*).

ἐξετάζειν 5mal bei Sir., 3mal = חקר; in der LXX 9mal (niemals für חקר). Das Simplex *ἐτάζειν* fehlt in Sir., steht in der LXX 13mal, 1mal (Job xxxii. 11) für חקר.

ἐρευνᾶν, *ἐξερευνᾶν* fehlt bei Sir.; in der LXX = חקר Jdc. xviii. 2 A, Regn. II x. 3, Par. I xix. 3.

Sehr beliebt (5mal) ist *ἐξερευνᾶν* (*ἐρευνᾶν* nur Koh. xii. 9 *α'*) bei den 'Drei'.

Im N.T. vgl. Cor. I ii. 10: *πάντα ἐρευνᾷ καὶ τὰ βάθη*.

(3) iv. 28b (33b) (*πολεμήσει*) *ὑπὲρ σοῦ* לך] *περι σου O* Or. X. 653.

Vgl. iv. 28a *περὶ* (*τῆς ἀληθείας*)] *υπερ* 46 alii Or.

Ex. xiv. 14 (*πολεμήσει*) *περὶ ὑμῶν*] *υπερ υμων* F M alii (19 min.) Philo Or. Eus. Chr. Cyr.

Smend 46 verweist auf xxix. 13 *πολεμήσει ὑπὲρ σοῦ* und Ex. xiv. 14, ohne die Variante zu nennen (siehe oben). Aus der Exodus-Stelle stammt die Präposition *περί*.

Es ist auffallend, daß Or. bei Sir. *περί* und bei Ex. *ὑπέρ* hat.

(4) v. 7 (9) *ἐξολῇ* תספה] *εξολοθρευσει σε O* La (*disperdet te*).

ἐξολλύναι nur hier in Sir., auch sonst in der LXX selten (3mal Prov.), bei Aquila 2mal. Das Simplex *ὀλλύναι* fehlt bei Sir., steht jedoch in der LXX öfter (23mal).

ἐξολεθρεύειν fehlt bei Sir., steht jedoch sehr oft in der LXX. Pe. 52

meint, daß die *O*-Lesart 'auf mißverstandenem ἐξολῇ' beruht. Dieses 'Mißverständnis' ist mir nicht erklärlich, ebenso wenig die Änderung. War eine andere hebr. Vorlage maßgebend?

(5) v. 8 (10) (ἐν ἡμέρᾳ) ἐπαγωγῆς עברה] εκδικησεως *O*; *obductionis et vindictae* La: lectio duplex.

ἐπαγωγή 'Heimsuchung', 'Plage', Lieblingswort des Sir. (9mal); sonst nur Dt. xxxii. 26 und Is. x. 4, xiv. 17, aber in anderer Bedeutung: 'Wegführung', 'Verschleppung'.

ἐκδίκησις ebenfalls Lieblingswort des Sir. (13mal), aber auch öfter in der LXX (über 60mal).

In *O* ist das bekannte ἐκδίκησις vorgezogen, zumal die Wendung ἡμέρα ἐκδικήσεως gebräuchlich ist, vgl. Dt. xxxii. 35, Jer. xxvi (xlvi) 10 u. ö. und im N.T. Lc. xxi. 22 (ἡμέραι ἐκδικήσεως). Auch in Verbindung mit καιρός wird ἐκδικήσεως gern verwendet, so im vorausgehenden Vers v. 7d ἐν καιρῷ ἐκδικήσεως und bei Jer. (4mal). Vielleicht ist ἐκδικήσεως V. 8 von V. 7d beeinflußt.

(6) vi. 28 (29) ἐπ' ἐσχάτων לאחור] υστερον *O*.

Vgl. Num. xxxi. 2 ἔσχατον אחר] υστερον N *L*.

ἐπ' ἐσχάτων bei Sir. 11mal; ὕστερον bei Sir. 2mal; in der LXX selten.

Ps. lxxii (lxxiii) 24 אחר ist ὕστερον Symmachus zugeschrieben (LXX μετά). Umgekehrt: Jer. xxxviii (xxxi) 19: ὕστερον] α' μετα.

Es mag sein, daß Num. xxxi. 2 ὕστερον von Symmachus stammt; sehr viele *L*-Lesarten überliefern verdeckte σ'-Lesarten, wie namentlich die prophetischen Schriften zeigen.

Im N.T. ist ὕστερον häufig (10mal) gegenüber ἐπ' ἐσχάτων, das in der Bedeutung 'zuletzt', 'schließlich' fehlt.

(7) vi. 37b διὰ παντός תמיד] ενδελεχως *O*; *maxime* La.

Vgl. Deut. xi. 12 διὰ παντός] α' ενδελεχως, ebenso Ps. lxviii (lxix) 24, cxviii (cxix) 109, Is. lii. 5, lx. 11.

Ps. l (li) 5 διὰ παντός] σ' ενδελεχως, ebenso Ps. lxx (lxxi) 7.

διὰ παντός bei Sir. 6mal; ἐνδελεχῶς bei Sir. 5mal, 2mal = תמיד; in der LXX 3mal im Pent. = תמיד. Aquila verwendet immer (6mal) ἐνδελεχῶς für תמיד. *O* bevorzugt ἐνδελεχῶς gegenüber διὰ παντός.

(8) vi. 37d (καὶ ἡ ἐπιθυμία) τῆς σοφίας (δοθήσεταί σοι) יחכמך] της συνεσεως *O*.

Vgl. i. 19 (24) συνέσεως] σοφια *O*; siehe unter IV (1).

Die wörtliche Übersetzung würde lauten: *καὶ ἡ ἐπιθ. σοφισθήσεταί σοι*, vgl. xxxviii. 24, 25, l. 28. Jedoch paßt zu *σοφισθήσεται* das Subjekt *ἡ ἐπιθυμία* nicht; es liegt somit freie Wiedergabe vi. 37d vor.

Die Stelle wäre eindeutig, wenn umgekehrt überliefert wäre wie i. 19 (24): *συνέσεως*] *σοφια O*; dann läge eine spätere, genaue Wiedergabe vor wie Is. v. 21 *συνετοί*] *α′ σ′ σοφοι*; ähnlich Jer. ix. 12 (11), xviii. 18, xxvii (l) 35. So aber bestehen zwei Möglichkeiten: (1) *O* hat ursprüngliches *συνέσεως* bewahrt, das in *σοφίας* nach H umgeändert wurde (dieser Weg ist jedoch nicht gut denkbar), (2) *O* (bzw. schon vorher GrII) hat *σοφίας* als Synonym von *συνέσεως* frei gewählt.

(9) xii. 14a (13) *τὸν προσπορευόμενον* חובר] *τον προσαγοντα O*.

προσπορεύεσθαι nur hier in Sir., auch in der LXX nicht oft, für קרב 7mal, für נגש 4mal.

προσάγειν bei Sir. 5mal; in der LXX öfter, gewöhnlich für קרב und נגש.

Die *O*-Lesart ist dem im vorausgehenden Vers 13b stehenden *τοὺς προσάγοντας* angepaßt. La *qui comitatur* ist genaue Wiedergabe von H.

(10) xiii. 25 (31) *κακά* רע] *πονηρα O*.

Vgl. xxvii. 22 (25) *κακά*] *πονηρα O*-V *L*; deest H: siehe IV (6).

Regn. I xxv. 28 *κακία*] *σ′ πονηρία*, ebenso *α′ πονηρία* Koh. vii. 16 (15), *α′ σ′ πονηρία* Jer. xii. 4.

Jer. xiii. 23 *κακά*] *α′ πονηρά*.

Koh. v. 12 *εἰς κακίαν*] *α′ εἰς πονηρόν*.

ix. 12 *κακῷ*] *α′ πονηρῷ*.

Jer. xi. 15 *τῆς κακίας*] *α′ πονηρά*.

κακός steht bei Sir. 28mal und *πονηρός* 36mal für רע, רעה. An beiden Stellen (xiii. 25, xxvii. 22) ist *πονηρά* gewählt worden, weil *κακός* allmählich von *πονηρός* verdrängt wurde. Besonders deutlich ist bei den 'Drei', namentlich bei Aquila, zu sehen, daß sie *πονηρός, πονηρία* gegenüber *κακός, κακία* LXX bevorzugen. Auch an solchen Stellen, wo in der ursprünglichen LXX die Wiedergabe von רע, רעה fehlt und erst sub asterisco von der hexaplarischen Rezension aus den Übersetzungen der 'Drei' beigefügt wurde, ist *πονηρός, πονηρία* gewählt worden:

Jer. v. 28 *α′ σ′ θ′* ※ *εἰς πονηρόν*; viii. 3 *α′ σ′ θ′* ※ *τῆς πονηρᾶς*; xiii. 10 *α′ θ′* ※ *τὸν πονηρόν*.

Ez. viii. 9 *οι γ′* ※ *τὰς πονηράς*; xxx. 12 *α′ θ′* ※ *πονηρῶν*.

Jer. xxxvi (xxix) 17 *θ'* ⁜ *ἀπὸ πονηρίας*.

xxvii. 22 (*τεκταίνει κακά*) mag die Wahl von *πονηρά* auch durch die Parallelstelle xi. 33 (*πονηρὰ γὰρ τεκταίνει*), wo das gleiche Verbum verwendet wird, beeinflußt sein.

(11) xiv. 3 *οὐ καλός* לא נאוה] *ουκ αγαθος O*.

καλός entspricht Sir. xli. 16 נאה und Cant. i. 5 נאוה.

ἀγαθός steht in der LXX fast immer, bei Sir. gewöhnlich für טוב. Sir. vii. 13 entspricht *ἀγαθός* נעם.

Die hebr. Vorlage war nicht für *ἀγαθός* maßgebend; es liegt einfacher Synonyma-Tausch vor.

(12) xv. 1. *ὁ ἐγκρατής* תופש] *ο ειληφως O-V*.

ἐγκρατής 4mal bei Sir.

λαμβάνειν 7mal bei Sir. In der LXX *λαμβάνειν* = תפש Regn. IV xiv. 13 A (*συλλαμβάνειν* B); Jer. xxvii (l) 24, xxviii (li) 32. Smend 139 verweist auf Jer. ii. 8, wo die gleiche hebr. Wendung תפשי התורה mit *οἱ ἀντεχόμενοι τοῦ νόμου* wiedergegeben wird.

GrII hat das seltene *ὁ ἐγκρατής*, das leicht in der Bedeutung 'der Enthaltsame' aufgefaßt werden konnte, durch das bekanntere *ὁ εἰληφώς* auf Grund von H ersetzt.

(13) xxxiii (xxxvi) 4b *ἐνώπιον* לעיני] *εναντιον O-V L*.

Vgl. xxxiii (xxxvi) 4a *ἐνώπιον* omnes לעיני.

ἐνώπιον bei Sir. selten (9mal); = לעיני 2mal, = לפני 1mal, = נגד 1mal.

ἐναντίον bei Sir. häufig (34mal); gewöhnlich = לפני, = נגד 3mal, = בעיני 2mal.

Im N.T. ist dagegen *ἐνώπιον* gegenüber *ἐναντίον* sehr häufig.

GrII hat das in Sir. häufige *ἐναντίον* gewählt, vielleicht auch um abzuwechseln, da *ἐνώπιον* bereits im gleichen Vers (4a) vorkommt.

(14) xliii. 12 (13) *ἐγύρωσεν* חוק] *εκυκλωσεν O-V*.

γυροῦν steht nur 2mal in der LXX, hier und Job xxvi. 10: חק חג ⁜ *θ' πρόσταγμα ἐγύρωσεν*. Die Jobstelle zeigt, daß die Variante חג (statt חוק) für *ἐγύρωσεν* Pate stand.

κυκλοῦν ist in der LXX häufiger (im N.T. 4mal) als *γυροῦν* (fehlt im N.T.); *κυκλοῦν* entspricht in Sir. 2mal und sonst in der LXX 3mal הקיף. *O* hat von GrII *ἐκύκλωσεν* übernommen, um das seltene *ἐγύρωσεν* zu verdrängen; damit kommt stilistisch unschön der gleiche Stamm zweimal in V. 12a vor: *ἐκύκλωσεν οὐρανὸν ἐν κυκλώσει δόξης*.

(15) xliii. 17 ὠδίνησεν יחול] συνεσεισε *O*.

Vgl. Ps. xxviii (xxix) 8a συσσείοντος α′ ὠδίνοντος יחיל.
8b συσσείσει α′ ὠδινήσει יחיל.

Statt ὠνείδισεν, das Rahlfs zu Unrecht im Text hat, ist mit A 248 *a* ὠδίνησεν zu lesen; ὠδίνειν חול steht auch Sir. xlviii. 19. Ebenso kennt Sir. xvi. 19 das Verbum συσσείειν = רעש und Sir. xxii. 16 das Subst. συσσεισμός (H fehlt). GrII hat יחיל statt יחול gelesen und es mit συνέσεισε übersetzt; er steht damit auf gleicher Stufe wie LXX Ps. xxviii (xxix) 8 (siehe oben).

Auf Grund der Ps-Stelle möchte man xliii. 17 συνέσεισε als ursprünglich und ὠδίνησεν als sekundär ansprechen, vgl. auch Jer. li (xxviii) 29 καὶ ἐπόνεσεν ותחול] σ′ καὶ ὠδινήσει. Aber GrII hat das seltsame ὠδίνησεν durch das bekanntere συνέσεισε ersetzt.

(16) xliv. 18 (19) (διαθῆκαι αἰῶνος) ἐτέθησαν נכרת] εσταθησαν *O L*; εστησαν V.

Die Wendung τιθέναι διαθήκην findet sich nur hier bei Sir.

In der LXX steht τιθέναι (כרת) δ. 4mal in der Gen. und 2mal in Job.

Dagegen ist ἱστάναι δ. häufiger, bei Sir. im gleichen Kap. Vers 20c ἔστησεν δ., ebenso xvii. 12a, xlv. 7a. Im Passiv steht xlv. 24 (30) ἐστάθη (εστη 248; *statuit* La) αὐτῷ διαθήκη.

In der LXX ist ἱστάναι δ. Deut. xxviii. 69 für כרת und 5mal in der Gen. für הקים verwendet.

O L haben somit die in Sir. häufiger vorkommende Wendung gewählt.

III

Leider ist H nicht zu allen Stellen erhalten. Als Ersatz kann vielfach Syr gelten, da Syr von H abhängig ist. Wenn somit *O*-Lesarten mit Syr übereinstimmen, kann man annehmen, daß sie auch mit H zusammengehen.

(1) i. 18 (22) ἀναθάλλων εἰρήνην καὶ ὑγίειαν ἰάσεως] αναθαλλει δε εν αυτοις κυριος ειρηνην μεστην ιασεως *O*; *replens pacem et salutis fructum* La.

ὑγίεια bei Sir. 5mal, = חיים 2mal, = שר 1mal (xxx. 16).

μεστός fehlt in Sir.; in der LXX nur 4mal. Ps. lxiv (lxv) 10 wird es Symmachus zugeschrieben (LXX ἐπληρώθη, α′ πλήρης). Steckt מלא hinter μεστήν, und kann man es mit *replens* zusammenbringen? Dagegen scheint die Stellung zu sprechen, die es als Äquivalent von ἀναθάλλων ausweist; *replens* ist innerlat. verderbt aus *repollens* (so La^G*Σ^).

Smend 12 weist darauf hin, daß ἴασις מרפא voraussetzen könnte; er sagt zur Variante μεστήν, daß die beiden Zeugen von *O* (253-Syh) den Vers 18b 'abwandeln'. Damit ist nicht gedient. Setzt μεστήν eine hebr. Lesart מרבה statt מרפא voraus? Dies vermutet Herk. 50 für *replens*; bestärkt wird er durch מסגיא Syr. Somit gewinnt die Annahme, daß μεστήν auf מרבה zurückgeht, hohe Wahrscheinlichkeit.

(2) i. 29 (37) ἐν στόμασιν (-ματι S)] ενωπιον *O* La (*in conspectu*) Co = Syr (לעין).

Vgl. xiii. 24 (30) ἐν στόμασιν (-ματι SA) על פי.
viii. 11b (14) τῷ στόματί σου = לפיך] *coram te* Arm = לפניך.
viii. 11a (14) ἀπὸ προσώπου ὑβριστοῦ מפני לץ.

Herk. 55 verweist auf Prov. xv. 14 und Neh. ii. 13, wo die gleiche hebr. Verlesung vorliegt:

Prov. xv. 14 στόμα δέ = ופי Qere, ופני Ketib.
Neh. ii. 13 καὶ πρὸς στόμα 𝔊* = ואל־פי, και κατα προσωπον 𝔊^79 93^ = ואל־פני 𝔐.

Es ist deutlich, daß in i. 29 und viii. 11b die beiden Lesarten לפי/לפני die Vorlage bilden, vgl. Smend 17, 79 und *Index* 216 zu viii. 11.

(3) xvii. 31 (30) καὶ πονηρός (sic B*–S* C; -ρον A alii Ra.)] και ανηρ ος *O*-V *L*: cf. Syr ברנשא.

Smend 162 nennt die Variante ἀνὴρ ὅς 'vollends entartet'. Herk. 160 und Pe. 148 dagegen möchten sie als ursprünglich annehmen; Pe. übersetzt: 'und der Mensch (erst), das Gebilde von Fleisch und Blut'.

Die Entscheidung ist schwer. Da auch Syr die Lesart 'Mensch' kennt, ist vielleicht ἀνὴρ ὅς als ursprünglich anzunehmen, aus dem πονηρός durch Verschreibung stammt.

(4) xix. 23 (20) πονηρία (*nequitia* La)] πανουργια *O*-V *L* = ערימותא Syr, *prudentiae nequitia* La^pc^: lectio duplex.

πονηρία in Sir. 10mal, gewöhnlich = רע, רעה.
πανουργία in Sir. 3mal, in der LXX immer (4mal) = ערמה.
Prov. viii. 12 (ערמה) hat Symmachus πανουργία (LXX βουλή).

Smend 177 hält πανουργία für ursprünglich. Pe. 162 erscheint es für wahrscheinlicher, anzunehmen, daß πονηρίᾳ zu V. 23b, dagegen σοφία zu V. 23a gehört. Es mag jedoch sein, daß G in ihrer Vorlage רעה las, während GrII (wie Syr) ערמה vor sich hatte, das mit πανουργία neu übersetzt wurde.

(5) xxiv. 14 (18) *ἐν αἰγιαλοῖς*] *εν εγγαδοις O* (*εν ενγαδοις* 253; בעין גד
Syh = Syr) –S^{c} (*εν ενγαδδοις*) *c*.

αἰγιαλός (Sing.!) nur noch Jdc. v. 17 A *παρ' αἰγιαλὸν θαλασσῶν*. Im N.T. ist *αἰγιαλός littus* häufig (6mal). Überall steht der Sing.; der Plur. ist verdächtig. Richtig hat bereits Herk. 191 *ἐν 'Εγγάδοις* (besser Ra. *ἐν Αἰγγάδοις*) als ursprüngliche Lesart erkannt, aus der *ἐν αἰγιαλοῖς* durch Verschreibung entstanden ist. Wir haben hier die gräzisierte Form *Αἴγγαδοι*, während sonst *Αιγγαδι*, *Εγγαδι* steht (so Ez. xlvii. 10, Cant. i. 14, Par. II xx. 2). Die Schreibweise *Αἰγγάδοις* (statt des sekundären *'Εγγάδοις*) ist durch *αἰγιαλοῖς* gewährleistet.

IV

In diesem Abschnitt sollen solche Stellen besprochen werden, wo in *O* Synonyma (oder parallele Wörter) stehen, die aber mit H nicht verglichen werden können, weil der hebr. Text fehlt.

(1) i. 19 (24) *καὶ γνῶσιν συνέσεως ἐξώμβρησεν*] *γνωσιν* (+*και δοξαν* 253: ex 19c) *σοφια εξομβρει O*; + *η σοφια L'*; *intellectum prudentiae sapientia compartietur* La.

σύνεσις bei Sir. sehr oft (30mal), gewöhnlich = בינה, דעת, שכל o. ä., nicht für חכמה. Das Adj. *συνετός* steht jedoch 1mal (iii. 29) für חכם: *συνετου*] *sapientis* La = H. In Syr entsprechen oft *σύνεσις* חכמתא (7mal) und *συνετός* חכימא (9mal).

Auch i. 19b hat in H vielleicht חכמה gestanden, das in GrII genau mit *σοφία* wiedergegeben worden ist. *O L* haben es von GrII übernommen und zum Subjekt gemacht; *L* und La haben zugleich eine Dublette. Vgl. zu vi. 37d unter II (8).

(2) i. 20 (25) *φοβεῖσθαι* (*τὸν κύριον*)] *αγαπαν O*.

Vgl. i. 10 *τοῖς ἀγαπῶσιν αὐτόν*] *τοις φοβουμενοις αυτον l* = Syr.

Zu i. 10 meint Smend 9, daß *φοβουμένοις* 'durch das Folgende erfordert' sei. Wenn man dies annimmt, dann muß man auch i. 20 (25) *ἀγαπᾶν* für ursprünglich halten, das durch den eingeschobenen Vers 21 (27) *φόβος κυρίου . . . ὀργήν* in *φοβεῖσθαι* umgekehrt worden sei. Jedoch ist i. 20 *φοβεῖσθαι* sicher ursprünglich, denn die 'Gottesfurcht' ist für Sir. die Grundlage der Frömmigkeit. Dagegen spielt für GrII die Gottesliebe eine wichtige Rolle; es ist jedoch nicht zu entscheiden, ob GrII aus theologischen Gründen geändert oder bereits in seiner Vorlage אהב gelesen hat.

(3) iii. 7 (8) δεσπόταις] *κυριοις O.*

Vgl. xxxi (xxxiv) 29 ὁ δεσπότης] *κυριος* 543.

Im Sing. wird δεσπότης im A.T. über 50mal von Gott verwendet, vgl. *Theol. Wörterb. z. N.T.* ii. 44 f. Selten steht es im Sing. vom menschlichen Herrn im Gegensatz zum Sklaven (so Sap. xviii. 11 δοῦλος ἅμα δεσπότῃ), dagegen öfter im Plur. von den Herren im Gegensatz zu den Sklaven und zwar im A.T. 2mal (Prov. xvii. 2, xxii. 7) und im N.T. 4mal (Tim. I vi. 1, 2, Tit. ii. 9, Petr. I ii. 18).

An den genannten ntl. Stellen stehen δοῦλοι (οἰκέται) und δεσπόται einander gegenüber. 'Für Past ergibt sich hier eine Differenz gegenüber Kol 3, 22 und Eph 6, 5, wo neben den δοῦλοι die κύριοι erscheinen' (*Theol. Wörterb. z. N.T.* ii. 47). Die gleiche Ersetzung von δεσπόταις durch κυρίοις haben wir an unserer Stelle. Vielleicht erschien dem Rezensor δεσπόταις zu stark (δεσπότης 'Despot', unumschränkter Herr).

Die Übersetzungen verwenden gewöhnlich *dominus* für δεσπότης. Damit ist aber nicht gesagt, daß sie κύριος in ihrer Vorlage gelesen haben. Auch La verwendet gewöhnlich *dominus*; manche Hss. haben genauer *dominator*, so Sap. xiii. 3 ὁ δεσπότης] *dominator* La; *dominus* La^{X} Spec.

(4) xix. 27 (24) ἑτεροκωφῶν] *εθελοκωφων O*-V 248–743 *a* La (*fingit se non videre*).

Beide Verba kommen nur hier im griech. A.T. vor. Das erste (ἑτεροκωφεῖν) ist sehr selten (bei Pape, *Griech.-Deutsches Wörterb.*, ist es überhaupt nicht aufgeführt). Das zweite (ἐθελοκωφεῖν) ist gebräuchlicher, aber auch selten; es steht bei Clemens von Alexandrien (*Strom.* vi. 65. 1): ἐθελοκωφῶσι τὴν ἀλήθειαν. Schleusner i. 674 und Smend 179 wollen ἐθελοκωφῶν vorziehen; aber richtig bemerkt Herk. 172, daß das äußerst seltene ἑτεροκωφῶν als ursprünglich beizubehalten ist. GrII hat es durch das bekanntere ἐθελοκωφῶν ersetzt.

(5a) xxiii. 22 (32) ἐξ ἀλλοτρίου] *εξ αλλου O*-V 248; *ex alieno matrimonio* La.

(5b) xxiii. 23 (33) καὶ ἐξ ἀλλοτρίου ἀνδρός] *και εξ αλλου ανδρος O*-V 248 La (*ex alio viro*).

ἀλλότριος bei Sir. oft (16mal); = זר 5mal, = נכרי 2mal.

ἄλλος bei Sir. 4mal (2mal im Prolog, 2mal = אחר).

In der LXX ἀλλότριος gewöhnlich = נכרי, selten = אחר. Dagegen *ἄλλος* gewöhnlich = אחר. Koh. vii. 23 (22) ist *ἄλλος* = אחר von Symmachus bezeugt (LXX *ἕτερος*).

GrII hat *ἄλλος* im weiteren Sinn ('ein anderer Mann', vgl. Regn. I x. 6 *εἰς ἄνδρα ἄλλον* אחר) genommen; *ἀλλότριος* 'fremd' erschien GrII unpassend.

(6) xxvii. 22 (25) *κακά*] *πονηρα O*-V *L*.

Siehe zu xiii. 25 (31) unter II (10).

(7) xli. 5b (8) (*καὶ συναναστρεφόμενα*) *παροικίαις*] *ευδοκιαις O* (-*κιας* 253)-V (*εν ευδ.*); *εν αμαρτιαις b*.

παροικία bei Sir. 4mal; in der LXX selten.

εὐδοκία bei Sir. 16mal, = רצון 8mal.

Die Entstehung der Lesart *εὐδοκίαις* ist schwer zu erklären. Hart 204 verweist auf Rom. i. 32 *ἄξιοι θανάτου εἰσίν . . . ἀλλὰ καὶ συνευδοκοῦσιν τοῖς πράσσουσιν*; aber diese ntl. Stelle kann nicht maßgeblich gewesen sein.

V

Sechs Stellen können genannt werden, an denen im Gegensatz zur ersten Übersetzung, die mit H übereinstimmt, eine andere von H abweichende Wiedergabe in *O* vorliegt. Diese Lesart verdankt ihre Entstehung entweder einer anderen hebr. Vorlage oder einer auf innergriech. Weg erfolgten Verdrängung der seltenen und mißverstandenen ursprünglichen Lesart.

(1) iii. 21 (22) *χαλεπώτερα* פלאות] *βαθυτερα O*-S[c] La (*altiora*).

χαλεπός nur hier in Sir.; *βαθύς* in Sir. nur noch xxii. 7 (H fehlt). Stand in der Vorlage עמוקות, das im Sing. (עמוקה) in dem rabbinischen Zitat Talm. Jerus. verwendet ist (vgl. Smend 29)?

Es ist nicht auszumachen, ob *altiora* La auf *βαθύτερα* oder auf *ὑψηλότερα*, das Theodoret kennt, zurückgeht (so Herk. 67).

(2) vi. 11 (*ἔσται*) *ὡς σύ* כמוך] *μετα σου O*.

Smend 55 meint, daß *O* in *μετὰ σοῦ* 'entsprechend dem *κατὰ σοῦ* V. 12' korrigiert habe. Dies ist nicht leicht einzusehen. Es könnte sein, daß in der hebr. Vorlage עמך stand.

(3) xiv. 16a *καὶ ἀπάτησον* (*τὴν ψυχήν σου*) ופנק] *και αγιασον O*-S[c]-V *L'*; *et iustifica* La.

ἀπατᾶν steht auch Sir. xxx. 23 = פתה mit dem gleichen Objekt: *ἀπάτα τὴν ψυχήν σου*. Die Änderung von *ἀπάτησον* in *ἁγίασον* ist nach Pe. 124

Tendenz (was näher damit gemeint ist, sagt Pe. nicht). Der Rezensor hat die besondere Bedeutung von ἀπατᾶν 'verzärteln', 'verwöhnen', 'ergötzen' nicht erkannt, sondern es in seiner gewöhnlichen Auffassung 'täuschen', 'verführen' verstanden und deshalb ἁγιάζειν gewählt. Ähnlich ist xxx. 23 ἀπάτα bereits von den alten Unzialen B-S* A in ἀγάπα geändert worden.

(4) xiv. 16b ζητῆσαι τρυφήν = H] μνησθηναι ζωην *O*.

Hat *O* bzw. GrII לזכר חיים gelesen? Der Gedanke 'des Lebens gedenken' ist blasser als der von H und G 'nach Lust und Üppigkeit verlangen' und sekundär. Die Wendung 'des Lebens gedenken' kommt Koh. v. 19 in der volleren Form 'der Tage des Lebens gedenken' vor: μνησθήσεται τὰς ἡμέρας τῆς ζωῆς αὐτοῦ.

(5) xlii. 25 (26) ἓν τοῦ ἑνός זה על זה] εως του αιωνος *O*.

Vgl. Ez. xxv. 15 ἕως αἰῶνος = 𝔐] εως ενος B *L'* Bo.

Es mag sein, daß die Änderung ἕως τοῦ αἰῶνος durch die orthographische Schreibweise αινος (diese ist nicht mehr handschriftlich bezeugt) statt ἑνός und durch die oft (bei Sir. 6mal) vorkommende Wendung ἕως (τοῦ) αἰῶνος (noch öfter steht εἰς (τὸν) αἰῶνα, bei Sir. 17mal) beeinflußt war; zudem paßte ἕως τοῦ αἰῶνος gut zum Verbum ἐστερέωσεν.

(6) xliv. 16 μετανοίας דעת] αιωνος *O*; διανοιας V.

μετάνοια steht nur hier bei Sir. Smend 421 hält διανοίας (= H), 'woraus vielleicht das αἰῶνος von Syroh. 253 entstellt ist', für ursprünglich. Es wäre aber auch möglich, daß αἰῶνος auf עד (aus דעת) zurückgeht.

Zu Beginn des Aufsatzes ist bereits die Frage aufgeworfen worden, ob der Wortschatz von *O*, der auf GrII zurückgeht, auch einen Dienst für die Bestimmung der Zeit von GrII leistet. Die Frage kann bejaht werden. Wie ich in meinem Beitrag zur Eissfeldt-Festschrift, 'Zum Wortschatz des griechischen Sirach' (*Z.A.W.*, Beih. 77, 1958, 274–87), gezeigt habe, hat die erste Übersetzung des Enkels (G) viele Vokabeln, die uns auch bei Aquila und Symmachus, ferner im N.T., begegnen. Diese Feststellung kann auch für den Wortschatz von GrII gemacht werden: manche in G häufig verwendete Vokabeln werden durch solche ersetzt, die zur Zeit des N.T. und der jüngeren griech. Übersetzer geläufig waren.

Besonders wertvoll für die zeitliche Festsetzung ist das Zitat xlviii. 10c aus. Mal. iv. 5 LXX (= iii. 24 𝔐), das im N.T. Luc. i. 17 wiederkehrt. Zur besseren Übersicht seien alle Texte zusammengestellt:

Sir. xlviii. 10c	להשיב לב אבות על בנים H ἐπιστρέψαι καρδίαν πατρὸς πρὸς (επι V) υἱόν (υιους *a*–534–613*) G ἐπιστρέψαι καρδίαν (plur. Syh) πατέρων ἐπὶ τέκνα *O*.
Mal. iii. 24	ותשיב לב אבות על בנים 𝔐.
Mal. iv. 5	ὃς ἀποκαταστήσει καρδίαν πατρὸς πρὸς υἱόν LXX.
Luc. i. 17	ἐπιστρέψαι καρδίας πατέρων ἐπὶ τέκνα.

Am besten ist von der ntl. Lukas-Stelle auszugehen, da sie zeitlich feststeht. Der Infinitiv ἐπιστρέψαι ist bereits aus Sir. xlviii. 10 G und H bekannt, kann also von hier stammen; er steht aber auch in *O* und kann GrII entnommen sein. Zu Mal. iii. 24 𝔐 (= iv. 5 LXX) besteht keine Beziehung.

Der Plural καρδίας ist auch von Syh xlviii. 10 bezeugt; er scheint aber nicht ursprünglich zu sein, sondern wurde infolge der beiden Plurale πατέρων und τέκνα später gesetzt.

Der Plural πατέρων entspricht dem Plural xlviii. 10 in H und *O*.

Die Präposition ἐπί steht auch xlviii. 10 in *O* und ist genaue Wiedergabe von על.

Die Lesart τέκνα ist äußerst wichtig, weil hier der Plural wie in xlviii. 10 H und *O* steht, und dann besonders, weil statt υἱός das Synonym τέκνον wie in *O* gewählt ist. Zum Vergleich kann auf folgende Stellen verwiesen werden:

Dt. xi. 21	υἱῶν] τεκνων 85mg 344mg.
Esdr. I viii. 81 (85)	υἱοῖς] τεκνοις A.
82 (85)	υἱοῖς B 19 55] τεκνοις ANrel. = Sixt.
Ps. lxxxix (xc) 16	τοὺς υἱοὺς αὐτῶν] σ′ ἐπὶ τὰ τέκνα αὐτῶν.
Job xvii. 5	ἐφ᾽ υἱοῖς] σ′ θ′ τέκνων.
Regn. III xiv. 3	α′ ※ τοῖς τέκνοις αὐτοῦ.
Job xxxix. 4	σ′ θ′ ※ τὰ τέκνα αὐτῶν.

Man kann deutlich beobachten, daß der Plur. τέκνα dem Plur. υἱοί vorgezogen wird; υἱοί hat ausnahmsweise seine feste Stelle (1) in den Ausdrücken υἱοὶ Ισραηλ, Ααρων, Αδαμ, ἀνθρώπων, ταύρων (Sir. xxxviii. 25) und mußte (2) als Parallelvokabel zu τέκνα im zweiten Halbvers, nämlich iii. 2b, xvi. 1b, xxx. 30b, gewählt werden. So hat auch GrII τέκνα 'Kinder' hier genommen, weil er υἱοί zu einseitig als 'Söhne' auffaßte, dagegen in *τέκνα* auch die 'Töchter' mit eingeschlossen wissen wollte.

Ein Rückblick zeigt, daß die von *O* überlieferten Vokabeln oftmals der hebr. Vorlage ihre Abkunft verdanken. Wo H fehlt, kann manchmal festgestellt werden, daß die Varianten mit Syr übereinstimmen. Da Syr gewöhnlich mit H zusammengeht, kann man annehmen, daß die Wortlautänderungen auch auf H zurückgehen.

Oftmals ist die Wahl der Vokabel dadurch bedingt, daß das von G verwendete Wort zur Zeit des zweiten Übersetzers oder Rezensors nicht mehr so gebräuchlich und gängig war. Gern wurden auch schwer verständliche und seltene Vokabeln durch leicht verständliche und häufig gebrauchte Wörter ersetzt.

Wenn völlig von G und H abweichende Wiedergaben von *O* überliefert sind, dann muß eine andere hebr. Vorlage angenommen werden, falls die Variante nicht innergriechisch verderbt ist.

Besonders wichtig sind solche Stellen, wo *O* eine ursprüngliche Lesart überliefert, die in den anderen Zeugen (also auch in den alten Unzialen B-S A) verderbt ist. Hier hat GrII auf dem Weg über *O* entweder die alte ursprüngliche Lesart bewahrt oder neu (nach H) übersetzt und dabei die richtige Vokabel getroffen.

INDEX DER VON *O* ÜBERLIEFERTEN UND IN DIESEM BEITRAG BESPROCHENEN VOKABELN

Vorbemerkung. Die Vokabeln des griech. Sir. sind bereits dreimal verzeichnet: (1) in der Konkordanz von Hatch–Redpath, (2) in dem *Supplement* dieser Konkordanz von H.–R. (Oxford, 1906), *Concordance to Portions of Ecclesiasticus with Hebrew Equivalents* (S. 163–96), (3) im *Index* von Smend.

Jedoch sind von Hatch–Redpath die Vokabeln der *O*-Rezension nur dann verzeichnet, wenn sie auch von S^c bezeugt sind, und dies ist nur selten der Fall, z. B. xii. 8 S^c *οὐ γνωσθήσεται* (*O* hat *ἐπιγνωσθήσεται*) unter *γιγνώσκειν* *Concordance*, S. 269, und *Supplement*, S. 170.

Häufiger hat Smend Vokabeln der *O*-Rezension in seinen *Index* aufgenommen, besonders dann, wenn er sie für ursprünglich hält.

Smend übt in seiner *Vorrede*, S. IX–XIII, (mit Recht) scharfe Kritik an den oben unter (1) und (2) genannten Konkordanzen von Hatch–Redpath; aber auch sein *Index* hat große Schwächen. Smend hat nämlich die von GrII stammenden Vokabeln nur schlecht oder gar nicht gekennzeichnet, so daß der Benützer nicht weiß, ob sie zur ersten griech. Übersetzung (G) oder zu GrII gehören. So notiert Smend in seinem *Index* S. 41 die oben genannte Stelle

xii. 8 unter γιγνώσκειν; vor xii. 8 ist das Zeichen ° gesetzt (laut *Vorrede* S. VI bezeichnet ° 'unsichere griechische Lesarten'). Jedoch ist γνωσθήσεται S^c keine 'unsichere griechische Lesart', sondern eine aus GrII stammende Neuübersetzung nach H; als solche sollte sie gekennzeichnet werden. Als weiteres Beispiel soll ἐθελοκωφεῖν genannt werden. Smend verzeichnet in seinem *Index*, S. 59, § ἐθελοκωφεῖν xix. 27 (das Zeichen § bedeutet, daß das genannte Wort nur im griech. Sir. vorkommt). Niemand kann wissen, daß ἐθελοκωφεῖν nur von *O*-V 248–743 *a* bezeugt ist, also von GrII stammt, und für ἑτεροκωφεῖν steht, das S. 103 als Hapaxlegomenon verzeichnet ist (hier steht wenigstens ein Verweis auf ἐθελοκωφεῖν).

Die in Klammern beigegebenen Vokabeln stammen von G, sind somit von Hatch–Redpath und Smend bereits verzeichnet. Wo kein hebr. Äquivalent angegeben ist, fehlt H zur Stelle.

ἀγαθός, ἀγαθά: ἐν τοῖς ἀγαθοῖς (χρήμασιν) αὐτοῦ בטובתו xiv. 5.
ἀγαθός (καλός) נאוה xiv. 3.
ἀγαπᾶν (φοβεῖσθαι) i. 20.
ἁγιάζειν: καὶ ἁγίασον (καὶ ἀπάτησον) ופנק xiv. 16a.
Αἴγγαδοι: ἐν Αἰγγάδοις (ἐν αἰγιαλοῖς) xxiv. 14.
αἰών: ἕως τοῦ αἰῶνος (ἓν τοῦ ἑνός) זה על זה xlii. 25.
αἰῶνος (μετανοίας) דעת xliv. 16.
ἄλλος: ἐξ ἄλλου (ἐξ ἀλλοτρίου) xxiii. 22, 23.
ἀνήρ: καὶ ἀνὴρ ὅς (καὶ πονηρός) xvii. 31.
βαθύς: βαθύτερα (χαλεπώτερα) פלאות iii. 21.
δόξα: δόξαν (δόμα) משאות xxxviii. 2.
ἐθελοκωφεῖν: ἐθελοκωφῶν (ἑτεροκωφῶν) xix. 27.
ἐκδίκησις: ἐκδικήσεως (ἐπαγωγῆς) עברה v. 8.
ἐκκλησία: ἐκκλησίας (ἐχθροῦ) קהל xlvi. 7.
ἐναντίον (ἐνώπιον) לעיני xxxiii. 4.
ἐνδελεχῶς (διὰ παντός) תמיד vi. 37.
ἐνώπιον (ἐν στόμασιν) i. 29.
ἐξολοθρεύειν: ἐξολοθρεύσει σε (ἐξολῇ) תספה v. 7.
ἐπιγινώσκειν: ἐπιγνωσθήσεται (ἐκδικηθήσεται) יודע xii. 8.
ἐρευνᾶν: μὴ ἔρευνα (μὴ ἐξέταζε) אל תחקור iii. 21.
εὐδοκία: εὐδοκίαις (παροικίαις) xli. 5.
εὐλογεῖν: ηὐλόγησεν (ἀνύψωσεν) ברך xxxvi. 9.
θεός: ὑπὸ θεοῦ (ὑπὸ κυρίου) בוראו iii. 16.
ἱστάναι διαθήκην: ἐστάθησαν (ἐτέθησαν) נכרת xliv. 18.
κατορθοῦν: κατώρθωσεν (ἀγαθῶσαι) המכלכל xlix. 9.
κυκλοῦν: ἐκύκλωσεν (ἐγύρωσεν) xliii. 12.
κύριος: κυρίοις (δεσπόταις) iii. 7.
κύριος: παρὰ τοῦ κυρίου (παρὰ τοῦ ὑψίστου) מיהוה xii. 2.
λαμβάνειν: ὁ εἰληφώς (ὁ ἐγκρατής) תופש xv. 1.
μελετᾶν: μελετήσει (τελευτήσει) יהגה xiv. 20.

μεστός: *μεστήν* (*ὑγίειαν*) i. 18.

μετά: *μετὰ σοῦ* (*ὡς σύ*) כמוך vi. 11.

μιμνήσκεσθαι: *μνησθῆναι ζωήν* (*ζητῆσαι τρυφήν*) xiv. 16b.

ὀλιγωρεῖν τῇ ψυχῇ: *καὶ μὴ ὀλιγωρήσῃς τῇ ψυχῇ* (*καὶ μὴ ὀλιγοψυχήσῃς*) ואל תקוץ iv. 9.

πανουργία (*πονηρία*) xix. 23.

περί: *περὶ σοῦ* (*ὑπὲρ σοῦ*) iv. 28.

πονηρός: *πονηρά* (*κακά*) xiii. 25, xxvii. 22.

πορνεία: *περὶ πορνείας* (*πρὸς νέους*) בזנות xlii. 8.

προσάγειν: *τὸν προσάγοντα* (*τὸν προσπορευόμενον*) חובר xii. 14.

σκέπη: *ἐν τῇ σκέπῃ αὐτῆς* (*ὑπ' αὐτῆς*) בצלה xiv. 27.

σοφία: *γνῶσιν σοφία* (*γνῶσιν συνέσεως*) i. 19.

σύνεσις: *τῆς συνέσεως* (*τῆς σοφίας*) *δοθήσεταί σοι* יחכמך vi. 37.

συσσείειν: *συνέσεισε* (*ὠδίνησεν*) יחול xliii. 17.

τέκνον: *ἐπὶ τέκνα* (*πρὸς υἱούς*) על בנים xlviii. 10.

ὑπερήφανος: *ὑπερηφάνων* (*ἀρχόντων* x. 14; *ἐθνῶν* V. 15) גאים x. 14; גוים V. 15.

ὑποσκάπτειν: *ὑποσκάψει* (*ὑποσχάσει*) יחפש xii. 17.

ὕστερον (*ἐπ' ἐσχάτων*) לאחור vi. 28.

ὕψιστος (*κύριος*) יהוה, אל v. 4.

SELECT BIBLIOGRAPHY OF THE WRITINGS OF GODFREY ROLLES DRIVER

ABBREVIATIONS: *A.f.O.* = Archiv für Orientforschung; *A.J.S.L.* = American Journal of Semitic Languages and Literatures; *Anal. Or.* = Analecta Orientalia; *A.O.* = Archiv Orientální; *B.A.S.O.R.* = Bulletin of the American Schools of Oriental Research; *B.S.O.A.S.* = Bulletin of the School of Oriental and African Studies; *C.Q.R.* = Church Quarterly Review; *E.T.* = Expository Times; *H.J.* = Hibbert Journal; *H.T.R.* = Harvard Theological Review; *J.B.L.* = Journal of Biblical Literature; *J.C.S.* = Journal of Cuneiform Studies; *J.E.A.* = Journal of Egyptian Archaeology; *J.J.S.* = Journal of Jewish Studies; *J.Q.R.* = Jewish Quarterly Review; *J.R.A.S.* = Journal of the Royal Asiatic Society; *J.S.S.* = Journal of Semitic Studies; *J.T.S.* = Journal of Theological Studies; *O.M.* = Oxford Magazine; *P.E.Q.* = Palestine Exploration Quarterly; *R.A.* = Revue d'Assyriologie; *TH.* = Theology; *T.Z.* = Theologische Zeitschrift; *V.T.* = Vetus Testamentum; *W.O.* = Die Welt des Orients; *Z.A.* = Zeitschrift für Assyriologie; *Z.A.T.W.* = Zeitschrift für die Alttestamentliche Wissenschaft; *Z.D.M.G.* = Zeitschrift der deutschen morgenländischen Gesellschaft.

1920

'The Linguistic Affinities of Syrian Arabic', *J.R.A.S.*, pp. 305–18.

1921

'Three Assyrian Roots', *J.R.A.S.*, pp. 389–93.
'The Meaning of קאת and קפד in Hebrew', *J.T.S.* xxii, pp. 382 f.
'The Natural and Commercial Products of Northern Kurdistan', *Asiatic Review*, xvii, no. 52, pp. 695–700.
'The Dispersion of the Kurds in Ancient Times', *J.R.A.S.*, pp. 563–72.
'Some Hebrew Roots and their Meanings', *J.T.S.* xxiii, pp. 69–73.

1922

'The Religion of the Kurds', *B.S.O.A.S.* ii, pp. 197–213.
'Studies in Kurdish History. 1. The Origin and Character of the Kurds', *B.S.O.A.S.* ii, pp. 491–511.
'Notes on Hebrew Lexicography', *J.T.S.* xxiii, pp. 405–10.
'On the Etymology of *marra* "hoe" in Latin', *Classical Review*, xxxvi, pp. 166 f.
Review: *The Book of Job* (C. J. Ball), *O.M.* xl, pp. 423 f.
Review: *The Aramaic Origin of the Fourth Gospel* (C. F. Burney), *O.M.* xli, pp. 88 f.

1923

'The Original Language of the Fourth Gospel. A Criticism of Dr. Burney's Thesis', *Jewish Guardian*, 5 Jan., pp. 8 f.

'The Original Language of the Fourth Gospel. A Criticism of Dr. Burney's Thesis', *Jewish Guardian*, 12 Jan., pp. 7 f.

'The Name KURD and its Philological Connections', *J.R.A.S.*, pp. 393–403.

'A New Seal in the Ashmolean Museum', *Journal of Hellenic Studies*, xliii, pp. 55 f.

1924

'Some Recent Discoveries in Babylonian Literature. I. The Epic of Creation', *TH.* viii, pp. 2–13.

'Some Recent Discoveries in Babylonian Literature. II. The Fall of Nineveh', *TH.* viii, pp. 67–79.

'Some Recent Discoveries in Babylonian Literature. III. The Righteous Sufferer', *TH.* viii, pp. 123–30.

'Some Recent Discoveries in Babylonian Literature. IV. The Death and Resurrection of Bel', *TH.* viii, pp. 190–7.

'The Root פרץ in Hebrew', *J.T.S.* xxv, pp. 177 f.

'The Origin of "Ḥireq Compaginis" in Hebrew', *J.T.S.* xxvi, pp. 76 f.

'The Sale of a Priesthood', *J.R.A.S.*, Centenary Supplement, pp. 41–48.

Review: *Geschichte des Volkes Israel* (R. Kittel), *J.T.S.* xxv, pp. 197–9.

Review: *Aramaic Papyri of the Fifth Century B.C.* (A. Cowley), *J.T.S.* xxv, pp. 293–303.

Review: *Comparative Grammar of the Semitic Languages* (De Lacy O'Leary), *O.M.* xlii, pp. 313 f.

Review: *The Babylonian Epic of Creation* (S. Langdon), *O.M.* xlii, pp. 382 f.

Review: *Oxford Editions of Cuneiform Texts: The Weld-Blundell Collection*, Vols. I, II (S. Langdon), *O.M.* xlii, pp. 530 f.

1925

Letters of the First Babylonian Dynasty.

A Grammar of the Colloquial Arabic of Syria and Palestine.

Nestorius: The Bazaar of Heracleides, newly translated from the Syriac and edited, with an Introduction, Notes, and Appendices (with L. Hodgson).

'The Modern Study of the Hebrew Language', in *The People and the Book* (ed. A. S. Peake), pp. 73–120.
'Aramaisms in the Fourth Gospel', *Jewish Guardian*, 6 Feb., p. 10.
'The Sale of a Priesthood', *J.R.A.S.*, p. 100.
Review: *Grammar of Palestinian Jewish Aramaic* (W. B. Stevenson), *J.T.S.* xxvi, pp. 210–12.
Review: *A Sumerian Reading-book* (C. J. Gadd), *O.M.* xliii, p. 205.
Review: *The Chemistry of the Ancient Assyrians* (R. C. Thompson), *O.M.* xliv, pp. 181 f.

1926

'Problems in the Book of Genesis in the Light of Recent Babylonian, Assyrian and Egyptian Research', in *The Book of Genesis*, 12th edn. (S. R. Driver), pp. 417–54.
'The Psalms in the Light of Babylonian Research', in *The Psalmists* (ed. D. C. Simpson), pp. 109–75.
'An Aramaic Inscription in the Cuneiform Script', *A.f.O.* iii, pp. 47–53.
'Corrections in "Letters of the First Babylonian Dynasty"', *Babyloniaca*, ix, pp. 38–40.
'Koschaker's Theory of the "Old Assyrian Laws"' (with Sir J. C. Miles), *Babyloniaca*, ix, pp. 41–65.
'The Aramaic of the Book of Daniel', *J.B.L.* xlv, pp. 110–19.
'The Aramaic Language', *J.B.L.* xlv, pp. 323–5.
'On Some Passages in the Books of Kings and Chronicles', *J.T.S.* xxvii, pp. 158–60.
Review: *Geschichte des alten Orients* (E. G. Klauber and C. F. Lehmann-Haupt), *A.f.O.* iii, pp. 80 f.
Review: *Le système verbal sémitique et l'expression du temps* (M. Cohen), *A.J.S.L.* xlii, pp. 134–7.
Review: *The Cambridge Ancient History*, Vol. III, *English Historical Review*, xli, pp. 424–7.
Review: *Geschichte des Volkes Israel*, 2. Band (R. Kittel), *J.T.S.* xxvii, pp. 211 f.
Review: *Grammaire de l'Hébreu Biblique* (P. Joüon), *J.T.S.* xxvii, pp. 212–15.
Review: *Šumer et Akkad: contribution à l'Histoire de la Civilisation dans la Basse-Mésopotamie* (C.-F. Jean), *J.T.S.* xxvii, pp. 216–18.
Review: *Sumerian Religious Texts* (E. Chiera), *J.T.S.* xxvii, pp. 219 f.
Review: *Israel and Babylon* (W. L. Wardle), *J.T.S.* xxvii, pp. 412 f.

1927

'The Evidence for the name "Yahweh" outside the Old Testament', in *Old Testament Essays* (ed. D. C. Simpson), pp. 18–24.

'A Sumerian Tablet at Oxford', *A.f.O.* iv, p. 26.

'Two Forgotten Words in the Hebrew Language', *J.T.S.* xxviii, pp. 285–7.

Review: *Hebräische Grammatik* (A. Ungnad), *A.f.O.* iv, pp. 107 f.

Review: *Cuneiform Texts from Cappadocian Tablets in the British Museum*, Part IV (S. Smith), *J.R.A.S.*, pp. 889–94.

Review: *A Grammar of Mishnaic Hebrew* (M. H. Segal), *O.M.* xlvi, p. 109.

1928

'Studies in Cappadocian Tablets', *Babyloniaca*, x, pp. 69–137.

'Some Hebrew Words', *J.T.S.* xxix, pp. 390–6.

'Studies in Cappadocian Tablets', *R.A.* xxiv, pp. 153–79.

'Studies in Cappadocian Texts', *Z.A.* xxxviii, pp. 217–32.

'The Original Form of the Name "Yahweh": Evidence and Conclusions', *Z.A.T.W.* xlvi, pp. 7–25.

Review: *Erklärung des Hohen Liedes* (G. Kuhn), *J.T.S.* xxix, pp. 211–13.

Review: *Textstudien zum Buche Hiob* (G. Richter), *J.T.S.* xxix, pp. 213 f.

Review: *Geschichte des Volkes Israel*, 3. Band, 1. Hälfte (R. Kittel), *J.T.S.* xxix, pp. 214 f.

1929

Articles on Assyrian Language, Bible (in part), Hebrew Language, Jehovah, and Semitic Languages, in *Encyclopaedia Britannica* (14th edn.).

'Some Hebrew Verbs, Nouns and Pronouns', *J.T.S.* xxx, pp. 371–8.

Review: *Aramäische Dialektproben* (G. Dalman), *A.f.O.* v, pp. 240 f.

1930

'Studies in the Vocabulary of the Old Testament. I', *J.T.S.* xxxi, pp. 275–84.

'A Magic Bowl', *R.A.* xxvii, pp. 61–64.

1931

'Studies in the Vocabulary of the Old Testament. II', *J.T.S.* xxxii, pp. 250–7.

'Studies in the Vocabulary of the Old Testament. III', *J.T.S.* xxxii, pp. 361–6.
'Studies in the Vocabulary of the Old Testament. IV', *J.T.S.* xxxiii, pp. 38–47.
'A Problem of River-traffic', *Z.A.* xl, pp. 228–33.
Review: *The Epic of Gilgamesh. Text, Translation and Notes* (R. C. Thompson), *J.E.A.* xvii, pp. 3 f.

1932

'The Aramaic *Papyri* from Egypt: Notes on Obscure Passages', *J.R.A.S.*, pp. 77–90.
'Two Sumerian Inscriptions at Oxford', *Orientalia*, i, pp. 86–88.
'Problems in "Proverbs"', *Z.A.T.W.* l, pp. 141–8.
Review: *Laut- und Formenlehre des Ägyptisch-Aramäischen* (P. Leander), *J.R.A.S.*, pp. 177–80.
Review: *Untersuchungen über literarische und exegetische Probleme des Buches Daniel* (H. Junker), *J.T.S.* xxxiii, pp. 434–6.
Review: *The Old Testament in Greek*, Vol. II, pt. iii (ed. A. E. Brooke, N. McLean, and H. St. J. Thackeray), *O.M.* l, pp. 709 f.

1933

'Notes on the Aramaic Inscription from Soudschin', *A.f.O.* viii, pp. 203–6.
'Cappadocian Texts at Oxford', *Anal. Or.* vi, pp. 69 f.
'Studies in the Vocabulary of the Old Testament. V', *J.T.S.* xxxiv, pp. 33–44.
'Studies in the Vocabulary of the Old Testament. VI', *J.T.S.* xxxiv, pp. 375–85.
Review: *Der Prediger* (Qohelet) *übersetzt und erklärt* (H. W. Hertzberg), *J.T.S.* xxxiv, pp. 419–21.

1934

'Hebrew Notes on the "Wisdom of Jesus ben Sirach"', *J.B.L.* liii, pp. 273–90.
'Ezekiel ii. 6: "Sitting upon scorpions"', *J.T.S.* xxxv, pp. 54 f.
'Studies in the Vocabulary of the Old Testament. VII', *J.T.S.* xxxv, pp. 380–93.
'Hebrew Notes', *Z.A.T.W.* lii, pp. 51–56.
Review: *The Mishnah, Translated from the Hebrew with Introduction and Brief Explanatory Notes* (H. Danby), *J.T.S.* xxxv, pp. 332 f.

1935

The Assyrian Laws (with Sir J. C. Miles).

'Problems in Aramaic and Hebrew Texts', *Anal. Or.* xii, pp. 46–70.

'Notes on the Psalms', *J.T.S.* xxxvi, pp. 147–56.

'Studies in the Vocabulary of the Old Testament. VIII', *J.T.S.* xxxvi, pp. 293–301.

'Linguistic and Textual Problems: Isa. xl–lxvi', *J.T.S.* xxxvi, pp. 396–406.

'Notes on the Text of Lamentations', *Z.A.T.W.* lii, pp. 308 f.

Review: *Rabbinische Texte* . . . (G. Kittel and K. H. Rengstorf), *J.T.S.* xxxvi, pp. 202 f.

Review: *Introduction to Semitic Comparative Linguistics* (L. H. Gray), *J.T.S.* xxxvi, pp. 418 f.

Review: *Babylonian Menologies and the Semitic Calendars* (S. Langdon), *O.M.* liii, p. 618.

Review: *Studies in the Book of Ezekiel* (J. B. Harford), *O.M.* liv, p. 140.

1936

Problems of the Hebrew Verbal System.

'Confused Hebrew Roots', in *Occident and Orient . . . Gaster Anniversary Volume* (ed. B. Schindler and A. Marmorstein), pp. 73–83.

'Sumerian ITU ŠE.GU(R).KUD', *A.f.O.* x, p. 362.

'Problems in Job', *A.J.S.L.* lii, pp. 160–70.

'Textual and Linguistic Problems of the Book of Psalms', *H.T.R.* xxix, pp. 171–95.

'Supposed Arabisms in the Old Testament', *J.B.L.* lv, pp. 101–20.

'Assyrian Sculpture in English Collections', *Museum Journal*, xxxv, p. 443.

Review: *The Vocalization of the Egyptian Syllabic Orthography* (W. F. Albright), *J.E.A.* xxi, p. 266.

Review: *The Letter of Aristeas* (H. G. Meecham), *O.M.* lv, p. 235.

1937

'Ecclesiasticus: A New Fragment of the Hebrew Text', *E.T.* xlix, pp. 37–39.

'A Babylonian Tablet with an Aramaic Endorsement', *Iraq*, iv, pp. 16–18.

'Linguistic and Textual Problems: Jeremiah', *J.Q.R.* xxviii, pp. 97–129.

'Linguistic and Textual Problems: Isaiah i–xxxix', *J.T.S.* xxxviii, pp. 36–50.

'Suggestions and Objections', *Z.A.T.W.* lv, pp. 68–71.

'Problems of Semitic Grammar', *Z.D.M.G.* xci, pp. 343–51.

Review: *The Stones of Assyria* (C. J. Gadd), *Burlington Magazine*, lxx, pp. 303 f.

Review: *Corpus Inscriptionum Iudaicarum*, Vol. I (J.-B. Frey), *J.T.S.* xxxviii, p. 305.

Review: *Occident and Orient . . . Gaster Anniversary Volume* (ed. B. Schindler and A. Marmorstein), *J.T.S.* xxxviii, pp. 306 f.

Review: *The Hebrew–Arabic Dictionary of the Bible known as Kitāb Jāmiʿ al-Alfāẓ (Agrōn) of David ben Abraham al-Fāsī the Karaïte*, Vol. I (S. L. Skoss), *J.T.S.* xxxviii, pp. 307 f.

Review: *Der Mišna-Traktat Tamid* (A. Brody), *J.T.S.* xxxviii, p. 308.

Review: *A Grammar of the Phoenician Language* (Z. S. Harris), *J.T.S.* xxxviii, pp. 309–11.

Review: *Biblia Sacra iuxta Latinam Vulgatam versionem . . .*, Vol. III, *J.T.S.* xxxviii, pp. 311 f.

Review: *Le Livre des Psaumes* (J. Calès), *J.T.S.* xxxviii, pp. 423 f.

Review: *Biblisches Reallexikon* (K. Galling), *J.T.S.* xxxviii, pp. 424 f.

1938

'Linguistic and Textual Problems: Ezekiel', *Biblica*, xix, pp. 60–69, 175–87.

'Hebrew *ʿal* ("high one") as a Divine Title', *E.T.* l, pp. 92 f.

'Linguistic and Textual Problems: Minor Prophets. I', *J.T.S.* xxxix, pp. 154–66.

'Linguistic and Textual Problems: Minor Prophets. II', *J.T.S.* xxxix, pp. 260–73.

'Linguistic and Textual Problems: Minor Prophets. III', *J.T.S.* xxxix, pp. 393–405.

'Old and New Semitic Texts', *P.E.Q.* lxx, pp. 188–92.

Review: *La Religion des Judéo-Araméens d'Éléphantine* (A. Vincent), *J.T.S.* xxxix, pp. 72–74.

Review: *L'Évolution religieuse d'Israël*, Vol. I (É. Dhorme), *J.T.S.* xxxix, pp. 74–76.

Review: *Systematische Wege von der Septuaginta zum hebräischen Urtext*, Vol. I (F. Wutz), *J.T.S.* xxxix, pp. 277–9.

Review: *The Music of the Sumerians and their Immediate Successors the Babylonians and Assyrians* (F. W. Galpin), *J.T.S.* xxxix, pp. 279–81.

Review: *Die Jesaja-Apokalypse: Jes. 24–27* (J. Lindblom), *J.T.S.* xxxix, pp. 420 f.

Review: *The Mandaeans of Iraq and Iran* (E. S. Drower), *Nature*, cxli, pp. 765 f.

1939

'Code of Hammurabi, §§ 117–119', in *Symbolae . . . Paulo Koschaker Dedicatae*, pp. 65–75 (with Sir J. C. Miles).

'The SAL-ZIKRUM "woman-man" in Old Babylonian Texts', *Iraq*, vi, pp. 66–70 (with Sir J. C. Miles).

'New Aramaeo-Jewish Names in Egypt', *J.E.A.* xxv, pp. 175 f.

'Problems in Job and Psalms Reconsidered', *J.T.S.* xl, pp. 391–4.

Review: *The Psalms Chronologically Treated with a New Translation* (M. Buttenwieser), *J.T.S.* xl, pp. 176 f.

Review: *Traité de grammaire hébraïque* (M. Lambert), *J.T.S.* xl, pp. 177–9.

Review: *The Herods of Judaea* (A. H. M. Jones), *J.T.S.* xl, pp. 179 f.

1940

'Ordeal by Oath at Nuzi', *Iraq*, vii, pp. 132–8 (with Sir J. C. Miles).

'Hebrew Notes on Prophets and Proverbs', *J.T.S.* xli, pp. 162–75.

Review: *The Cuneiform Texts of Ras Shamra-Ugarit* (C. F. A. Schaeffer), *J.T.S.* xli, pp. 60 f.

Review: *The Fauna of Ancient Mesopotamia as Represented in Art* (E. D. van Buren), *J.T.S.* xli, pp. 61 f.

Review: *Cylinder Seals: A Documentary Essay on the Art and Religion of the Ancient Near East* (K. Frankfort), *J.T.S.* xli, pp. 62 f.

Review: *Manuel d'archéologie biblique* (A.-G. Barrois), *J.T.S.* xli, pp. 63 f.

Review: *Midrash Rabbah* (ed. H. Freedman and M. Simon), *J.T.S.* xli, pp. 64 f.

Review: *The Tell-el-Amarna Tablets* (ed. S. A. B. Mercer), *J.T.S.* xli, pp. 192 f.

Review: *Études sur le récit du paradis et de la chute dans la Genèse* (P. Humbert), *J.T.S.* xli, pp. 193 f.

Review: *Problemas de Topografía Palestinense* (A. Fernández), *J.T.S.* xli, p. 224.

1942

'Notes on the Psalms. I. 1–72', *J.T.S.* xliii, pp. 149–60.

1943

'Notes on Some Recently Recovered Proper Names', *B.A.S.O.R.* xc, p. 34.
'Critical Note on Habakkuk 3^7', *J.B.L.* lxii, p. 121.
'Witchcraft in the Old Testament', *J.R.A.S.*, pp. 6–16.
'Notes on the Psalms. II. 73–150', *J.T.S.* xliv, pp. 12–23.

1944

'Hebrew Notes', *J.R.A.S.*, pp. 165–71.
'Uncertain Hebrew Words', *J.T.S.* xlv, pp. 13 f.
'Seals from 'Amman and Petra', *Quarterly of the Department of Antiquities in Palestine*, xi, pp. 81 f.

1945

'New Aramaic Documents', *Bodleian Library Record*, ii, pp. 123 f.
'Jehoiakin in Captivity', *E.T.* lvi, pp. 317 f.

1946

'Mistranslations', *E.T.* lvii, pp. 192 f.
'Mistranslations', *E.T.* lvii, p. 249.
'On תפשי המלחמה (Num. 31^{27})', *J.Q.R.* xxxvii, p. 85.
'Theological and Philological Problems in the Old Testament', *J.T.S.* xlvii, pp. 156–66.
Review: *Les Verbes à allongement vocalique interne en sémitique* (H. Fleisch), *Africa*, xvi, pp. 55–57.
Review: *Kleine Lichter: fünfzig Bibelstellen erklärt* (L. Köhler), *J.T.S.* xlvii, pp. 75 f.
Review: *The Hebrew–Arabic Dictionary of the Bible known as Kitāb Jāmiʿ al-Alfāẓ (Agrōn) of David ben Abraham al-Fāsī the Karaïte*, Vol. II (S. L. Skoss), *J.T.S.* xlvii, pp. 209–11.

1947

'On a Passage in the Baal Epic (IV AB iii 24) and Proverbs xxxi. 21', *B.A.S.O.R.* cv, p. 11.
'Additions to the Cuneiform Syllabary', *J.C.S.* i, pp. 47–49.

'Mistranslations', *P.E.Q.* lxxix, pp. 123–6.
'Mistranslations in the Old Testament', *W.O.* i, pp. 29–31.
'Oriental Chronicle', *J.T.S.* xlviii, pp. 125–8.
Review: *The Gilgamesh Epic and Old Testament Parallels* (A. Heidel), *O.M.* lxv, p. 313.

1948

Semitic Writing: from Pictograph to Alphabet (Schweich Lectures, 1944; revised edn. 1954).
'Gender in Hebrew Numbers', *J.J.S.* i, pp. 90–104.
'Hebrew Studies', *J.R.A.S.*, pp. 164–76.
'Mistranslations', *P.E.Q.* lxxx, pp. 64 f.
'Misreadings in the Old Testament', *W.O.* i, pp. 234–8.
'Oriental Chronicle', *J.T.S.* xlix, pp. 248–56.
Review: *Associations of Cult Prophets among the Ancient Semites* (A. Haldar), *J.R.A.S.*, pp. 64–66.
Review: *Studies in Biblical Law* (D. Daube), *J.T.S.* xlix, pp. 185 f.
Review: *The Cairo Geniza* (P. Kahle), *O.M.* lxvii, p. 62.
Review: *Ideas of Divine Rule in the Ancient East* (C. J. Gadd), *O.M.* lxvii, pp. 141 f.
Review: *Early Traditions of Israel* (C. A. Simpson), *O.M.* lxvii, p. 171.

1949

'New Aramaic Documents on Leather', *Actes du xxie Congrès International des Orientalistes*, pp. 108 f.
'Ugaritic and Hebrew Problems', *A.O.* xvii, pp. 153–7.
'Hebrew Notes', *J.B.L.* lxviii, pp. 57–59.
'New Hebrew Manuscripts', *J.Q.R.*, N.S., xl, pp. 127–34.
Review: *Joel Studies* (A. S. Kapelrud), *J.R.A.S.*, pp. 212 f.
Review: *The Targum of Isaiah* (J. F. Stenning), *O.M.* lxviii, pp. 106 f.

1950

'Problems of the Hebrew Text and Language', in *Alttestamentliche Studien Friedrich Nötscher . . . gewidmet*, pp. 46–61.
'Hebrew Notes on "Song of Songs" and "Lamentations"', in *Festschrift für Alfred Bertholet*, pp. 134–46.
'Difficult Words in the Hebrew Prophets', in *Studies in Old Testament Prophecy* (ed. H. H. Rowley), pp. 52–72.

'L'Interprétation du texte masorétique à la lumière de la lexicographie hébraïque', *Ephemerides Theologicae Lovanienses*, xxvi, pp. 337–53.
'New Hebrew Scrolls', *H.J.* xlix, pp. 11–21.
'Note on a Phoenician Inscription of Ptolemaic Date', *J.E.A.* xxxvi, p. 82.
'New Hebrew Manuscripts', *J.Q.R.*, N.S., xl, pp. 359–72.
'The Plague of the Philistines (1 Samuel v, 6–vi, 16)', *J.R.A.S.*, pp. 50–52.
'Hebrew Roots and Words', *W.O.* i, pp. 406–15.
'New Aramaic Documents', *Z.A.T.W.* lxii, pp. 220–4.
'Chronicle: Old Testament', *J.T.S.*, N.S., i, pp. 242–6.
Review: *Origin of Language* (A. Jóhannesson), *O.M.* lxviii, p. 503.
Review: *Philo's Bible* (P. Katz), *O.M.* lxix, p. 138.

1951

The Hebrew Scrolls (Friends of Dr. Williams's Library, Fourth Lecture, 1950).
'On the Hebrew פצירה (1 Sam. xiii. 21)', *A.f.O.* xv, p. 68.
'Problems in the Hebrew Text of Proverbs', *Biblica*, xxxii, pp. 173–97.
'Hebrew Scrolls', *J.T.S.*, N.S., ii, pp. 17–30.
'Ezekiel's Inaugural Vision', *V.T.* i, pp. 60–62.
'Hebrew Notes', *V.T.* i, pp. 241–50.
'Chronicle: Old Testament', *J.T.S.*, N.S., ii, pp. 240–5.
Review: *The Old Testament and Modern Study* (ed. H. H. Rowley), *C.Q.R.* clii, pp. 6–8.

1952

The Babylonian Laws, Vol. I (with Sir J. C. Miles).
Corrections to new impression of Brown, Driver, Briggs, *A Hebrew and English Lexicon*.
'Three Notes', *V.T.* ii, pp. 356 f.
'Chronicle: Old Testament', *J.T.S.*, N.S., iii, pp. 303–11.
Review: *Introduction to the Old Testament* (R. H. Pfeiffer), *C.Q.R.* cliii, pp. 530 f.

1953

'Seals and Tombstones', in *Annual of the Department of Antiquities of Jordan*, ii, pp. 62–65.
'Once again the Judaean Scrolls', *J.Q.R.*, N.S., xliv, pp. 1–20.

‘Two Astronomical Passages in the Old Testament’, *J.T.S.*, N.S., iv, pp. 208–12.
‘On Psalm 35^{16}’, *T.Z.* ix, pp. 468 f.
‘Hebrew Poetic Diction’, in Supplement to *V.T.* i, pp. 26–39.
‘Chronicle: Old Testament’, *J.T.S.*, N.S., iv, pp. 300–10.
Review: *The Zadokite Fragments and the Dead Sea Scrolls* (H. H. Rowley), *H.J.* li, pp. 301–3.

1954

Aramaic Documents of the Fifth Century B.C.
‘Ezekiel: Linguistic and Textual Problems’, *Biblica*, xxxv, pp. 145–59, 299–312.
‘Reflections on Recent Articles’, *J.B.L.* lxxiii, pp. 125–36.
‘Problems and Solutions’, *V.T.* iv, pp. 225–45.
‘Babylonian and Hebrew Notes’, *W.O.* ii, pp. 19–26.
‘Some Hebrew Medical Expressions’, *Z.A.T.W.* lxv, pp. 255–62.
Review: *Archaeology and the Religion of Israel* (W. F. Albright), *H.J.* liii, pp. 82 f.

1955

The Babylonian Laws, Vol. II (with Sir J. C. Miles).
‘Problems in the Hebrew Text of Job’, in *Wisdom in Israel and in the Ancient Near East* (ed. M. Noth and D. Winton Thomas), pp. 72–93.
‘Notes upon Notes’, *Biblica*, xxxvi, pp. 71–73.
‘Amos vii. 14’, *E.T.* lxvii, pp. 91–92.
‘1. Ben Sira, xxxiii. 4; 2. Jeremiah, xii. 6’, *J.J.S.* v, pp. 177 f.
‘Two Misunderstood Passages of the Old Testament’, *J.T.S.*, N.S., vi, pp. 82–87.
‘Birds in the Old Testament: I. Birds in Law’, *P.E.Q.* lxxxvii, pp. 5–20.
‘Birds in the Old Testament: II. Birds in Life’, *P.E.Q.* lxxxvii, pp. 129–40.
‘Hebrew Seals’, *P.E.Q.* lxxxvii, p. 183.
‘Proverbs xix. 26’, *T.Z.* xi, pp. 373 f.
‘A Hebrew Burial Custom’, *Z.A.T.W.* lxvi, pp. 314 f.
Review: *Discoveries in the Judaean Desert I: Qumran Cave I* (D. Barthélemy and J. T. Milik), *H.J.* liv, pp. 104–6.
Review: *Recueil des tessères de Palmyre* (K. Ingholt, K. Seyrig, J. Stanley, and A. Caquot), *J.R.A.S.*, p. 172.
Review: *Die Palästina-Literatur* (P. Thomsen), *J.T.S.*, N.S., vi, p. 117.

Review: *Dictionnaire des inscriptions sémitiques de l'Ouest*, I, II (C.-F. Jean), *J.T.S.*, N.S., vi, pp. 117 f.

Review: *Kleine Schriften zur Geschichte des Volkes Israel*, II (A. Alt), *J.T.S.*, N.S., vi, pp. 118 f.

Review: *The Ancient Near East in Pictures* . . . (J. B. Pritchard), *J.T.S.*, N.S., vi, p. 254.

Review: *Miscellanea Biblica B. Ubach: Scripta et Documenta*, I, *J.T.S.*, N.S., vi, p. 255.

Review: *Das Buch Ijjob hebräisch und deutsch* (F. Stier), *J.T.S.*, N.S., vi, p. 259.

Review: *The Brooklyn Museum Aramaic Papyri* (E. G. Kraeling), *P.E.Q.* lxxxvi, pp. 91–94.

Review: *Qataban and Sheba* (W. Phillips), *Royal Central Asian Journal*, xlii, pp. 46 f.

1956

Canaanite Myths and Legends.

'Mythical Monsters in the Old Testament', in *Studi Orientalistici in onore di Giorgio Levi Della Vida*, i, pp. 234–49.

'Three Technical Terms in the Pentateuch', *J.S.S.* i, pp. 97–105.

'Two Astronomical Passages in the Old Testament', *J.T.S.*, N.S., vii, pp. 1–11.

'Correction', *J.T.S.*, N.S., vii, p. 352.

'Two Problems in the Old Testament examined in the Light of Assyriology', *Syria*, xxxiii, pp. 70–78.

'On Job v. 5', *T.Z.* xii, pp. 485 f.

'Technical Terms in the Pentateuch', *W.O.* ii, pp. 254–63.

'Hebrew Mothers (Exodus i. 19)', *Z.A.T.W.* lxvii, pp. 246–8.

Review: *The Diacritical Point and the Accents in Syriac* (J. B. Segal), *B.S.O.A.S.* xvii, p. 182.

Review: *Donum Natalicium Henrico Samueli Nyberg oblatum* (E. Gren, B. Lewin, H. Ringgren, and S. Wikander), *J.S.S.* i, pp. 177 f.

Review: *The Hebrew Scripts* (S. A. Birnbaum), *J.T.S.*, N.S., vii, pp. 262 f.

Review: *The Ḫab/pirū* (M. Greenberg), *J.T.S.*, N.S., vii, pp. 264 f.

Review: *Ancient Near Eastern Texts* . . . (J. B. Pritchard), *O.M.* lxxiv, p. 262.

1957

Aramaic Documents of the Fifth Century B.C., abridged and revised edition.

'Presidential Address: Le Congrès international pour l'étude de l'Ancien Testament, Strasbourg, 1956', in *Volume du Congrès* (ed. P. A. H. de Boer), pp. 1–7.

'Problems of Interpretation in the Heptateuch', in *Mélanges bibliques rédigés en l'honneur de André Robert*, pp. 66–76.

'Glosses in the Hebrew Text of the Old Testament', *Orientalia et Biblica Lovaniensia*, i, pp. 123–61.

'Aramaic Names in Accadian Texts', in *Scritti in onore di Giuseppe Furlani*, pp. 41–57.

'On *ana utūnim nadû*', *A.f.O.* xviii, p. 129.

'Waw Explicative in Amos vii. 14', *E.T.* lxviii, p. 302.

'Three difficult words in *Discipline* (iii. 3–4, vii. 5–6, 11)', *J.S.S.* ii, pp. 247–50.

'A Lost Colloquialism in the Old Testament (1 Samuel xxv. 6)', *J.T.S.*, N.S., viii, pp. 272 f.

'The Scrolls from the Dead Sea: the Riddle Unriddled', *Royal Central Asian Journal*, xlvi, pp. 235–7.

'Acc. šimê/îtān "two evenings"', *Z.A.*, N.F., xviii, pp. 307 f.

'On עלה "went up country" and ירד "went down country"', *Z.A.T.W.* lxix, pp. 74–77.

Review: *The Assyrian Dictionary of the Oriental Institute of the University of Chicago*, V, VI (ed. A. L. Oppenheim and others), *J.S.S.* ii, pp. 387 f.

Review: *Concordance of Ugaritic* (G. D. Young), *J.S.S.* ii, p. 389.

Review: *The Dead Sea Scrolls of the Hebrew University* (E. L. Sukenik), *J.T.S.*, N.S., viii, pp. 141–3.

1958

'Notes on Isaiah', in *Von Ugarit nach Qumran* (Festschrift für Otto Eissfeldt, ed. J. Hempel and L. Rost), pp. 42–48.

'Introduction', in *Our Bible and the Ancient Manuscripts* (F. G. Kenyon; 5th edn. revised by A. W. Adams), pp. 11–16.

'Geographical Problems', *Eretz-Israel*, v, pp. 16–20.

'Once again: Birds in the Bible', *P.E.Q.* xc, pp. 56–58.

'On ḥēmāh "hot anger, fury" and also "fiery wine"', *T.Z.* xiv, pp. 133–5.

Review: *Rückläufiges hebräisches Wörterbuch* (K. G. Kuhn and others), *J.S.S.* iv, p. 148.

Review: *The Scriptures of the Dead Sea Sect in English Translation with Introduction and Notes* (T. H. Gaster), *J.T.S.*, N.S., ix, pp. 347 f.

1959

'Heb. לילית "goat-sucker, night-jar" (Is. xxxix, 14)', *P.E.Q.* xci, pp. 55–58.

Review: *Die mythologischen und kultischen Texte aus Ras Schamra übersetzt* (J. Aistleitner), *J.J.S.* x, pp. 181 f.

Review: *Supplementum ad Lexicon in Veteris Testamenti Libros* (L. Koehler and W. Baumgartner), *J.S.S.* iv, pp. 147 f.

Review: *Die Palästina-Literatur: eine internationale Bibliographie* (P. Thomsen), *J.T.S.*, N.S., x, pp. 119 f.

Review: *La Règle de la Guerre des Fils de Lumière contre les Fils des Ténèbres* (J. Carmignac), *J.T.S.*, N.S., x, pp. 120 f.

Review: *Aspects of the Dead Sea Scrolls* (ed. C. Rabin and Y. Yadin), *J.T.S.*, N.S., x, pp. 121–4.

Review: *Le Livre des Hymnes découvert près de la Mer Morte* (A. Dupont-Sommer), *J.T.S.*, N.S., x, pp. 124–6.

Review: *Gesammelte Studien zum Alten Testament* (G. von Rad), *J.T.S.*, N.S., x, pp. 356–9.

Review: *The Riddle of the Scrolls* (H. E. Del Medico), *J.T.S.*, N.S., x, pp. 359–61.

1960

'A Confused Hebrew Root (דמם, דמה, דום)', in ספר טור־סיני, pp. 1–11.

'Abbreviations in the Massoretic Text', *Textus*, i, pp. 112–31.

Review: *The Assyrian Dictionary of the Oriental Institute of the University of Chicago*, III, IV (ed. A. L. Oppenheim, E. Reiner, and others), *J.S.S.* v, pp. 156–8.

Review: *Semantic Notes on the Hebrew Lexicon* (J. L. Palache), *J.S.S.* v, pp. 423–5.

Review: *Kleine Schriften zur Geschichte des Volkes Israel* (A. Alt), *J.T.S.*, N.S., xi, pp. 361–6.

Review: *Le Rouleau de la Guerre* (J. van der Ploeg), *J.T.S.*, N.S., xi, pp. 366–9.

Review: *The Apocalypse of John* (C. C. Torrey), *J.T.S.*, N.S., xi, pp. 383–9.

1961

'Oriental Studies and the Oriental Institute', *Oxford*, xvii, no. 2, pp. 56–67.

Review: *The Treasure of the Copper Scroll* (J. M. Allegro), *J.S.S.* vi, pp. 275–8.

Review: *Animal and Man in Bible Lands* (F. S. Bodenheimer), *J.S.S.* vi, pp. 289–92.

Review: *Zum Alten Testament und seiner Umwelt: ausgewählte Aufsätze* (W. Baumgartner), *J.T.S.*, N.S., xii, pp. 61–64.

Review: *The Moabites* (A. H. van Zyl), *J.T.S.*, N.S., xii, pp. 64–66.

Review: *Die Palästina-Literatur: eine internationale Bibliographie* (P. Thomsen), *J.T.S.*, N.S., xii, pp. 66 f.

1962

'Plurima Mortis Imago', in *Essays and Studies in honour of Abraham A. Neuman*, pp. 128–43.

'The Resurrection of Marine and Terrestrial Creatures', *J.S.S.* vii, pp. 12–22.

Review: *Discoveries in the Judaean Desert II: Les Grottes de Murabbaʿât* (P. Benoit, J. T. Milik, and R. de Vaux), *H.J.* lx, pp. 164–71.

Review: *The Scroll of the War of the Sons of Light against the Sons of Darkness* (Y. Yadin), *H.J.* lx, pp. 351–3.

Review: *The Assyrian Dictionary of the Oriental Institute of the University of Chicago*, VII, XXI (ed. A. L. Oppenheim and E. Reiner), *J.S.S.* vii, pp. 95–98.

Review: *L'Égypte et la Bible* (P. Montet), *J.T.S.*, N.S., xiii, pp. 118 f.

PRINTED IN GREAT BRITAIN
AT THE UNIVERSITY PRESS, OXFORD
BY VIVIAN RIDLER
PRINTER TO THE UNIVERSITY

492.082
T45